THE POLITICAL HISTORY OF NEWFOUNDLAND
1832-1864

CANADIAN STUDIES IN HISTORY AND GOVERNMENT

A series of studies edited by G. S. French, sponsored by the Social Science Research Council of Canada, and published with financial assistance from the Canada Council.

The Jesuits' Estates Question, 1760–1888. By Roy C. Dalton

The Franchise and Politics in British North America, 1755–1867. By John Garner

Land Policies of Upper Canada. By Lillian F. Gates

The Political History of Newfoundland, 1832–1864. By Gertrude E. Gunn

The Mark of Honour. By Hazel C. Mathews

Church and State in Canada West, 1841–1867. By John S. Moir

The Politics of the Yukon Territory, 1898–1909. By David R. Morrison

The Emergence of the Federal Concept in Canada, 1839–1845. By William Ormsby

Soldiers of the International. By William Rodney

The Clergy Reserves of Upper Canada. By Alan Wilson

THE POLITICAL HISTORY

OF NEWFOUNDLAND

1832-1864

Gertrude E. Gunn

UNIVERSITY OF NEW BRUNSWICK

UNIVERSITY OF TORONTO PRESS

© University of Toronto Press 1966
Toronto and Buffalo

Reprinted 1969, 1977, 2017

First paperback edition 1977

ISBN 978-0-8020-1656-0 (cloth)
ISBN 978-0-8020-6323-6 (paper)

PREFACE

THREE DECADES of disorder followed the establishment of representative government in Newfoundland in 1832. These decades have never been closely studied in a published work. D. W. Prowse in his *History of Newfoundland* (1896), which is still the standard, general, and popular work on the colony, offered intermittent glimpses and explanations of the political scene, interspersed with anecdote and recollection. Writing at random from Colonial Office records and for a wide public, he did not attempt a systematic narrative of political events or a detailed analysis of cause and effect. In such a work, a close study of discordant politics and dubious motives seemed to him neither necessary nor discreet. He declined the task of entering into the long discussion about responsible government, and he intimated that he had had to walk delicately in order to avoid offence.

Some historians have gone to Prowse and to a handful of local chroniclers for opinions, extracts, and abridgements. Others, basing their work largely on that of their predecessors, have described the "evolution" of the colony from representative to responsible government and related the political struggles of the first half of the nineteenth century to the contemporaneous contests in the rest of British North America and to the fixed and changing policies of the Colonial Office. Their stress has been on Newfoundland's general conformity to, and occasional deviation from, the pattern of political and constitutional development in the colonies. The political history of Newfoundland has, therefore, been related by, or derived from, those who were more or less involved in their own narration and anxious to gloss, vindicate, condemn, or ignore; or it has been condensed by those who were intent upon placing the island in a general context.

At the close of his book, *The Establishment of Constitutional Government in Newfoundland, 1783-1832*, which expounds the thesis that the colony was "retarded" and representative institutions were belatedly established, A. H. McLintock described the institution of the long-anticipated legislature as "but the prelude to years of internal political strife, economic chaos, and religious discord." There seemed to be a need for a return to the documents for a study focused on the pressures and processes which ensured for Newfoundland a political story peculiarly its own. This investigation of the structure of the early political parties, of the causes of popular tumult, and of the effects of constitutional changes, was undertaken, therefore, to fill this need.

ACKNOWLEDGMENTS

THE WRITER expresses her gratitude to the Beaverbrook Foundation for Overseas Scholarships which made possible her researches in England.

The advice and encouragement of Dr. Gerald S. Graham, King's College, University of London, director of the thesis, are most gratefully acknowledged. Acknowledgment is also made for the kind assistance of Mr. Taylor Milne and the staff of the Institute of Historical Research, University of London, to the officials and staff of the Public Record Office, the British Museum, the Gosling Memorial Library in St. John's and the libraries of the University of Nottingham, the Colonial Office, the Commonwealth Relations Office, the Royal Commonwealth Society, and Canada House, London. Thanks are due, too, to Mr. Watson Jamer, Agent-General for the Atlantic Provinces, London, and to Mr. John Goodrum of Job Brothers Limited, Liverpool. Extracts from the Newcastle Papers are published with the kind permission of the Trustees of the Newcastle estates.

This work has been published with the help of a grant from the Social Science Research Council of Canada, using funds provided by the Canada Council.

CONTENTS

PART I

REPRESENTATIVE GOVERNMENT

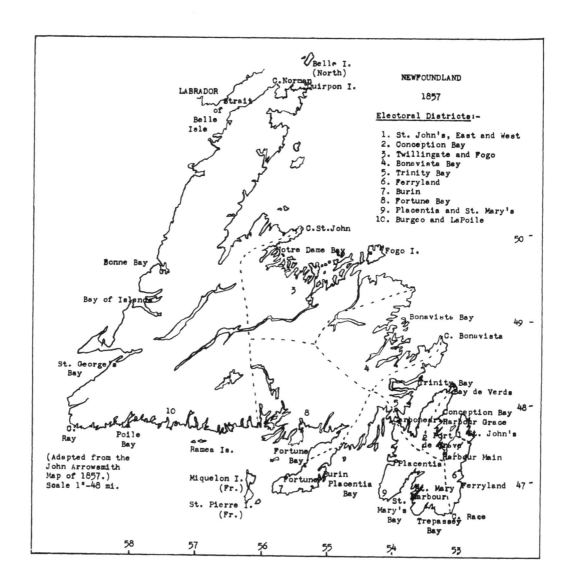

NEWFOUNDLAND

1857

Electoral Districts:-

1. St. John's, East and West
2. Conception Bay
3. Twillingate and Fogo
4. Bonavista Bay
5. Trinity Bay
6. Ferryland
7. Burin
8. Fortune Bay
9. Placentia and St. Mary's
10. Burgeo and LaPoile

(Adapted from the
John Arrowsmith
Map of 1857.)
Scale 1"-48 mi.

CHAPTER ONE

THE ESTABLISHMENT OF REPRESENTATIVE GOVERNMENT, 1832

ON JUNE 7, 1832, the day the Reform Bill received royal assent, the Whigs introduced their bill to provide Newfoundland with an elective assembly. After two centuries of illicit settlement and eight years of colonial status, the island was to acquire "the transcript of the constitution" which had been given the other colonies of British North America. The Governor had urged that representative government was ill suited to the condition of the population and for a time the Colonial Office had hesitated and considered alternatives. But pressure from the political reformers, the resident merchants, and the inhabitants of Newfoundland had its effect on a ministry which had championed the principles of political freedom and parliamentary reform. Doubts and objections were laid aside and it was hoped that a system which had brought advantages to other colonies would produce similar benefits in Newfoundland.[1] It was a concession in which idealism, economy, and expediency were inextricably mixed. From the more mature colonies there was already much evidence of its power to disrupt.

Newfoundland had only emerged in 1824 from its protracted minority under maritime government. It had been relieved of the obsolete laws protecting the monopoly of the West Country fishing merchants and had acquired a civil governor, Sir Thomas Cochrane, an official council, and a revised and extended supreme court. This break with the past did not satisfy the small group of reformers who had called for an end to autocratic government. They immediately renewed their pressure for a local legislature, arguing that such a body would best foster the interests and develop the resources of the country and eradicate the evils of long neglect.[2] The leading spirits in this agitation were Dr. William Carson, a Scottish physician, and Patrick Morris, an Irish merchant, both residents of St. John's.[3] Carson, the District Surgeon, was a fearless, formal, and dogmatic liberal of the early nineteenth century who had championed the cause of democratic reform in Newfoundland ten years earlier and had earned the odium of the admiral-governors with his pamphlets advocating civil government, a local legislature, and the appropriation and cultivation of Crown lands.[4] Morris was an impetuous, witty, and voluble pamphleteer and demagogue who had followed Carson into the political arena in 1825 and whose literary efforts were a stimulus in the renewed campaign for representative government.[5] A reform committee again became active and petitions were framed and forwarded from St. John's and the principal outports.[6] One of these, bearing the signature of 2,500 of the inhabitants, confronted Lord Goderich and Lord Howick in the Colonial Office soon after the Whigs took office in November 1830. It urged the concession on the grounds of the island's commercial importance, its vast acreage of uncultivated soil, its rights as a British North American colony, and its need for local legislation.[7] The Colonial Office response was to ask the Governor for a report on the wisdom of establishing local self-government.[8]

Sir Thomas Cochrane was a naval captain of forty-two whose only apparent qualification for the civil administration of Newfoundland, in the throes of political agitation and post-war depression, was a period of service on the North Atlantic Station (see Appendix A). A naval career which had begun, ostensibly, at the age of seven under his father, Admiral Sir Alexander Cochrane, had equipped him with Tory principles, a quarterdeck manner, and a love of ceremony, dignity, and lavish display. He had begun his government in St. John's with the construction of an enormous residence whose cost, five times the original estimate, had led the Treasury to veto his subsequent extravagant schemes for public works. But he had addressed himself with sense and energy to the task of alleviating some of the evils by which the colony was beset. He had recognized the folly of the established system of unconditional government assistance to the destitute and improvident and had attacked this problem by employing pauper labour in beginning the first roads from the capital. He had decided that agriculture, though unlikely ever to become a major pursuit, might be fostered sufficiently to remove the threat of famine recurrent with failures of the fishery. To this end he had begun, under his Commission, to grant small holdings at a nominal quit-rent to applicants who would cultivate the soil. He had deplored the total absence of municipal government and by-laws in St. John's and the consequent prevalence of squalor and disorder, and had urged the citizens to form a town council with powers of assessment. Hopes for this had foundered on factionalism and aversion to direct taxation, and the Colonial Office had refused to impose a town charter by Imperial act. He had sought to end the system under which the Chief Justice, combining legislative powers with judicial functions, was authorized to determine to what extent the laws of England were applicable to Newfoundland. He proposed that such laws as were suitable to the colony be selected from the British statutes, to be enacted, with supplementary laws, as a code for the island. This question was in abeyance when discussion about representative government was renewed.[9]

The Governor was informed by the Colonial Office that the population had increased to the point where pressure for some change could not long be resisted and he was asked whether the inhabitants yet included sufficient persons qualified to manage public affairs.[10] Despite his admitted reluctance to jeopardize his popularity with the substantial merchants who had rallied to the cause, Cochrane felt that he could not conscientiously give it his support. He said that although the inhabitants numbered some 60,000 persons, there were in the community only two classes of persons—the small group comprising the merchants and their agents, and the large one comprising the fishermen whom they supplied. The wealth, intelligence, and respectability which he considered indispensable for membership in the assembly were confined to the mercantile class, but at all seasons the merchants and their agents tended to be tied to the demands of the trade. They seemed fully occupied in procuring supplies and provisions, in outfitting the fishery for seal and for cod, and in disposing of the catch and settling the accounts of a business conducted almost entirely in terms of credit and truck. Merchants who resided in St. John's might conveniently offer themselves as candidates, but he doubted that respectable persons could be found to represent the outports. In some of these only the agents would be eligible and in no season, he said, could an agent absent himself from his post. Moreover, during the long winter the eastern outports were ice-bound and the absence of roads made access to the capital almost impossible. Another difficulty was that, save for a few outports, the whole of the population was scattered sparsely along the deeply indented eastern and southern coasts. For Cochrane, the "lower orders" were ruled out as potential representatives by poverty and ignorance, as well as by the nature of their calling, and between these and the merchants there was virtually no middle class of professional men, shopkeepers, and farmers from which legislators could be drawn. In his opinion, the present system was well suited to a colony whose people were as yet merely "children of a larger growth." He maintained that the group behind the agitation was very small and had resorted to deception in obtaining signatures for the petitions.[11]

Cochrane pointed out, too, that the resident merchants had thrown their weight behind the movement for a legislature when Huskisson, as Colonial Secretary, had recommended that the expenses of the civil establishment in Newfoundland be met by a duty on most of its imported supplies.[12] Free importation of supplies necessary for the fishery had long been the mercantile tenet and the Colony's expenses had hitherto been met from the revenue raised on imported spirits, supplemented by Parliament's annual grant.[13] Cochrane's Attorney-General, James Simms, equally opposed to an assembly, declared that it could only be a creature of the merchants, experimenting in measures designed to advance the mercantile interest rather than the welfare of the island. Nor, he said, could most of these merchants be identified with the permanent interest of the colony, since they were frequently replaced by younger partners from the west of England, or retired to England when they had acquired fortunes or become insolvent.[14]

Although the Governor failed to stress the ambivalence arising from the perpetual debtor-relationship in which the fishermen stood with the merchants, this conflict of obligation and resentment supplied yet another reason for hesitation about an elective assembly. The truck system could scarcely fail to breed in the fishermen dependence and improvidence on the one hand and distrust and suspicion on the other. It was insidious and self-perpetrating for it loaded the fishermen with debt, but did not induce them to save, and it cast the merchants as exploiters, but kept them as indispensable props.

The organization of the resident fishery had previously been largely feudal, the fishermen, as employees, turning over their catch to the exporting merchant in return for the gear and supplies necessary for the fishing season and for sufficient food and clothing to keep themselves and their families through the year.[15] Under this system, the merchants assumed the duty of supporting the fishing population, like serfs, in good times and in bad. The former were able to amass large fortunes and the latter to live at a subsistence level. The growth of the population, however, led to a gradual modification of this system and found the merchants increasingly anxious to transfer the obligation of supporting the fishermen in bad times to the government. In outline, the practice in the shore-based cod fishery was this: The fisherman boat-owner went to his merchant in the spring and obtained on credit food and equipment for the three- or four-month season. At its close he returned with his catch, dried and cured, to set off against his account. The prices of the spring supplies and of the fish were set by the merchant and the quality and value of the fish determined by his culler. In good years a fisherman might wipe out his debt and obtain a balance in cash or, as was usual at this period, in notes for goods. In bad years there might be no balance and he might not cover his debt. The merchant might, or might not, tide him over the winter and refit him on credit for the next season, but successive bad fisheries burdened the fisherman with debt and made the merchant adamant about further advances. Then the fisherman, with no savings, with no alternative employment, and with no source of food save a small and sometimes failing "potato patch," turned to the government for relief.

The ship fishery for seals, which took place in March and April, and for cod, which lasted from June till October at Labrador, was also based on this system of credit and truck. These fisheries were conducted by a "planter"—that is, a shipowner or skipper—with a hired crew of fishermen who were paid not in wages but in half the proceeds of the voyage, the planter taking the balance. The merchant, as mortgagee, furnished the necessary supplies to the planter on the security of the proceeds of the voyage. Since his loan was usually about one-third of the estimated proceeds, these proceeds were actually distributed in thirds among planter, crew, and mortgagee.[16] An account based on the experience of Philip Henry Gosse, who served as a junior clerk in an establishment at Carbonear in 1827 and 1828, relates that the amounts due to the crews were paid, amidst vehement disagreements, partly in cash and partly in notes for goods.[17]

The planters were a growing class of fishermen in the east-coast outports, especially in Conception Bay. According to Gosse, they numbered seventy in a population of 2,500 at Carbonear in 1828 and included several "worthy and respectable" persons whose houses afforded the only society the town possessed.[18] Although some of the planters grew prosperous, many of them remained in or fell into the debtor class. For them, as for the individual fishermen, the vagaries of wind and weather, ice conditions and bait supply, French competition and fluctuating prices, brought good years and bad and sharp changes of fortune.[19] The hired fishermen claimed the right to "follow" the planter's fish and oil into the hands of his supplier, the produce of the voyage being by law (5 Geo. IV, c. 51) subject in the first place to payment of wages. In a case of insolvency, the current supplier was the privileged creditor, after the satisfaction of wage claims on the proceeds of the voyage (c. 67). These devices for protecting the interests of fishermen and merchants provided the grounds for much dispute and litigation, and there were frequent civil suits before the local magistrates. Since the magistrates were for the most part, and inevitably, drawn from the merchant class, it often happened that the judge and the defendant were one, or that their interests were identical. Their rulings were so frequently biased as to make the inhabitants mock the magistracy and the justice dispensed by these courts.[20]

By setting the prices for the material supplied for the fishery, and by paying for the fish and oil at prices determined by themselves, the merchants secured their profits and insured themselves against the risk of a small catch, a bad cure, or a poor market, and against the possibility that the fishermen might, dishonestly, fail to bring their fish to the supplier. Prices on account were double the retail prices in England and were always higher in the outports than in St. John's.[21] The prices to be paid for the fish and oil in St. John's and the outports were never known when the supplies were taken up in the spring, but were decided by the principal merchants, meeting together in July or August, on the basis of price reports from abroad. Once the price had been "broken" the only adjustments were made in favour of the merchants, the price dropping with reports of bad markets, but remaining steady when reports were good.[22] In January and February of 1832 there were mass meetings of fishermen between Carbonear and Harbour Grace to attempt a combination which would compel their merchants and employers to adopt a different mode of dealing with them, as to the price given for fish and oil and the prices paid for supplies. A proclamation was issued declaring such meetings illegal.[23] There had been, however, with the increase in the population and the contraction of larger mercantile houses after the Napoleonic War, some growth of competition from shopkeepers with small capital, and from traders in schooners along the coasts. These persons imported goods for retail or purchased from the merchants with cash, fish, and oil.[24] Some fishermen were, therefore, able to avail themselves of cheaper prices and these shopkeepers and traders were to become the nucleus of another social class. One observer described the "fishocracy" in the last quarter of the century as comprising (1) the principal merchants, high officials, and some lawyers and medical men; (2) small merchants, important shopkeepers, lawyers, doctors, and secondary officials; (3) grocers, master mechanics, and schooner holders; and (4) fishermen.[25]

A further ground for hesitation about conferring a popular franchise was the nearly equal division of the inhabitants into Protestants and Irish Roman Catholics (see Appendix E, Table I) and the tension which existed between the two groups. The danger of arousing sectarian strife in the island had been one of the factors in the decision to leave at rest the question of local government in St. John's,[26] but in his despatches adverse to a legislature Cochrane made no specific reference to sectarian and "racial" difficulties.[27] The census of 1827 showed the people in the districts in and about St. John's, Ferryland, and Placentia and St. Mary's to be predominantly Roman Catholic, those in Bonavista Bay, Trinity Bay, Fortune Bay, and Twillingate and Fogo to be predominantly Protestant, and those in Conception Bay and Burin to be almost equally divided as to creed (Appendix E, Table II). An unspecified number of the Protestants in 1827 were Dissenters from the Church of England, and by 1836 these, chiefly Wesleyans, numbered just under one-third of the Protestant population. In Conception Bay their strength was approximately that of the Anglicans, and in Burin it was greater. The merchants were, with very few exceptions, Protestant, as was half the fishing population, while the Roman Catholics, most of them southern Irish in origin or descent, were principally of the fishing and debtor class. The tendency of Roman Catholics, Anglicans, and Dissenters to cluster in separate harbours and coves, the isolation imposed in summer by occupation and in winter by absence of roads, and the thin and irregular attendance at the few schools supported by the Society for the Propagation of the Gospel and by the Roman Catholic Church,[28] all served to foster a peculiar outport insularity and a spirit of exclusive sectarianism. In St. John's and the larger outports of Conception Bay where Protestants and Irish Catholics were in habitual contact, the population seems to have lived, as in Ireland, in an uneasy state of suspicion and aversion. P. H. Gosse wrote of the mockery to which the Irish of Carbonear and other harbours subjected the Protestant fishermen from the north shore of Conception Bay, the latter being mild and guileless "giants" with peculiar manners and idiom and a strong dread of their tormentors. He declared that in 1827 amongst the Protestant population of the island there was "an habitual dread of the Irish as a class which was more oppressively felt than openly expressed and ... an habitual caution in conversation to avoid any unguarded expression which might be laid hold of by their jealous enmity." He adds, "It was very largely this dread which impelled me to foresake Newfoundland as a residence in 1835; and I recollect saying to my friends that when we got to Canada, we might climb to the top of the tallest tree ... and shout 'Irishman' at the top of our voices, without 'fear'."[29]

The attitude of the Irish can be traced to the factors which led to their influx, to the prejudices they brought with them, and to the conditions they met and aggravated; that of the Protestants was a response to the reputation of the Irish for moving from docility to individual and concerted disorder. Famine and the suppressive laws against Irish industry during much of the eighteenth century, economic and political unrest towards its close, and the hope of high wages and speedy employment during and after the long wars with the French had stimulated the emigration from Ireland of thousands of individuals characterized by a very low standard of life and by a decided animus against English law, English landlords, and the English Church. The earliest Irish settlers, apparently of a superior type, were "youngsters" or "green" men engaged at Waterford and Cork by West Country fishing masters bound for the season in Newfoundland. The practice seems to have been to sign these servants for two summers and the intervening winter, and many of them remained in the island, marrying into the families of the planters or settlers.[30] The influx of hungry and destitute Irish peasants who came to join their relatives and friends during the eighteenth century was less happy. Much of the fourfold population increase between 1713 and 1756 was accounted for by these arrivals from Ireland; by 1752 the Irish numbered some 3,000 persons, or about half the population. Their numbers and their refusals to take the oath of abjuration aroused the anxiety of the naval captains who were present during the summer. In the winter when there was little employment and a high consumption of rum, they lived in idleness, drunkenness, and disorder. Irish names figure largely in eighteenth-century reports of felonies and brawls and in the heavy sentences of the courts.[31]

In 1784 a proclamation of religious liberty coincided with the arrival of the first Roman Catholic priest, the Prefect Apostolic, Dr. J. L. O'Donel. His activities, a source of complaint to some of the Protestant merchants and officials, promoted the growth of a vigorous Roman Catholic spirit which found its expression not only in the Church but in the Benevolent Irish Society, founded as a non-sectarian organization in 1806.[32] As the eighteenth century closed, unrest in Ireland and the "United Irish" rebellion accelerated emigration from that un-happy country. Some of the new arrivals had links with the rebels. In 1800 the projected massacre of the people of St. John's by Irish malcontents in the garrison and United Irishmen in the town was averted by the information given and the influence exerted by Bishop O'Donel. In 1801 he rendered patriotic service by instructing his priests to "inculcate a willing obedience to the salutary laws of England, and to the commands of the Governor and magistrates" and to dissuade their people from conspiring with the "infidel French."[33]

During the prosperity of the war years, hopes of high wages induced thousands of poor and ignorant Irish to emigrate, while thousands more booked passage on the security of possible employment. Between 1811 and 1830 some 24,000 of these persons arrived in the appalling filth and overcrowding of the emigrant ships. In this period, outbreaks of typhus raged through the squalor of St. John's. The newcomers who obtained employment found at the end of the season that the deduction of their passage money from their wages left them nearly pen-niless.[34] Mounting prices thereafter kept them in the servitude of debt.[35] Those who failed to find employment remained derelict and destitute in the midst of the winter population, which passed the time in idleness and the consumption of rum. In 1815, when the population of St. John's was about 10,000, nightly armed patrols were necessary to guard the wharves and other property.[36] After the war, when prices and demand for cod fell, continued emigration augmented the debauched and idle floating population, aggravated the recurrent famine conditions and food riots, and worsened outbreaks of lawlessness and insubordi-nation. In some of the outports, only the presence of a naval or military detach-ment kept the populace in order through the long winters.[37]

Reforming zeal, political ambition, and mercantile self-interest would seem to have led the various proponents of representative government into denying or blinding themselves to the existing conditions or into using them as arguments for the change. Thus Morris, in undertaking to disprove the assertions of the Society for the Propagation of the Gospel that society in Newfoundland was retarded and degraded, resorted to attacks on the undeniable injustices and neglects in the colony's past. He declared that the island had reached the age for self-government.[38] Ignoring the dissensions which had arisen, he made it a grievance that the government had not established a civic administration in St. John's. He called for the establishment of constitutional government and an end to the "quackery" about alternatives. He called, too, for the full development of the resources of the island to support its increasing population.[39]

In the reformers' arguments, assertions about the need to foster agriculture, about the potentialities of the soil, and about the enthusiasm for its cultivation had a prominent place. A petition of 1830, referring to "millions of uncultivated acres," announced that the colonists had discovered in the capabilities of the soil "new and unbounded sources of profitable employment."[40] In 1831, however, the Governor informed Lord Goderich that so far from applications for 500,000 acres having been received, as had been alleged, 15,000 acres was the total in demand.[41] The fact was that in the known and accessible parts of the island the thin soil, the need for repeated fertilization, and the short and unreliable growing season gave the fishermen little incentive to extend their "potato patches" or to take up full-time farming. Little was known of the interior beyond the fringe of forest from which firewood was cut, and what had been seen consisted of barrens and ponds, scrub vegetation and rock.[42] Since the land had never been systematically explored, assertions about its arability were baseless and largely disproved in the course of time.[43]

Diplomatic arrangements which, by allowing international competition, had deprived the colony of the right to exploit to the full its resources in the fishery, had also curtailed its use of the soil. Although there was productive land on the west coast, particularly about St. George's Bay, the prohibition against settlement on the "French shore" shut the colonists off from legal title and protection. The Treaty of Versailles of 1783, which ceded St. Pierre and Miquelon to France in full right, had established the limits between which French subjects could take and cure fish on the Newfoundland coast, the Treaty shore being defined as extending from Cape Bonavista on the east, around the northern and western coasts, south to Cape Ray. By a controversial Declaration appended to the Treaty, Britain had promised to prevent her subjects from interrupting by competition the prosecution of the French fishery, and to remove, for that purpose, such fixed settlements as were formed. The French interpretation of the Declaration as a guarantee of "exclusive rights" was to be a source of dispute and a block in negotiations for more than a century. Less drastic concessions were made to American fishermen by the Convention of 1818 when they were given rights of competition but not of interference with the expansion of settlement. The Convention conceded to American subjects the right to take fish on the south coast from the Ramean Islands to Cape Ray and on the west coast north to the Quirpon Islands, and to dry and cure their fish within their defined limits on the south coast, but only in such places as were and remained unsettled. Similar fishing, curing, and drying rights were conferred for the south coast of Labrador.

While size,[44] needs, length of settlement, and growth of population suggested that it would be invidious to withhold representative government from Newfoundland, there were, as have been noted, several reasons for believing that its advocates were not entirely scrupulous and that its concession might be less than a boon. Cochrane's objections were founded in the belief that the circumstances of the colony did not yet warrant so fundamental a change.[45] He proposed instead a legislative council with powers to enact laws, not at variance with the principles of the British constitution, for the interior government and policing of the island. Alternatively, he suggested that corporations be established for some of the towns and that the existing council of five officials be enlarged to comprise fourteen members, half of them representing the government and the rest the "influential" part of the community, this Council to draft laws for enactment by Parliament. He advocated the imposition of a duty on spirits to provide further revenue, the revision of the Judicature Act, and improvements in the magistracy. Such changes would be sufficient, he thought, for the colony's needs.[46] James Simms, his Attorney-General, believed that giving the council a popular aspect might satisfy those who complained of unconstitutional government.[47]

For some time the weight of Cochrane's arguments had their effect at the Colonial Office. It seemed that the project for a legislature would be abandoned and some alternative measure adopted to give the inhabitants a share in the management of their affairs.[48] In July 1831, however, the pressure for a legislature was astutely renewed in the House of Commons by the Tory member for Worcester, George Robinson, a partner in Robinson, Brooking, and Garland, principal merchants in the Newfoundland trade, and a member of the island's political committee. He opposed the vote of £11,000 for the civil establishment of Newfoundland, declaring that if the colony were given a legislature it would never ask the House for another farthing. Debates about the Reform Bill intervened, but on the evening of its third reading Robinson revived the question at a time and in a manner calculated to win Whig and Radical support. His arguments for economy and justice in the government of Newfoundland won him the backing of the Radicals and he extracted from the Ministry the equivocal assurance that steps were about to be taken to extend to Newfoundland "as much freedom as was compatible with local circumstances."[49]

As 1831 ended and 1832 began there was a flurry of activity on the Newfoundland question. The Governor arrived for interviews with the Colonial Secretary and departed for Paris, convinced his opinion had prevailed. Robinson's partner, T. H. Brooking, came from St. John's to press the case for his fellow-petitioners.[50] James Stephen, as legal adviser to the Colonial Office, prepared, on the basis of his nineteen years of experience, a lengthy report on the value and limitations of colonial legislatures, and offered his recommendations for Newfoundland.[51] By mid-January, after the "fullest and most deliberate consideration," the decision had been taken to grant the colony the constitution it had asked.[52] Surprised and chagrined, Governor Cochrane could only assure Lord Goderich that he would forward the new arrangements as though they had originated with himself.[53]

The constitution was embodied in four documents. These were the brief Act which empowered the Crown to exercise the prerogative in establishing a legislature, the Governor's Commission, his Instructions, and the Proclamation for an election.[54] Together these provided that Newfoundland should have an assembly of fifteen persons elected from nine defined districts, and a nominated council of seven named persons with both legislative and executive functions. The franchise was to be very wide, the vote being given to all registered male householders, either tenants or owners, who had been resident in the island for a year. It seems to have been decided that an adequate franchise could only be secured by making no stipulation whatever about property valuation, annual rent, annual income, or literacy. The qualifications for candidates were to be the same, except that they must prove two years' residence. The revenue from the Imperial customs duties was to be at the Assembly's command, except for a sum of £6,500 reserved for certain official salaries; the reserving clause was to be repealed when the Assembly had passed a Civil List Act satisfactory to the Home Government.

Although Newfoundland was granted the British North American "transcript" of the British constitution, the Colonial Office had deep misgivings about the provision for a legislative council. Stephen, in his report, had condemned these councils as "scarcely more useful than popular." He said that in theory the council's function was to check the radicalism of the assembly and to free the governor from direct conflict with the elected members. In practice, he said, such councils acted only as defenders of their own privileges or as agents for the governor in unpopular measures; they relieved the governor from the responsibility he should bear without enhancing his authority. Far better, in Stephen's opinion, was the system in British Guiana where nominees and representatives were united in one legislative body. If such a body were established in Newfoundland, he believed that its members, too, would "mutually enlighten, assist and check each other" and the governor feel the full weight of his own responsibility.[55] With this view Goderich and Howick concurred.[56] It is surprising, therefore, that the Colonial Office chose to commit again what it had decided was a practical error.

It seems that Lord Goderich was influenced in his decision by the considerations of precedent and expediency raised by Stephen. The latter had pointed out that the Governor could be directly and lawfully authorized in his Commission to convoke an amalgamated body, but that such a Commission had never yet been issued. Further, the process of giving effect to a new constitutional theory would undoubtedly subject the Government to embarrassment in the House. The need to defend a novel constitution could be avoided if both branches of the Newfoundland Legislature could be induced to pass an act of union. This would provide for the admission to the Assembly of a certain number of government officers, *ex officio*, and for the dissolution of the Legislative Council.[57] Goderich instructed the Governor to propose such a bill, suggesting that three nominated members, the Colonial Secretary, the Attorney-General, and the Collector of Customs should sit in the Assembly and that the full Council should be retained only as an advisory body.[58] Lest the Assembly be hesitant about subverting the newly won constitution and the Council reluctant to pass a self-denying ordinance, Cochrane was to prepare opinion in advance by emphasis on Lord Goderich's strong desire for the union, and by judicious reference to disharmony in the other North American colonies.[59] Clearly, the Secretary of State hoped that gratitude might effect what convenience seemed to forbid. Aware of the deficiency of legislative experience in Newfoundland and of the disparity in the condition of its inhabitants, convinced of the wisdom of establishing an amalgamated body, the Colonial Office of 1832 lacked the flexibility and the resolution to undertake the experiment.

A second error the Colonial Office sought to avoid was the erection of an assembly in which the interests of St. John's would predominate at the expense of those of the widely scattered and sparsely settled outports. Earlier, before his conversion to the cause, Lord Howick had twice informed the House of Commons that there seemed no ready answer to this problem.[60] By February 1832, the decision having been taken, he could assure the petitioners of Poole, anxious for their long-vested interests in supplying the outports, that effective measures would be taken for obviating the difficulty.[61] The measures would appear to have been electoral divisions which would ensure the under-representation of the commercial capital, a household franchise which would admit all but transients, and a members' qualification which would secure sufficient candidates. The census of 1827 showed that the population of 59,000 was distributed in nine more or less distinct areas of settlement, groups of outports, on the eastern and southern coasts. This suggested a basic constituency of about 6,500 persons, but only in the four most populous districts, St. John's, Conception Bay, Trinity Bay, and Bonavista Bay, was this standard approached. The capital and Conception Bay were given three and four members respectively, the latter places one member each. The other five outport districts were below the standard, but four were given a member each, and the fifth, Placentia and St. Mary's, which contained a Roman Catholic population on the shores of adjoining south coast bays, was given two. In an assembly of fifteen members, the five smallest outport districts, with just over one-fifth of the population, would be proportionately over-re-presented by two-fifths of the members, while St. John's, with almost one-fourth of the population, would send only one-fifth (see Appendix E, Table I). There is no evidence that Cochrane suggested a political significance in the distribu-tion and concentration of Roman Catholics and Protestants in the several districts, but rather some evidence that he did not.[62] If he did make such a suggestion verbally, it would seem to have been dismissed as a problem to be solved within the colony.

The Governor's interviews with Lord Howick were apparently unfortunate. It was reasonable to assume, and Cochrane did assume, that his knowledge of the colony would be invaluable, but there was a gulf between the Governor and the Parliamentary Under-Secretary which seems to have been widened by their conferences about Newfoundland. Howick, seven years Cochrane's junior, was a didactic and dogmatic Whig, beginning a career in colonial management which was to be distinguished by a belief in representative institutions and a desire to lessen the economic and governmental burdens of the mother country.[63] One of his contemporaries has noted Howick's contempt for the opinion of others and the tenacity with which he clung to his own.[64] Cochrane declared that his opinions on the electoral divisions and qualifications were received in a petulant manner and with such an assumption of superior local knowledge that he resolved to make no further observations unless specifically asked.[65] Thus, the Governor's belief that the arrangements were injudicious seems to have been dismissed as a continuance of Tory obstructionism.[66]

As an illustration of Whiggish faith in the panacea of parliamentary bodies under executive control, the constitution of 1832 is ideal. There is evidence of the hypnotic power of the parliamentary model in the colony's pressure for in-stitutions whose limitations were elsewhere giving rise to complaint, and in the Colonial Office reluctance to impose a variant which they hoped the colony might have the wisdom to adopt. A representative body which was the empirical growth of centuries was conferred overnight upon a raw settlement which had grown up in illegitimacy and neglect; a franchise which was but a radical aspi-ration in the mother country was bestowed at once on unlettered fishermen whose existence she had only just ceased to ignore ; and an upper chamber which was the natural expression of aristocracy in the old land was presented to a rude colony where nearly all lived by catching or trading in cod.

CHAPTER TWO

THE GENESIS OF PARTY, 1832-1836

EXCEPT in the capital, the general election in the autumn of 1832 engendered little excitement and a Assembly of Protestant and mercantile aspect was formed (See Appendix B, Table I). At Placentia and St. Mary's one of the two mercantile members chosen was a Roman Catholic and at Conception Bay a coalescing agreement brought the return of two Protestant merchants and two Roman Catholic "dealers" (persons who dealt or traded directly with a merchant).[1] In most of the outports the election does not seem to have been contested, but in St. John's four candidates stood for the three seats. They were Dr. Carson, the veteran reformer, William Thomas, a prominent merchant, Patrick Kough, a prosperous contracting carpenter, and John Kent, an auctioneer and commission agent. Of these, Dr. Carson was not returned. Prowse, the island's standard historian, has attributed Carson's defeat to the "proverbial fickleness" of the public and to an electioneering trick which ensured Kough the votes of the Wexford Irish. Carson himself alleged that candidates Kent and Kough brought forward swollen "tallies" of voters in order to crowd his voters from the poll.[2]

The pettiness and the small scale of the election at St. John's might tempt one to dismiss it as a municipal contest conducted at a low level; yet, since it inaugurated three decades of violent party strife, it bears closer examination. Of the three victorious candidates, Willam Thomas clearly represented the resident mercantile interest. He was a substantial merchant and gentleman-farmer whose family connection with the island went back to Cromwellian times. As deputy chairman of the political committee, he had in recent years been in the van of the movement for a local legislature.[3] Like the officials of the colony he was a member of the Church of England. As a native, as a man of wealth and respectability, and as an advocate of an assembly, his qualifications were high, and he was apparently able to command support from all sections of the community. Patrick Kough was a well-to-do tradesman, a native of Wexford, and a Roman Catholic, whose skill and reliability had brought him responsible work at Government House and had earned him official esteem.[4] His election called forth a petition from Dr. Carson who issued the first of his calls for the purity of parliaments, declaring that Kough's employment as a contractor for the government disqualified him from membership in the Assembly.[5] This protest may have stemmed in part from personal chagrin, but to a man who had been fighting for almost a quarter of a century against despotism and officialdom in Newfoundland, the presence in the first Assembly of one who owed his advancement to official favour seemed ominous. Carson's initial defeat at the polls was probably due to the fact that he lacked the talents of a popular demagogue. His fearless, reasoned arguments against the old system had made him bitter enemies among its defenders, but such arguments were not those to rally the support of an illiterate labouring people. He seems to have been a man who could dilate upon grievances without arousing the aggrieved.[6]

If Thomas and Kough represented conservative elements in the community, and Carson an intellectual liberalism of limited appeal, John Kent, then only twenty-six, could be termed a colonial reformer of the school of Howe, Papineau, and Mackenzie. He seems to have given some attention to proceedings in the North American colonies and he declared that Newfoundland must not look with complacency on what it had achieved. In his address to the electors of St. John's, he said:

Our constitution has, as yet, only half developed itself; but in that partial development a sufficient evidence is given of the desire of power to hedge around its prerogative with a force ductile to its will, but irresponsible to the people. In a council nominated by the Governor, composed of those holding office under the Government, or expectants for the place, and in which the leading interests are unrepresented, oligarchical principles must prevail. The task of prostrating those principles or of so modifying them as to make them useful now devolves on the people.... Your extensive franchise, amounting to almost universal suffrage, will enable you to do this.[7]

The appearance of a "popular" candidate caused some uneasiness among those who had favoured representative government, but who did not look for radical reform. The Governor observed that some of the first promoters of the constitution were beginning to have second thoughts.[8] One of these, Henry Winton, editor of the *Public Ledger,* objected (September 18, 1832) to Kent as a newcomer qualified neither by length of residence nor by personal attainments to represent St. John's, the inference being that political opportunism rather than the interest of the colony was Kent's guiding principle. Kent had arrived in St. John's only eleven years earlier and did not occupy a significant place in the commercial life of the capital.[9] He had, however, as a fellow-emigrant from Waterford, come under the wing of Dr. Michael Anthony Fleming, the Roman Catholic Bishop, whose sister he was later to marry.[10] When Kent, irritated by the *Ledger*'s aspersions, informed the public, with youthful rashness, that though he were an imbecile an irresistible influence would carry him into the House,[11] the *Ledger* and the community could be in no doubt as to what influence was meant. Nor did the Bishop deny that he had used or would use influence with his flock; rather he issued a statement supporting Kent and justifying by paternal analogy his right as Bishop to do so.[12] At this, the *Ledger,* on September 21, adopted a threatening tone, urging the disgrace of clerical interference in political matters and stating that if Dr. Fleming wished to retain the respect of the community, he owed it to himself to retire from the contest. It announced that the Bishop was not, as he appeared to think, beyond the reach of the press which had only begun to deal with him, and advised him that in his collision with it he should not overrate his strength. This provoked a mass meeting at the Roman Catholic chapel at which two resolutions were passed, one lauding Dr. Fleming for his efforts on behalf of the people, the other denouncing Winton for attacks on the Church and the Bishop.[13] The Governor was told that the Bishop was present at the hustings on Kent's behalf.[14]

If the Governor, like Winton, saw a significance in this politico-religious combination, he gave no hint of it to the Colonial Office. A whole year was to elapse before he wrote a despatch describing the Kent-Fleming alliance.[15] Nor could a perusal of the colony's newspapers remedy this failure, since Cochrane had made no arrangement for the regular transmission of these to the Colonial Office.[16] The Governor was, in fact, a most haphazard correspondent. After ignoring the political scene for long periods he would pen lengthy, chaotic despatches describing events several months old.[17] Informed of an established trend, the Colonial Office could then only labour in its wake with tardy advice.

Lord Goderich had instructed the Governor that the constitution would provide him with a "large scope for the exercise of circumspection and industry."[18] Accordingly, Cochrane opened the Legislature in January 1833 with a ceremony which was designed to show that the Crown had not abdicated its function in the colony and with an address which called for unity of purpose and action in the new era. Glossing over late events, he congratulated the House on the complete harmony of the eight-day election in St. John's. He informed the members that their legislative tasks and responsibilities were great. He promised co-operation with them in all measures for the improvement of the island, stressing his detachment from all local influence and from all hope of personal gain.[19]

The vice-royal party had scarcely departed when the voice of democracy was heard contending against the influence of the Crown. Brown, a Roman Catholic member for Conception Bay, moved a resolution that the House proceed to the election of their own officers. The Governor had been instructed to maintain his right of appointment and Brown's motion was referred to the Committee on Privileges.[20] Although the Committee reported that the right belonged to the House, the members compromised by appointing the persons already named the Governor, a concession which the democrat, Kent, decidedly opposed.[21] Early in the session Brown gave notice of another attempt to purify the House of official influence by announcing a bill to prevent contractors with the Government and Government officers from sitting in the Assembly. This was clearly aimed at removing Patrick Kough and the Colonial Treasurer, Newman Hoyles. In this effort Brown also failed, for though he piloted the Bill through a divided House, it was amended in the Council and the session closed without its enactment.[22] A desire to avoid setting an awkward precedent in so limited a society apparently made the House reluctant to finalize such a bill.[23] Nor was Brown's third effort more successful. Facts were necessary to substantiate a claim that there was a Church of England monopoly of office. He moved for a return of the last census which would show the number of each religious creed and the names and creeds of the public officers. The Governor refused the request until the House should vote an appropriation for a new census.[24] For the moment the reformers were checked.

The democratic element in the Assembly was a significant factor in ensuring the rejection of the Colonial Office proposal for the union of the two legislative bodies. Laid before the House on January 9, it was rejected unanimously and without discussion.[25] Cochrane's analysis of the grounds for the refusal was no doubt correct. He said that the "democrats" feared the ascendancy of nominated councillors in their midst, while the more conservative members, the "constitutionalists," feared the establishment of an unbridled democracy in which nominees would be outvoiced and outvoted by representatives.[26] For opposite reasons both groups wanted the Legislative Council.

Since the Council could not be abolished, the Governor suggested that it be enlarged from six members to nine or ten, and made more representative by selecting half its members from the principal inhabitants. Accordingly he submitted a list of merchants. Further, he suggested the need for a separate executive council of officials and senior persons, since he believed it an anomaly that he must consult as advisers the very people who had already decided for or against the measure on which he desired advice. He also made a strong plea for the removal of the Chief Justice from the Council on the grounds that his political duties interfered with his judical ones, and that persons who collided with him in political matters might attribute political motives to his conduct on the Bench.[27]

Within a month these constitutional anomalies had produced a crisis. The Assembly had passed the colony's first Revenue Bill which laid small duties on wines and spirituous liquors from British and foreign sources. The Bill was rejected in a Legislative Council of four when Chief Justice R. A. Tucker, presiding, declared dogmatically that the duties were neither legal nor expedient. In this stand he was backed by the Attorney-General, who had opposed the granting of representative government. They argued that the Bill conflicted with the Imperial Act (6 Geo. IV, c. 114) which already taxed these items and that it discriminated against British produce.[28] Tucker said that the state of Newfoundland did not permit a double tax and maintained that so far from being ready for a legislature, the island was not far removed from "primitive barbarity," that the people were illiterate, and that the means were lacking to advance education and religion. He did not concede, it may be noted, that a colonial revenue might remedy these defects.[29] Further, he told the Council that if the Bill were passed, he would render it abortive from the Bench.[30] The Assembly declared that they could not but "consider the course pursued by the Council as manifesting a feeling more calculated to check the early operation of the Assembly than to promote the best interests of the Colony . . ."[31] Cochrane was inclined to agree, the Bill having been passed by the persons who had a real stake in the island and having been rejected by the officials who had not. He repeated his request for a separate executive council.[32]

On the immediate question of ensuring a revenue for the island, the Colonial Office acted with as much vigour as the Governor could desire. Tucker's stand was condemned and his conditional resignation confirmed.[33] Parliament was approached for a "last" grant for Newfoundland.[34] The Council and the Assembly were assured that the Revenue Bill was valid and advised that in future they must provide for their own expenditure.[35]

On the broader question of constitutional amendment, the Colonial Office was still as hesitant as it had been concerning amalgamation. The Governor's Instructions authorized him to call one Council and must be amended if he were to call two. After so short a trial it was apparently inconvenient for the Secretary of State to have to seek an amendment. Since the removal of the Chief Justice from the Council would have to be effected in the same way, neither of these changes were sanctioned. Members could be added to the Council by the issue of royal warrants, however, and three of Cochrane's slate were approved.[36]

Since these decisions of May 1833 were not conducive to legislative harmony but produced instead the opposite effect, they will be examined more closely. The officials as a group having proved obstructive, the Governor recommended the addition of a mercantile element to the council which would, presumably, provide a body more receptive to the measures of the mercantile Assembly. For the Colonial Office such a change seemed to need no defence and from the Governor's list of "suitable" gentlemen they chose the first three: John Dunscombe, William Thomas, and John Garland. Since the Governor had stressed the difficulty of finding respectable persons from the outports who could spare the time for the sessions, it is not surprising that his nominees were all residents of St. John's. But, having urged the dearth of respectable persons as a reason for refusing a legislature, he ensured, by priority of recommendation, that two of these persons, Speaker Garland and Mr. Thomas, would be removed from the House.[37] These merchants were no doubt willing to become "Honourable" councillors and to leave the debates of the Assembly in order to exert their influence in the Council, and Cochrane was undoubtedly predisposed to choose as his councillors those whom he chose to meet socially. If his aim, however, were to alter the composition of the Council so as to make it more harmonious with the Assembly, it was unwise to risk an unwanted alteration in the latter. Although the Assembly could be termed mercantile, there were already within its walls two reformers, Brown and Kent, who were vocal in questioning the establishment. Others might join them as seats were vacated. The Governor may have calculated the risk and decided to take it, although his despatches suggest that it had not seriously occurred to him.[38]

On the religious question, the discontent among Roman Catholics and Dissenters about appointments to office of which Brown's resolution was a symptom, the Governor kept official silence. Perhaps his answer was his solid slate of Church of England councillors, but in making his selection he may not have deigned to notice the question at all. Although the population of St. John's was two-thirds Roman Catholic, most of the Catholics were members of what Cochrane termed, in the phrase of the day, the "lower orders." Of the rest, there were a few substantial citizens—merchants, professional men, and shopkeepers—from whom he could have chosen, had he been so disposed.[39] Apparently he numbered none of these among the principal inhabitants of St. John's. Whether he acted from religious bigotry or from social prejudice, or from both, his selections served to focus the ambitions of the Catholics upon the elected Assembly.

Certain coincidences of persons and events in 1833 may have played their part in the Colonial Office decision not to alter the constitution of Newfoundland and in the choice of a replacement for the recalcitrant Chief Justice. When the constitution came before the Colonial Office for review in the spring of 1833, Lord Stanley had just replaced Lord Goderich as Colonial Secretary in the Whig Ministry. His attention was engaged by the problems posed in the West Indies by the abolition of slavery and the regulation of apprenticeship.[40] It happened also that in March the Attorney-General of Upper Canada, Henry John Boulton, had been dismissed at Lord Goderich's direction for pursuing an obstructive course in the Assembly of that colony. Boulton and the Solicitor-General had twice opposed the admission to the House of the reform agitator, William Lyon Mackenzie. Their failure to support the policy being attempted by the Government led Sir John Colborne to ask for their removal.[41] In June, Boulton arrived in England to exonerate himself with the Secretary of State. Asserting that the Governor had not informed him of his policy, Boulton seems to have vindicated himself to Stanley and he was promptly appointed Chief Justice of Newfoundland.[42]

The Governor had stressed the need for care in the selection of a new Chief Justice.[43] The man required for Newfoundland should be an experienced barrister, well versed in English criminal law, able to devise enactments or a code applicable to the island, and to undertake the remodelling of the courts and of judicial procedure.[44] Boulton, by training and experience, undoubtedly had these qualifications. His career began in 1807 with law studies, first under his father, the Solicitor-General of Upper Canada, and then in London from 1811 to 1814. There followed two years at Oxford, after which he was called to the Bar. In 1818 he became Solicitor-General of Upper Canada, and in 1830 Attorney-General. He was familiar with the functioning of colonial legislatures and anxious to continue his career in the colonies. In all these respects he seemed ideal for his dual tasks in Newfoundland, and the Colonial Office was pleased that so favourable an opportunity had presented itself of providing for him.[45] He seemed to the Office a practical person, in contrast to his apparently unsound and eccentric predecessor.[46] While his record indicated that he was also conservative, opinionated, and stubborn, these characteristics may have counted in his favour with Lord Stanley, lately Chief Secretary for Ireland and fresh from his spirited opposition to Daniel O'Connell on the question of the Irish tithes; Boulton's determined stand against another demagogue may have created a bond of sympathy between the two men which made the Secretary receptive to his explanations. Stanley, though serving with the Whigs, was essentially conservative himself, moving, after he left the Whigs in 1834, towards the right and protectionist wing of the Tory party. The analyst of his colonial policy has pointed out that Stanley was characterized by an essential disbelief in free institutions for the colonies, by an aristocratic dislike for factious demagogues, and by a total failure to understand or to sympathize with colonial aspirations.[47] Boulton's conservatism may, therefore, have been a factor in his appointment. But he seems to have been selected mainly because he was available and aggrieved, and because he was an experienced and energetic man, professionally qualified to do much for an infant colony.

When the second session of the Assembly was prorogued in October 1833, the Governor was able to forward for approval sixteen useful Acts.[48] Half of these provided the first municipal regulations for St. John's, Harbour Grace, and Carbonear, while the rest were of a more general nature, including a Quarantine Act, a Barristers' Qualifications Act, and an Act restoring to Dissenting ministers the right to celebrate marriage.[49] These were only the beginning of a heavy legislative programme which called for enactments of criminal law, for harbour regulations, and for the establishment of a savings bank, and, when a revenue was secured, for roads, schools, lighthouses, constables and magistrates, a militia, and a census.[50]

Before the House met again it proved necessary to hold an election to fill one of the two vacancies caused by the removals to the Council.[51] Two candidates presented themselves for the seat left by William Thomas: a Roman Catholic shopkeeper, Timothy Hogan, and the reformer, Dr. Carson. The election of Kent in 1832 had evidently made the Roman Catholic clergy fully conscious of what they could do in exerting influence for the candidate they preferred. This time the favourite was Dr. Carson, who was not a Catholic, but who had set up a reform newspaper, the *Patriot,* and whose election the Bishop freely advocated from the pulpit. Hogan appears to have been a rather independent Roman Catholic, not amenable to clerical pressure in the political field, and with Protestant friends. Strong measures were taken by the Bishop and his priests to secure Hogan's withdrawal as a candidate. There were hints, veiled or explicit, that Roman Catholics who voted for or dealt with the man might be denied the sacraments. After three months, cut off from his church and faced with financial ruin, Hogan withdrew from the election and made a public apology to the Bishop.[52] Winton of the *Ledger,* on December 10, 1833, aroused as he had been by the Kent-Fleming combination, took up Hogan's case, deploring strenuously the growing priestly influence in politics. Although the newspaper was ostensibly anti-Catholic in the political sense only, its attacks on the clergy provoked counter-attacks from the Roman Catholic pulpit.[53] The Bishop afterwards declared that he had had to resort to this means of defence because all newspapers were closed to him, but the fact seems to be that he did not try their columns.[54] The outbursts from the pulpit served as incitements to mob violence, and a hostile crowd assembled before Winton's house on Christmas night and was dispersed with some difficulty by the few troops of the garrison.[55]

Cochrane found himself in difficulties, with sharp criticism from the Colonial Office and concerted hostility from an incipient Roman Catholic party. Lord Stanley made it clear that he held the Governor more than a little responsible for the disturbances. Cochrane, he said, had been remiss in not reporting the depleted state of the garrison and imprudent in recommending Thomas for the Council, in view of the "insubordinate spirit" in St. John's.[56] The Colonial Office had been given no reason to apprehend these troubles. It was now learned that the Bishop and his flock seemed disposed to play the "game" which had for so long been going on in Ireland.[57] The Governor protested that the mandamus having arrived, he had had to remove Thomas to the Council, and that he had not anticipated that the Bishop would again enter the election field.[58]

On the night after the disturbances, while feeling still ran high, a public meeting was held at which Carson, Kent, Morris, and other reformers were conspicuous. Four resolutions of an inflammatory nature were passed. These expressed the determination of the meeting to counter a despotic attack on liberties, to inquire from the Governor the reason for outrages by the troops, to thank Dr. Fleming for the calming influence he had exerted, and to offer sympathy and aid to those injured or jailed. There followed a number of public exchanges between the Bishop and the Governor. The Bishop declared that

Cochrane, by placing the Government's advertising in the *Ledger*, countenanced the editor's criticisms of him; this the Governor denied. The Bishop then distributed his own account of an interview with the Governor phrased so that the latter seemed to imply that the magistrate and the military commandant were solely responsible for the use of the troops; this the Governor also denied. In January 1834 a series of letters began to appear in the *Patriot* accusing the Governor of bigotry, injustice, and despotism. When Cochrane was about to sue the proprietor and the printer, Father Troy, a priest in the Bishop's household, announced himself to be the author. The Governor at once transferred the suit, though he declared that neither the priest nor the Bishop seemed literate enough to compose the letters. He attributed them to a man of radical political views, a schoolmaster named John V. Nugent, brought by the Bishop from Waterford. Cochrane believed that the Bishop condoned the letters and that he had sanctioned an "irresponsible re-opening of the sectarian wound" as part of a scheme to establish a Roman Catholic political ascendancy. He declared that the Bishop and his clergy were catering to the passions of the lower four-fifths of the population of St. John's in order to "convert a naturally quiet and well-disposed people into engines of violence and disorder."[59]

So violent were the *Patriot*'s attacks upon the Governor that he felt constrained to point out to Stanley that they were being directed to his eye.[60] He believed that Carson forwarded the newspaper regularly with a view to making good an initial boast that it would take but twelve months to achieve the Governor's recall.[61] Cochrane did not hesitate to retaliate. On the grounds that he could draw no funds for the salary of District Surgeon until the Assembly voted its first Supply Bill in 1834, he abolished Carson's office and when the Assembly voted a salary for the position, he altered its scope and gave it to another physician, Dr. Edward Kielly, who was to be Carson's adversary in the celebrated case of *Kielly* v. *Carson*.[62]

The new session of the Assembly began with a sharp contest for the Speakership between Carson and T. R. Bennett, the Protestant merchant who was the member for Fogo. The doctor declared that three members, Patrick Kough, Newman Hoyles, and Charles Cozens, a recent bankrupt, were ineligible for their seats and could not vote for a Speaker. Brown objected to John Martin, the Protestant member for St. Mary's, who as a mercantile agent did not, technically, occupy his own premises. Since the four members voted on the question of their own eligibility, they retained their seats and Carson's opponent became Speaker.[63] Having failed to expel the members odious to them the reformers drew up a petition for the dissolution of the Assembly and the election of another, and by exhibiting it at the Roman Catholic chapel after mass, obtained the signatures of some 2,000 persons, the Bishop's being third. The Governor was informed that priestly pressure had been exerted on the parishioners, that some of the signatures and marks were fraudulent, and that very few non-Catholics had signed.[64] In a report to Cochrane, with which James Stephen concurred, the Attorney-General of the colony declared that there were no valid grounds for the dissolution.[65] Whatever the law on matters of eligibility in England, it was not applicable to the colony unless the Assembly chose by legislation to make it so.[66]

The activities of the new Chief Justice convinced the reformers that another enemy had arrived in the colony. Their suspicions were aroused when in December 1833, shortly after his arrival, Boulton altered the rules for the em-panelling of Supreme Court juries. The effect of the change, if not the motive behind it, was almost to eliminate Roman Catholic jurors who were likely to be of radical persuasion, for the Sheriff was instructed to constitute the juries by ballot and subsequent strike-off from a restricted Grand Jury list for which few but merchants and Protestants could qualify.[67] In January 1834, Kent and Brown launched an enquiry in the House into the timing and nature of this change, but Boulton wrote to a member of the Colonial Office that his efforts to regu-larize the proceedings of the Supreme Court were appreciated by all who were capable of forming an opinion on such matters.[68]

There is no doubt that Boulton was convinced that he must take an im-mediate stand against judicial laxity and against lawlessness and insubordina-tion. No less than twelve persons arrested for capital felonies were awaiting indictment by a Grand Jury and arraignment before him in the Supreme Court.[69] The fishing season over, large numbers of idle persons roamed the capital and lounged about its grog-shops, while the press, the politicians, and the priests kept the recent by-election fever high. Boulton believed that the arts of a few "designing" persons working upon the religious prejudices of the Irish Roman Catholics were making the people as discontented as Daniel O'Connell him-self could desire.[70] Indeed, complaints by these "designing" persons were not long in finding their way to O'Connell, after Boulton, with a steady indifference to opinion, had conducted the trials with his new juries and under his new rules and had pronounced the death sentence upon six of the offenders. O'Con-nell passed on to the Colonial Office a remonstrance about changes in the procedure of the Supreme Court and a petition that two of the death sentences be remitted.[71] The Bishop himself, forwarding through O'Connell a petition on behalf of the children of a convicted murderess, depicted the Chief Justice as a Tory whose judicial decisions were the product of political bias, bigotry, and sadism.[72]

As President of the Council, Boulton was in a position to frame criminal law as well as to administer it from the Bench. He therefore devised a bill which passed the Council and the Assembly and which came to be known to the reformers as "Mr. Boulton's Criminal Code for Newfoundland" (4 Wm. IV, c. 5 (Nfld.)). To them it was a source of grievance and agitation not only because of the discretionary rights of punishment it conferred upon the three judges, but also because it seemed to give them, as prison administrators, inquisitorial powers before and after conviction.[73] It did, in fact, give the judge wide powers of banishment and punishment, with provisions for whipping, hard labour in iron clogs or shackles, and solitary confinement, as well as powers to regulate prison discipline and diet. For James Stephen, however, under whose review passed all colonial laws, it seems to have been a satisfactory application of English laws to the Newfoundland situation.[74]

A further source of grievance to those who saw the Chief Justice as an op-presser was his Act to incorporate a Law Society and to regulate the admission of barristers and attorneys to practise in the courts (c. 23). This Act, with its provision that subsequent to its passage none but those called to the bar in Great Britain or qualified by five years' service with a practising Newfoundland attorney might practise in the colony, was interpreted as a device to close the bar to local aspirants and to deny justice to persons who could not afford the fees charged by the qualified few.[75]

The reformers were too few in number to prevent the passage of bills with which they did not agree or to impose their will upon the House. Kent, for instance, would have had the members say in the Reply to the Governor that Sir Thomas had been "induced" to believe military power was necessary to support the civil power in the colony; in this he was overruled.[76] During 1834, with a mercantile majority, with a merchant as Speaker, and with a young barrister, E. M. Archibald (son of S. G. Archibald, the Speaker of Nova Scotia), as Clerk of the House,[77] the course of legislation and debate was relatively smooth. The legislative output was almost double that of 1833, much of it, understandably, being mercantile in character.[78] Sir Thomas felt that it was the best House Newfoundland could ever expect; any change must bring a deterioration, and the next election, he was sure, would mean the return of ten Roman Catholics. Already, he said, six of the thirteen members then attending were under the orders of the Bishop, so that none of the rest dared absent himself for a day.[79]

It is not surprising that the Assembly prepared a measure (c. 14) to increase the number of representatives, as they were authorized to do by the Imperial Act. The bill provided for the return of twenty-five members by subdividing the existing nine electoral divisions so as to create twenty-four districts each returning a single member, except the city of St. John's proper, which would return two. The objects appear to have been to remove obscurities about district boundaries, to relieve members of the strain of constant attendance, to provide a wider basis for the selection of committees, and to secure the return of members independent of the Bishop's influence. Although Sir Thomas could not see that an increase of members was yet warranted, he pointed out to the Colonial Office, as the bill's proponents pointed out to him, that if the bill were not confirmed it might be difficult to obtain its re-enactment in a subsequent session or in a new Assembly. Since it carried, necessarily, a suspending clause, he recommended that confirmation be withheld until its expediency had been demonstrated.[80] The drafters apparently hoped, though in the absence of accurate statistics on religious distribution they could not be sure, that the redivision would bring a majoriy of Protestants. When the census of 1836 revealed a preponderance of Protestants in thirteen of the twenty-four districts (Appendix E, Table II) the new Governor recommended in the most decided manner that the bill should be sanctioned.[81]

In June 1834 Governor Cochrane received his first intimation that he was to be removed from Newfoundland before the end of the year, ostensibly because his period of service had expired.[82] Actually, Lord Stanley, who left the Colonial Office in June, and his successor, Sir Thomas Spring Rice, seem to have decided that there could be no hope for improvement in the unsatisfactory state of the colony under a governor who had rendered himself unpopular with a large portion of the population. When Cochrane protested that Goderich had assured him of a reasonable tenure of office under his new Commission, or a larger colony to govern, Spring Rice remained adamant. There was nothing on paper to support the Governor's contention and he saw no reason to reverse Stanley's decision.[83] Cochrane's tardy reports and explanations, as well as his extravagance, may have contributed to an impression that he lacked the qualities of a good colonial governor, for he never received another appointment from the Colonial Office. Cochrane himself suspected that complaints from various quarters had prejudiced the Office against him, for he was at odds not only with Carson, the Bishop, and the reformers, but with an importunate landowner, and with the Ordinance Department.[84] With the Treasury, too, he was in disrepute. By August the Commissioners had decided that he had so deviated from their instructions for the disposal of the parliamentary grant as to incur personally a very serious responsibility.[85] He was partly responsible, too, in Stanley's view, for the disorders of the previous December. The Governor's original objections to the granting of a legislature, his pessimistic predictions, and his disposition to oppose rather than to conciliate could scarcely fail to suggest that the constitution could only be given a fair test under a new administrator.

The man selected for this task was, like Cochrane, without experience in civil administration. He was Captain Henry Prescott of the Royal Navy, a fifty-one-year-old Whig, a veteran of the Napoleonic War and of responsible missions on the coast of South America, and the son of an admiral who had been on the Newfoundland station (see Appendix A). Although his background, like Cochrane's, was naval, Prescott had won his promotion to captain not through jobbery by his father, but through distinguished service. In almost all other respects, too, he seems to have been unlike Cochrane. On hearing that Prescott had been appointed, an officer under whom he had served wrote to congratulate the Colonial Office, saying that they could not have chosen an officer with sounder judgment or with more propriety of character; he was a man of complete discretion and incorruptible integrity and as an administrator he would not fail to be "steady, impartial, and considerate."[86] His despatches from Newfoundland go far to confirm this description, being characterized, like his speeches, by calmness, deliberation, and precision.[87] James Stephen seems to have regarded him as an exemplary governor, a man of "excellent sense and temper."[88]

Captain Prescott arrived at St. John's on November 3, 1834, and Cochrane departed in the same week, complaining that his "fair fame" had been sullied, and that he had incurred "all the penalties of imbecility and impropriety without any ostensible cause." He declared that only thirty householders in the whole island disapproved of his government, that these were under the influence of the Bishop and Father Troy, and that Kent openly boasted that his representations to O'Connell had helped to remove the Governor from office.[89] As Sir Thomas and his daughter drove to the ship down the street named in his honour, the assembled mob hooted and threw mud,[90] Father Troy having, reportedly, recommended from the pulpit a derisive farewell.[91] So closed a vice-regal career of eight years.

To allay intense party feeling and to lessen the sectarian content of island politics, Captain Prescott believed it imperative to adopt for himself a rule of entire impartiality.[92] To this end, immediately Sir Thomas had sailed, he instructed the Attorney-General to discontinue the suit against Father Troy.[93] Six months after his arrival he was able to report that the course he had set himself had thus far kept him from attacks by the press of either party and that he was "in habits of civility and, in some degree, of kindness with Dr. Fleming."[94] The Governor's early efforts to lower the political temperature of the colony were, however, thwarted and almost nullified by the inflammatory activities of the Chief Justice and the Bishop.

As in Upper Canada, Boulton's stern, uncompromising disposition seems to have blinded him to the virtue and necessity of tempering zeal with discretion and legalism with flexibility. Governor Cochrane's parting advice had been that he continue to act with a scorn for "spurious popularity" and with a "steady indifference to public opinion." Boulton's efforts from the Council and the Bench to regularize the law of Newfoundland and to sweep away eccentric customs suggest that this counsel accorded so well with his own principles as to be superfluous.[95] By the summer of 1835 he had rendered himself so odious to the advocates of popular rights that he had repaired to England to urge, unsuccessfully, that he be transferred to another colony.[96] In 1834 he had introduced a bill which, had it passed the Assembly, would have extended to the island the English law of real property, with inheritable succession in land, and would have replaced the customary law by which landed property was distributed as real chattels.[97] He attempted by a series of judicial decisions to revolutionize the credit arrangements under which the fisheries had long been conducted. He ruled that a planter's past creditors, rather than his current supplier, had prior claims to his fish, oil, and gear. He altered a writ of attachment so as to make it possible for a planter's boat and gear to be attached for debt during the fishing season. He decided that a fishing servant did not have the right to follow the fish and oil for his wages. Convinced that the system was unsound, he ignored its long history and the precedents of his own Court.[98] His decisions, by lessening the confidence with which fishermen hired themselves to impoverished planters, earned for him a place among the oppressors of Newfoundland. He was, on the other hand, viewed with great favour by the wealthy merchants. The Governor urged that Boulton's removal would be a happy event since his popularity with the merchants made for the strongest party feelings.[99]

In May 1835 Boulton's triple role in a case of contempt of court did much to exacerbate political feelings in the colony. The *Patriot*, the organ of dissidence in Newfoundland, had used some remarks by the Chief Justice in the Supreme Court as the basis for a derisive article on the merits of hanging. Boulton cited the editor, R. J. Parsons, for contempt, and acting alone as prosecutor, judge, and jury, heard the case and passed a sentence of great severity. This sentence, and Boulton's questionable method of conducting the case, increased the existing excitement and led to the formation of a Constitutional Society whose immediate purpose was to free the editor and to remove the Chief Justice. There were rumours that a mob planned to pull down the courthouse to release Parsons, and the garrison was installed as a precaution.[100] Petitions from the prisoner and 5,000 of his supporters were despatched to the Colonial Office.[101] They resulted in immediate instructions that the Governor should free Parsons and repay his fine. While the Law Officers of the Crown defended Boulton's right to sentence for contempt of himself in office, they declared that propriety should have led him to follow the English practice, which was to make a deposition, to secure an indictment, and to bring the accused to trial by jury.[102] When Boulton heard that the sentence had been remitted, he pressed for a transfer from the colony on grounds of personal danger to himself and his family.[103] His failure to secure a West Indian appointment was, he said a "grievous disappointment."[104]

Boulton's fears for his physical safety were not unwarranted for in May 1835 Henry Winton of the *Ledger* had been the victim of an outrageous assault in which his ears were cut off.[105] As the outspoken opponent of clerical influence in politics, Winton had drawn frequent denunciations from the Roman Catholic pulpit, denunciations which extended to all Roman Catholics who patronized the *Ledger* as subscribers or advertisers.[106] Goaded by the spiritual influence being used against him, Winton was occasionally intemperate in his observations, making, for instance, derogatory remarks about the nuns brought to the colony by Bishop Fleming. This had resulted in a meeting of Roman Catholics at which his article was censured.[107] In May 1835 he was waylaid near Carbonear by a group of masked men armed with knives. The Governor believed that repeated tirades from the altar and the pulpit had prompted the assault and that the perpetrators might well believe they had performed a meritorious act.[108] Despite large rewards offered by the Government and the merchants, the culprits were not revealed and the Governor understood that the whole affair was a matter for rejoicing among the lower order of Roman Catholics.[109]

Prescott's efforts to lessen the spirit of religious party were counteracted in 1835 by an incident in the Roman Catholic outport of St. Mary's when bad feeling between the inhabitants and the mercantile establishment, Slade, Elson and Company of Poole, culminated in the destruction of some of the company's property. The company's agent and the clerks were the only Protestants in the community. The former, John Martin, appears to have been a pompous, self-important little West Country man.[110] Acting in his triple capacity as agent, district magistrate, and member for St. Mary's, Martin provided the Governor and Council with an *ex parte* account of the affair which alleged that the local priest had instigated and led his parishioners to the attack. According to this report, the priest had tried unsuccessfully to secure public use of a ship's room (a shore site for the curing and drying of fish) claimed by the company. The report also alleged that he had erected a church without permission upon company ground, and, on behalf of the inhabitants, had requested from the company a substantial advance of supplies. When the chief clerk, obeying his instructions, refused this request, simmering hostility had burst into violence and a valuable fish flake was destroyed. The constables who arrived on the colonial brig found a populace solidly resistant to their efforts to find and arrest the culprits.[111] A Bench warrant from the Chief Justice compelled the priest to appear, not in the Southern District Court at St. Mary's, but, after a long winter journey overland, in the Supreme Court at St. John's. There Boulton's charge to the Grand Jury secured an indictment. When sympathizers with the priest tried to arrange for Roman Catholic counsel on the grounds that no Protestant barrister could be trusted to conduct the defence, the Chief Justice, with his colleagues, indignantly refused to permit unqualified counsel in the Court and charged the petitioners with great disrespect to the bar and the Bench.[112] Boulton's conduct was strongly commended by the mercantile community,[113] and as strongly condemned by almost 9,000 other persons.[114] His accusers were advised that they must appeal formally to the Privy Council if they wished an enquiry into the alleged maladministration of justice.[115]

Excitement about the case was kept high by a series of postponements which entailed more journeys for the priest, with the result that he became, not unnaturally, a near-martyr in the eyes of his people. The delays, which prolonged the case for eighteen months, stemmed from two causes—the resistance of the culprits to arrest and the reluctance of Martin and his clerk to leave their posts to appear for the prosecution. To make the arrest the Governor, on the advice of his Council and with the sanction of Glenelg, proposed to send to St. Mary's by naval frigate a detachment of troops, accompanied by a magistrate and an officer of the law, a naval vessel being necessary because the Assembly had decided to eliminate the appropriation for the brig.[116] It was May 1836, however, before the frigate arrived in St. John's, and before it could be sent to St. Mary's the culprits surrendered, apparently induced to do so by a pastoral letter which the Bishop published after the Governor's proclamation had appeared. Although the Bishop's letter advised obedience, its tenor was somewhat less than pacific:

... the object ... is evidently to exhibit the character of the people ... as turbulent, in order to prove the value to the government of individuals in high places who will not be trammelled by the fetters of the law when the object is coercion of the people. The natural question then is, how shall you defeat the machinations of your enemies? Simply by not suffering yourselves to be led astray from the paths of rectitude, by reverencing the laws and respecting the authorities.[117]

Five months later, while the case was still in progress, he published another letter in similar vein, implying that the case had been prejudged and that no priest could expect justice in a Newfoundland court.[118] Nor was the sense of grievance among Roman Catholics dispelled when, in May 1837, the priest was finally acquitted, the prosecution abandoning the charges against him when Martin's story was shown to contain exaggeration and misrepresentation and when his clerk, the principal Crown witness, failed to appear.[119]

In the belief that a letter of admonition from the Court of Rome might persuade Bishop Fleming to abandon his venture into Newfoundland politics, the Colonial Office had in 1834 begun discreet negotiations to call his conduct to the attention of the Pope. Extracts from Governor Cochrane's despatches were sent to Lord Palmerston at the Foreign Office.[120] These were forwarded by him to the British Minister at Florence and by the Minister to a British agent at Rome. In September 1834 the Colonial Office learned that Cardinal Bernetti, the Vatican Secretary of State, would convey to Dr. Fleming and his clergy the Pope's disapproval of their role in Newfoundland elections.[121] Cardinal Bernetti's promises, however, were not implemented for when the British agent called to ascertain whether a letter had actually been sent, he was told that the Cardinal had fallen ill and had forgotten to inform his successor about the matter. The latter, Cardinal Capaccini, seems to have temporized, saying that the moment was unfavourable to bring the affair to the attention of the Pope, but that he himself would write a private and friendly letter to the Bishop and would later mention it to His Holiness.[122] Judging by the events of 1835, the deterrent effect of the Cardinal's letter was negligible. The Bishop's reply to it was compounded of denial, self-justification, and counter-accusation. Shrewdly, in view of the papal sentiments about liberals, he transferred this label to his political opponents, Roman Catholic and Protestant, whom he described as dangerous innovators.[123]

In May 1835 Prescott reported that the measures taken by the Colonial Office to close the Bishop's political career had completely failed. He forwarded to the Secretary of State a document drawn up by a Roman Catholic, whom Prescott described as a respectable and industrious tradesman, who had incurred by his political independence the wrath of the Bishop and his clergy. The tradesman described the measures taken against him because he had supported Carson's opponent in 1833 and because he subscribed to the *Ledger*. He was denied the rites of the Church; from the pulpit Father Troy had proscribed trade with him and had declared that he must be made a beggar before he could become a good Catholic; placards had been posted which warned against any dealings with him. The man was but one of several respectable Catholics in the same plight, wrote the Governor, but the others were too apprehensive of the power of the priests and the effect of denunciation to lay their cases before him.[124] There is copious evidence that many other Catholics endured similar penalties and were left no recourse but published apologies to the Bishop, death-bed recantations, or departure from the island.[125]

Once again the Colonial Office sought to restrain Bishop Fleming. Unwilling to attempt direct intervention with the Roman Catholic clergy of the colony, the Colonial Secretary sought the aid of Dr. Bramston, Vicar Apostolic of London, before whom in July 1835 the cases of Winton and the Catholic complainant were laid. Although Dr. Bramston had no official authority over the Bishop, it was hoped that his remonstrances would have great weight.[126] In the same month Dr. Bramston wrote a letter of kindly admonition to the Bishop, asking that he use his spiritual influence to restore harmony to the colony.[127] The Bishop's reaction was extreme resentment that Governor Prescott had preferred "highly criminating" charges against him.[128] His reply was a long complaint about the whispering slander spread by his supposed friend, the Governor, which he described as part of a "vile" campaign by Boulton, Winton, the officials, and the merchants to rout Catholicism from Newfoundland.[129]

In 1836 efforts were made at the Colonial Office to have Bishop Fleming and Father Troy, the most political of his priests, removed from the colony. Glenelg, the Colonial Secretary, assured Palmerston that the admonition from Rome had had no effect and that the island was tormented and the Catholic population driven to the "most atrocious extremes" by the conduct and language of the Bishop and Father Troy.[130] After the St. Mary's affair he became convinced that Palmerston should make further representations to the Court of

Rome, asking that the Bishop and some of his priests be replaced.[131] Once again the Foreign Office embarked on its circuitous negotiations via Florence and Rome. In May, Glenelg advised the Governor of the result. The Congregation of the Propaganda had addressed a reprimand to the Bishop which Glenelg hoped would obviate the need for more vigorous and decisive measures.[132] Shortly after receiving this second admonition from Rome the Bishop proceeded to England. His object was to bypass the Governor and to urge in person that the Colonial Office grant him a portion of Ordinance Department land for the erection of a church and other buildings, a grant which he seemed to think had been postponed for sectarian reasons rather than by interdepartmental delays.[133] While in England he applied to Glenelg for all the statements made to his prejudice, and the Secretary felt that he could not, in fairness, refuse to supply at least the substance of these.[134] That the Colonial Office found the Bishop's visit somewhat disruptive may be deduced from Stephen's later graphic description. He appeared to Stephen to be a person whose "constitutional vehemence was exceedingly great, and ... very little kept in check by culture of any kind, or, in plainer terms, ... a very irascible and coarse-mannered man."[135]

By February 1835 the Governor had come to believe that the aim of the Roman Catholic clergy might be a wholly Roman Catholic Assembly.[136] In the *Patriot* of April 28, 1835, Dr. Carson wrote that Catholics were being driven to this aim by an official policy designed to keep Roman Catholics from seats in the Council and from offices in the Government. His letter, prompted by an unconfirmed rumour that the Crown Surveyor, a Congregationalist and a newcomer, was to be made a councillor, was a rhetorical outburst in the manner of his Nova Scotian contemporary, Joseph Howe. He wrote that the Surveyor, with no stake in the colony, could only be interested in his salary and fees, and that holding a place at will under the Government, he must have a dominant motive to support it in every measure, right or wrong. He referred to similar complaints being voiced in other North American colonies and to his hope that a reformed government in the United Kingdom would have meant the extension of justice to Newfoundland and an end to exclusion for religious belief. He pointed out that the Council contained neither Roman Catholics nor Wesleyans, though the former numbered nearly half the population. There were, he said, at least two Catholic gentlemen in the Assembly whose education and talents justified their elevation to the Council, though he admitted that they would not "attach themselves to the sleeves" of the official members. He thought, however, that such appointments would do much to strengthen Prescott's Government and to harmonize the people. But he added:

Why do I write? The country is not yet sufficiently enlightened for the operation of reason founded on justice. Agitation must be kept up—the high spirits of a high-minded people must be cherished and supported—they must be aroused to the pure love of liberty, to the utter detestation of all tyrants, and of all manacles.... Submission never gained a point in politics—it has only the effect to confirm pride and foster presumption.

While Prescott's aim was to restore harmony in Newfoundland, he had selected as his guiding principle neutrality rather than concession to popular pressure. Whether his resistance to this pressure stemmed from what Carson believed to be a lack of enlightenment, or from capture by his official and mercantile advisers, or from a conviction that ability rather than religion should be the primary qualification for office in Newfoundland, does not appear. Certainly he embarked on no programme of radical innovation in the matter of appointments. To have done so would no doubt have subjected him to hostility from his Protestant councillors and others. His first list of nominees for a vacancy in the Council gave priority neither to the Surveyor nor to the reformers, but to a Presbyterian merchant who was, he believed, free from party feelings.[137] With this choice Glenelg agreed.[138] The Governor's nominees from the popular party were Carson himself and two merchants who were not members of the Assembly.[139] One of the latter was Patrick Morris who did, in fact, become a councillor and Colonial Treasurer in 1840.[140] For Morris, the Governor seems to have had a qualified admiration, regarding him as a man deserving recognition for his own merits and as a person able, if willing, to reconcile the extreme elements in the two parties. In 1835, as a reformer and advocate of the people's rights, Morris had violent feelings, but the Governor felt that, as a probable member of the second Assembly, he should be conciliated.[141]

Encouraged by improving revenue, the first Assembly passed useful legislation in 1836. The appropriation for roads, under £1,000 in 1834 (4 Wm. IV, c. 25), was raised to eight times that figure (6 Wm. IV, c. 15). The first Act for the encouragement of education was passed (c. 13) allotting £2,100 annually for five years for elementary schools, and authorizing the Governor to set up district school boards of mixed denomination. Provision was made for a census (c. 4). As the session ended, however, the Governor noted that it had become increasingly difficult to secure sufficient attendance.[142]

Would it be wise to dissolve the first Assembly at the end of 1836? This was the question which had troubled the Governor in February 1835 when he was presented with a bill for limiting the duration of assemblies to four years. His assent to it would make an election mandatory in 1836 and the results might, he thought, be undesirable:

The spirit of Party, and especially of religious party, is very strong at this moment and would be displayed in its utmost extent ... at a general election. We have unfortunately an illiterate and vulgar Roman Catholic Bishop, whose dependent Clergy, being principally of his own choice, too closely resemble him in character. Should the Assembly be dissolved according to the provisions of this Act, there should be no discretionary power left to the Governor to avail himself of a favourable and tranquil opportunity to proceed to a new Election; and we should have the Priesthood urging on the Roman Catholic population to vote for Representatives of their nomination.

... However unimportant the object may appear to the eye of reason when it is considered that there are no religious privileges, no preferences or distinctions of any kind, yet certain it is that the Parties above named deem it of the highest consequence to secure the return of Members; and their nominees have hitherto been pseudo Patriots, professed enemies of all taxation, violent Declaimers against what they term the enormous salaries of public Functionaries, and Opposers of every necessary measure of finance.

It is to be hoped that a steady and impartial conduct on the part of the Executive may ultimately in some degree allay this feeling, and indeed had we such a Roman Catholic Bishop as formerly presided here and whose memory is still revered, I should be under no apprehension on this subject.

He advised that confirmation be withheld from the Act and that he be authorized to ask the House for a similar one which would, if passed in 1836, permit the Assembly to continue until 1840.[143] To this plan Lord Aberdeen would not lend himself. He reminded Prescott that the quadrennial principle was correct and said that a particular inconvenience should not be allowed to prevail against it. Nor could he see any reason why the influence of the Roman Catholic priesthood should be expected to operate more advantageously in one year than in another. However, he refused to sanction the Quadrennial Act because of the objectionable term "Colonial Parliament" in the preamble.[144] Glenelg, succeeding Aberdeen, was more receptive to the Governor's request. Having just learned of the treatment meted out to Winton and others, he could well believe that an election in a time of excitement might return immoderate and unqualified legislators. If Prescott could, by influence and persuasion, induce the House to modify the Act, he might do so, but he was advised to avoid controversy.[145] In this course the Governor was partly successful in 1836, securing a measure which provided that dissolution might be postponed until January 1, 1838.[146]

In February 1835 Prescott had recommended that two changes precede a general election. He agreed with some of his councillors that the franchise, virtually universal, should be limited to those occupying houses valued at £10 a year. Rents tended to be high in the colony, so that such a franchise would still include much of the humblest class in the colony, but might diminish the influence of the Roman Catholic clergy.[147] Aberdeen had informed him, in reply, that however inconvenient the franchise of 1832 might prove, the Imperial Act did not empower the King to revoke it.[148] The Governor at the same time had asked that the Representation Act of 1834 be confirmed because it increased the number of members and defined several districts in which the Protestants predominated. He hoped that an increased membership would give greater confidence to the "well-disposed" and raise them above their apprehension of the mob constantly thronging the gallery of the House. Although most of the members were, he said, respectable in "propriety and character," they had in 1835 "betrayed a lamentable deficiency of moral courage," particularly in voting the supplies.[149] This request also fell to the ground because the Act would have established an electoral district extending as far as Bonne Bay on the west coast, thereby infringing, in the opinion of the Home Government, the rights of the French on the Treaty shore.[150]

It was a moment for amendment of the constitution, or for departure from the formula itself; but the challenge was not met. The Governor had prescribed two remedies; but the Colonial Office had hesitated to approach Parliament for the one and the Foreign Office to annoy the French with the other. The composition of the Assembly was in jeopardy; but neither the Governor nor the Colonial Office had suggested that the amalgamation scheme of 1832 might be imperially imposed. Although radical actions in the Lower House were known to produce conservative reactions in the other, the Whigs retained their faith in the self-rectifying power of the constitution.

Despite his fear that an election might produce an intractable House, the Governor decided in the spring of 1836 that the Assembly should not be recalled after prorogation. The Council had succeeded in amending the Quadrennial Bill so that the life of the Assembly might be prolonged until January 1838, but in April 1836 the latter body petitioned the Governor to be relieved of duty at the end of the session. They announced that they had only agreed to the amendment in order to secure the enactment of the quadrennial principle. They declared that political ignorance had been the rule at the election of 1832, but that much of this had been dispelled, and that the people, enlightened now as to their own interests and the function of Assembly, should be allowed to choose new members, if that was their wish. Prescott feared that if he refused the request and took advantage of the authorized extension there would be suspicion of secret interference and collusion with the Council. This, he thought, would engender agitation and petitions, increase ill-feeling, and lead to the election of members more vehement than might otherwise be expected. He thought that something might be gained by a display of openness and generosity and much lost by a compulsory dissolution in 1837 when party feeling might be running very high. Although the House contained, in his opinion, some excellent individuals, he was apprehensive about the effect of depleted attendance.[151]

Thus, in the autumn of 1836, with neither of the electoral modifications suggested by the Governor, the colony faced its second general election. At its first, the mass of the fishing population, economically dependent on the Protestant mercantile class and politically unaware, had been content to return their merchants or those whom these commended. The small group of vocal liberals who had worked with the resident merchants to win representative government had shown themselves unwilling to leave the prize to their late allies. In their effort to convert a mercantile Assembly into a popular one, they could play upon the resentment of the fisherman towards his supplier and employer, they could foster the hostility of Irish Catholic for English Protestant, and they could rely upon the influence of an Irish Bishop who did not scruple to supplement persuasion with the spiritual weapons of the Church.

CHAPTER THREE

THE ASSERTIVE ASSEMBLY, 1837

GOVERNOR PRESCOTT's fears that the general election in 1836 would produce a radical change in the composition of the Assembly proved correct. At dissolution the House contained nine representatives of the Protestant mercantile interest, Dr. Carson, and five Roman Catholics, of whom two, like the doctor, were declamatory reformers. In the election of November 1836 the mercantile party won only four seats, Dr. Carson was again returned, and the rest of the candidates elected were, with one exception, Irish Roman Catholics. With several vehement advocates of popular rights, and with planters and dealers to lend them support, a reform party of Catholics would control the House (see Appendix B, Table II).[1]

This result was achieved by a united Roman Catholic vote, or by acclamation, in the districts in which Catholics were predominant, and by intimidation and violence at Conception Bay and St. John's. In the capital, organized intimidation secured the withdrawal of an independent Catholic and two Protestant mercantile candidates and the return of the "popular" candidates, Carson, Morris, and Kent. These were actively supported from the hustings by the Catholic clergy. Clerical exhortation, cudgels, stones, and threats had their effect. Despite the presence of the garrison at the courthouse, many householders dared not vote in defiance of the mob and, in the interest of peace, the field was soon left to those favoured by the priests.[2] At Harbour Grace in Conception Bay the disorders were similar but more violent, for there the few constables were helpless. The first tally of five voters to come forward for a Protestant merchant was severely beaten and the rest of his voters were too cowed to appear. After several days of street brawling, assault, and intimidation, the election closed with the withdrawal of this candidate and his colleague and the return of their opponents.[3]

A significant event occurred on November 9 while the elections were still in progress in some districts. At the Governor's command the Council assembled to consider complaints from the magistrates at Harbour Grace that, as a result of obstruction to the free exercise of the franchise, there had been an "undue return" of members for Conception Bay. What followed may bear the interpretation of a curious accident, or as the reformers contended, it may not. From his office the Colonial Secretary, James Crowdy, produced, as relevant to the discussion, the election writ for Conception Bay. Chief Justice Boulton at once pointed out that the writ did not bear the Great Seal and that the document, and therefore the election, could not be valid. With this view the Attorney-General agreed.[4]

This verdict of invalidity by his legal advisers placed the Governor in a dilemma. There had been no seals affixed to any of the nine writs for the election; nor, according to the Colonial Secretary, had there been any on those issued for the election of 1832; thus the legal status of the first Assembly, as well as of the one being elected, was in question. Prescott decided, however, that his only course was to allow the election to continue and to prorogue the Assembly until he had received a ruling from London. Inexperience and the influence of his advisers seem to have induced him to make this reference. That he hoped for a decision which would permit him to convene the new members may be inferred from his pressure for a quick reply and from his stress on the need to hold a session at the beginning of 1837 to vote the supplies for the year. The Colonial Office answer was prompt, but in support of the stand taken by the colonial officials. Privately, Stephen and Glenelg seem to have felt that the Chief Justice, in zeal for correctness and the public good, had erected a minor error into a major difficulty.[5] However, without referring the question to the Law Officers of the Crown, they decided that the objection raised by Boulton had no valid answer in point of law and that it could only be met by an Imperial Act to legalize the writs or by the issue of new writs for another election. The first course being ruled out by the delay it would involve, the Governor was advised to take the second.[6]

When this decision was made known in St. John's in January 1837, there was naturally profound resentment and suspicion in the ranks of the elected reformers. One member declared that the failure to seal the writs was a deliberate omission, a reserve device to prevent the formation of a liberal House.[7] Glenelg regretted the inconvenience, but disclaimed all responsibility and ascribed the error to the unfamiliarity of the public officers with the formalities of elections.[8] There could be little doubt, however, that the reformers, if re-elected, would have more to say on the question of the writs.

The result of the November election had convinced some of the merchants that representative government should be completely abandoned.[9] Their chagrin may be gauged from the reaction of the *Ledger*, whose editor wrote (Nov. 25):

We have in innumerable instances reiterated the truth that His Majesty's Government committed a very serious error in rendering the principles of democracy so large an ingredient in the constitution of this country; that the elective franchise must be very considerably narrowed indeed, before the form of government which has been given to us can possibly answer the purposes for which it was intended .... But the history of the last week or two induces us to think that we have not proposed a sufficient remedy ... and that however limited the elective franchise may be made, the same evils will abound so long as we have for the most part a Catholic population controlled in their every movement by an ignorant, a vicious, and a political priesthood.

He urged respectable inhabitants to prepare for Parliament a statement of the evils produced by the constitution of 1832 and a prayer that it be rescinded and the colony left with the Governor and Council. He lent his columns to a letter exhorting the "Sons of England and Scotland" to fight the influence of bigotry and superstition and to join in petitions for redress. If, said this correspondent, a remedy did not come from the Imperial Government, the merchants had a weapon close at hand, the patronage of trade, and with this they could defeat the "monsters" in their attempt at exclusive dealing and political monopoly.

The Governor was not yet prepared to recommend the abrogation of the system. He believed that it had produced much good in the construction of roads, bridges, and lighthouses, the establishment of a savings bank, the encouragement of education, and the promotion of useful institutions, and that the evils besetting it could be cured. Since the franchise could not be narrowed, he proposed several measures which he believed would ensure that it could be exercised freely and fairly. He suggested that to prevent the transit of the lawless mob from place to place the nomination of all candidates should take place in all districts on the same day and that the returning officer in each district should appoint deputies so that polling might take place simultaneously in all parts of the district. He recommended again that the Representation Act of 1834 be confirmed, the census just taken having indicated that under the Act a Protestant majority of one might be elected. He pointed out that the Act's redefinition of some of the districts might lessen the provocations to violence and might, in the event of appeals from undue returns, increase the prospect of a fair decision from the Assembly. He suggested that the Imperial Government should modify the one objectionable clause in the Act by setting the western limits of the new district at Cape Ray rather than at Bonne Bay on the French shore. If the Act could not thus be altered and approved, he asked that its terms be given effect by proclamation, a course which he thought should not raise objections, since the Assembly had already approved the principle of the Act.[10]

The Colonial Office did not question the expediency of these remedies, but it informed the Governor that they were impracticable and contrary to law. The Royal Proclamation, with its provisions for electoral procedure, was, in effect, a Charter which the King could neither revoke nor amend through his unaided prerogative, and Glenelg was apparently not inclined to seek the permissive legislation which would be required from Parliament. Nor could the Representation Act be made law as Prescott had suggested, since the King was not empowered to confirm or proclaim parts of an Act to the exclusion of other parts. For the great social evil which had appeared in the colony, the coincidence of religious and political differences, Glenelg could suggest no effectual cure except "in the diffusion of sound knowledge and in the prevalence of a better understanding of the real principles and obligations of Christianity."[11]

The Governor asked also for an increase in the military and naval support on which he might call in the event of disorders. He requested a permanent addition to the three military companies at St. John's so that occasional detachments might be made. He suggested, alternatively, that part of a regiment be stationed in Harbour Grace and Carbonear to ensure that elections there, if required again in 1837, might not be marred by violence. He thought too that a second naval vessel should be allotted in 1836 for the protection of the fisheries so that one ship might be available in the event of disturbances in the outports.[12] Glenelg believed that it was useless to approach Parliament for any permanent increase in troops, in view of the pressure for drastic reductions in the colonial garrisons, and because it would certainly be urged that the unrest in Newfoundland was only transitory. However, appreciating that the Governor could not acquiesce in the rule of violence, he arranged that Prescott might call upon the commanders of the naval and military stations at Halifax for a vessel or a company of soldiers, but only if such a requisition became absolutely necessary.[13]

The election disturbances were followed by criminal proceedings in the Supreme Court before Chief Justice Boulton and his assistants. He seems to have countered timidity and unreliability in the witnesses and leniency in the jury with vigorous rulings on evidence and verdicts, and with heavy sentences on those found guilty.[14] When Glenelg had reviewed all the cases and the inevitable petitions, he declared that the sentences passed on at least three of the petitioners—a year's imprisonment and large recognizances of the peace—were needlessly severe, considering the crudeness of the jail and the quality of the diet. He advised the exercise of mercy and the immediate liberation of these three prisoners, and authorized the Governor to remit the other sentences, wholly or partially, at his own discretion. He noted that Boulton was charged in the most comprehensive terms with "having in his judicial decisions been biassed by his political feelings"—with having suggested evidence, suppressed cross-examination, overruled verdicts, and so regulated prison discipline and diet as to persecute those he had confined. Glenelg did not doubt that if these charges were well founded, the Assembly would make an enquiry and demand a remedy from the Crown.[15] The Chief Justice may have been animated in his proceedings by zeal for the law and by a desire to set stern precedents and deterring examples, but he had left himself open to the suspicion that he had used the Bench for party vengeance. This suspicion the reformers, already armed with many grievances, would not hesitate to cultivate.

The reformers, despite their protest about the invalidation of the November election, proved to be the gainers by the decision or conspiracy, for in June 1837 they swept the field (see Appendix B, Table III). The merchants, apparently convinced that they could not now dominate the House, would not submit themselves to another contest. The Protestant barrister elected for Fortune Bay refused to take his seat.[16] With the *Ledger* urging the abolition of the Assembly, it may be suspected that many of the merchants were of the same mind, and, persuaded that they could not regain political power, believed that the situation might be retrieved by the return of candidates deficient in education, status, and means. Daniel O'Connell pointed out in the House of Commons in 1842 that it was a singular circumstance that two of the persons most complained of as unfit for membership were returned by Protestant districts. He had been told that this had grown out of a "combination among the Protestant merchants not to take a seat in the Assembly, even though they should be elected." The firm of Robinson, Brooking, and Garland seems to have had a part in the return by Trinity of one of these "unfit" persons, a vehement local eccentric—fisherman, messenger, and constable—whose regular income was but £10 a year. The man who replaced the mercantile member for Fogo was a servant whose master reportedly sanctioned his absence for half the man's expected sessional remuneration.[17] The formation of a demonstrably incompetent, sectarian, and vulgarian House might serve to discredit the representative system and to block the radicals in their course. The argument that the House had become such a body was, in fact, one to which some merchants would soon resort.[18] The Governor's first report on the new Assembly was far from favourable. He told Glenelg that the House was composed, with few exceptions, of "violent leaders—themselves governed by the Roman Catholic priesthood—and of individuals of the humblest class to whom the sum of forty pounds expected to be allotted to outharbour members was a matter of high consideration, and a principal if not the only inducement to their becoming representatives."[19] After two years of experience with this Assembly, Prescott wrote for the Colonial Office another appraisal of the House, describing the members for St. John's, Placentia and St. Mary's as excitable agitators and those for Trinity, Fogo, and Burin as "low." One member for Conception Bay was "untractable" and another, too, was "low." The member for Ferryland was a prosperous but vulgar planter and the member for Bonavista Bay was an impoverished lawyer, dependent upon the favour of the House.[20]

From the opening of the session on July 3, 1837, until prorogation four months later, the Governor and the Council were faced with a hostile and determined Assembly. A perusal of the *Journal* for the session goes far to corroborate Prescott's assertion that the principal object seemed to be "the display of party feelings, the reward of friends, and the punishment of foes."[21] The proceedings were marked by an insistence on privilege, a conviction that grievances were to be exposed and remedied, and a desire for vengeance and the spoils of office. The trend of the session was set on the first day when Carson was elected Speaker, when Morris called for an enquiry into the administration of justice, and when the House resolved to appoint their own officers.[22]

The resolution on appointments brought the Governor into immediate conflict with the members, because Glenelg, looking to Parliament for analogy, had instructed him to maintain the Crown's right to appoint by refusing to sanction salaries for persons chosen by the House.[23] When the Governor sent down these instructions, they were read, laid upon the table, and disregarded, the House proceeding at once to a choice of their officers.[24] They informed the Governor that they would not be awed, intimidated, or compelled to recede from their conscientious decision, that they had in the past been directed to colonial rather than to parliamentary usage, and that the right of appointment was exercised by the assemblies of Nova Scotia and New Brunswick, and no longer disputed in Upper Canada and Prince Edward Island.[25] The Governor countered by refusing to receive the Address in Reply if he were waited on by the House with their new officers, but he compromised by accepting it from a selected delegation.[26] Glenelg, reviewing the matter, decided he must retreat from his stand if the Assembly had correctly cited colonial precedents. However, the Crown-appointed officers must be upheld while enquiries were made. The Governor was told to refuse to sanction any device by the Assembly for the payment of their new officers unless salaries were also reserved for the old.[27] Thus the ground was laid for a continuation of the dispute.

In the first week of the session accumulated grievances found expression in addresses asking the Governor for a score of detailed returns.[28] These addresses seem to have been prompted by a relief that there had been three conspiracies against the Roman Catholic inhabitants of the colony—that they had been the victims of a deliberate maladministration of justice, of repeated attempts to depict them as lawless and violent, and of a sinister plot to wrest from them the political power they had won. The Assembly sought evidence on the proceedings and rules of the Supreme Court, on the trials for malicious destruction and rioting, and on the discovery of the unsealed writs. The Governor declined to send down Glenelg's despatch ordering the remission of the three sentences. He refused to ask the public officers to furnish sworn affidavits with their returns. He would not demand the presentation of private correspondence, of letters exchanged by subordinate officials, or of statements of their agreements on fees.[29] In his opinion, compliance with the Assembly's requests would lead to no other end than "interminable hatred and recrimination."[30]

If the Assembly failed to clarify the affair of the writs, they did succeed in discovering in it an odd collection of hasty opinions, inconsistencies, and misstatements. Glenelg had declared that a body chosen on informal writs could have no legal authority.[31] The House therefore sought to establish whether the Acts of the first Legislature were invalid and they resolved to ask the Governor to take legal opinion on the matter.[32] Since the reformers had objected to many of the enactments of the former Assembly, it was clear that the new House would be unwilling to confirm all the legislation of the old. They had already condemned the Act (6 Wm. IV, c. 11 (Nfld.)) regulating the press.[33] The Governor had informed them that the writs of 1832 might, after all, have been sealed and therefore valid, and that his original statement had been based on information which was "at least doubtful, if not positively incorrect." He thought the point immaterial. The members announced that they found it more than surprising that his advisers should have succeeded in deluding him for seven months. They demanded to see all the writs, hinting that if they were not produced the supplies would be jeopardized. The Colonial Secretary, Crowdy, then explained to the Governor why he had been much shaken in his opinion that the writs of 1832 had gone out unsealed. His first impression was that the seals had been deemed unnecessary and removed prior to issue of the writs. Now, however, some of the returning officers remembered that the seals had been affixed. The Governor agreed to let the members see the writs in the Secretary's office. After a thorough inspection a committee of five produced a most ambiguous report, saying that it was "merely possible the seals had once been attached," but that it appeared to them "nearly an impossibility that they had been detached subsequently to their issue."[34] It seemed, therefore, that the writs for all elections had gone out unsealed.

The suspicions of the House about the writs were not dispelled. Nugent, the chairman of the committee, believed that if the procedure had been straightforward the documents themselves would not have been cut, but the seals merely detached so as to leave their impression on the paper. In his view, the Colonial Secretary's recollection of the affair had conveniently changed when he had realized that the early legislation might be lost.[35] The Governor sent one of the early Acts to Glenelg for submission as a test case to the Law Officers of the Crown, declaring that it was hopeless to expect this Assembly to pass a comprehensive act validating past legislation.[36] However, this problem was averted when Glenelg informed him of the Law Officers' advice that no informality in the writs could affect the measure in question.[37] Although one anxiety was thereby removed, Prescott believed that the conduct of the Colonial Office had been unfortunate. He felt that Glenelg had increased the difficulties of governing the colony by his initial failure to refer the writ question to the Law Officers—that had he done so in December 1836 the candidates first elected might have taken their seats and much excitement and agitation been prevented.[38]

With Morris as chairman, another committee launched an investigation into the administration of justice since the arrival of Boulton. The members sought principally to establish that Boulton had altered the method of empanelling juries in December 1833 before being sworn into office, and that he had put the new system into operation without observing the stipulation of the Judicature Act that three months must elapse after promulgation of the change. They sought also to show that he had by his judicial decisions tried to alter the fishery customs in defiance of the law, proclamation, and precedent. They were anxious also to show that unduly high court fees and a monopoly of the bar by a few lawyers made for a virtual denial of justice to the people.[39] The attempt to prove a premature and therefore illegal alteration in the method of summoning juries was frustrated by the refusal of the Clerk of the Court (E. M. Archibald, who was also Clerk of the House by Crown appointment) to produce the relevant documents, a refusal the Governor supported on the grounds that the correspondence was private. He advised the House that Boulton had been installed in November. Petitions were drawn up on the state of justice, agriculture, and the fisheries, and decisions made to send a delegation to London and to ask for the removal of Boulton from the Bench of Newfoundland.[40]

Suspicion of the Assembly made the Council vigilant in the extreme.[41] Of the thirty-two bills passed by the Lower House only ten were forwarded to the Home Government for confirmation. Early in the session the House framed a series of bills to effect changes in the administration of justice, but the intervention of the Council under Boulton prevented these from becoming law. The Council rejected bills to regulate prison discipline, to provide for the incorporation of lawyers, to appoint three sheriffs with fixed duties and fees, and to require public officers to detail and to swear to their returns. The councillors blocked, by means of amendments, bills to regulate the terms and sessions of the Supreme Court and to authorize summary proceedings in the circuit courts.[42] Prolonged disputes arose over the four major bills of the session and since these disputes throw considerable light on the differences between the Assembly and the Council and on the state of party feelings, they will be examined in some detail.

The Assembly regarded as an infringement of their privileges the Council's suggested amendments to the Revenue Bill. By one of these the Council sought to specify how the amount subtracted from revenue for the expenses of collection should be allocated. By the other they tried to change the wording of the Bill so that it would last, not for one year, but until the end of the next session. On these points the Assembly were adamant. When the Bill was sent up a second time, the Council renewed their objections to the duration clause. Convinced, or purporting to be convinced, that there was a sinister motive for the pressure for this amendment—the intention of the executive to postpone the calling of another session—the Assembly refused to extend the time of the Act. The Council gave way, still contending that their principle was correct.[43]

At the beginning of the session the Governor announced that the Education Act of 1836 had met serious impediments, its operation in most places being neither "cordial nor complete."[44] Some of the boards had ruled that the Bible must be admitted to the schools, and Roman Catholics, unwilling to expose their children to Protestant teaching, would not allow them to attend.[45] In 1837 the Assembly attempted to amend the Act in such a way as to exclude the Bible. They introduced a clause providing that no book objectionable to any member of any religious denomination should be brought into a school. This clause the Council amended to provide that no child should be required to use a book disapproved of by its parents. Since the Assembly interpreted this as a device to allow a child to introduce any book approved by his parents—including the Bible—the amended Bill was defeated.[46]

The Assembly's Road Bill for 1837 (1 Vict., c. 2) appropriated almost £17,000 for the making and repairing of roads and bridges and named for the first time the commissioners, who were to serve under a Board of Control appointed by the Governor. Objecting strongly to the amount of the vote and to the failure to give the Board sufficient control over its expenditure, the Council attempted amendments, which the Assembly countered by resolving that it was impermissible for the Council to amend a money bill. The Council persisting in their objections, the Assembly informed them that apart from rejecting the Bill outright, their only course was to present their objections in conference. Then the Assembly would prepare a new Road Bill "if they saw not in the amendments suggested a spirit of hostility to the public welfare, a concealed desire to impede public improvement, a studied inclination to fritter away the time, and to fling embarrassments in the pathway of that branch of the Legislature, or a latent wish to insult a body who have no disposition to reciprocate...." A conference having failed to settle the matter, the Assembly, in an effort to coerce the Council into assent, "tacked" the appropriations to the general Supply Bill. This mixed bill the Council rejected in the most decided terms, saying that they would not be induced to deviate from their stand by considerations of temporary expediency. Finally, the Assembly relented by sending up a separate Road Bill with the requested provision for control and this the Council passed.[47]

The Assembly, reviewing the road controversy in a petition to the Queen, implied that it had stemmed entirely from the Council's reluctance to provide employment for the poor and to open communications between the outports.[48] That is, they attributed to the Council of officials and merchants the motives of the transient West Country profiteer—the desire to focus the attention of the people entirely upon the fishery, to retain the supplying monopoly, and to prevent the opening of the country to settlement and agriculture. Since the construction of roads might in time jeopardize the domination of the merchants, they were unlikely to greet with enthusiasm a large expenditure on roads. Again, since the revenue was raised by duties payable in the first instance by the merchants, with the everpresent risk that these could not be redeemed from the fishermen, the suppliers had a strong interest in preventing anything which might cause taxation to soar.[49] The abuses inherent in a system of uncontrolled appropriation and expenditure for roads could scarcely fail to have this effect and the merchants could therefore join self-interested resistance with the objections on principle to which the Chief Justice gave voice.

The Assembly's determination to allow the Council no control in the appropriation of money led to a rancorous dispute about the vote for supplies. The Council's aim was to compel the Lower House to follow the practice of the assemblies in the other North American colonies where resolutions on each item were sent up for the Council's approval before being embodied in the Supply Bill, or where several distinct bills were prepared.[50] Having obtained a separate Road Bill, the Council went on to insist on separate bills covering the grants for civil government, for legislative contingencies, for poor relief, and for occasional items.[51] The Assembly's Supply Bill contained several marked inequalities in the grants to constables, which gave rise to the suspicion that the increased sums were rewards for political support and the decreased ones penalties for opposition. For example, salaries of constables in the Roman Catholic districts of Placentia and Burin were double those in other districts. The reduction of the salary of the Ferryland constable was believed to stem from his failure to vote for the successful candidate there.[52] To these variations, negligible in themselves, the Council objected.[53] Boulton had maintained that one of the chief difficulties in securing a proper administration of justice was the close control exercised by the popular body over magistrates and constables, the disposition to vary the salaries at pleasure, and the consequent reluctance of these persons to enforce the law with "vigilance, firmness, and promptitude." He thought that these salaries should be incorporated in a general grant for executive distribution.[54] The Council thought likewise. They objected also to the attempt of the representatives to determine without check their own sessional pay, to the amount of the vote for legislative contingencies, and to what they deemed inadequate provision for certain of the public services.[55] In these objections the Assembly refused to see anything but a desire to impede and embarrass. Finding that the Bill had been shelved for three months, they returned it to the Council and were informed again that several bills would be necessary for the several classes of grants. To leave the members in no doubt about their will, the councillors returned the Bill with radical amendments to no less than thirty-five of its clauses. The dispute ended in failure to vote the supplies for the year and in high exasperation on both sides. For example, Nugent, a member particularly odious to the Council, reported that no one would come to the bar of the Council to receive the Assembly's final message. He flung it inside, whereupon the President, Boulton, shouted twice in the loudest accents that it should be kicked out.[56]

In response to the petitions from both bodies, Glenelg in February 1838 relayed "Her Majesty's mediation" in a tactfully equivocal despatch. This commended the Council's principles for the future while awarding the immediate victory to the Assembly. He said that if the Assembly were not prepared to leave the initiation of money grants to the Crown, as was the practice in Parliament, they should see the necessity of following colonial practice in order to give the Council the means of passing on specific expenditure. He pointed out that if the members submitted to no control save the rejection of the whole vote, they either subjected the colony to great inconvenience, as in this instance, or forced the Governor and Council into agreement against their judgment. He trusted that the representatives would see the propriety of giving control to the Council in the matter of sessional pay and suggested that the legislative contingencies might be reduced. There seemed, he said, no grounds for impugning the motives and honesty of the Assembly, but if the charges were true, an effective censure might be expected from the inhabitants. None of the reasons advanced by the Council for rejecting the Bill seemed sufficient and if it were returned it should be given their assent.[57]

The evils inherent in the constitution and in the condition of Newfoundland had appeared and the attempts at palliation had begun. The Assembly believed that their grievances demanded a delegation to England. One of their chief aims was to effect the removal of the Chief Justice who had, they contended, made the Bench ancillary to party vengeance, and whose presence, they declared, was inconsistent with the public good.[58] As the session drew to a close, Boulton attempted to silence those who urged that he be removed. He began proceedings for libel against Morris, Nugent, and Kent because a speech arraigning his conduct, delivered by Morris in the Assembly and printed for the House, had been circulated in St. John's. Since Morris and Nugent were delegates for London, it was suspected that Boulton meant to see that they did not depart.[59] But this design, or the attempt to vindicate himself in the colony, was thwarted when the defendants objected successfully to the jurisdiction of his Court, the assistant judges ruling that the Supreme Court was improperly constituted without Boulton, who acted as his own counsel.[60] In January 1838 the delegates and the Chief Justice sailed for England to continue there the colony's disputes.

CHAPTER FOUR

THE DELEGATION OF 1838

THE DECISIONS of the Newfoundland reformers in the closing months of 1837 to petition for a redress of grievances and to send a delegation to London were made at a time when the political unrest of two decades in Lower and Upper Canada was reaching its climax. In November and December this unrest flared out in the brief and abortive armed uprisings of Papineau's *patriotes* in the Richelieu Valley and of Mackenzie's rebels in North Toronto.[1] As news of the rebellions reached Newfoundland, there were predictable reactions from the leading political journals. The *Patriot*, on December 30, 1837, though it disapproved of the hasty appeal to arms, hoped that the rebels would succeed, while the *Public Ledger* on January 2, 1838, avowed that there was cordial sympathy between the "turbulent demagogues" of Newfoundland and the "seditious" inhabitants of Lower Canada. It urged the Government, on January 5, to take early and strong measures to support the judges and the law and it assured its readers that the "rigid impartiality" of the Chief Justice and his peculiar firmness and energy of character qualified him in a singular way for his tasks in Newfoundland.

Whatever their degree of sympathy with the rebels, the reformers had in the session of 1837 shown their familarity with the proceedings of the Assembly of Lower Canada in respect to impeachment and supply. Thus, the attack on Chief Justice Boulton, the enemy of Irish dissidence and customary law, bore a resemblance to that on Chief Justice Sewell, the opponent of *la survivance française*. The principal charge in the unsuccessful impeachment of the latter before the Privy Council in 1815 had been that of publishing on his own authority the Rules and Order of Practice for his court. Boulton was being accused of an illegal alteration in the rules for the empanelling of juries. Again, the first efforts of the Newfoundland Assembly to acquire unquestioned control over placemen and finance were probably inspired not only by the struggle in Upper and Lower Canada, but by Papineau's ninety-two resolutions of 1834 and his clear desire to make the representative body the controlling authority in government.[2] Again, a reforming and predominantly Irish Assembly in Newfoundland could look to a predominantly French-Canadian Assembly in Lower Canada for precedents in fighting the ascendancy of the conservative and English governing clique. In the alliance of the liberal Dr. Carson with Morris and the Irish and of the liberal John Neilsen with Papineau and the French, one could push the analogy further. But although the struggle in Newfoundland had its nationalist and Catholic aspect, the aspirations of the Irish reformers seem to have been for change within the British tradition. According to Morris, who was stung by charges that the Assembly was disloyal, neither he nor his colleagues had received letters from the Lower Canadian rebels and although Dr. Carson had received circulars from the Canadian reformers earlier in the decade, he had decided, after consultation with his friends, that it would be imprudent to link Newfoundland with the Canadian disputes.[3] The editor of the *Patriot* admitted, on March 3, 1838, to a correspondence with the Montreal *patriote* journal, *La Minerve*, and declared that the colony and the Canadas undoubtedly had grievances in common. Newfoundland's loyalty had not evaporated, he said, but he added, provocatively, that he would not predict how long it would last if wrongs were not redressed.

In the early months of 1838 the Newfoundland delegates were pressed in Ireland and in London to appear before political meetings in order to foster excitement about the plight of Irish Catholics in Newfoundland and about the state of the North American colonies. They were urged to lend themselves to the Tory attempt to oust the Melbourne Ministry which had just persuaded Lord Durham to undertake a mission of enquiry in the Canadas. The reformers refused the overtures so made, being convinced that they could expect no remedy from a Tory Government.[4] At least one Tory journal, the London *Spectator*, assured them, however, that they, like colonial delegations of the past, could expect little from the vague promises of the Whig ministers and the procrastinations of Glenelg.[5]

Of the several matters which the delegates had been instructed to treat, two related to Chief Justice Boulton. They were to submit a petition which embodied ten major charges against him and a prayer for his removal, and they were to ask that in future no judge should sit in the Council.[6] Since the petition dealt with acts of misconduct imputed to Boulton in his judicial capacity, Glenelg referred it to the Privy Council for consideration by the Judicial Committee.[7] The delegates had apparently arrived in London neither authorized nor prepared to submit a formal case, and three expensive months were thus to elapse before they and the Chief Justice were ready for Privy Council adjudication.[8] As early as January, however, Glenelg, acting on Prescott's strong recommendation, had determined that, irrespective of the Privy Council's decision, Boulton was to be removed from his seat in the Council.[9] The pronounced differences between the two legislative bodies had convinced him that the combination of judicial with political duties in a small community "unhappily much divided into parties" could scarcely fail to impair confidence in the administration of justice. New Instructions would be issued on this point and Prescott was to make it known that the change rested on a general and permanent principle.[10]

The Privy Council hearing took place in the first week in May. The Chief Justice presented to their Lordships a detailed defence against the Assembly's charges of maladministration of justice through political bias. He claimed that his changes in the method of summoning juries and his decisions on fishermen's wages were legally sound and expedient. He denied that he had set aside the law of current supply. He gave reasons for his conduct of the several election trials, for his triple role in the prosecution of R. J. Parsons in 1835, and for his attempted suit against the Assembly's delegates to London. He submitted a testimonial from his colleagues in the Supreme Court which declared in the strongest terms that malevolence and utter disregard for truth were leading characteristics of the prosecuting party.[11] The Assembly's case was presented by the famous liberal advocate, Dr. Stephen Lushington. Morris, describing the masterly presentation, said that Boulton's humiliation was such that he was moved by compassion for the man. In the opinion of Morris, Boulton's case fell on the affidavit from the Supreme Court, which Lord Denman called a most partisan production.[12] On July 5 the Judicial Committee reported in the following terms:

... we have not found anything to justify the terms ... of the Memorial, "That Your Majesty would be pleased to purify the Bench of Justice ... by the Removal of the Chief Justice," inasmuch as we have not found any ground for imputing to the Chief Justice any corrupt motive or intentional deviation from his duty as a Judge and we feel it incumbent upon us to express disapprobation at the language and conduct adopted as being unjust towards him personally and which is inconsistent with the respect due to the High Office he was filling.

We regret to be under the necessity of reporting that we have found in some of the transactions brought under our consideration so much of indiscretion in the conduct of the Chief Justice, and that he has permitted himself so much to participate in the strong feelings which appear unfortunately to have influenced the different parties in the Colony, (although we do not feel that his judicial proceedings have been affected thereby) that we feel it our duty to state that we think it will be inexpedient that he should be continued in the Office of Chief Justice of Newfoundland.

Accordingly, the Secretary of State was instructed to inform Boulton that he would not resume his position in the colony.[13]

Despite the rebuke administered to Boulton's accusers, the Assembly had unquestionably triumphed. According to the *Public Ledger* of August 21, the *Patriot* was exhorting Boulton's victims to rejoice at his downfall. On August 17 the *Ledger* denounced Glenelg for the removal, but assured its readers that Boulton would be given a more lucrative appointment in a larger colony. However, when Boulton, his judicial conduct apparently vindicated by the Report, promptly applied for a position elsewhere, the Colonial Office replied that another appointment was virtually ruled out by the verdict on his partisan behaviour. Nor was any prospect held forth for a pension from the Treasury or the Assembly.[14] Thus, Boulton, after two dismissals from high office involving severe financial loss, was forced at the age of fifty, with a family of eight, to return to private practice in Upper Canada. He was the scapegoat not only of the popular party, enraged by his bias in the Council and by his inflexibility on the Bench, but of the Colonial Office which had assigned him to these incompatible offices, had upheld him in both while his conduct exacerbated party feelings, and had abandoned him when the anomaly they had created could no longer be ignored. It is scarcely surprising that within a year Boulton had turned his back on Colonial Office patronage and, reversing the principles of a life-time, had declared himself a supporter of responsible government for Upper Canada.[15] The Colonial Office, too, seems to have drawn a lesson from the unfortunate Boulton appointment, selecting as the new Chief Justice, J. G. B. Bourne, a Fellow of Magdalen College, Oxford, whom Glenelg believed to have not only sound legal knowledge, but the wisdom to abstain from political matters.[16]

To most of the other questions which they had been authorized to submit, the delegates drew less satisfactory answers. On behalf of the Assembly they urged the removal of all restrictions on the cultivation of the soil, declaring that the sale of Crown lands at a stipulated price, as in British North America and Australia, was inappropriate to Newfoundland. The absence of roads, the differences in accessibility and quality of the land, and the need to encourage settlement and cultivation, seemed to them to argue for varying prices, for conditional free or quit-rent grants to fishermen, and for payment and confirmation of title to present occupiers who had made improvements.[17] They asked also that Crown lands and ship rooms, and the revenue from these, be placed at the disposal of the Assembly.[18] Glenelg signified that he would be willing to transfer control and revenue to the Assembly only upon the passage of a bill modelled on the recent Acts of New Brunswick and Upper Canada, which provided for sale of all waste lands at public auction to the highest bidder at a fixed upset price. He would not agree to the suggestion that the Assembly rather than the Executive Government should conduct the administration and sale of the lands.[19] The problem of bridging these differences and of devising a Crown Lands Bill satisfactory to the Assembly, the Council, and the Home Government was to persist until 1844.[20] To a related request for Imperial aid in the development of the island, in the form of grants for roads and bridges and a geological survey, Glenelg replied that Parliament would be unwilling to vote such sums. He suggested that the Assembly employ for these purposes the large revenue they expected from the sale of Crown lands.[21]

The delegates advanced two other proposals for increasing the revenue of the colony. They renewed the demand, first made in 1834, for a reduction in the reserved salaries in return for a Civil List Act making permanent the reduced salary scale.[22] Glenelg pointed out that while New Brunswick and Nova Scotia granted a Civil List to the Crown, the sum in each was larger than the £6,550 now deducted by the Crown from the Newfoundland revenue, whereas the cost of living was, he understood, higher in Newfoundland than in the mainland colonies. Unless the Governor recommended reductions of salary, he could not entertain the proposal for a decreased Civil List.[23] The delegates renewed earlier objections to the absence of all control over the expenses of collecting the Imperial duties, and pledged the House to enact a bill securing the salaries of customs officers. They also asked for the withdrawal of the Collector of Customs and his replacement by a lesser officer.[24] The Treasury, with whom these decisions lay, deemed the first change unnecessary and the second inexpedient.[25]

Three grievances about appointments to office were brought to Glenelg's attention. The delegates asked that "systematic" exclusion of Roman Catholics be forbidden, that minor offices in the gift of the Crown should be given to natives or residents of the island, and that pluralities in major offices should be abolished.[26] On the last two points, they extracted from Glenelg a qualified agreement. On the first point, he denied that there was any design to maintain a Protestant monopoly.[27] The delegates then produced comprehensive lists showing that out of about a hundred offices, only three were held by Roman Catholics, seventy of these having been filled since the Emancipation Act, and forty by or under Governor Prescott.[28] When the question was referred to Prescott, he submitted a detailed analysis of all appointments made since his arrival, vindicating himself, at least to Glenelg, from the charges that religion rather than seniority, capacity, or prior arrangement was with him the decisive factor in selection.[29]

The question of the fisheries was one on which both parties in the colony could agree. The Assembly's petition on the fisheries urged the inequality of the competition faced by Newfoundland fishermen because of the French insistence on exclusive use of much of the Treaty shore, the use by the French of buoyed hooks on the Grand Banks, and the fact that the French and American fisheries were upheld by bounties totalling five times the revenue of Newfoundland. It asked for the restoration of concurrent fishing rights on the whole French shore, or compensation for exclusion, and for Imperial bounties.[30] Neither bounties nor compensation were promised and the delegates had to leave with an inconclusive reply to the petition.[31]

The major constitutional problem was that of easing the relations between the Council and the Assembly. In a petition despatched to forestall or counteract the complaints of the delegates, and laid before Parliament on July 30 by Lord Aberdeen, the merchants of St. John's declared that the root of the trouble lay in the composition of the Assembly. The present character of the Assembly they traced to the nature of the franchise: the low qualifications for electors and candidates had brought the return of unscrupulous agitators and low persons who were the ignorant tools of a powerful Roman Catholic clergy; the latter unlike the fishermen and the merchants who were bound by common interests and mutual dependence, had no stake in the colony, but had from the beginning exercised political influence in an irresponsible and pernicious manner. Commenting on this document, the Governor once again recommended Imperial measures to bring the Representation Act of 1834 into effect, pointing out, too, that a property qualification of £300 or £500 for candidates might do much to remedy the situation. Once again his proposed alterations were rejected as beyond the competence of the Crown. In Stephen's view, the evils complained of could be redressed if these "gentlemen of property and education would employ their legitimate influence to secure to themselves seats in the . . . Assembly."[32] After interviews with ex-Governor Cochrane and George Robinson, Glenelg informed Prescott that the remedy lay with the inhabitants themselves and in the Governor's continuing endeavours to protect the rights and liberties of all and to moderate party animosity.[33]

The Assembly declared that the evils stemmed from the composition of the Council. They advanced suggestions for the reform of that body, one of which, the removal of the Chief Justice, was put into effect. They asked also for the separation of the Council into executive and legislative councils and for the "infusion of the representative principle" into the latter.[34] By the summer of 1837, when Nova Scotia complied with instructions originally sent in 1832, the separation into two councils had become general in the North American colonies. In Nova Scotia four members of the Assembly were introduced into the Executive Council, and in New Brunswick Sir John Harvey added to his Council members enjoying the confidence of the House.[35]

Representation of the Assembly in an executive council was not asked for by the Newfoundland reformers, apparently absorbed in the conflict with their rivals as legislators. They did suggest, however, as an alternative to the addition of representative persons to the Upper House, the scheme of Lord Goderich which had been so hastily rejected in 1833, the amalgamation of the two legislative bodies, with three officials of the Crown meeting with the elected members.[36] Morris, in a published letter to Lord Durham, whose short-lived mission to the

Canadian provinces did not permit him to visit Newfoundland, denounced the Legislative Council as a useless incumbrance composed of placemen and officials, of "birds of passage and birds of prey," a body in no way comparable to the House of Lords. He believed that only the reform or abolition of these bodies could prevent the separation of the colonies from the mother country. For Newfoundland he favoured, despite the strictures of Lord John Russell about elective councils, the formation of a legislative council through election by the Assembly. He viewed with even more favour the amalgamation plan of 1832.[37]

Governor Prescott gave Glenelg his decided opinion that the abolition of the Legislative Council and the introduction of three officials into the Assembly would, in the circumstances of the colony, be a dangerous experiment. The officials, he said, would have no weight in the House and he doubted whether all the authority of the Government would be sufficient to induce them to submit to the discomforts of such a position. From the loss of the Legislative Council as a check upon violent and democratic proceedings, he could only anticipate great inconvenience. Nor did he think any practical benefit could be derived from separate councils, since the present body in its executive proceedings seemed to give the Assembly no cause for jealousy. If there were to be a change, he suggested one along the lines of Sir John Harvey's in New Brunswick, the formation of an executive council by the union of four official members with two members of the Assembly nominated by himself, the latter members to retire should they fail to be elected to a future House. If there were to be no separation, but the enlargement of the Council by the addition of representative members, he foresaw some difficulty in finding members from the outports. Membership had hitherto been limited to residents of St. John's by the need for rapid assembly in the event of an emergency. The nature of society in the outports, he said, imposed severe restrictions on a choice of members and of the few he could select, he feared that all would claim remuneration for the time spent in the capital. He suggested three persons for the Legislative Council, two of them, Morris and Doyle, being Catholics, reformers, and members of the Assembly, and the third, Robert Pack, being a merchant and farmer of Carbonear, who had sat in the previous House.[38]

The Colonial Office, studying these recommendations in November 1838, appeared to find them rather inconclusive and with Lord Durham about to make recommendations for the government of the North American colonies, were reluctant to make any fundamental changes in the constitution of Newfoundland.[39] Glenelg said he was willing to entertain any address which the Assembly chose to submit on the separation of the councils, together with a thorough report from the Governor on persons he might nominate. He would give no opinion on Prescott's suggestion that two members of the Assembly be admitted to the Executive Council, save that he could not permit such persons to be considered as representing the local Government in any way, or used as the agents through which the Governor transmitted messages.[40] On this point, the Governor assured him that he contemplated no change in the usual mode of communicating with the House, but he pointed out that such councillors might occasionally and conveniently explain to the Assembly the plans and ideas of the Government. Prescott's suggested additions to the Legislative Council were not made, none of the three persons being then available, nor did the Governor implement his own suggestion that executive councillors be chosen from the Assembly. He reported in January 1839 that the difficulty of making a selection from the popular members would prevent him from making an immediate change.[41]

During the early months of 1838, while the delegation waited upon Glenelg, Bishop Fleming was again in London on the same errand. His purpose was twofold—to complete his negotiations for a portion of Ordinance land and to refute a heavily documented statement which the Governor, at Glenelg's request, had prepared in September 1837.[42] The Bishop had been absent from the island during most of 1837 in Ireland, England, and Rome. On his return to St. John's in the autumn he had learned that a mass of evidence against him had been collected from many sources. His second visit to London followed promptly.[43]

If any reproaches had been made to the Bishop during his stay in Rome in 1837, they do not seem to have induced him to greater restraint. His pastoral letter in the *Patriot* of December 30 of that year had informed his flock that "despite the artifices of the enemy" he had persuaded the British Government to accede to his wishes for a grant of land, and that all the representations against his behaviour—"the designs of the enemies of religion, the malevolence of the wicked"—had brought to him proportionately greater favours of consolation from the Pope. These expressions seemed to lend force to the plea the Governor had made six months earlier for Dr. Fleming's removal: "Never was there a more inviting field than this for the healing efforts of a truly pious, enlightened, upright and benevolent Roman Catholic Bishop. It is the greatest of our wants, and his arrival would be hailed with infinite satisfaction by every reflecting and well disposed person in this Community, whether Catholic or Protestant."[44]

Through Foreign Office channels this description of a desirable bishop had been forwarded to Rome.[45] Glenelg, however, had confessed himself pessimistic about the result, saying that statements to the prejudice of the clergy were received with jealousy by the Court of Rome, and that counter-statements and a plea of zeal for the Church and the papal authority tended to disarm censure and to result in intervention devoid of the necessary vigour.[46] Stephen, in a minute which deplored the "humiliating necessity" of appeals to Rome against this "incendiary priest," had written: "I suspect that the Pope secretly enjoys the power of keeping a whole English colony in a ferment which His Holiness alone can quell and which remains a standing monument of the fact that this Protestant country cannot entirely shake off its dependence even in this nineteenth century on the Papal power."[47]

The Foreign Office agent in Rome was determined that the Papal Court should not be able to plead ignorance of the charges against the Newfoundland clergy. He produced for the Pope's perusal a long statement in Italian setting forth the details of the intensive campaign carried on during the Bishop's prolonged absence by his assistant, Father Troy, against the few Catholics who had tried to maintain their political independence. This gave circumstantial accounts of frequent denials of religious rites, physical expulsion from the chapel, and diatribes from the pulpit and the altar. The Pope, he reported, had at once seen the necessity of stopping this course of conduct and the Propaganda had despatched letters ordering the Bishop to suspend at once any priest who intervened in political affairs. To Fleming himself there had been administered what was hoped would be an effective rebuke. Cardinal Capaccini, Secretary of State at the Vatican, though he allowed the agent to see the instructions despatched to the Bishop for the removal of Father Troy, would not allow him to make a copy for the Foreign Office, fearing that the Papal Government might be placed in an embarrassing position if Fleming refused to comply with the orders—a refusal for which the Cardinal seemed prepared.[48]

While unknown to the Bishop these negotiations were going on in Rome, his application for the Governor's voluminous indictment was causing the Colonial Office much embarrassment. There could be no doubt but that party animosity and personal hostility in the colony would be greatly inflamed if the Bishop read the statements from his various accusers. These had, however, already been shown to Boulton for the preparation of his defence before the Privy Council. Stephen wondered if they could, with fairness, be concealed from the Bishop. Could the Bishop be told that the Secretary of State was prepared to give an opinion on his conduct based on evidence Fleming had not seen? Stephen would not say outright that the previous decisions about this documented enquiry had been "injudicious," but he was certain that they had led the Government into "as awkward a predicament as could well be imagined." If the Bishop were refused, he would certainly apply to his friends in the Commons; he must therefore be answered at once, further silence being "so discreditable that Lord Glenelg could hardly hazard it.[49] Since the Bishop's friends numbered Hume and O'Connell, and since Sir William Molesworth was in a few days to move a want of confidence in Glenelg and the Ministry, there were good and immediate grounds for Stephen's apprehension.[50] Accordingly, he drafted, and had the Under-Secretary approve, a carefully tactful letter which declined, in the interests of the future tranquillity of Newfoundland, to permit an examination of the controversial documents, or to pursue the subject further. This was not sent. The Bishop renewed his reproaches and Stephen his pressure for an end to Glenelg's silence. Finally, in April an interview was granted to the Bishop and he was told that the Minister, having given close attention to all the evidence, had concluded that no decision could be pronounced in London upon events so remote in time, and upon statements which depended so heavily upon minute recollection and accurate appreciation of motive. Further, the Minister acknowledged himself to be without power either to censure or to acquit members of the Roman Catholic clergy. He hoped that the Bishop would, in the interests of his flock and of the colony as a whole, see the wisdom of abandoning the discussion.[51]

The Bishop had now definitely secured the land on which he had set his heart and he seems to have given way to Glenelg's appeal, declaring that he too desired the restoration of harmony in Newfoundland.[52] The admonitions and instructions from Rome which he found awaiting him in September 1838 seem, too, to have had a salutary effect. Shortly after his return to St. John's he published a letter exhorting Roman Catholics to forgive their enemies and to make them their friends.[53] Within a year the Governor was able to report that overt clerical interference in political matters had subsided. Father Troy, transferred to Placentia, disappeared from the centre of the political scene. Nevertheless, Prescott was inclined to feel that Glenelg's course had aggravated rather than lessened ill-feeling in the colony. After the Minister's resignation in 1839, Prescott informed the new Colonial Secretary, Lord Normanby, that the conduct of the Colonial Office in the Fleming affair had been decidedly injurious. The investigation the Governor had been required to make had raised and then disappointed great hopes for a redress of grievances. It had made him the victim of the Bishop's unceasing resentment and it had led to "no practical benefit, or indeed to a decision of any description," an outcome which he thought must have been foreseen from the first.[54] Among the extreme elements of the Protestant party, the grant of land to the Roman Catholic Church was a source of complaint. The *Ledger's* pronouncement seemed calculated to offset the mollifying influence of the concession. The grant convinced the editor that Glenelg was "ready to sacrifice everything to the clamours of a noisy, turbulent, disaffected rabble" and that his government of the colonies must end in disaster and contempt.[55]

The reformers, through their petitions and delegation, had achieved in 1838 a very limited victory. They had extracted promises on the questions of Crown lands, a Civil List, and appointments to office. They had secured the removal of Chief Justice Boulton from Newfoundland and the closing of the Council to the Bench of the Supreme Court. They had failed to obtain the other constitutional changes they had sought—the separation of the Council into two bodies, a democratic alteration in the composition of the Upper House, or the formation of a single amalgamated House. Their failure to penetrate the Council would make the triumph over Boulton a hollow one indeed.

CHAPTER FIVE

THE CONTEST WITH THE COUNCIL, 1838-1841

WHEN the session of the Legislature began in the summer of 1838 it became clear that the intervention of the Colonial Office had not improved relations between the Council and the Assembly. The mutual suspicion and jealousy and the insistence upon rights and privileges which had crippled their proceedings in 1837 had not been removed.

The most urgent requirement was the passage of the Supply Bill which had been rejected in 1837, but despite Glenelg's recommendation, it was for some days in jeopardy in the Council.[1] Two factors were at work. One was the equivocal nature of Glenelg's advice about the immediate and the future mode of voting supplies. The other was mercantile bitterness at the success of the Assembly in effecting the removal of the Chief Justice. The merchants were determined to express, however futilely, their conviction that the charges against Boulton had been baseless by refusing to sanction the vote for the expenses of his accusers. This they believed they could do by insisting on the principle of separate resolutions or separate bills recommended by Glenelg, despite the fact that he had advised them not to reject the Supply Bill again. Their cause was lost when one of their number, Thomas, was induced by his reading of the Glenelg despatch to cast his vote with the official members in favour of the Bill. Intense indignation from his mercantile colleagues and from the *Ledger* greeted this desertion. The three mercantile councillors entered a protest against the Bill, which reiterated Glenelg's own strictures about multifarious grants over which the Council had no control. They objected to this method of forcing through items known to be objectionable to the Council, citing the prohibition against mixed bills contained in the Instructions, and declaring that there were no grounds for reversing the stand taken by the Council in the last session.[2] The Governor, reviewing the dispute, believed that it would be altogether inexpedient to withhold his assent to the Bill.[3]

Emboldened by this success to ignore the course prescribed by Glenelg, the Assembly prepared a similar mixed Supply Bill for the ensuing year. This time the Council took a stand upon principle and insisted upon separate bills. The Assembly, faced by the threat of more financial embarrassment to the colony and to themselves, complied with this demand to the extent of preparing three bills, one for the support of the civil government, a second for the defrayal of legislative contingencies, and a third for the payment of the legal expenses incurred by the delegates in London. This last measure was rejected outright by the Council when the official members agreed with their colleagues that these unauthorized costs should not be defrayed from the public revenue.[4]

Although the Contingency Bill passed into law, the Council, influenced perhaps by Glenelg's remark about the desirability of retrenchment, expressed strong objections to the growth of the Assembly's expenses, alleging that the vote for 1838, more than £3,000, one-sixth the net income of the colony, was triple that for 1836.[5] The Assembly countered by declaring that the Council had compiled the figures with deliberate inaccuracy.[6]

Anxiety for the public service and the vote for official salaries seems to have prompted the Council to concur in the Supply Bill. They did protest, however, about the inclusion of a clause naming the commissioners for the disbursement of poor relief. Since the Governor was not inclined to raise obstacles or to appear to have a personal feeling in the matter, he gave his assent, but he applied to Glenelg for guidance. It seemed to Prescott a rather presumptuous irregularity that the Assembly should name the commissioners and empower them to appoint their own secretary and to remunerate him with an unspecified sum from the funds allotted. This provision, like the naming of all the commissioners in the Road Acts of 1837 and 1838, seemed to Prescott to stem from jealousy of the executive and from the idea that anything wrested from Her Majesty's Government, parent or local, was a triumph.[7] The sessions of 1839 and 1840 were to be bedevilled by the Assembly's obstinacy about the naming of commissioners.

At the close of the session the House addressed the Queen in terms of injured virtue, declaring that against their judgment, but for the sake of harmony, they had acceded in several matters to the demands of the Crown and of the Council. In order to obtain the Governor's assent to the Revenue Bill they had met his request for a supplementary grant to the Collector of Customs for the collection of colonial duties, although they were still awaiting an answer from the Imperial Government to their prayer for the reduction of his salary. Pending the settlement of the question of their right to appoint their own officers, they had voted two sets of salaries. They had, at the Council's insistence, voted the appropriations in three separate bills. This conciliatory disposition, the Council, they said, had failed to match, having rejected one of the bills and maligned them upon another.[8]

In a second address the Assembly declared that the legislative precedents of former years and the island's peculiar social structure were strong arguments for the continuation of the miscellaneous Supply Bills. They would, they said, willingly consent to the origination of all money grants by the Crown if they were allowed, like the House of Commons, to exert control over public officers. Or they might agree to the preparation of separate bills, if the relations between the Council and the Assembly were parallel to those between these bodies in the other North American colonies. They contended that they were not. They argued as follows: Whereas the fostering care of the Imperial Government in the Canadian provinces and New Brunswick had promoted agriculture and had created a native gentry with interests in the country common to those of the body of the people, the policy towards Newfoundland had been totally different and had produced a unique situation. This policy had been first to forbid residence, then to restrain settlement, and later to hinder and decry agriculture. The result was that there was no native gentry, no resident landowning class, from which councillors might be drawn. There were but two classes. One, the mercantile, was composed of "merchants and adventurers," non-native, and to some extent non-resident, together with officials of the Government, also outsiders. The other class comprised the fishermen. The merchants, because of a desire to retain their supplying monopoly, were consistently opposed to agricultural development and intent only upon self-aggrandizement and withdrawal. The natives and residents, on the other hand, sought through the Assembly to promote the prosperity and development of the island. The composition of the Council endangered their measures, hence their reluctance to abandon mixed Supply Bills.[9] To this analysis of the causes of legislative disharmony and this plea for their mode of voting supply, Glenelg replied that the Queen's decision was that the Council had asserted a principle which was "just and constitutional and essential to the good Government of the Colony."[10]

Hypersensitivity and an inflated view of the privileges of the Assembly, derived perhaps from the successful impeachment of the Chief Justice and the quashing of his suit against the three members, seems to have led the House in the summer of 1838, at the instigation of Kent and Carson, to adopt a course of action ill calculated to enhance the reputation of that body. On August 6 high words were exchanged in the street between Kent and Kielly, the surgeon who had supplanted Carson as government medical officer in 1834. The quarrel seems to have arisen over some statements made by Kent in the Assembly about the management of the hospital and to have ended with derisive remarks and a threatening gesture by the doctor. Kent repaired to the House and complained that Kielly by so attacking him had been guilty of a gross breach of the privileges of that body. On a warrant from the Speaker, Kielly was brought before the bar of the House to listen to the charge and to be informed that his only course was to apologize and to throw himself on the clemency of that body. Kielly responded with further derogatory remarks about Kent and was remanded to the custody of the Sergeant-at-Arms. Two days later, on again being brought before the House, he refused to make a dictated apology. The Speaker then issued warrants for his confinement in the local jail, from which he was shortly freed on a writ of *habeas corpus*. Assistant Judge Lilly of the Supreme Court, who issued the writ, delivered judgment to the effect that the Assembly did not have the right either by analogy with the House of Commons or by derivation from parliamentary practice to try and to punish summarily for an alleged breach of privileges, and that the Speaker's warrant was legally informal and insufficient for Kielly's committal.[11]

Instead of acceding to this judgment, the House determined to push the matter further. The barrister, Bryan Robinson, who had taken up Kielly's case, had issued writs on Kielly's behalf against the Speaker and several members and officers of the House. Robinson was Master in Chancery of the Legislative Council and since the House could not proceed against him for contempt, they resorted to the somewhat futile gesture of passing and later rescinding a resolution not to receive him as bearer of messages from the Upper House. They considered a motion that the proprietor and printer of the *Newfoundlander* be brought before the bar for a breach of privileges in the publishing of the adverse judgment. Their most decisive step was to order the Sheriff to produce Dr. Kielly. On being told that the accused had been freed, the Speaker issued warrants for the arrest of Judge Lilly and the Sheriff. The Sergeant-at-Arms, complying, marched these gentlemen, to the great merriment of the following throng, through the streets of St. John's, first to the House and then to confinement in his own home. The Governor decided that he must put an immediate end to these questionable and degrading proceedings. In order to allow cooler judgment to reassert itself, he prorogued the House for a week and the prisoners were set free.[12]

In the autumn of 1838 Kielly's action for false imprisonment came before the Bench of the Supreme Court. The defendants entered a plea of privileges of the House. The principal arguments for the plaintiff were "that the Newfoundland House of Assembly being not quite seven years old, and this being the first case of the kind, no usage or custom could be contended for, that there was no analogy between the origin, constitution, or jurisdiction of the House of Assembly and that of the House of Commons; that the ... Assembly was not a court; and ... that the pretended warrant was bad ...."[13] Judgment was delivered at the end of December for the defendants, Judge Lilly dissenting. Lilly, who was serving on the Bench in a provisional capacity, was believed to have relied upon E. M. Archibald, Clerk of the Court and Clerk of the Assembly, in preparing his dissenting judgment, pronounced a most able one by the Colonial Office.[14]

The implications of the judgment in favour of the House were not lost upon the merchants who were the outspoken critics of that body. The Governor predicted that if the precedent were allowed to stand there would be a frequent and improper use of such privileges, Dr. Carson already being assertive on the subject.[15] Mercantile pressure and support apparently induced Kielly to enter an appeal, as a test case, to Her Majesty in Council.[16] This case, *Kielly v. Carson and others*, first came on for hearing in January 1841 and was re-argued on May 23, 1842, before ten Lords of the Privy Council. On January 11, 1843, Chief Baron Parke announced that their Lordships would advise the Queen to reverse the decision of the Supreme Court. Of the House of Assembly he said: "They are a local legislature, with every power reasonably necessary for the proper exercise of their functions and duties; but they have not, what they have erroneously supposed themselves to possess, the same exclusive privileges which the ancient law of England has annexed to the House of Parliament."[17] Thus a case which began in undignified displays in the streets of St. John's ended in the establishment of a precedent on the question of the inherent privileges of colonial assemblies.

In 1838 and 1839 the Kielly affair served to aggravate the disharmony in the island. For eight months the Governor was without any pronouncement from Glenelg on the correctness of his course in proroguing the Assembly, while doubts about the propriety of his conduct and rumours of an official reproach were fostered by the reformers.[18] Glenelg's delay seems to have been caused in part by a reference to the Law Officers on the privileges question. Their views, though inconclusive, were adverse to the Assembly.[19] When Glenelg's despatch finally arrived in April 1839, the Governor arranged for its immediate publication, an action which Carson and his supporters declared to be highly improper, in view of the appeal pending to the Privy Council.[20] Earlier, in January, the Governor had informed Glenelg that the resentment harboured against him had so impaired his usefulness in the colony that, in the interests of tranquillity, he felt he should resign.[21] Glenelg, however, saw no reason to avail himself of this proposal.[22]

The most significant result of the abortive arrests was an increase in the odium in which the Assembly was held by the principal merchants and a concerted effort by these merchants and their West Country associates to discredit that body with Parliament. The attack was launched in December 1838 with a petition to the Queen from the Chamber of Commerce of St. John's reciting the whole mercantile case against the Assembly. Once again Her Majesty was informed that the island's society contained only two classes—the merchants, who were the capitalists and employers, and the fishermen. This time, however, she was assured that it was the latter class which was transient and that save for a few honourable native-born persons its membership was constantly changing, with immigration to the United States and replacements from Ireland. The address declared that the Catholic inhabitants were peaceable when not stirred up by agitators and priests, but that under the influence of these they habitually surrendered their free and independent exercise of the franchise and resorted to violence to prevent its exercise by others. The result had been the return of a set of unprincipled and unqualified members who had obstructed the course of justice, illegally arrested a judge of the Supreme Court, appropriated public funds for their own use, and engaged in disloyal correspondence with the Canadian rebels. Nevertheless, these persons were certain to be re-elected. The petitioners complained that as a result of the disturbed state of the colony the value of property had decreased while the rate of insurance had gone up. While they were willing to go on paying taxes at the current rate, they refused, as property-holders and taxpayers, to be ruled by those who were neither. Representative government, they said, had been conferred in an "evil hour" and they now insisted that abrogation of the Legislature was the only means to restore harmony. Such local enactments as were necessary could be made by the Governor and an enlarged nominated Council.[23] To this address the Queen, on her Minister's advice, made no reply.[24] In February 1839 this petition was followed by a similar one from merchants, traders, and shipowners at Conception Bay.[25]

During the autumn of 1838 the merchants of Liverpool, Poole, and Bristol despatched petitions to Glenelg complaining of the arrest of Judge Lilly and voicing fears for their property and for the prosperity of the colony. They requested that troops be sent for the winter and that measures be taken to arrest the evils produced by the elective franchise.[26] At the same time Tory newspapers in Great Britain joined in vehement denunciation of the Roman Catholic party in Newfoundland, and were quoted extensively in the columns of the *Public Ledger*.[27] The autumn petitions were followed in the late winter and early spring of 1839 by another set from the merchants of Liverpool, Torquay, Dartmouth, and Teignmouth. The first of these suggested that the state of Newfoundland would damage mercantile credit in Europe, that insufficient supplies would be procured and sent, that the fisheries would be prosecuted on a reduced scale, and that the inhabitants would suffer much privation. It asked for an immediate remedy. The other three petitions were couched in similar terms, but demanded as a remedy the abolition of the Legislature and the abrogation of the Charter.[28]

The reformers were not passive before this attack. Four members of the Assembly attempted a refutation of the charges levelled by the Chamber of Commerce. They asked for an investigation into the situation in the colony and declared that the Council was opposed to everything liberal and that any representations from that quarter were aimed at discrediting Her Majesty's Government with the Tory Opposition.[29] An address to the Queen bearing almost 3,000 signatures directly impugned the charges made by the Liverpool merchants and denied the need for coercive measures. It declared that Liverpool's hostility could be traced to the merchants' loss of power following the grant of representative government and it asked for a commission of enquiry.[30] From Harbour Grace and Carbonear came a similar petition.[31] Perhaps the most eloquent of the Assembly's defenders was Patrick Morris. Admitting the respectability of those who had made the charges, he declared that the only one with a basis of fact was the regrettable Kielly affair. From this, he said, the Assembly, after the initial step, had felt it awkward to recede, and the opponents of representative government had seized upon it with great avidity. He did not dispute the fact that the clergy played a prominent political role, but he did deny that the inhabitants were lawless and that property was insecure, that the people were unfit for elective government, that the Assembly had squandered the revenue, and that the members had engaged in treason.[32]

The Chamber of Commerce had entrusted their petition to the former Colonial Secretary, Lord Aberdeen, who presented it to the House of Lords in April 1839, after a speech which enlarged upon the "wretched and distracted" state of the colony. He was not, he said, ready to support the prayer for abolition of the Legislature, but he thought that there were ample grounds for an enquiry, and that no remedy could be expected from the Government. Reviewing for the edification of the peers the influence of the Catholic clergy and the composition and conduct of the Assembly, he said that he would not enquire into the motives of those who had introduced this constitutional experiment, but he was sure they must now wish to amend it.[33]

Lord Normanby, who had in March succeeded the harassed Glenelg as Colonial Secretary in Melbourne's Ministry, was not yet in a position to make an adequate reply to this speech. As Aberdeen had suggested, however, he probably knew, as late Lord Lieutenant of Ireland, better than any other how the influence of the Catholic clergy could operate at elections. On the previous day he had written to the Governor for a comprehensive and dispassionate report on the state of the colony, directing his attention particularly to the recent allegations of decay in trade and industry and of the withholding of supplies.[34] He therefore informed the Lords that he would at a later date report the Governor's views and that he saw no reason yet for the extreme remedy of abrogation or for a parliamentary enquiry.[35]

Lord Durham then presented the petition drawn up by the inhabitants to counter the charges from Liverpool. The abrupt termination of Durham's mission to British North America had, as he now intimated, prevented him from gaining a first-hand knowledge of the political state of Newfoundland.[36] His *Report* had said that the Assembly had signified their intention of making an appeal to him "respecting some differences with the Governor, which had their immediate origin in a dispute with a Judge." But, the *Report* had continued, owing probably to the difficulties of communication between Quebec and St. John's, he had heard no more from the Assembly until his return to England, when he had received an address expressing regret at his departure. (According to the *Public Ledger*, July 20, 1838, Prescott had been invited to meet Durham and the lieutenant-governors of the Lower Provinces at Quebec in September 1838, but had declined because his presence was indispensable in Newfoundland. Prescott informed the Assembly that he had received no letters from Durham about the interests of the colony.)[37] Lord Durham, with "no information whatever, except from sources open to the public at large," had confined his report on Newfoundland to two brief paragraphs, one of which read:

I know nothing, therefore, of ... Newfoundland, except that there is, and long has been the ordinary collision between the representative body on one side, and the executive on the other; that the representatives have no influence on the composition or proceedings of the Executive Government; and that the dispute is now carried on, as in Canada, by impeachments of various public officers on one hand, and prorogations on the other. I am inclined to think that the cause of these disorders is to be found in the same constitutional defects as those which I have signalized in the rest of the North American Colonies.[38]

Durham now asked for a parliamentary enquiry.[39]

Other peers gave their views. Lord Ripon, who as Lord Goderich had been largely responsible for the concession of an Assembly, believed that the causes of the dissension were not inherent in the constitution he had drawn up and that whatever the outcome, it had been politic to make the experiment. Lord Brougham, whose malignance had done much to undermine the Durham mission, echoed Durham's call for an enquiry. He wondered whether the British constitution could be successfully applied on so small a scale, but would insist that a strong case be made for revoking it. Lord Aberdeen pointed out that the persons who had been most active in procuring the Legislature were now most desirous for the repeal. He personally felt that it was too late for a remedy by accommodation. Lord Normanby brought the discussion to a close by expressing great confidence in the judgment of Captain Prescott and the hope that the Governor might presently induce the Assembly to adopt a more proper mode of behaviour.

Aberdeen's speech provoked Patrick Morris to another of his eloquent outbursts. He deplored the "hasty and inconsiderate manner" in which Aberdeen had entertained the "calumnies" of the petitioners. Such charges, if true, seemed to Morris to warrant the impeachment of the late Secretary of State for a gross dereliction of duty. He reiterated his faith in the Newfoundland constitution, saying that he had sat at its cradle and did not want to follow its hearse. He entertained the strongest faith in the "miraculous power of free British institutions," believing with Sir James Mackintosh that they were "the parent of arts—the parent of commerce—the parent of wealth—the parent of every virtue." He fervently hoped that Aberdeen would not succeed to the Colonial Office.[40]

Lord Normanby's record as Lord Lieutenant gave the Catholic party in Newfoundland reason for optimism.[41] He had won the support of many Catholics in Ireland and that of O'Connell by the way in which he had consulted Catholic prelates and politicians, appointed Catholics to executive posts, and removed magistrates for political partisanship. These measures had earned him the distrust of the Orange party and had subjected him to suspicion from the Protestants and

to attacks in the press.[42] In Newfoundland the *Ledger* believed that his appointment to the Colonial Office might be a threat to the Protestant basis of the
Empire.[43] As it happened, however, Normanby held the appointment very briefly—
the Whigs were defeated in the House of Commons in May, 1839, but on Peel's
being unable to form a government, they returned to power, Normanby resuming
his office until August, when he was replaced by Lord John Russell--and the
speculation and fear that the Colonial Office might adopt a vigorous pro-Catholic
policy soon subsided.

The dispassionate report which Normanby had requested from the Governor
arrived on August 5.[44] Although Stephen at once pointed out that it merited the
most serious attention,[45] its length and its controversial contents, as well as the
coming change in the parliamentary members of the Colonial Office, interposed
a delay of two months between receipt and reply. On several points, Prescott's
despatch served to lessen anxiety. He reported that the evil of clerical interference in politics had virtually ceased since the Bishop's return in September 1838,
although the Bishop himself was estranged and refused invitations to Government House. He denied that there was a progressive decay in the Newfoundland trade. It was possible, he said, that the highly coloured accounts of terror
in Newfoundland which had appeared after the arrests of August 1838 had deterred some merchants from sending out the normal bulk of stores and provisions.
He noted that the revenue from imports for the year ending March 1839 was
substantially less than that for the previous year—a decline for which the arrests
and a degree of overstocking may have been jointly responsible. As for the
security of property under the law, he declared that he could see no just cause
for apprehension. After reviewing the course of political and legislative dissension since his arrival, he reaffirmed his belief that, despite these troubles, the
colony had benefited from the constitution and that it should not be abolished.
He said: "The existing dissensions proceed very much from the natural mortifica-
tion which the richer and more intellectual part of the Community feel at being
excluded from the influence which they should naturally possess and at finding
themselves subjected in a certain degree to the control of People unfit for their
station as Legislators, and who certainly must be deemed in various particulars
their Inferiors." These distinctions were, of course, increased by the coinciding
religious distinctions.

While the Governor deplored the recent behaviour of the Assembly, he admitted
that the Council too was at fault and prone to misrepresentation and exaggeration.
Since 1837 they had adopted a negative role, originating almost no legislation and
confining themselves to the prevention of evil. In a frank appraisal of the members of both bodies, he described the difficulties of working with the Speaker,
Dr. Carson, who, though seventy years of age, seemed to him to have the "immature judgment of youth, without the calmness and moderation which seem
naturally to belong to age." Thus, private communication between himself and
the Speaker, which might have averted public disputes, was rendered virtually
impossible. Of the other three popular leaders in the Assembly, Nugent had
made the Governor the object of personal attacks, Morris had good intentions,
despite his tendency to be swept away by his own oratory, and Kent had of late
become calmer and more reasonable. He described a cleavage in the Council,

in which he found himself in accord with the views of the Attorney-General and the Colonial Secretary, while the Collector of Customs and the four mercantile members, including his own nominee whom he had believed free of party spirit, seemed, in their opposition to the Assembly's measures, to be dominated even yet by the influence of Boulton.

In distributing the blame for the uneasy situation in the island, Prescott remarked that the conduct of the Home Government had been in some respects distinctly injurious. The charges of weakness and ineptitude which had culminated in Glenelg's resignation may have encouraged the Governor to add his own brief indictment of that unhappy Minister. He cited the futile enquiry he had been ordered to make into Bishop Fleming's conduct and the immediate admission of Boulton's objection to the unsealed writs, a decision later reversed. He complained that the delegates having made against him certain charges of contempt which Glenelg had decided were unfounded, the Minister had not so informed the delegation or the Assembly, with the result that Nugent had been able to publish a letter alleging that the Governor had been privately reprimanded for his conduct. He complained also of Glenelg's embarrassing delay in approving the abrupt prorogation of the Assembly. He stated his belief that Glenelg had on January 10, 1839, made an unwise concession to the Assembly. This was the acknowledgement of the right of the House to appoint their own officers when the present incumbents had been provided for, the decision being based on the practice in two of the North American colonies. In the present state of affairs, he thought it more convenient that the Clerk should be dependent upon the executive. The concession would tend to increase presumption and encroachment by members whose feelings seemed to him too coarse for proper appreciation. He now believed that Newfoundland had never had a governor as unpopular as himself. Referring to his offered resignation, he said that his successor would probably be able to do something for the peace of the colony, since he would begin without these counts against him and would be hailed with satisfaction.

Once again Prescott repeated his view that the best remedy for the colony's political ills would be an Imperial Act putting into force, with some modifications, the provisions of the Assembly's Representation Act of 1834. An increase of members from the more minute division of districts must, he said, be accompanied by a property qualification for representatives; otherwise the fact that the sessional remuneration was more than the average fisherman's annual income would induce large numbers of ill-qualified persons to come forward. He suggested that the qualification be set at £500 in lands, tenements, or vessels. He suggested further, in a supplementary letter, that the Imperial Act should contain a clause enabling the Governor-in-Council to make provisions for simultaneous nomination and simultaneous polling.[46]

However highly the Colonial Office rated the report, it was not one which could conveniently be laid before the House of Commons. Prescott's strictures upon Glenelg's conduct which, Stephen remarked in his minute, were based on incomplete knowledge of attendant circumstances, would certainly provoke comment embarrassing to the Whigs. A bill to abridge the constitution of Newfoundland, if less dangerous than the recent attempt to suspend the Assembly of

Jamaica, which had brought down the Whigs, could not fail to evoke searching questions from the Tories on the wisdom of the original liberal grant, and spirited opposition from the Radicals and Irish members to a contraction of the democratic franchise. Stephen thought that the despatch should be answered by advising the Governor to ask the Assembly and Council for the bill he had suggested; in view of the recent proceedings in Parliament, they might be willing to comply. If they refused to re-enact what the Legislature had already substantially passed, he thought that Parliament might then be more favourably disposed towards such a bill.

Russell agreed with Stephen and asked the Governor whether the colony would effect the suggested remedies.[47] The Governor replied that he was certain that it would not, pointing out that since the changes would be opposed by the persons against whose "undue ascendancy" they were intended to operate, no beneficial result could reasonably be expected from the attempt to obtain such a bill. Defending his request for Imperial legislation, he wrote: "A measure which will balance religious and political interests in a Community equally divided into Catholics and Protestants, which will prevent the condensed and therefore preponderating influence of the former, put an end to the application of physical force under spiritual direction at Elections, and secure to every one the quiet exercise of his right to vote, cannot, I think 'increase the existing discontents.'"[48]

Lord John would not be persuaded. He informed the Governor that he was against parliamentary interference except as a last resource and "as a case of absolute and overwhelming necessity." He was not yet prepared to admit that such a case had arisen. While he agreed that the present members were unlikely to subvert their own ascendancy, he believed that the force of public opinion and the opposition in other quarters of the excluded influential class might be effective. There could, in any case, he said, be no appeal to Parliament until a dissolution and general election had been tried in the colony. He was encouraged by Prescott's assurances that permanent injury to trade was unlikely, that property was safe, and that several sound local measures had been passed. His hope was that there would be a progressive improvement in the composition and temper of the House, which, though slow, would be preferable to a violent change. He was fully aware that the Governor faced an arduous task of conciliation and he assured him that in this task failure would be no disgrace. He would have the full support of the Colonial Office.[49]

The tasks confronting Prescott—of persuading the Council and the Assembly to adopt a conciliatory attitude, of following advice from England, of protecting the rights of the Crown, of curbing the assumptions of the Assembly, and of securing the passage of necessary legislation—were tasks before which even a colonial governor with long years of experience in the arts of dealing with recalcitrant legislatures might have quailed. Such experience Prescott certainly lacked and if five years of coping with the combatants in Newfoundland had given him a commanding knowledge of that arena, they had also made him decreasingly flexible and increasingly unpopular. Never a courtier, and now resigned to his unpopularity, he was determined still to govern as firmly and as fairly as he could. His views on the political state of the colony in the summer

of 1839 are disclosed in two succinct comments in his unsigned, but later acknowledged, article in a London magazine. Of himself, he wrote, anonymously:

> I believe that few men could have been found more willing and more able to act upon an
> enlightened policy and to administer justice with strict impartiality . . . but if he or an angel
> from heaven were to drop down in order to adjust party feuds, to still the storm of religious
> rancour, to satisfy to the full the aspirations of one party, and to mitigate the virulence of an-
> other, and to hope for an impartial judgment upon his conduct in the end, his hope would
> be vain indeed.

As for the Assembly, as then composed, he said:

> Any undue assumption of authority . . . must be promptly checked; but it will be time enough
> to apply for the interposition of Parliament when its misconduct shall be of such a nature as
> to make apparent its utter incapacity and unfitness for its designed purpose, and the impos-
> sibility of good government and commercial prosperity existing in conjunction with it.[50]

When the session began in May 1839, it was immediately clear that the Assembly,
under Carson, in their relations with the Governor and Council, were more determined than ever upon a jealous assertion of rights and privileges. Risking a direct
collision with the House, Prescott refused to grant to them the right to make
a temporary appointment to the office of clerk, the Crown-appointed Clerk,
Archibald being absent in England. Carson, threatening resignation and a remonstrance to the Queen, took his stand not only upon the principle conceded
in January by Glenelg, but upon the grounds that Archibald had been an opponent of the House, notably in the cases of the *Assembly* v. *Boulton* and *Kielly*
v. *Carson*, in which latter case he was understood to be acting in England. For
a time it seemed that proceedings would be suspended.[51] In some alarm, Normanby, who had so recently defended Prescott's conduct in the Lords, wrote
that the occurrence seemed to him "peculiarly ill-timed and inconvenient" and
that while he approved of the Governor's zeal for the Crown, he thought that
the concession made by Glenelg might have been extended, with little damage,
to cover a temporary appointment. Nor was he surprised that the Assembly felt
some dissatisfaction with Mr. Archibald. If, therefore, they persisted in their
claim, Prescott was to give way.[52] As the Governor had hoped, however, the
Assembly rescinded their resolutions against his acting Clerk, and allowed him
to perform his duties. Prescott expressed surprise at the implied censure in the
Minister's despatch, saying that the result seemed to justify his stand as "one
of temperate and judicious fairness."[53] Normanby assured him that he did not
doubt his "temper, prudence, and public spirit."[54]

Another attempt was made to free the House of the supposed influence of the
Crown. The members tried to expel a Roman Catholic colleague, member for
Conception Bay, who had accepted from Prescott a post as stipendiary magistrate.
A bill empowering the House, in certain circumstances, to declare a seat vacant,
and authorizing the Speaker to issue a warrant to the Governor for a writ of
election, had, in the previous session, failed to pass the Council. Now, taking
their stand upon several Imperial Acts, the House insisted that they had had from
the beginning, by analogy and derivation, an inherent right to declare seats vacant,
and that if the larger House of Commons needed such constitutional restraints
on the power of the Crown, these were even more requisite in a fifteen-member
Assembly where "the Crown could easily produce at any time and for any purpose

a majority subservient to the will of the Executive at the sacrifice of the privileges of the Assembly." The Governor refused to issue a new writ until he had received the opinion of the Law Officers in England.[55] They reported that he had been correct in refusing, since the disqualifications provided by statute for the House of Commons were inapplicable to a colonial assembly, and even the Commons had never claimed the right, "by its own authority, of disqualifying persons elected by the people and not disqualified by the Common Law."[56] The onus was therefore on the Assembly to devise a bill for the vacating of seats.

Had the Assembly not been so intent on protecting their rights and privileges, they might have been able to devise legislation which would have passed a watchful Council and conformed to instructions from the Home Government. Patience and prudence, even at that date, might have allayed the suspicions to which their precipitate course had given rise. But the virtues of moderation and gradualism had no appeal to the aged and obstinate Carson or to the Irish leaders who dominated the House. In 1839 and 1840, spurred on rather than deterred by mercantile opposition and Westminster's attention, the House continued to act with belligerence.

This attitude led to the failure in both years of the acutely needed Poor Relief Bill.[57] Although, following Glenelg's advice, they abandoned the attempt to "tack" the poor relief clauses to the Supply Bill, they persisted in their attempt to name the commissioners, on the grounds that Normanby had not expressly forbidden this.[58] The latter had said that he could see no reason in this case for withholding from the executive their "appropriate function" of appointing public officers, and that colonial experience had shown that the appointment of commissioners by legislatures was amongst the "most fertile sources of abuse and misapplication of the Public Revenue."[59] Acting on this principle and on this despatch, the Council amended the Bill to provide for the appointment and payment of the commissioners by the executive. The Assembly declared that the Council had made these amendments because they knew that such amended bills always failed in the Lower House. They declared also that their mode of appointing commissioners was more constitutional because it was done by the voice of the three branches.[60] However, the Bill appeared to Russell to be open to the objections made by the Council. He believed that the Council should not agree to named persons whom they considered unsuitable and that it was a "wise but not invariable rule" to leave such nominations to the Governor.[61] The outcome was that the Governor, as an emergency measure and at the Assembly's request, had to appropriate from the colonial Treasury a stipulated sum for the relief of the poor.[62]

The controversy did further damage to the Governor's standing with the reform party. In the autumn of 1839 when he was obliged to draw funds on his own authority, the *Patriot* condemned the act as irresponsible and a demonstration of the need for an executive council responsible to the people. When, at the opening of the special session in January 1840, he called for a Poor Relief Bill, again declaring against the naming of commissioners, the *Patriot* announced that the Governor acted under the influence of those who were strenuously attempting to abridge the rights of the people. For the *Patriot*, Prescott's policy was now without a single redeeming quality. If he wished he could instruct the Council to pass the Bill and could influence his officials; instead he seemed to the *Patriot* to be a "panderer and a partisan." The editor doubted whether Boulton himself had done one-tenth as much harm as had Prescott in the sessions of 1839 and 1840. He would leave Newfoundland "one of the most unpopular Governors that ever misruled our ill-used country."[63]

The legislative record for 1839 and 1840 was a continuation of the tale of antagonism and disharmony between the Council and the Assembly. By dint of public recommendation, and through the absence of a mercantile member, the Governor managed to ensure the passage by the Council of the Assembly's bill for the supplementary expenses of the late delegation.[64] However, despite his efforts, the Contingency Bills of 1839 and 1840 were not enacted. In 1839 the Council objected to what they considered was undue remuneration to the members of the Assembly and to the chairmen of committees, as well as to minor servants of the House. In 1840 the Governor asked the Assembly to prepare a Contingency Bill embracing the undisputed items, but the Assembly bluntly declined to accept his advice.[65] Kent declared in the House that the Council and their supporters, having failed to get the constitution abrogated, were obstructing the contingencies in an effort to harass and tire "every honest and independent" man from taking upon himself the duty of a representative.[66] The Assembly's response was to send up Contingency Bills for the past and current session which included all the provisions objected to by the Council. When the Council proved obdurate, the Assembly protested to the Governor against all, "even the slightest" interference in their votes for remunerating their officers and servants, citing precedents in New Brunswick and Prince Edward Island; any pronouncement on wastage must come from the public.[67] The Governor was obliged to adopt, at the request of the Assembly and upon the advice of the Council, the irregular course of issuing warrants to defray the undisputed items and to rely on the House to pass an Indemnity Bill in the next session.[68]

There were quarrels over other measures. The Road Bill and the Loan Bill for road construction were rejected by the Council in 1839 on the grounds of the decreased revenue, the large amount of unexpended money voted in the Road Act of 1838, and the outstanding debt incurred by the Loan Act of the same year.[69] Despite Prescott's call in 1840 for a prudent reduction that year in the appropriation for roads, the Assembly reintroduced, unsuccessfully, these two road measures.[70] The year 1839 saw, too, the unanimous rejection by the Council of the Jury Bill which attempted to remove the choice of jurors from the discretion of the Sheriff and to provide instead a residence and property qualification.[71]

The extent of the differences between the Council and the Assembly may be judged from the fact that of the twenty-four bills introduced by the latter in 1840, only ten received the Council's assent. The rest failed through rejection or amendment. Bills to establish a grammar school at Carbonear and an academy at St. John's foundered upon the obstacle of religious instruction. A Crown Lands Bill drawn up by Morris contained expensive machinery of commissioners and provisions for free grants. Other bills which did not become law were those to provide for the vacating of seats, to ensure accurate returns from officials, to regulate the office of the Sheriff, to ease rules for the registration of voters, to prevent fraud in the sale of imported articles, to provide for the collection of revenue on the coast of Labrador, and to subsidize shipbuilding in the colony.[72] As the Governor remarked at the close of the four-month session of 1840, the results did not appear to correspond with the duration.[73]

At the close of the session of 1839, an Assembly of eight members had adopted an address drawn up by Nugent which recited many old complaints and reviewed the struggle with the Council. The Council opened the session of 1840 with a counter-address which informed the Governor that the Assembly's claims to consideration might be estimated from their own admission that they had fallen into bad repute with the Governor, the Judges, the Council, the mercantile community, and the press. Prescott suggested to Russell that if the Assembly's address were found to contain grievances already settled much good might be done by saying so. After examining the charges against the Governor, Russell wrote that he did not hesitate to express his strong dissent from the opinion of the Assembly. The Governor's conduct of his very arduous duties did not, in Russell's opinion, give the slightest foundation for impugning his justice and impartiality. His conduct indicated rather "an earnest desire to act fairly and impartially" and had earned Her Majesty's approval. "Under circumstances of considerable embarrassment," wrote the Minister, "you have in no degree deviated from the line of your duty." In his reply to the opposing addresses, Russell disclaimed any right to interfere between the two bodies. He said, however, that the Home Government did not believe that the Council had exceeded their constitutional powers, or shown a determination to impede public improvement and to deprive the Assembly of their privileges. He hoped that the differences between the two bodies were transitory and that the Assembly, by showing some forbearance, would gain back the respect of the classes they had alienated. If they did not, an investigation must be undertaken, he said, to discover why "a system of free government should have failed in producing its natural happy results." This might, he suggested, lead to a remodelling of the system of representation and to an alteration in the franchise. He hoped that parliamentary intervention would not be necessary and that Her Majesty might not be forced to the "painful conviction" that the form of government and the manner in which it was exercised were inapplicable to the condition of Newfoundland.[74]

The Assembly had not demanded responsible government, though this was foreshadowed in the prayer for such a reform in the Council as would harmonize the two bodies, and for instructions that the executive should be "protective of the interests and liberties of the people in their representatives."[75] Carson did not advocate for Newfoundland the change urged by Joseph Howe in Nova Scotia and Robert Baldwin in Upper Canada—the construction of an executive council which could command a majority in the popular branch. On November 2, 1839, he informed the readers of the *Patriot* that the colonies already possessed responsible government—that it lay in the device of impeachment and in reprimand by the Governor's superiors. This pronouncement was greeted by the editor with scorn. A fortnight later (Nov. 16) this journal began to publish Howe's masterly *Letters to Lord John Russell*. These letters were Howe's response to the doctrine propounded by Russell in June 1839 that the essence of colonial government was an executive council under a governor receiving instructions from the Crown on the responsibility of the Secretary of State. They painted a satirical picture of a governor struggling in the thrall of his life-councillors to follow his instructions from the Crown and they made an eloquent plea for nothing less than the rights of British subjects.[76]

Howe's *Letters* were followed by, if they did not specifically evoke, Russell's circular despatch of October 16, 1839, which authorized governors to change their executive councillors at will upon motives of public policy. Its object was to strengthen the hands of the governors in the resistance to responsible government—to confer upon them a freedom of action which would allow them to control or to dismiss refractory councillors—but not to permit the collective dismissal of the Council on the demand of the House. Howe saw that the despatch could be made the basis for such a demand. His resolutions of 1840 in the Nova Scotian House produced not the dismissal of the Council but the removal of the Governor, who was bound by his contrary instructions.[77] The *Patriot* interpreted the despatch as a warrant for a change of department heads when the public had declared against their policy, and as a device for the coercion of the councillors. Governor Prescott made no public interpretation of Russell's doctrine nor did he mention it in opening the session of 1840. To have done so would probably have been deemed a declaration of intention. Kent called attention to the omission and questioned the moral courage of the Governor and the integrity of the Secretary of State.[78]

If Prescott was not prepared to dismiss some of his councillors and to replace them with reformers, he was ready to try the effect of appointing a reformer to office. He seems to have made his first approaches to Patrick Morris in 1839, for on September 14 the *Patriot* called attention to this member's unwonted concern about the passage of the Supply Bill and the salaries of public officials. At the opening of the session in January 1840 Morris spoke in terms of studied conciliation. He disputed the perennial charge that the merchants were opposed to the building of roads and declared that the interests of the merchants and the people were indivisible.[79] In March 1840 the Governor informed Russell that Morris had accepted the office of Colonial Treasurer and that he hoped this selection from the popular party would promote tranquillity.[80]

The appointment gave rise to complaints from both parties. The *Ledger* on March 3, 1840, condemned it as a clear recognition of the principle of conciliation to men who would never be permanently conciliated, and as another deplorable concession by the Colonial Office. A few days later, on March 7, the *Patriot* commended it, but insisted that Morris must forfeit his place in the Assembly. The Assembly's reaction was similar. Resolutions were passed against the presence of persons appointed to office after election.[81] Before the close of the session the Governor had obtained a warrant for the removal of Morris to the Council and in May 1840 St. John's faced a by-election to fill his place in the Assembly.[82]

With the conservatives standing aloof, it seemed that there would be no contest for the vacated seat. A policy of total abstention was urged by the *Ledger* which maintained that no gentleman would offer himself. "Since the knaves have it," wrote Winton on May 5, "let them keep it; the *trumps* will come out by and by." One candidate appeared, the merchant, James Douglas, a Scots Presbyterian who had long been known as a liberal. At the request of his friends among the Dissenters and Roman Catholics he announced his intention of running and was nominated by Nugent, Kent, and a fellow-merchant, the Roman Catholic, Lawrence O'Brien.[83] The *Patriot*, as the organ of the reform party, on May 9 called for perfect unanimity in his support.

Unanimity there was not to be, for Bishop Fleming, breaking his two and a half years' silence on political questions, called upon O'Brien to become a candidate. On the Sunday three days before polling was to begin, his officiating priest read from the altar a letter exhorting the congregation to support their religion by voting for O'Brien.[84] The *Patriot*, in vigorous language, deplored this sudden sectarian rift in the party, saying that there could be no doubt about the superior candidate. Douglas, it said, was a staunch and intelligent liberal and a firm supporter of Catholic rights, while O'Brien was a "hard dealer" with no discernible qualifications. The editor noted, however, that O'Brien, now backed by Kent, had declared himself to be "sustained" by all those to whom the electors had hitherto looked as guides. Nominated by Nugent and Kent, O'Brien appeared on the hustings accompanied by three priests and vociferous supporters. Politico-religious harangues and unruly scenes between the rival Roman Catholic factions followed, the priests, according at least to the indignant *Patriot*, going so far as to wield horsewhips to quell opposition. There were factional street fights and danger to life and property. During the week the Bishop addressed the Roman Catholic electors from his residence and on the Sunday after mass his priests convened and addressed an election meeting outside the chapel. Reporting the meeting, the *Patriot* declared on May 27 that while these appeals to religious bias had perhaps been justified in earlier days by the evils then to be overcome, they could no longer be tolerated. With the constables powerless to cope with the disorders, the Governor ordered troops to be stationed near the polls, prepared to act upon the requisition of the magistrates.[85]

In his despatch to Russell on the course of the election, Prescott wrote that want of judgment and firmness in the Returning Officer, a former servant of the reforming House, prolonged the election for eighteen days and that "throughout the whole period ... during the hours of polling the Priests were in the Polling-Room or on the Hustings encouraging the voters on one side, and browbeating and reproaching those on the other; and at other times constantly canvassing for votes, and using such arguments of excitement and spiritual intimidation as are known to be too powerful with the uneducated portion of the Roman Catholic Community." In the circumstances, he said, the original indifference of the merchants disappeared and was replaced by indignation at the conduct of the priests and a desire to help the independent Catholics in their efforts for Douglas. He was certain that, left to themselves, the lower orders would have given O'Brien little support. When it was found at the end of polling that O'Brien had won, the supporters of Douglas alleged that the Returning Officer, a Roman Catholic, had been overawed by the priests present at the polls, and that instead of using his own judgment when qualifications were questioned, had deferred in every instance to the opinion of Nugent, manager of the O'Brien campaign. They declared that the said Nugent had stated in the polling-room that his candidate need only have a majority of votes in the book, since he, Nugent, would be the judge should the matter come before the Assembly.[86]

For Prescott the unexpected renewal of priestly intervention was the most deplorable and inexcusable feature of this election. He had, he said, seized opportunities of proving to Roman Catholics that they were not debarred from official position. Yet, he said, Dr. Fleming "without the slightest reasonable pretext, or any rational motive, but apparently from a pure love of dissension" had again blown up the flames of religious strife. He had "produced a new discord in a community which appeared to be subsiding into peace and tranquillity." The Governor informed Russell that the Irish priests employed in electioneering were uneducated and vulgar, which, he thought, must be a fact well known to the superiors of the Church in Europe. It seemed to him essential for the peace of the island that the Bishop should be more than a man of great religious zeal. He must also be "calm and considerate, a lover and promoter of peace, and capable of appreciating and responding to an impartial conduct on the part of the supreme and local government." The Governor gave the Colonial Office a timely warning. There was to be a general election in the spring of 1841 when a repetition of clerical interference in the several districts might be expected to produce more serious disorders, or even fatalities. He was convinced that the Bishop's continued presence was incompatible with the welfare of the colony and that no governor could obliterate religious jealousy while Dr. Fleming remained.[87]

Once again the Colonial Office faced the problem of securing papal intervention. For Stephen these applications to Rome were full of "embarrassment and inconvenience." "I believe," he wrote, "that the Pope is not sorry to teach us that so long as we refuse to acknowledge his power in theory, he can make us feel the reality of it in fact." On Russell's behalf he intimated to the Foreign Office that it would be useful if their agent at Rome conveyed an unofficial hint that unless some steps were taken to remove Dr. Fleming from Newfoundland, the Colonial Secretary must in future "decline to accede to any applications for pecuniary grants, or salaries to Roman Catholic Bishops and Priests in the Colonies."[88] In September 1840 a second bargaining device came to Russell's hand. He learned that Prince Metternich had solicited unofficially that the British Government should procure the admission of the Latin Bishop of Taute to be Vicar-Apostolic of the Latin Church of Corfu. Accordingly, Russell advised Palmerston that he would give the requisite instructions to the Lord High Commissioner of the Ionian States as soon as the Court of Rome gave an assurance that they would make a serious enquiry into the conduct of Bishop Fleming. This information was conveyed to Metternich in November. In the same month the Foreign Office agent laid the whole case against Dr. Fleming before the Cardinal Secretary of State and was shortly informed that the Pope, in high displeasure with the Bishop, had ordered that he be summoned to Rome. The letter of summons was shown officially to the agent in the hope that the British Government would immediately accede to Metternich's request. Close questioning by the agent, however, failed to elicit a definite guarantee that Bishop Fleming would not return to Newfoundland. With Metternich's assurance that it was not intended to allow the Bishop to resume his position, though he was to be heard before being condemned, Lord John had to be content.[89]

To the Bishop's plaintive enquiry about these Colonial Office representations to Rome, Russell replied, bluntly, that they had been made necessary by the fact that the Pope's authority was the only one to which Dr. Fleming considered himself subordinate and on whose justice he confidently relied. When the Bishop later learned that his removal was the subject of discussion among eminent statesmen, he renewed his protests, saying that as a British subject he should be given a chance to vindicate himself. He now said it must be his spiritual conduct which was being condemned. He pledged his firm support to a new governor if he were, what he said Prescott was not, a man of honour.[90] It must be assumed that Dr. Fleming's explanations and promises in Rome and his good works in Newfoundland (a cathedral, a monastery, and the introduction of a second order of nuns) were sufficient to dispel the papal displeasure, since he continued his labours in the island until his death in 1850.[91] His energies seem to have been absorbed in these tasks of expansion for after 1841 references to his political activities disappear from the official despatches.

That the behaviour of the Roman Catholic clergy had been reprehensible was a point on which Winton of the *Ledger* and Parsons of the *Patriot* agreed. Their views about the significance of the election were different. For Winton it demonstrated that the united efforts of the Protestants and the intelligent and respectable Roman Catholics could not compete with the influence wielded by "wily and cunning" priests playing on the "grossest superstition." It proved to him that only solution was the abolition of the Assembly—the solution shunned, he said, by the "radical" Governor and by the "radical" Home Government, bound to Daniel O'Connell.[92] For Parsons, whose candour was marked if not animated by political opportunism, it was a hopeful portent that the election had brought about the co-operation of the mercantile and the Douglas party, the latter being, he said, the real liberals. He praised this junction of the capitalists and the people.[93] The old party, he said, had now split into the "despotic" Toryism of the Bishop and the "independent" liberalism of Douglas. The *Patriot* announced that it would adopt a new course. In 1836 and 1837, in the campaign to unseat the "Tories," it had "blazoned their ill-deeds and suppressed their good ones for the country's good" and when it had found that the people were still attached to their merchants, it had called in the aid of religious prejudice. The result, it now admitted, had been "tragedy": many Roman Catholics had been unable to find employers; the "reformed" House had shown itself incompetent to legislate; and import duties had driven up the cost of bread. A reaction had set in and this Kent and Nugent were seeking to counteract by raising again the religious clamour. The *Patriot* warned, however, that a real union of the merchants and the liberals could not be effected until the former adopted the tenets of the latter, whose "Grand Radical principle" was "the unlimited improvement of the country— in its roads and its agriculture—in its fisheries and in its mineral resources—thus affecting the improvement of the people by giving them an increase of employment and consequent happiness, and protecting their industry by a *Responsible system of Government!*" Influence from any quarter in favour of this doctrine of the people's party would be welcomed by the *Patriot*.[94]

Within a month of the election an appropriate political vehicle had been designed. This was the Natives' Society, whose objects, as stated by the President, Dr. Kielly, were not only benevolence among the native-born but, significantly, the promotion of unity and the advancement of the general interests of the colony through co-operation with the "peaceable, orderly, and well-disposed inhabitants."[95] That it was the nucleus of a rival political party was immediately and jealously recognized by the Benevolent Irish Society. Parsons made clear the political aims of the "Natives" by pointed remarks about the failure of the native-born to return a single representative to the Assembly and about the means by which they had been coerced and cajoled into lending themselves to the "usurpation of aliens." "This night," he said, "we proclaim ourselves a people." Not long afterwards he announced that the character of the old West Country merchants had been unjustly fixed upon their successors in Newfoundland. He said that it was an "unpardonable error ever to have included the unostentatious, open-handed merchant as an enemy of popular rights or public improvement." The people, he said, could hope for nothing without their merchants. The reformers had fought placemen, but the liberals must turn upon the present system of colonial government, with the improvement of the island's resources as their object.

Before the new movement could gather strength, and before the papal summons had arrived for the Bishop, the death of a member for Conception Bay made necessary another by-election. This was set for the late autumn when merchants, planters, and fishermen were free to turn their attention to politics. As early as June the Governor wrote to Russell of his anxiety about election proceedings in a locality where the civil power could not, as in St. John's, be supplemented by the military. In November, three weeks before the contest was to begin, the stipendiary magistrate of Harbour Grace informed him that two Roman Catholic candidates had appeared, Edward Hanrahan and James Prendergast. The former was receiving active support from the clergy, with the usual exhortations from the altar, and party spirit was consequently running high among the Catholics. The candidates were said to be about equal in condition, men of humble means, but whereas Prendergast had shown some independence of the clergy in temporal matters, Hanrahan was understood to be subservient. Opinion in the Colonial Office was that nothing could be done. As Stephen noted, in what was presumably a reflection on the state of the Whig Ministry, "only a very rash and strong government would brave the unanswerable charge of partiality in attempting to put down this clerical-political interference."

As the Governor had anticipated, the election was marred by disorders. It began quietly, but on November 30 two magistrates reported violence at Carbonear, with attacks on Prendergast's supporters, and asked for a military force. No such request arrived from the stipendiary magistrate and the requisitioners, merchants, were informed that troops could not be sent and that they, with their special constables, must exert themselves to keep the peace. On December 5 the Governor convened his Council, laid before them various representations made to him by the magistrates, and asked for an opinion on the despatch of troops. The Council decided unanimously that the lateness of the season, the limited period until the close of the election, and other circumstances, made it impracticable to send a detachment. It is possible that both the Governor and the Council were not unwilling to see the situation deteriorate.

The violence increased as the polling drew to a close. On December 8 five magistrates sent details of a riot at Carbonear in which some of them were injured. One had received a possible skull fracture, an elector had been shot in the hip, six others had suffered bullet wounds, a house had been burned, and another partly destroyed. The Returning Officer had to close the poll since the civil power could not preserve the peace. A meeting of the Council followed promptly and this time they advised the despatch of troops. The hope was that with the support of a hundred soldiers the magistrates could identify and arrest some of the offenders, and that the troops could be billeted at Harbour Grace as long as their presence was necessary. The detachment, with the advantage of favourable winter weather, was able to cross Conception Bay and arrived at the critical moment. Their presence proved sufficient to restore order without bloodshed and some of the rioters were arrested.

Because of the violence there was no return from the town of Carbonear and the House ending legally in May, the Governor decided not to issue a writ for another by-election. In his opinion the responsibility for the "detestable results" at Conception Bay must be laid at the door of the Bishop for permitting his clergy to take part in a "degrading and unnecessary" contest. Although they had ultimately exerted themselves to repress the riot, he could not see that their merit in this was any greater than that of an arsonist who first set a fire and then tried to smother the flames. He could see no justification whatever for the clergy's role in the election. He felt he must ask for an additional company of troops and a barrack in which they could be permanently stationed at Harbour Grace.[96]

In the Colonial Office three questions arose from this second disorderly by-election: Should the Governor's conduct be approved? What should be done about the electorate at Carbonear? Should the Newfoundland garrison be increased in order to discharge police duties?

Russell for the first time withheld approval of the Governor's course. He informed the Governor that he had failed in his duty, in that, without waiting for the advice of his council, he should on his own responsibility have sent off troops upon the first requisition.[97] This "prompt and absolute condemnation" evoked from Prescott a detailed and reproachful explanation of his motives. He had consulted his Council as a duty and not to escape his own responsibility, and had found that their opinion coincided with his own. He believed that military power should always be used as a last resource. He pointed out that rioting, in the strict sense, had not taken place until two hours before the close of polling. He realized that had he sent the troops upon the first requisition the disorders would have been prevented, but said that he would then have had to defend himself against plausible charges of attempting to overawe the electors. Instead, he now had grounds for asking the Assembly for an improvement in the election law and an "advantage over the factious leaders and demagogues in the House never before possessed." He dwelt upon the difficulties and risks of transporting and billeting troops at that season. Since Russell, he said, seemed to have overlooked the fact that he, as the Governor, was bound to consider the character and motives of his requisitioners, he would not enter upon that aspect of the matter, but he was convinced that in the Carbonear affair he was less open to censure than in any other part of his conduct. The troops, he declared, had arrived at exactly the right moment, early enough to prevent human sacrifice, late enough to make absurd any assertions about his "appetite for blood."[98]

As to the people of Carbonear, it seemed obvious to Stephen that the Irish colonists there were a body of men who were more savage than civilized and as little qualified to hold the franchise as "so many Malays." He recommended that the vote be withdrawn from this "herd of wild people."[99] With this opinion Russell agreed. He instructed the Governor to convey to the House the Minister's "decided opinion that Carbonear ought no longer to be a polling place." He should also inform that body that unless punitive and preventive measures were taken by the Legislature and the Executive, representative government in Newfoundland would fall into general reproach.[100] The Governor replied that the disfranchisement of Carbonear, even if it could be affected, would merely free the lawless portion of the inhabitants there to roam about the district and to interfere at other polls.[101]

On the question of additional troops, the Colonial Office answer was, from the Governor's point of view, equally unsatisfactory. Russell reminded him that the proper mode of preserving the peace was through an effective police force or a local militia which the colony should itself organize and finance. If only a minority of the population of Conception Bay was ill-disposed, he could not see why the peace could not be kept by the combined efforts of the majority and the local officers of the law.[102] The Governor could not have been more pessimistic about the chances of securing a Militia Act. He referred Russell to the abortive attempt of 1834 when the Assembly had contained "superior" persons. The occupations and dispersed state of the population and the difficulties of finding suitable officers would prevent him from recommending such a measure. He remarked, ruefully, that he had "succeeded very ill" in informing the Home Government about the nature of the present House if it was thought that such a measure, proposed by him, could succeed.[103]

The Governor himself proved to have been too sanguine about the temper of the Assembly. The *Patriot*, however, in its new role, did not look for much from the session of 1841, since there had been no infusion of new members. For this, said Parsons, the Governor was to blame: he had produced the crisis by appointing a poor Returning Officer at St. John's and by failing to afford protection at Conception Bay.[104] Prescott made a strong plea for an election law which would ensure for all the free exercise of the franchise. He pointed out that if, in the two largest districts, which returned seven of the fifteen members, elections could only be carried out under the protection of bayonets, the inevitable inference must be that the island was unfit for a representative system. The Assembly was unmoved. The members regretted to learn that there had been, in his opinion, circumstances which called for legislation, but they promised no such measure. Instead they declared that the Governor had had no right to issue the by-election writ without an official intimation to the Speaker of the death of the late member.[105] Four days later the Governor asked to be relieved of his post.[106]

The Solicitor-General introduced an electoral bill on January 15. At its second reading the House, girding for controversy, asked the Governor for all the documents on the disorders at Conception Bay. These he refused to furnish on the grounds that no good could ensue and that the events at Carbonear were notorious. He gave the Assembly due warning that if the session produced no election law, he would decline to take the responsibility of issuing writs for a general election in the spring. He would not render himself accountable for the probable bloodshed, but would refer the question to the Home Government for decision.[107] He informed Lord John that those who profited from intimidation and violence had set themselves to defeat all his efforts in the cause of order.[108]

The Electoral Bill which the Assembly finally sent up to the Council on March 19 provided that there should be a forty-day period between the issue of the writs and the day of nomination, that polling should take place in all districts simultaneously and continue for four days, and that unregistered householders should be allowed to vote on furnishing evidence of residence. To this Bill the Council made several amendments, apparently designed to accelerate the elections and to diminish the opportunities for disorder. They reduced the periods specified by ten and two days respectively and made more stringent the registration provision. They also expunged a provision for election expenses which they deemed to be an unnecessary money vote. These amendments made the Bill too odious to the Assembly to gain their assent. The Council rejected the Assembly's Bill of March 15 to provide for the taking of votes by ballot.

Since nineteen other measures failed to become law through the intervention of the Council, the Assembly had ample grounds for their annual assertion that the Upper House acted from a desire to obstruct. The members complained to the Queen at the end of the session that they had not been met in a spirit of reciprocity, but had been "encompassed by difficulties, impeded by embarrassment, and subjected to great personal injury." They laid at the door of the Council the blame for the failure of the Supply Bill—to which the Assembly had incorrigibly added the contingency clauses—three Education Bills, three Road Bills, the Jury Bill, and the Bill for the vacating of seats. They found fault with several clauses in the Council's version of the Crown Lands Bill and claimed that that body had deliberately inserted a money vote into the Bill to ensure its rejection.[109]

Earlier in the session the Assembly had again asked Her Majesty to separate the Council into two bodies.[110] This change the Governor was not prepared to advise.[111] On March 30 Russell informed the members curtly that there were several "other questions" relating to the affairs of Newfoundland which must precede consideration of the establishment of an executive council.[112] Russell's irritation was understandable for three days earlier he had been obliged in the House of Commons to agree to a Tory motion for a select committee on Newfoundland.[113]

PART II

CONSTITUTIONAL CHANGE

CHAPTER SIX

CONSTITUTIONAL REVIEW, 1841-1842

THE WHIGS' HESITATIONS about bringing the political state of Newfoundland to the attention of Parliament stemmed from reluctance to expose themselves to attacks from the O'Connellites and the Radicals, with whom they were in uneasy alliance, and from the Tories, whose strength was mounting. On March 15, 1841, James Stephen, commenting on one of Governor Prescott's despatches, remarked that if no interests but those of Newfoundland were to be taken into account, it would not be difficult to conclude that Parliament ought to interfere. Such a proposal, however, involved "questions of far greater importance" of which he could not take the measure.[1] On January 11, 1841 the London *Times* had published a leading article comparing "Popish Priests" in Ireland with those in Newfoundland. Discussions in the House of Commons in which this comparison was pursued and disputed, pressure to disfranchise part of the Newfoundland electorate, or proposals to change or abrogate the constitution, might well embarrass the Whigs.

The Tories had been considering what might be their best approach to the Newfoundland situation. On March 18 Lord Stanley, acknowledging Newfoundland papers sent him by Peel, wrote that the state of the colony had long been critical and that there were ample grounds for an enquiry. He noted, however, that all the topics were precisely similar to those which agitated Ireland and that the debate and enquiry, if entered upon, would turn on "religious dissentions of a most rancorous description."[2] Next day in the House of Lords, Aberdeen presented a petition from the Chamber of Commerce of St. John's which detailed recent disorders and asked for a radical change in the constitution which would give permanent security to rights and protection to life. He declared that events had proved that the enquiries promised by official persons were useless and that Parliament must undertake the task. As evidence that a crisis had arrived, he cited the religious factor in the election violence and read out the Governor's refusal, in the absence of a revised election law, to call a general election.[3] For the Government, Normanby deprecated the call for an enquiry, at least until further news should arrive from the colony. The failure of Normanby and his successor, Russell, to lay before Parliament the detailed report requested two years earlier from the Governor was the subject of private discussion among Gladstone, Stanley, and Peel. Gladstone understood that the suppressed despatch made large admissions. He believed that the Government's refusal to table it might be the basis for a good motion, and that if they did produce it, it might furnish grounds for a committee. He was, however, "quite alive to the delicacy of the subject, and the difficulty of avoiding, what he at the same time admitted it was most desirable to avoid, the introduction of the religious question." It was Stanley's opinion that there was little sectarian animosity in Newfoundland and that the trouble sprang primarily from the fact that the more respectable Roman Catholics refused to be "Priest-led."[4] Russell evaded the embarrassment of tabling the despatch in the House of Commons by informing the Opposition that to do so would be undesirable for the public service. He advised Sir John Pakington that he had no objection to his motion for a select committee on Newfoundland, though he was not ready to say what measures he would adopt in respect to the colony. On the day before Pakington's motion, on the grounds that in the absence of statements from all the interested parties the matter was not ripe for discussion, he attemped to set aside the Orders of the Day. However, upon Peel's insistence that the interposition of other business would create a dangerous precedent, he gave way.

In introducing his motion, Sir John Pakington mentioned but did not dwell upon religious animosity in Newfoundland—"happily unknown elsewhere in the Empire." In his opinion, the constitution of 1832 had been given prematurely. He questioned the expediency of giving representative government to "small states and infant colonies" and doubted that the "peculiar circumstances" of Newfoundland had been properly considered. He reviewed the religious and class divisions and referred to the composition and conduct of the Assembly—to the expenditure, the assumption of privileges, and the campaign against the Chief Justice. He said that he would enter upon the enquiry unpledged to any course and believing that repeal of the constitution should be a last resort.

Russell's reply epitomized the Whigs' approach to the problem of the colony and disclosed the party's reasons for caution. He announced that he would propose his remedial measures, if any, without reference to the Select Committee, but said that he thought it desirable for some members of the House to acquire information on the state of the colony. Size, he maintained, should have no bearing upon the granting or withholding of a constitution. He pointed out that the Governor had said that the colony had benefited from the grant. Admittedly there might be found facts and actions "very strange and discordant" to the notions of Parliament, but impropriety was no ground for removing a constitution and the present evils were preferable to a return to arbitrary government. He confessed he should "entertain some doubts of the attachment of a House of Commons to a representative constitution which would consent to the repeal of the constitution of a colony unless on the very strongest grounds." This remark being greeted by cheers, friendly and hostile, he observed that the members were perhaps thinking of the Government's recent and, as he now admitted, ill judged attempt to suspend the Assembly of Jamaica. What he wanted for Newfoundland, he said, was an impartial committee. For this reason he asked that haste be avoided. Both Joseph Hume and Daniel O'Connell asked that the enquiry be carried on with the full knowledge of the colonists and that these be given a chance to come forward.[5]

As it happened, however, the enquiry was a very abbreviated one, the evidence taken almost entirely *ex parte*, and no report laid before Parliament. The Select Committee sat during May and broke up with the dissolution of Parliament in the summer of 1841. When the Tories succeeded to office in September, Lord

Stanley, the new Colonial Secretary, who had been on the Committee, decided that it should not be reappointed.[6] Neither the delegation appointed by the Assembly nor the Governor reached England before the enquiry was adjourned on May 25.[7] However, a mass of printed documents covering the ten-year period under investigation was furnished by the Colonial Office to the twelve members of the Committee.[8] The seven persons who gave evidence were Sir Thomas Cochrane, three merchants, a merchant's clerk, a Roman Catholic physician who had left the colony after denunciation for his political independence, and an artillery captain who had been stationed in St. John's for five years and had there been converted to Catholicism.[9] Only this witness had been in the island since 1839.

Since his departure from the colony in 1834 events there had strengthened Cochrane's conviction that the granting of the constitution had been a grave error. He informed the Committee that Newfoundland was still no more than a "great ship with stages lying around her," that the island could produce neither a class of agricultural proprietors nor sufficient respectable candidates for the Assembly, and that it would be impossible to find suitable persons for the Council in the Catholic shopkeeping class (pp. 7-9, 14). With this view, T. H. Brooking (pp. 23, 45) and Robert Job (pp. 58-59), principal merchants and signatories of the petition for representative government, agreed. The latter said that most of the members of the Assembly were "passive tools" in the hands of the priesthood, and both advised the abolition of the Legislature.

These merchants and the third, Ewen Stabb, made tacit admission of economic factors in the mercantile pressure for abrogation. Brooking asserted that despite an increase in public expenditure the value of property in the outports had decreased and that his firm was withdrawing its capital entirely from Newfoundland (p. 43). Stabb, who said that he had decided in 1839 that the island was neither suitable nor safe for his family, traced the alleged depreciation in property value to ineffective protection from the law (p. 70). Brooking also gave it as his view that in the absence of bounties to support the fishery, there should be no duties on imported food (p. 44). Job testified that the political consciousness which had appeared since 1832 had led the Roman Catholic seal fishermen of St. John's into the habit of combination for higher wages, with the result that he now resorted to Trinity Bay for Protestant crews (pp. 60-63).

Questions were asked about the controversy over roads. Stabb declared that there was no systematic or judicious road-building programme and that most of the construction had been useless, badly done, and undertaken for private gain (p. 72). It seemed significant to Brooking that all the road commissioners named by the Assembly in 1838 were members of the majority party in the House (p. 39). Dr. Shea gave no support to the reformers' contention that the merchants opposed the construction of roads from the capital because they wished to maintain a monopoly of the winter supply trade by keeping St. John's inaccessible in that season (p. 96). However, the mercantile clerk, Thomas Browning, who had formerly served in a firm at Conception Bay, testified that the fishermen of the outports had no protection against arbitrary charges for provisions taken up in the autumn and that the prices were always higher in the outports than in the capital. He said also that most planters were kept in a state of perpetual dependence upon their merchants, since they seldom knew the expense of the supplies they had taken up in the spring until their return from the fishery. For this reason, planters tended to think their suppliers extortionate and to dislike trusting them with political power pp. (109-12). Brooking told the Committee that three out of every four men supplied by his firm were debtors (p. 22).

In their recommendations for constitutional change, Brooking and Cochrane were in substantial agreement. The former admitted frankly that it was not "quite congenial" to the feelings of Englishmen to be governed by universal suffrage. Though the present Assembly exercised, he said, a "tyranny," a restriction of the franchise would only result in an "oligarchy." He thought, therefore, that there should only be the nominated Council with power to frame laws for confirmation in England. This body might be supplemented by municipal councils, though he believed a renewal of the party contest might occur in these (pp. 43-5). Sir Thomas recommended a reversion to government by Governor and Council and the omission of municipal corporations (p. 11). Lord Stanley put to Brooking a series of questions on the possibilities of an amalgamated legislature and was told that such a body would probably be unworkable (p. 46). It seems clear that the principal merchants had decided that nothing would serve but the abolition of representative government.

Arriving too late to be heard by the Committee, the four delegates from the Assembly presented their case in a series of letters to Lord John Russell. They countered the charges about the composition and conduct of the House with charges about the motives and methods of the accusers. They argued that self-interest rather than concern for the island lay behind the mercantile pressure for the abolition of the Legislature. The merchants had joined in the call for representative government in 1831 because they had realized that popular petitions tended, in any case, to succeed and that with legislatures in the other colonies, a change was inevitable in Newfoundland. They had thought that they would have the people's votes at their command and would dominate both branches of the Legislature, but when they had found that the Assembly was not to be theirs they had begun to press for abolition. They had been ousted from the Assembly when the people had realized that the House was not representative and that, instead of passing measures for the improvement of the colony, the members were concentrating on restrictive and exclusive legislation. As examples of legislation detrimental to the public interest, the delegates cited the Acts dealing with public nuisances, banishment, road labour, bastardy, registration of voters, incorporation of lawyers, protection of game, management of the hospital, and protection of bait. The merchants had then embarked on a campaign to hound and discredit the members and to destroy the Assembly, in which scheme they were being assisted by the Governor, the officials, and the press. They had captured the Governor and all new and potentially liberal arrivals by the spread of falsehood and by the threat of public ridicule, and they wielded a solid influence through the Chamber of Commerce and the Council. The whole basis of the mercantile opposition to the Assembly was fear that agriculture would spread and destroy their monopoly and this opposition had found its expression in the unrelenting obstructionism of the Council.[10]

The merchants and the delegates in their concern, respectively, to suppress and to save the Assembly, were careful to depict the political scene in Newfoundland in strong and simple strokes. Earlier in the year, however, the Colonial Office had been supplied by a disinterested observer with a more detailed and objective picture of parties, factions, and alliances. During his survey for the Royal Engineers, Sir Richard Bonnycastle had gathered information directly and indirectly about the economic, social, and political state of the colony and had submitted to Russell his findings and suggestions. He defined two political parties in St. John's—an "ultra" Tory party, composed of officials and merchants and a "moderate" Reform party, composed of members of the educated middle classes and the mass of the people. His sympathies, so far as they were engaged, appear to have been with the "Natives" who held the balance and who did not yield, he said, to the "absurd pre-eminence in thought, rank, and puerile precedence" claimed by the Tories, or to the "rash, ill-devised, undigested schemes" of the most excited of the Reformers. Since the Natives' Society advocated reform and opposed priestly power in politics, and since it contained the germ of colonial independence, it could, in Bonnycastle's opinion, be a "most useful engine, if managed by skilful hands." But the government officials in their treatment of the Irish Catholics seemed to him to have displayed neither skill nor knowledge of human nature. Politically, the Roman Catholics were divided between the "Mad Dogs" or independents and the "Priests' Party," led by the vigorous Bishop and his strongly prejudiced and poorly educated clergy from remote parts of Ireland. Ambitious and bigoted though Dr. Fleming may have been, said Bonnycastle, he had nevertheless been much maligned and most injudiciously treated by the underlings of the government, who had discussed him with undisguised contempt in articles, allegedly sanctioned by Government House, in a low and scurrilous newspaper, the *Times*, which was edited by several leading officials. The idea was much fostered that the priests aimed at winning power through elections, but Bonnycastle doubted that there was such a design.

It seemed to Bonnycastle that a great change would be necessary to bring about a new order of things. He advocated a civil governor rather than a naval man whose preconceived notions of discipline were not likely to reconcile "petty but vexatious jarring interests." He suggested that arrogant subordinate officials be removed and all officials be forbidden to take part in newspaper warfare. He proposed the formation of two councils as in Canada—a salaried executive council of merchants of both religions and an entirely distinct legislative council. Both councils, he thought, should be open to members advanced from the Assembly, but closed to the Colonial Secretary and the Collector of Customs, whose standing in society seemed to him unwarrantably high and whose tenure of office prevented them from giving the Governor real opinions. The Governor, he said, with every desire to please and to accommodate differences, had wholly failed. What was required in his successor was "firmness, the actual exercise, literally, of the *suaviter-in-modo* with the *fortiter-in-re* carried to their full extent by a person of strong powers of mind, deep knowledge of human nature, and from situation, above attack."[11]

Another major submission on the Newfoundland problem came from E. M. Archibald, who for eight years had been Clerk of the Assembly. Archibald looked for a gradual decrease in party jealousy and strife as the number of small agricultural proprietors near St. John's increased, as education weakened clerical influence in politics, and as more merchants became full-time residents with a property stake and a settled interest in the welfare of the colony. Much of the trouble might have been avoided, he believed, had the establishment of the Assembly been preceded by a trial with a preliminary legislative body. He suggested three remedial measures—an increase in membership as provided by the Assembly's Representation Bill of 1834, higher qualifications for electors and candidates, and election regulations which reduced the polling period to one day. He thought that it might be useful to try the experiment of amalgamation if the House were composed of equal numbers of nominated and elected members, and if the power of initiating money votes were vested in the Governor. He suggested that the qualifications for electors in the outports be (1) freehold ownership or occupancy under a twenty-year Crown lease of lands or tenements valued at forty shillings a year and (2) for tenants, one year's residence at a rent of five pounds or, in the absence of rent, two years' occupancy. He suggested also that resident agents be specifically authorized to vote in the name of their absent employers. For St. John's he would ask that the voter occupy a dwelling at an annual rent of ten pounds. He would require candidates to have two years' residence and property valued at £500, or an annual income of £100.[12]

When Sir Richard Bonnycastle prescribed for Newfoundland a civil governor of statesmanlike sagacity and skill, he may well have been thinking of a person of Lord Sydenham's calibre. In 1841 there became available a man whom the Governor-General himself had described as a "pearl of civil governors."[13] This was Sir John Harvey (see Appendix A) whose eminently successful administration in New Brunswick had terminated in abrupt recall when he chose, at the end of 1840, without reference to the Governor-General, to reopen negotiations with the Governor of Maine on the renewed boundary dispute with that state.[14] In February 1841, bitter about his sudden dismissal after forty-seven years in the public service, and devoid of private means, Harvey had enlisted the support of the Marquis of Anglesey under whom, as Lord Lieutenant of Ireland, he had served as head of the police. Anglesey recommended Harvey very strongly to Lord John Russell, describing him as a "good and zealous and clever" man. His "zest," said Anglesey, sometimes carried him a little beyond discretion, but it was known that he had done much to promote harmony in New Brunswick.[15] Almost immediately Russell recommended the appointment to the Queen.[16] Prescott's resignation was accepted on his return to England in May. In September Harvey arrived in St. John's.[17]

Sir John's formal Instructions did not state that the constitution was to be in abeyance until the political situation had altered, or until appropriate constitutional changes had been devised and put into effect, but it is clear from the despatches exchanged during his first months in Newfoundland that he had been told to exercise discretion, study the situation, and render carefully considered advice. His own view was that he was both Governor and investigating Commissioner.[18]

Harvey's reputation had preceded him to Newfoundland where he was believed, according to the *Patriot* of June 2, 1841, to have leanings towards the popular branch of the Legislature. In New Brunswick, acting as a patriot governor and, like Sydenham, as his own prime minister, he had, without overturning the Assembly's initiative and supremacy, maintained a harmony unmatched by the other North American colonies. Handsome, confident, and persuasive, he had purchased support by lavish hospitality and by concurrence in that large expenditure of public funds for parochial rather than provincial purposes which had followed upon the surrender of the Crown lands revenue to the Legislature in 1837. The prosperity of the Assembly and the system of initiating money votes by legislative committee, with individual members supporting each other's projects on a *quid pro quo* basis, if not conducive to the welfare of the province as a whole, had fostered content among the members, support for the Governor, financial subsidies for his establishment, and rejection of the "objectionable principle" of responsible government. Sir John's own tactics had helped to ward off this principle. In order to promote harmony between the dominant Assembly and the Executive Council and to influence legislation, he had, on his own initiative, met the Assembly's request for representation in the Executive Council and had chosen as councillors two members, one of them the Speaker himself, who enjoyed the confidence of the House. Later, upon receipt of Russell's despatch of October 16, 1839, he had made public his readiness to dismiss at pleasure recalcitrant office-holders and had managed thus to cow certain members of his Legislative Council who dissented from his policies.[19] The *Patriot* welcomed his appointment to Newfoundland, but, with its new stress on the need for responsible government, warned that Sir John would lose his laurels unless he brought the Council into line with the Assembly.

The Governor began his administration with his characteristic buoyancy and blandishment. A week after his arrival he sent home a group of effusively loyal addresses of welcome and remarked that it was a hopeful sign that the Roman Catholic clergy showed a disposition to forget the past and to inculcate harmony from the pulpit.[20] He set out to ingratiate himself with the Benevolent Irish Society by the manner in which he broke the news that the Queen had refused for a second time to assent to the Act for their incorporation. It had seemed likely to the Home Government that an exclusively Irish body whose rules were unspecified might deviate, when incorporation had placed it beyond the power of the law courts, into political activity, and that this might start a trend in the colony for the chartering of hostile "national" bodies, none of which could be dissolved except by the local Legislature.[21] Harvey's course was to congratulate the Society on the failure of the Act because it might have left them open to the suspicion that the Society had motives other than benevolence.[22] Three months after his arrival he informed Lord Stanley that popular esteem had already enabled him to do much in the promotion of harmony. He had persuaded all parties and creeds to unite in one general address of congratulation on the birth of the Prince of Wales and had supported the formation of the non-sectarian Agricultural Society, of which he had become Patron. Upon Sir John's methods of acquiring popularity and securing peace, Stephen permitted himself a cautious comment: perhaps, he said, the Colonial Office tended to depreciate unduly this talent of governing mankind, exerted in places where "no man enjoys advantages of birth, rank, or fortune which enable him to receive with real indifference the flatteries, or at least the elaborate courtesies of the Representative of his Sovereign." To dispense them successfully was, he said, Sir John's "peculiar talent."[23]

Flattery, however, could not reconcile the reformers to the apparent suspension of the constitution. On October 3 the *Patriot* deplored the Governor's failure to issue writs for an election. Three days later Harvey wrote the first of his three despatches on the revision of the constitution. He had found not only flourishing trade, an ample revenue, and a successful fishery, but a general loyalty to the Crown, an absence of political excitement, and a desire to bury the past. He believed that the suspension of the constitution had had a moral effect and would serve to repress any undue violence at an election, should he be authorized to convene another Assembly. He suggested that the constitution be modified by adding a property qualification for candidates, by doubling the number of representatives through subdivision of the electoral districts, and by providing for simultaneous elections. He would stipulate that there be a two years' residence qualification for voters with the hope that the Assembly might later add other qualifications. He asked also for separate councils, pointing out that under the present system the Governor was inconveniently identified with the acts of the Legislative Council. The Legislative Council ought to be enlarged, he said, by the addition of members representative of the community and the Executive Council ought to contain three government officers and three members from each of the legislative bodies.[24]

On the question of how these or other modifications might be effected, Stanley and Stephen differed. The latter, still reluctant to recommend parliamentary intervention, thought that Sir John, with his singular skill in the arts of conciliation, might induce the Assembly to pass, with a suspending clause, the suggested measure, which might then receive royal assent or be ratified by Imperial legislation. But the Minister was not inclined to subject the Governor's skill to such a test. He remarked that a "fatal objection" to this course would be the necessity of calling together the Assembly in its present form.[25] He advised Harvey that the modifications must emanate from Parliament.[26]

Stanley was already reasoning his way towards the establishment of an amalgamated legislative body. Would it not be better, he asked the Governor, to abandon the "fancied analogy" to Parliament and to combine the two jealous bodies? The Crown would then no longer be forced to act in a separate council as a "counterpoise to the democratic spirit," but could exercise its influence in the Assembly.[27]

Stanley's queries about amalgamation crossed a second despatch from Harvey who was having misgivings about his own proposals. He had discovered the society of Newfoundland to be very unlike that of New Brunswick, where the Assembly, like the two councils, was composed largely of men of property and ability. He now doubted that there were in Newfoundland sufficient persons of "respectability, intelligence, and attainments" from which to construct two councils and an increased assembly. He had therefore turned, like Stanley, to Lord Goderich's amalgamation plan. He suggested, however, that the proportions in a united House of twenty-four members be fifteen representatives to nine nominees, five of the latter being officials. He suggested also an executive council like that of New Brunswick, with four officers of the Government and three members of the Assembly chosen by himself. The chief difficulty, he said, would lie in reconciling the inhabitants to the constitution of what they termed "that

Dutch Slave Colony," British Guiana. However, on the basis of what he had so far accomplished, he believed that he could, by promising a permanent increase in population, induce the moderate elements to agree to the scheme.[28]

In a complete reversal of the views he had expressed in 1831, Stephen now confessed himself an "entire Dissentient" from the Goderich proposal of 1832, though he acknowledged that he had prepared every word of the draft. Apparently overlooking the fact that he had also prepared the advisory minute on which it was based, he now said that it was perfectly consistent to write such drafts and to dissent from the policy of them:

Experience has convinced me that in the Constitution of Colonial Governments our forefathers were far wiser than their descendants and it is a maxim with me admitting of no single exception, that the model of Governor, Council and Assembly is on the whole the best for every Colonial Society, great and small, of which the Inhabitants are of the English race. I think so about the Australian Colonies, except perhaps where the intention is to convert the Colony into a great Gaol for transported Convicts, and I believe that a Single Chamber, composed partly of elected and partly of nominated members, must turn out to be nothing more nor less than a pure Democracy. The nominated members will either form a distinct party and consolidate the opposite party, and be overpowered by them—or they will shrink from so invidious a position, and rescue their independence from suspicion by an exaggerated and extravagant exhibition of it. In either case, the Governor will be left to contend with the Assembly single-handed. The case of Guiana is on many accounts inapplicable. The Court of Policy is not an Assembly. The Governor is himself a Member of it. It is kept in check by the College of Keisers and of Financial Representatives, and by the mixed population, European and African, and above all, the Sovereign has a Legislative power.[29]

This declaration of a lack of faith in the amalgamation principle did not deter Lord Stanley. The principle had been broached in 1840 by Lord John Russell for New South Wales and was the basis of Stanley's New South Wales Government Act in 1842. The Act provided for a legislative council of thirty-six members, of whom one-third should be nominated and the rest elected on a moderate property qualification, and it empowered the governor to return bills with amendments for the council's reconsideration.[30] By March, Stanley had decided on a similar bill to effect a union of the two Houses in Newfoundland. Such a union would, he thought, with a discreet governor, be a satisfactory and workable solution of the colony's political problems. The decision having been taken, Stephen announced himself "at once and entirely silenced," though he pointed out that his views were based on those of Sir George Arthur, lately Lieutenant-Governor of Upper Canada, whom he continued to regard as the highest authority on the subject.

Still to be met were objections and criticism in Parliament. While amalgamation might be effected by the issue of a new commission to the Governor, the franchise could not be restricted without reference to Parliament. Stephen believed that the most convenient means of implementing the several changes would be by a short permissive act. Stanley, however, doubted that the House of Commons would be "satisfied to vest in the Crown a somewhat undefined power of limiting a boon already granted." This might lead to justifiable charges that Newfoundland had no fixed constitution, but was subject to "capricious changes at the instance of the Ministers of the day." It was decided that the bill must be detailed.[31]

The Newfoundland Bill was outlined by the Minister in the House of Commons on May 26, 1842. It provided for what he termed two "nominal restrictions in the franchise. The minimum electoral qualification in country districts was to be the undisputed, even if unauthorized, possession of a forty-shilling freehold, upon which the person was resident, whether paying rent or not, while the corresponding qualification in the towns was to be occupancy of a house with an annual rent of five pounds. Candidates must have an annual income of £100 or incumbrance-free property to the value of £500. Money votes were to be originated by the Crown. Finally, the Bill called for the abolition of the Legislative Council and the establishment of a single chamber of twenty-five members, ten of them nominated by the Crown. Stanley defended this as an arrangement which would aid the legislative process and the despatch of public business, so often hindered in the past, he told the House, by preoccupation with questions of precedence and dignity. He admitted that the amalgamation plan did not have the general consent of the colonists, but their consent, he asserted, had been given to the other proposals.

His old enemy, O'Connell, at once informed the House that the assertion was untrue. He declared that the residents, none of whom had appeared before the Select Committee, had been extremely ill used by the past and present governments. He poured scorn on the Bill, saying that the proposed electoral qualifications would transfer the franchise from the many to the few and that the amalgamation scheme was a mere mockery of representative government. He pointed out that with ten nominees in the Assembly only three elected members need be of the Government's persuasion to give the Government complete sway.[32]

By the time of the second reading debate two months later, O'Connell had received a letter from Dr. Fleming which satisfied him that Stanley had failed to keep a pledge to the delegates that he would consult them prior to constitutional change. He was convinced that the Secretary of State was acting at the behest of a small party seeking to destroy a constitution which obstructed their monopolizing interests. Since Stanley had brought forward the Bill when those who would protest were absent, O'Connell moved for a postponement of three months to permit the receipt of communications from the colony. Joseph Hume, supporting this motion, alleged that the object of the Bill was to give the representation to the merchants of London, Liverpool, Bristol, and Dartmouth. He declared also that Stanley himself had done the initial damage to the colony by sending out the discredited Boulton as Chief Justice. The Minister, he said, had long had a prejudice against Newfoundland. Stanley defended himself and his Bill against this attack by stating that the colonists were having a fair hearing through the debate in the House. He had abstained from using the evidence of the Select Committee and was restoring a constitution suspended by the Whigs. He argued the need for haste, saying that the colony's Revenue Act had already expired. He claimed that extensive disfranchisement would be avoided by a loose interpretation of the forty-shilling freehold clause, and affected not to see how ten nominees could swamp fifteen representatives in the amalgamated legislature.[33]

When the debate was resumed in August, objections to the failure to give the colonists a voice, to the principle and proportions of the amalgamation scheme, and to the restriction of the franchise were variously stressed by members of all groups in the House. Charles Buller, the colonial reformer who had served with

Durham and who had had a large share in the drafting of the Bill for New South Wales,[34] believed that a delegation from Newfoundland could have presented a strong case at the bar of the House. He was opposed both to the number of Crown nominees and to the limitation of the franchise. Sir Howard Douglas, a strong Tory and a former Governor of New Brunswick, condemned the constitution of 1832 as an "immature seizure on liberty"—as a grant which should not have been made in the absence of a qualified electorate. Now, because modification seemed a lesser evil than abrogation, he supported the raising of the franchise qualification and, very reluctantly, the amalgamation experiment, maintaining at the same time that if a colony were not ready for the whole British constitution, it was not ready for representative government at all. Two Houses were needed for a proper balance, with the Crown acting as a counterpoise to the democratic principle. In his opinion, colonial councils had already been infused with too much democracy and he feared that when the Legislative Council was restored in Newfoundland there would be a demand that councillors be elected. An intimation of Whig support for the Bill came from the former Under-Secretary of State for the Colonies, R. V. Smith. He suggested that amalgamation be only a four- or five-year experiment and that alterations in the franchise be made in Newfoundland. It had been Lord John Russell's intention, he said, to introduce such a bill. Stanley then announced that he would accept these two suggestions and would ask only for a two-year residence qualification for voters. Henry Labouchere, who had also served as Colonial Under-Secretary with the Whigs, called the members' attention to the fact that Stanley had agreed to abandon the most objectionable part of what had been a "dangerous" bill. Despite the efforts of O'Connell, who complained that the Assembly of Jamaica had been given another trial, and of the Radicals, who called for delay, the House went into Committee. Although there was opposition to each of the clauses, and in particular to the provision for amalgamation, the Bill was passed with a comfortable margin, maintaining an average of 87 votes in the House of 100.[35]

The Bill was preceded to the House of Lords by an address of complaint from Newfoundland.[36] There was some desultory criticism from two Whig peers, one of whom presented a petition from a person purporting to be the agent of the suspended Assembly, but no delay was interposed by the Lords, presumably anxious like the Commons for the August recess—a factor which may have entered into Stanley's calculations—and on August 12 the Bill (5 and 6 Vict., c.120) received royal assent.[37]

If the late introduction of the Bill were not a device to forestall protests from the colony, this was its effect. Information about the measure was late in reaching Newfoundland, impressively signed petitions could not be produced with facility in mid-summer, and there was, of course, no Assembly to authorize and despatch a delegation. Although changes in the franchise and a reconstruction of the Assembly were being mooted in February, the terms of the Bill were not known in St. John's until late in June, when Bishop Fleming sent his complaint to O'Connell.[38] As a first reaction, on June 29, 1842, both the conservative *Times* and the liberal *Patriot* had expressed approval, although the latter called for the simultaneous introduction of responsible government. The *Patriot* apparently looked for valuable co-operation between the merchants and the liberals in the

House, but further consideration of the terms of the Bill led the editor on July 13 to denounce it as the "pencil sketch" of a man with bandaged eyes. On August 25 he announced himself to be surprised and disillusioned to learn that Harvey himself had suggested the amalgamation experiment and had entirely overlooked the principle of responsible government. He declared that no change had been necessary except this reform of the Council and he predicted that the merchants would become all-powerful in the new House.

This fear Captain Prescott had already expressed. The former Governor, in retirement "without any mark of approbation," had been asked by the Colonial Office in June for his opinion of the Bill. He had replied, stiffly, that it seemed a strong suppressive measure.[39] His own recommendations had been, as in the past, for increased representation and a higher qualification for candidates.[40] Expanding his view of the Bill in a second letter, he said that it might have been useful in 1832 as a means of testing the preparedness of the colony for representative government, but now it would seem to be punitive and to place the island in mortifying contrast with smaller colonies like Prince Edward Island and Bermuda. He thought that Dr. Fleming's party would object to the lessening of their influence, that most of the councillors would feel a loss of dignity in being members of the Assembly, and that if legislative power became fixed in a few officials united with the wealthy merchants, the improvement of the island might be postponed to the "supposed interests of Commerce."[41]

Sir Thomas Cochrane had governed for six years with an executive council alone, had objected to the constitution of 1832, and had been disregarded. Captain Prescott had struggled for six years with two hostile legislative bodies, had advised against their amalgamation, and had been ignored. Now Sir John Harvey, new to Newfoundland, but experienced in civil government and skilled in conciliation, was to put the new constitution to its test.

CHAPTER SEVEN

THE AMALGAMATED LEGISLATURE, 1842-1848

UNDER the amalgamated system in Newfoundland there would be ample scope for Sir John Harvey to play the roles of diplomatist and politician. The Governor's duty, as Lord Stanley described it, was to "hold the balance and act as mediator between the contending parties in politics and religion."[1] His initial task, therefore, was a strategic distribution of Crown nominees in the Council and the Amalgamated Legislature.

The election of December 1842 was unmarred by violence or open intimidation. One incident did cause some irritation in St. John's. This was the arrest of the candidate, J. V. Nugent, for non-payment of libel damages. The Governor took disciplinary action against the Protestant police magistrate for the timing of this arrest and the conservative candidates dissociated themselves from it. They were defeated in the polling.[2] The suspension of the constitution would seem to have had a chastening effect on candidates and electors and the admonitions from Rome on Bishop Fleming and his clergy. Sir John had used his powers of persuasion on the Bishop,[3] and neither during nor after the campaign did the Governor prefer any complaints about political harangues from the pulpit or about the presence of priests on the hustings. The opportunities for disorder had been lessened by the provisions in the Imperial Act for simultaneous and shortened elections. Further, the increased qualifications for candidates and electors may have eliminated some of the wilder spirits in both categories and encouraged some of the more substantial inhabitants to offer themselves for election. Two of the members returned by Conception Bay and the member for Twillingate and Fogo were Protestants and principal merchants; the Protestant barrister returned by Fortune Bay adhered to the same party; and the members for Bonavista and Trinity Bays were both Protestant and native-born. Of the other nine persons returned, all but two were Roman Catholics. Party affiliations would be dubious until the session had begun, but the *Patriot* on December 28 anticipated that the "liberals" would have a majority of two among the fifteen elected members.

In choosing his councillors and his nominees for the Assembly, Sir John Harvey had the advantage of a year's acquaintance with the political, social, and religious scene, and with the opinions, prejudices, and ambitions of those he might call. In October 1842 he summoned seven persons to the Executive Council, four of them officers of the government. The executive councillors were Attorney-General J. A. Simms, Colonial Secretary J. A. Crowdy, Colonial Treasurer Patrick Morris, Surveyor-General J. Noad, and William Thomas, W. B. Row, and Dr. William Carson. The first six of these were also to be nominated members of the Assembly and it was anticipated, correctly, that the seventh, Dr. Carson, would be elected for St. John's.[4] The nominated members of the Assembly were brought to eight by the addition of a Protestant and a Roman Catholic merchant from the old Council, and to ten, after the election results were known, by the addition of another Protestant merchant and John Kent, the Catholic reformer (see Appendix B, Table IV). The Governor hoped that his selections would balance the parties in the House.[5] The newspapers, characteristically, looked for evidence of his political sympathies. The *Ledger* (quoted in the *Patriot* of September 28) deplored the elevation of such "questionable men" as Morris and Carson to the Council and the *Patriot* on October 5 complained that six of the nominated legislators, presumably those who were of the Church of England, were "red-hot priest hunters and anti-liberals" in whose hands the Governor was already a tool.

Sir John informed Lord Stanley that he did not propose to identify himself with either party. His aim was rather to command a majority upon any question in which either of the parties concurred in his views, by requiring concurrence from the official members, on pain of loss of office. He reminded his councillors and office-holders that he was empowered by Lord John Russell's despatch of October 16, 1839, to retire them at pleasure. This power, he said, had increased his responsibility to the Crown and to the people. In his first address to the Council, he set out his own doctrine of responsible government. He maintained that he was responsible solely to the Queen and to the people for the administration of affairs and the machinery of administration, and that the executive councillors, the law officers, and the department heads owed a direct responsibility to him alone. Opinion at the Colonial Office, was that Sir John would have done better had he refrained from enunciating an abstract theory on a dangerous subject.[6]

In the selection of the officers of the House, Sir John was anxious to have the effective voice. He had informed Stanley that he was opposed to the re-election of Carson as Speaker and that he favoured the resumption by the Crown of the privilege of naming the Clerk.[7] On the first point, Stanley expressed his decided opinion that the Speaker should not be an executive councillor. The Speaker, he said, should be as little as possible a party man; it seemed to him that the election of a member of the Government to this post would give it so decided a political character as to divest the officer of all pretence to impartiality.[8] When the matter arose at the opening of the session, a deputation from the elected members asked Harvey to forbid the nominated members to vote for a Speaker. This request he refused, apparently believing that to comply would clear the way for the election of Carson or one of his party. The result, which could scarcely have surprised the Governor, and which he did not forestall, was the election of the Colonial Secretary to the chair.[9] It was not a result which Stanley thought desirable and he informed the Governor that the two positions seemed incompatible, but he did not instruct that there be another election.[10] On the question of the Clerkship, Stanley had pointed out the difficulty of taking from the Assembly the privilege already granted.[11] However, the Crown-appointed Clerk, Archibald, was elected to the position. The *Patriot* (January 18) deplored the failure of the two Protestant "native" members to support the native-born candidate for this post. Sir John had had his way and the members an intimation of the power of the Governor in their midst.

The Speech from the Throne, ingratiating in tone and formidable in length, and the complete and grateful concurrence of the Reply, might be said to define the respective roles of the Governor and the Assembly in the session of 1843.[12] The Governor pointed out the financial problems raised by the legislative hiatus of 1842 and suggested how they could be solved. The Assembly passed the suggested bills: a Revenue Act (c. 5) which provided for a substantial increase in tariffs; a Loan Act (c. 23), and an Indemnity Act (c. 30). They passed other financial measures which in the past would have given rise to long and bitter disputes, including an Appropriation Act (c. 24) with grants for the payment of the legal and other expenses of the delegations to London. The Road Act (c. 4) vested in the executive the appointment and payment of commissioners. The Civil List Act (c. 12) made the unreduced reserved salaries a permanent charge upon the revenue of the colony. Another vexed question was settled by the passage of a bill to regulate the trial of controverted elections by a committee of the house (c. 3). The Education Act (c. 6) attempted to meet the recurring sectarian difficulties by providing that Protestant and Roman Catholic boards be appointed by the Governor for each district, and that the majority of members on each Protestant board should be of the majority denomination of the district. The Act also provided that each board should make rules to be confirmed by the Governor, that the total annual grant of £5,000 should be apportioned to each district and to each board, and that the Governor should appoint an inspector. Departing from conventional usage, the Governor sent the Assembly in mid-session a cordial message of thanks for legislation already passed.[13] As the session drew to a close, he reported to Stanley with some complacency that the House had shown a disposition to "confer increased powers and repose increased confidence in the Executive."[14] At the end of the session, he congratulated the members on their productive labours, placing upon public record the high degree of satisfaction he had derived from "a most important and interesting Session."[15]

Reporting upon the system to Stanley, Harvey wrote that it so admirably suited the needs of the colony that he believed most of the influential inhabitants would agree to a petition against its lapse in 1846. Much credit for its success was due, he said, to the skill and judgment of the Speaker and to Newfoundland's comparative freedom from the "contagion of Democratic principles" raging in the other North American colonies. This had been demonstrated, he thought, by the equanimity with which the members had accepted the principle of conceding to the Crown the initiation of all grants of money in aid of the public service. He wrote that the community as a whole approved of the Amalgamated Legislature, the merchants because the obstructive power of the Assembly had been neutralized, the Liberals because they had been met in a conciliating spirit by their late opponents in the Council. The only real objection he had heard was to the great influence thrown into the hands of the Governor and he admitted freely that the success of such a system depended entirely upon a governor's "moderation, judgment, and discretion."[16]

The press, however, was opposed to the system. The *Patriot* of May 17 admitted that beneficial legislation had been passed, but reminded its readers of the displacement of the officers of the Assembly, of the salary provided for the Sheriff, and of the introduction of a Militia and a Crown Lands Bill, neither of which it deemed suitable for the island. On April 26 the *Times*, which had looked for the destruction of the "misused powers of an intolerant faction," expressed disillusionment at the bargaining methods and mutual favours, and above all, at the appointment of the reformer, Nugent, to be Inspector of Schools. The *Ledger*, April 21, regretted that "declamatory agitators" had not been restrained by the presence and example of men of "moderate and correct" views. Later, on May 9, it also deplored what it alleged to be reckless expenditure on roads. The Governor declared that these newspaper objections were made only for the sake of consistency and he dismissed the press as a negligible factor in public opinion.[17]

That the press was not a factor to be ignored in St. John's was made clear when Parsons, editor of the *Patriot*, was elected to fill the seat vacated by the death of Dr. Carson.[18] (It was said in St. John's that Dr. Carson's death had been hastened by the Privy Council's decision against the Privileges of the Assembly.[19]) Parsons, who was one of the colony's most vociferous advocates of "natives' rights" and of responsible government, was apparently regarded with some distrust by both major parties. The *Ledger* of May 30 hinted that certain "Conservative gentlemen" would express their disapproval of the conduct of their mercantile colleagues in the session of 1843 by voting for the "greatest political scoundrel" available. On June 18, after the election, it announced that many Conservatives had stood aloof in the conviction that one good mercantile member could do nothing in the Assembly. It noted also that the Roman Catholic clergy, whose political intervention Parsons had criticized, had given him no support. Parsons was elected by a slight majority over his opponent, a substantial Presbyterian merchant.

Consistent with its pressure for responsible government, the *Patriot* of August 30 was highly critical of the appointments made to the Executive Council in the summer of 1843. Only one of these, the appointment of O'Brien, the Liberal member for St. John's, to replace Dr. Carson in the Council, met its approval. Harvey raised the number of councillors to eleven by the appointment of four Protestants, two, Bryan Robinson and Thomas Ridley, being members of the Assembly and two, T. R. Bennett and Robert Job, being merchants who had failed in 1842 to win seats for St. John's and Trinity Bay.[20] In order to retain their positions, councillors chosen from the Assembly were to be required, as in New Brunswick, to retain their seats in the House in subsequent general elections.[21] So far from feeling himself bound to make his selections from the elected majority party in the Assembly, the Governor seems to have regarded these selections as a means for mollifying jealousy and weakening the will to obstruct. He informed Stanley that his power of appointment gave him a cheap and expedient means of purchasing good will.[22]

On one of his appointments the Governor found himself subjected to criticism from another quarter. To Chief Justice Bourne, the selection of the barrister, Bryan Robinson, for the Council, following upon the election of Colonial Secretary Crowdy to be Speaker, seemed evidence that these gentlemen had some financial hold upon the Governor. Between Bourne and Robinson relations had long been bad. Early in the year the young barrister had laid before the Colonial Office a long statement charging Bourne with discourtesy, prejudice, ill-temper, and ignorance, charges which he later declined, for reasons of expense, to lay before the Privy Council. Incensed, the Chief Justice, adopting the methods of Nugent, with whom he was friendly, prepared for the Colonial Office a lengthy counter-charge denouncing as politically corrupt the Governor's financial relations with Robinson, Crowdy, and others. Statements were laid before Stanley by the other parties in the affair.[23] It emerged that Harvey had arrived in the colony heavily in debt, that his principal creditor at home had employed Robinson to present his bill, and that the Bank of British North America in St. John's had been unwilling to accept Harvey's personal effects as security for his private borrowing. Suspecting, he said, that this refusal stemmed from political motives—an attempt to gain power over him—Harvey declined a private loan from a director of the Bank and accepted the sum from Crowdy instead. The contention of the Chief Justice was that there was a traceable connection between these transactions and Crowdy's plural and remunerative offices, and Robinson's elevation to the Council. He cited, among other things, the Governor's recommendation that Robinson be paid for his advice upon amendments to the criminal law. He alleged that when Sir John's bid for a supplemental salary had failed, Robinson's efforts in the Assembly had secured him a secret fuel and light allowance.[24] After due consideration, Stanley decided that Bourne had failed to prove his charges of reciprocal favours, and the Chief Justice, like his two predecessors, was removed from Newfoundland. Advising Sir John of the outcome, Stanley added the stern admonition that his conduct in accepting loans from persons upon whom he could confer advantages was "incautious and ill-considered" and that he must exercise greater circumspection.[25] Discovering that his pronouncement had been published by the councillors in the colony's newspapers without the final paragraph of reproach to Sir John, Stanley insisted that the entire despatch be given a permanent place in the Minutes of the Council.[26] The whole affair seems to lend force to Bonnycastle's point that the Governor of Newfoundland ought to be "from situation above attack."

Although it might be unfair to Sir John to suspect a private reason for his satisfaction about the increasing colonial revenue,[27] it must be said that ample funds were indispensable to his method of government. In New Brunswick it had been said that he had bought co-operation by creating offices, by dispensing hospitality, and by condoning lavish expenditure by the Assembly, and that he had been rewarded or bought by the Legislature by increases in his salary and by grants for his residence.[28] In Newfoundland these techniques were in evidence. Scathing comments on the distribution of patronage were made by both parties, the *Ledger* declaring frequently and vehemently that the Governor had put himself entirely in the hands of the radicals.[29] Shortly after a sanguine forecast of revenue, Harvey asked Stanley for permission to ask the Assembly for an increase in salary. For Stephen this raised the question of whether or not the Colonial Office expected a governor to live as a "grandee." Harvey, he thought, lacked the "courage to be frugal and the capacity to rule mankind without appealing to their eyes and their palates." For such a man an income of more than £3,000 seemed an indispensable instrument.[30] Stanley was prepared to sanction an application for £500 if the Assembly were willing to make this a permanent grant to all governors, for he did not want them to become pecuniary dependents of the House. He warned Harvey that in seeking the grant he must not expose himself to the risk of a failure which would prejudice his office. Instead he should privately and previously ascertain the views of the members.[31] Before the close of the session of 1844, Harvey had found it wise to abandon the idea of an increase. He had learned that while sixteen of the members would support a permanent grant, the rest, a majority of the elected members would not. He understood that the Assembly would have made the grant to him personally and he remarked that his enquiries had been useful in apprising him of the esteem in which he was held.[32] They had also shown, although he did not remark on this, that despite his blandishments the Liberals remained a coherent group.

In the session of 1844 the Governor's relations with the Assembly were marked by successful promotion of, and tactful acquiescence in, public expenditure. He was able to persuade mercantile members to agree to several measures furthering the internal interests of the island. Their approval of the appropriations testified, he said, to their "good sense, moderation, and even liberality of sentiment."[33] Grants were made (7 Vict., c. 9) for roads to a total of £40,000. Although the power of initiating these grants rested with the Governor, he found it convenient in 1844 to make a partial surrender of his initiative by sanctioning numerous petitions for construction presented by members on behalf of their districts. He thought that this departure from his Instructions could be offset by reserving to himself the power to refuse any bill for roads which had objectionable provisions, and by insisting that priority be given to the completion of roads already begun.[34] Stanley warned him, however, that he must maintain the full rights of the Crown.[35]

The proceedings of the session were on the whole less amicable than those in 1843 and only sixteen bills, as compared with a previous twenty-five, were presented for the Governor's signature. A Crown Lands Bill (c. 1) was passed which placed the revenue from waste lands in the hands of the Legislature. However, a number of other controversial measures were introduced, discussed at length, and rejected or postponed. Among these were a bill brought in by Kent to define the powers and privileges of the Assembly, one by Nugent to regulate the calling of juries, and one by Robinson to provide for a more efficient administration of justice in the outports.[36] The Governor thought that the frank airing of views had been useful and that crude legislation had been avoided.[37]

The most politically significant bill of the session was one providing for a reversion, with some modifications, to the former constitution of the colony. This was drawn up and proposed by Richard Barnes, member for Trinity Bay. He was a native and a Wesleyan and, according to Sir John, not an adherent of the Government.[38] Nor, judging by the tenor of the debates, was he, like some of his Dissenting compatriots, a supporter of the Liberal party of Kent and Nugent. He proposed that after September 1, 1846, the colony should have separate executive and legislative councils and an elected assembly of twenty-five members. He proposed also simultaneous elections, a two-year residence qualification for electors, and Crown initiative in money votes. His bill provided for a new subdivision and rearrangement of the electoral districts, which, like the controversial bill of 1834, raised the number of districts to twenty-four.

In introducing the measure Barnes's stress was upon the need for a return to the orthodox parliamentary system of two legislative chambers. He set forth graphically his objections to the Amalgamated Legislature:

... when I remember that the present system with all its power to originate evils, may possibly become permanent, and as a chain upon our necks, keep us licking the dust for perhaps half a century to come, I am emboldened to come out upon the subject and make an attempt to arouse the Legislature to a sense of its duty, to induce it to stand erect and look out upon society, and join it in the march of civilization and improvement, as a legitimate child of the parent stock, and not as an ill-favoured brat, with a badge of disgrace upon its forehead.

He warned that the present system, without the traditional British system of checks and balances, was a potential despotism, although the present Governor and his councillors might be virtuous men. But, he said, "the safety with which we may handle and listen to the rattle of one serpent which has lost its sting is no protection against the attack of another from which the venom has never been extracted." What was the attitude of the Colonial Office and the British Government? Perhaps they thought that Newfoundland had not shown her readiness for a more advanced form of government. How could they be convinced that this was not so? The colony must demonstrate a growing restlessness under its degrading constitution and prove that it valued rational liberty. The members should throw off their servility to the Governor and give leadership to the country.

Barnes made two major objections to the amalgamated system. One was that it might permit taxation without representation. He pointed out that in the previous session only four elected members had been present in the Committee of Ways and Means, that one of these had been in the Chair, and that the mover of all the duties had been an officer of the Government. If it chose, the executive could, by corrupting only three representatives, grasp unlimited powers of taxation and expenditure. He refused to believe that amalgamation could be an experiment intended for application to other British colonies. His second objection was that in the Assembly both the representative and nominated members were impeded in the free expression of opinion. The latter could be swamped by the votes of the former and could not, as in the Legislative Council, exercise their deterrent power over legislation. This must force them into attempts to corrupt the representatives and the price of bought votes would soon soar. Alternatively, the Governor might displace councillors who failed to give his policies support, but in such dismissals the people would have no voice.[39]

In the discussion which ensued the Catholic Liberals subjected the electoral divisions to a suspicious analysis and alleged that Barnes's motives were primarily sectarian rather than constitutional. Kent declared that the object of the Bill was the reduction of Roman Catholic strength in the House.[40] Before the second reading, his party convened a public meeting to organize opinion against the Bill and to devise means of preventing its passage. O'Brien, Kent, and Nugent rang the changes upon the old theme of attempted Protestant domination. O'Brien insisted that the Bill was ingeniously contrived to return three times as many

Wesleyans and other "Sectarians" as Roman Catholics. Kent claimed that there was no need for such a scheme because Catholic constituencies were always ready to return Protestant Liberals when they could find them, as had happened in the election of Carson and later Parsons for St. John's. Nugent purported to find that eighteen Protestant districts had been devised, five more than had been attempted in 1834. He was able to point out what he considered intentional anomalies in the over-representation of Protestant Trinity Bay and Fortune Bay and the under-representation of Catholic St. John's. He outlined a scheme to block the progress of the Bill by successive adjournments and the appointment of a citizen's committee. A series of resolutions was passed. One commended the existing arrangement of districts and another condemned minute subdivisions as tending to throw the representation of the outports into the hands of a few mercantile houses. It was resolved to petition the House to reject the Bill. Kent made the indisputable point that Barnes had shown inconsistency in deploring the association of the Council with the Assembly while entrusting to this joint body the formation of a new constitution.[41]

Parsons based his objection to the Bill on the absence of any provision for responsible government. He would ask that with the separation of the councils there should also be the establishment of the British system of cabinet responsibility.[42] He moved at the meeting for a speedy restoration of that form of government which afforded a "faint outline" of that of the mother country.[43] In further support of the Bill in the Assembly, Barnes said that although it did not explicitly recognize the principle of responsible government, he thought that this principle was "virtually comprehended." Selections for the Executive Council would continue to be made from the representative branch and would lead to a "due share" of responsibility to the wishes of the Assembly.[44]

Barnes entered little into the charges of an ulterior sectarian motive in the Bill. He argued instead that fifteen members were too few to provide a choice for committees, a variety of talent, and a division of labour. Increased membership would, he said, prevent the domination of one party and give the House the benefit of more enlightened opinions. He was opposed to a further increase in the representation of populous St. John's and Conception Bay and defended as just his allocation of members to those small outport districts which his opponents termed "close boroughs." Nugent argued in reply that they should not establish an abuse which the English Reform Bill had so lately corrected. Kent's contribution was a long review of the political struggle in Newfoundland and a recitation of the good results of the Amalgamated Legislature, a form of constitution he was not disposed to abandon in haste.[45] It seems fair to conclude that the opposition of the Catholic Liberals stemmed from the fear that they would be supplanted in the House by Protestant merchants and a Liberal party drawing its support from Dissenters and natives.

The Governor took steps to secure the withdrawal of the Bill. He advised his councillors that he thought the present constitution had not had a sufficient test, that public opinion had not yet been expressed, and that the measure was therefore premature. Barnes was induced to withdraw the Bill on the understanding that the Governor would submit it for Lord Stanley's consideration.

Harvey, personally opposed to the change, found it satisfactory that the Catholic members had made a stand against it.[46]

The *Times*, one of the organs of the mercantile party, commenting on April 17 on the events of the session, advocated not a reversion to the old constitution, but the suspension or abrogation of representative government. With due allowance for editorial exaggeration and an attempt to catch the eye of the Secretary of State, its description of the Amalgamated Legislature suggests that for nominated members and merchants, the Assembly was often an uncomfortable place:

> We cannot ... as honest recorders of passing events, abstain from ... remarking ... that in the General Assembly of late, there has not only been an absence of that decorum and dignity which should distinguish a deliberative body; but a violence of manner and a coarseness of speech which have gone far to disgust the more civilized portion of the community.... Does a member of the Council freely express an opinion? He is branded as a traitor to the people's cause, or as an hireling whose wages are honour. Does a merchant, with a capital embarked in the trade of the country, venture to oppose some sweeping motion that would jeopardise his property? He is hooted as a monopolist and an oppressor, as a self-interested maintainer of abuse and fraud, or a relentless tyrant with his foot on the neck of the poor!

The writer was sure that if a correct report of these proceeding reached England, the colony's unfitness for representative government would be recognized and Lord Stanley would arrange for its suspension.

Since legislation on the future form of the Newfoundland constitution would be required in 1845, or at latest in 1846, Stanley asked the Governor for his views and for his comments on the suitability of the local bill.[47] Harvey, replying in October 1844, emphasized that though the Amalgamated Legislature had worked well, there had been no material change in the composition of the community and that if there were to be a reversion to the former type of government, there must also be "*salutary* precautions and securities." In making his preliminary recommendations, he followed the framework of the bill proposed by Barnes, with its provisions for two distinct councils and an assembly of twenty-five members. He advised that the executive council be constructed upon the principle already recognized by Lord Stanley—presumably the combination of officials with legislators from both branches. He called for a legislative council of at least ten members who should be nominated by the Crown, but be rendered to some degree independent through holding their seats for life. He thought that if the Council included a certain number of officers of the government, no further precautions need be taken for representing and sustaining the influence of the Crown in that body. He suggested that the Crown should appoint to the Assembly three *ex officio* members "for the purpose of representing the local Government in that Body, of introducing, explaining and vindicating its measures, and taking part in all its debates, with or *without voting*." Expanding on this, he wrote:

> To the absence of some such precautionary measure as the presence of a few *ex officio* members in the Assembly of Lower Canada I have often been disposed to refer most of those violent Legislative proceedings which, based upon false premises and wilful misstatements, led to the adoption of inflammatory resolutions and other measures of an ultra and revolutionary tendency which a little temperate and well timed explanation *might* have averted.

He would have the elected members chosen at simultaneous elections in all districts, the districts being arranged when a new census had been completed, and the candidates required to bear a part of the election costs. Since any member of the Assembly who introduced a bill to alter the electoral districts exposed himself to the charge of acting in the interests of religious party, he believed that these alterations, like the constitutional modifications, should be effected by the Imperial Parliament.[48]

In 1845, with the legal term of the experiment half over and with constitutional revision in the air, the weaknesses of the Amalgamated Legislature were becoming more apparent. Only sixteen bills were enacted and apart from one providing, in anticipation of new constitution, for the taking of the census, and another regulating by duties and fines the sale of bait fish for export, most of the legislation was of a routine nature.[49] Reviewing the session on March 28, the *Ledger* remarked that much of it had been occupied in debating the Jury Bill which had eventually been laid aside, and that little good or evil had been accomplished. Most of the members had abandoned "honour and principle" and the few who had not could not extricate the Assembly from the disrepute into which it had fallen with sober-thinking observers. In these circumstances, it said, the less the House did, the better.

The Governor, too, had become reluctant to urge the Assembly to pass much legislation. Writing to Stanley in April, he referred for the first time to the absence of the usual "salutary constitutional checks" and of the opportunity for a free discussion and full investigation of all measures in an upper house. He had been instrumental, he said, in discouraging the passage of several crude and discreditable measures, but he admitted that in the small Assembly certain members were able to avail themselves of means to appropriate for their districts more than their share of public funds. Due to the "superior leaven" in the House, he thought that there was probably less use of these devices than in some of the North American colonies. He admitted that the enthusiasm for road building was still resulting in the passing of larger road grants than he had recommended.

With these reservations, Harvey still regarded the Amalgamated Legislature as a "well-contrived political machine for raising and appropriating to the general improvement of the colony such an amount of revenue as its trade and resources could reasonably afford." In what had been an arena of bitter dispute, there were now what he termed "moderate" discussions, with merchants and planters surpassing official members of the government in backing appropriations for public use. Personal and party violence had, he said, been softened, and both sides had been practically convinced of the great advantage derived from the exercise of a "due degree of moderation and mutual forbearance." These qualities, he did not doubt, would be conspicuously displayed when the Legislature was again separated into two branches. He recommended the Amalgamated Assembly as a most excellent school of training for future rational and practical legislation. He denied the charge that it was a "mere court of Provincial Parliament in which to register and give effect to the suggestions and recommendations of the Governor." He declared that it was not possible for any body to have acted more independently and patriotically, or more in accordance with the "well-understood wishes and interests of the people." Stephen apparently could not forbear calling attention to the equivocal nature of this report, which he described as a "eulogy of Lord Stanley's constitution" and an explanation of why the "least possible use" had been made of it.[50]

Having said, if ambiguously, that the time was ripe for a constitutional change, the Governor wrote privately that the present constitution could safely be renewed for another year or two. Public opinion, he said, would not be decidedly against the re-enactment. Selecting on this occasion, as an organ of public opinion, an unnamed newspaper of large circulation, presumably the *Patriot,* and ignoring the newspapers which urged an end to the Amalgamated Assembly or to representative government itself, he enclosed a leading article which argued that unless responsible government were to be introduced, the people should declare against a return to the old system. He explained that there would be no violent degree of dissatisfaction should it prove inconvenient for the Minister to introduce a new constitution.[51] In reply, Stanley asked to be supplied with distinct recommendations before the parliamentary session of 1846.[52]

When Sir John's recommendations arrived in November 1845 he was found to have abandoned one of his major proposals—that of introducing official members into the Assembly. He had come to the conclusion that this, with its implication that the people of Newfoundland were less fitted for political privileges than those in other colonies, would give ground for too much dissatisfaction. He now said, expansively, that any form of constitution would work well, and that the presence in the Assembly of some executive councillors, whose seats in the Council depended upon re-election to the House, would give the Government an adequate voice in that body. He suggested that he, with his Council, should undertake the revision of the electoral districts on the basis of the completed census, which had disclosed a population of 96,000. They would work on the principle of one representative for every 4,000 of the inhabitants.[53] Stanley asked that a complete bill in draft form be sent immediately for his use.[54]

With this bill in the course of preparation, Harvey informed the House at the opening of the session of 1846 that a new constitution would almost certainly be conferred. As a precaution against Parliament's delay, however, he asked that the Revenue Bill contain a clause extending its life until the end of the next ensuing session. At once the Liberals expressed alarm at being asked to authorize taxes of unlimited duration. They believed that such authorization would allow the Minister to suspend the constitution indefinitely. Kent, who had been serving with relative docility as a nominated member, spoke with admiration of the Governor's "simplicity and candour," but he made a statement which seemed to herald his return to active politics and to mark out the line the Liberal party would follow. Hitherto, Parsons, associated with Kent and his colleagues, but ambitious for the ascendancy of a rival "Native" Liberal party, had been the most vocal proponent of responsible government. Now, significantly, Kent observed that if responsible government were in operation, the objection being made to a passage in the Speech from the Throne might compel the councillors to retire.[55] A month later he brought in his resolutions on the applicability of the responsible principle of colonial government to any future form of constitution ceded to Newfoundland.[56]

Kent's resolutions were based on the Harrison Resolutions carried in the Canadian Parliament of September 3, 1841, the interpretation of these by the late Governor-General, Lord Metcalfe, and on the Proceedings of the Nova Scotia Assembly, March 5, 1844. The Harrison Resolutions had called for a governor responsible to the Imperial authority alone, but acting with advisers who formed a provincial administration and who had the confidence of the representatives of the people. This arrangement was to guarantee that the "well-understood wishes and interests of the people" should at all times be "faithfully represented and advocated." They stipulated also that the people had the right to expect from such an administration a constant exertion to see that the Imperial authority was exercised in accordance with their wishes and interests.[57] Metcalfe had been unwilling to concede that the Harrison Resolutions meant full cabinet responsibility, party government, and party patronage. But, "provided that the respec-tive parties engaged in the undertaking be guided by moderation, honest purpose, common sense, and equitable minds, devoid of party purpose," he had seen no difficulty in carrying on responsible government. He understood the Resolutions to mean

that it should be competent to the Council to offer advice on all occasions, whether as to patronage or otherwise; and that the Governor should receive it with the attention due to his constitutional advisers, and consult with them on all occasions of adequate importance, and that there should be a cordial cooperation and sympathy between him and them; that the Council should be responsible to the Provincial Parliament and people; and that when the acts of the Governor are such as they do not choose to be responsible for, they should be at liberty to resign.[58]

What Kent ostensibly proposed, then, was not the full doctrine of responsible government being propounded by Howe in Nova Scotia and Baldwin in Canada, but a qualified version by which the Colonial Office, through its governors, might still hope to resist the concession of party government demanded by the reformers.

In support of his resolutions, Kent argued that tradition and loyalty should spur the colony to win responsible government: "We must participate in the spirit of our sires—we must endeavour by infusing the spirit of freedom into our institutions, to keep pace with the progress of reform and the growing intelligence of the age." He urged the members not to be deterred, by fears of alarming the mother country, from seeking what had been yielded to neighbouring colonies. The climate of opinion in England had changed, and even influential men who believed that further concessions to the colonies would sever the Imperial connection would support such concessions in order that the parting should be temperate. The problem in Newfoundland was, he said, political apathy, that general lack of interest in party movements produced by a system which had elevated political leaders and removed them from the theatre of agitation. Was the colony therefore to revert to the old constitution which had given so much dissatisfaction in the past? It was not any peculiarity in society which had caused the failure of that system, but the inherent defect in the system itself. If it were restored, he forecast that it would work at most for three or four years, if novelty and the influence of the Governor were able to induce persons of influence to undergo the ordeal of election. Some argued that the colony was not yet ready for responsible government, but he asked whether Christianity would ever have been introduced if the apostles had waited for complete purity in society. He declared, like Lord Durham, that the present system made it impossible to form a responsible Opposition of men ready to take office, and that until the system was changed Opposition leaders could only be wild demagogues.[59]

Unreadiness for responsible government or the inapplicability of the system to Newfoundland were the arguments of those who opposed Kent's resolutions. Barnes reminded the members that they had lost one constitution and were "on their knees" looking for its restoration. They were not in a position to dictate the spirit in which this should be worked, but should rather show themselves able to use the powers they had.[60] Robinson, for the mercantile party, saw no reason for the colony, with its own history and its own intelligent public men, to attach itself to the skirts of Nova Scotia.[61] The Governor informed Stanley that he had always regarded the principle of responsible government as utterly inapplicable to the administration of colonial affairs, "if not positively inconsistent with the relation of a British Colony to the Parent State." He pointed out that the resolutions were passed by only ten votes to nine and that the yeas were all Roman Catholics, with one exception—a Protestant dependent upon Catholic constituents. He declared that he had totally abstained from interference in the matter, that he had not tried to prevent the affirmative vote of his Catholic councillors, and that he regarded the question as "entirely unimportant."

Quite obviously, however, the Governor did attribute significance to the resolutions, for in the same despatch he observed that they contemplated nothing less than the "absolute surrender into the hands of the popular branch . . . of the nomination to all offices within the Colony." He now suggested that the restoration of the former constitution be only a four-year experiment, to be followed by a decision on a permanent form of government suitable to the colony. His objections to responsible government were still those he had had in New Brunswick: there was an inadequate number of suitable persons to form two distinct and efficient party administrations; the Crown would be required to surrender essential prerogatives to a party government; the Governor, responsible only to the Crown, could not undertake to be guided at all times by councillors responsible to a representative body. He would rather abandon the monarchical principle than acquiesce in the transfer of the power of appointment into the hands of the people. Nor did he think that such a transfer could be advocated by any loyal British subject.[62] Gladstone, serving briefly as Colonial Secretary after the resignation of Stanley, was saved from the difficulty of making a pronouncement on this question by the fact that the Assembly did not embody the resolutions in an address to the Crown.[63]

A month after the introduction of the resolutions the Governor was faced with another resurgence of political feeling, evoked this time by his proposal for the establishment of a militia. The expansionist mood of the United States during the eighteen-forties had resulted in pressure from Britain on her North American colonies for the setting up of local defence forces. Harvey, with his military background, was particularly anxious for the enactment of a creditable Militia Bill, and anxious, too, for obvious reasons to secure its passage before the expiration of the Amalgamated Assembly. The Bill, as drawn by the Attorney-General, provided for the registration of male inhabitants, for an annual one-day muster, and for emergency call-up. It provided also for various penalties and for court martial.[64] Opposition from the Assembly was apparently to be disarmed by active support for the Bill from the nominated Catholic members, Morris and Kent.

On March 11 the Governor's message was brought down to the House by Morris in his capacity as executive councillor and on March 17 the Governor reported to the Colonial Office that prospects for a militia were favourable.[65] Next day, however, the *Patriot* published an outspoken attack on the Bill. The force proposed would draw men away from the fishery while providing no real protection for the colony because of its open seaboard. Further, it would be "dangerous and impolitic" to countenance the Bill because it threatened a loss of constitutional liberty and an approach to despotic military government. The *Patriot* added some caustic comments on the transformation of "fiery democrats into staid admirers of fusty forms and ceremonies" and obedient servants of the Governor. There followed organized demonstrations against the Bill, including a procession through the capital and the posting of placards of warning to Kent and Morris.[66] On March 23 Kent referred in the House to the threatening placards and announced that he would not risk his popularity by further support of the Bill. The Governor, he said, did not want to push through a measure obnoxious to the people. All he desired was the registration of the male population. Morris spoke of warnings that he would be shot through the heart if he persisted in his course. He said that he would now agree only to the principle of the Bill—registration and annual drill.[67] The Governor then advised Gladstone, euphemistically, that there was some demur to be overcome.[68]

The debate continued, with men from the outports thronging the gallery to give vigorous opposition to the Bill.[69] Their noisy presence lent force to Nugent's contention that there were dangers in arming neighbouring communities of different religions. These dangers had been remarked on as early as March 13 by the *Ledger*, which seemed to anticipate an "O'Connellite" reign of terror. Kent remarked, however, that if the people were disposed to violence, they were already armed with sealing guns. He maintained that a militia was preferable to a voluntary force of "Orange yeomanry." Parsons proposed that Britain should send a steam-powered naval force for the island's defence, while Barnes advocated a force of professional soldiers. The original Militia Bill was withdrawn and a second, couched in more general terms, was introduced. To the indignation of the gallery, Kent defended this Bill at some length, contrasting Newfoundland's attitude with the example set by the other colonies.[70] However, the fulminations of the *Patriot*, together with public meetings and petitions in which the editor was a moving spirit, had their effect. The second Bill, to the disappointment and disgust of the Governor, had to be abandoned before the close of the session.[71]

Since the Assembly's approval was not to be sought for that other piece of controversial legislation, the draft Constitution Bill, this was sent to the Colonial Office at the end of the session, after receiving the sanction of the Council. The councillors themselves, Protestant and Roman Catholic, had, on the basis of the new census and without making any major alteration in the electoral districts, drawn up provisions for the return of ten additional members by doubling the representation from several of the existing districts. With an approach to a basic constituency of 4,000 persons, and with a population of 50,000 Protestants to 46,000 Roman Catholics, it seemed fair that these arrangements might be expected to bring the return of thirteen Protestants and twelve Catholics. The Bill's other major provisions were for the establishment of separate and distinct legislative and executive councils.[72]

There was some discussion in the Colonial Office, as in 1842, as to whether Parliament should be asked for a detailed or a permissive Newfoundland Act, and on the possibility of postponing legislation for a year, since the Assembly had been induced to make the Revenue Act effective until January 1848. The Peel Ministry was in a uneasy position after the five-month debate on the repeal of the Corn Laws, and there was a natural reluctance to introduce late in the session any measure which might increase difficulties in the House of Commons.[73] Harvey suggested that to avoid disappointment in Newfoundland the Bill should be passed immediately, but with a clause instructing the Governor to withhold the warrants for a general election until June 1847. This would allow the Assembly to be convened before the expiration of the Revenue Act. Stephen, however, objected to this plan on the grounds that the Colonial Secretary should not, at so late a period of the session, "hazard all the inconvenience of bringing in a Bill which (for reasons requiring no particular statement) would infallibly and strongly be opposed." He confessed that he would rather have some disappointment in Newfoundland than an "ill-timed and embarrassing controversy in the House of Commons." It was decided to renew for one year, until September 1, 1847, the Act of 1842.[74]

For a second time a Newfoundland Constitution Bill coincided with significant events in the political history of the mother country. The Bill was introduced on June 25.[75] This was the day on which the Corn Law Bill was carried on the third reading. In the evening a combination of Whigs, Radicals, and Irish Repealers defeated the Ministry on the Bill for coercion in Ireland.[76] The Whigs under Russell succeeded to office in July, with Earl Grey, the former Lord Howick, as Colonial Secretary. The Newfoundland Bill was not withdrawn by the Whig Ministry, under whose auspices it had an unobstructed passage through both Houses.[77]

The news that the new constitution was to be postponed would undoubtedly have caused much chagrin and frustration among the Liberal aspirants, but in the great disaster which overwhelmed St. John's on June 9, 1846, political emotions were inevitably for a time submerged. On that day a tremendous fire raged through the city for ten hours, fanned by a strong west wind and fed by the wooden buildings with their vast stores of oil and combustible materials. The best efforts of the Governor, the garrison, the fire brigade, and the citizens were of no avail. By nightfall, when the fire had burnt itself out, the two principal streets had been devastated for more than a mile, 2,000 buildings including sixty mercantile establishments had been destroyed, and 12,000 of the 19,000 inhabitants had been rendered homeless. Among the buildings consumed were the Customs House, the courthouse, the two banks, one with the office of the

Colonial Treasurer, the Anglican church, and the Roman Catholic convent and school.[78]

Next day the Governor with his advisers took practical steps to meet the great emergency and to prepare for the restoration of the still smouldering city. He appointed a relief committee, placed an embargo on the export of provisions, chartered two vessels to bring food from New York and Halifax, and despatched circular letters to the other North American colonies and to the consuls at New York and Boston. A proclamation was issued for the reconvening of the Amalgamated Legislature on June 16.[79] At the brief session a law was passed to regulate the rebuilding of St. John's, with provisions for widened streets and firebreaks, for stone or brick construction within a specified area, and for compensation for appropriated land.[80] It seemed that the way had been cleared for the building of an improved city. When the Whigs came into office in July, Parliament granted a sum of £30,000 for relief purposes. In addition, the Queen issued a letter to her two Archbishops asking that congregations be invited to contribute to a fund for Newfoundland, and provisions, subscriptions, and grants were sent from the several North American colonies.[81]

Sir John Harvey's role in the relief and rebuilding of St. John's was cut short by his transfer in August 1846 to Nova Scotia, the administration for which he had asked earlier in the year.[82] The general esteem in which he was held at the close of his administration in the island was in marked contrast with the partisan bitterness his predecessors had evoked. On July 17, shortly before he sailed, there appeared in the *Ledger* an informed and realistic letter of appraisal and eulogy, signed "K," which attributed the Governor's arts, not to any dissimulation in his character, but to a profound knowledge of human nature and to a realization that he must minister even to its weaknesses if he were to govern successfully. This, on the evidence, could certainly be termed a fair and succinct estimate of Sir John. There had been, and there long would be, criticism of his system and of his devices for assuaging political jealousy and securing acquiescence. He had oiled the political wheels with charm and with public money and had given the island a respite from agitation. He had eased the legislative process and had persuaded the members of both parties to co-operate with him and with one another. He had come to the colony at a critical moment when class and sectarian bitterness and executive inexperience and ineptitude had brought the operation of the conventional form of representative government to a halt. It is tempting to suggest that had he been appointed and an amalgamated legislature established a decade earlier the political struggle might have been waged with less rancour. He left the island as a new phase of that struggle loomed ahead— as new conflicts were being threatened by the determination of one party to steer Newfoundland in the constitutional wake of the neighbouring colonies.

Pending the appointment of a new governor, the duties of administration devolved upon Colonel Law, the senior military officer in Newfoundland. These duties were made more arduous by a destructive tempest in September, by the appearance of the dreaded potato blight, and by the competitive pressure of the inhabitants of St. John's for compensation from the fire relief funds. In November, Colonel Law reported that the principal uninsured sufferers from

the fire had received almost the whole amount of their losses and that con-
continued direct relief was having a most demoralizing effect. He suggested,
therefore, that the balance of the funds be left with, and expended at the discretion of, the Secretary of State. He recommended that a portion of the money
be used for rebuilding the Anglican church, an expense which must otherwise
be borne by the shopkeepers of St. John's who had not, he said, like the lower
orders, received the amount of their losses.[83] Lord Grey then made a decision
which was to give rise to that sense of grievance always evoked in the colony
by any suspicion of sectarian favouritism. The Queen's letter had not specifically
asked for, or indeed mentioned, contributions for rebuilding the church. However, on the basis of Colonel Law's despatch and recommendation and of his
own belief that the donors expected such an allocation, the Minister, as he was
later to explain to the House of Lords and in his book on his colonial policy,
reserved half of the Letter Fund, some £14,000, for this purpose.[84] In December,
Colonel Law called the final session of the Amalgamated Legislature to pass a
Loan Bill, to vote a sum for the relief of the stricken outports, and to render
less stringent and expensive the provisions of the Rebuilding Act, which were
already giving rise to complaints.[85]

The new Governor, Sir John Gaspard LeMarchant, arrived in St. John's on
April 22, 1847. Sir Gaspard, like his predecessor, had had a distinguished military
career, but, unlike Sir John, no experience in governing a colony (see Appendix
A). Although he was personally unknown to Lord Grey, his family had Whig
connections and his brother was serving as Secretary to the Board of Trade in
the Russell Government. The *Patriot* on February 6 had greeted the news of
Sir Gaspard's appointment coldly, forecasting that he would institute no new
policy, but would fall immediately under the influence of his officials. Ten days
after his arrival this journal on May 3 criticized him roundly for the range and
nature of his activities, which it declared to be those of a missionary and a dust-
man, rather than of a governor. In the same issue it condemned him for his
reply to a petition from the people of St. John's for further allotments from the
relief funds. He had said that the money was now to be used for the assistance
of the outports and for public buildings and public works in the capital, in order
to obviate the need for heavy taxation of those who already supported the poor
through employment and advances. When the Governor deemed salutary for
the colony a day of public fasting and humiliation, the *Patriot* of May 24 gave
vent to a scathing comment on the subject of hypocrisy coupled with misappro-
priation of the "people's money."

In his report to Grey on the allocation of the funds, LeMarchant followed
Law's recommendation that no more money be devoted to the relief of individuals. He proposed that the residue be spent on public buildings, works,
and amenities in St. John's, not only for the improvement and security of the
city, but also to relieve from taxation the mercantile class upon whose restoration
to prosperity the well-being of the colony largely depended.[86] Grey agreed that
this seemed the most beneficial mode of using the money.[87] The Governor recommended and the Minister sanctioned expenditure on certain public works,
including water tanks, a new cemetery, repairs and alterations to Government
House, and construction of a Marine Parade.[88]

Sir Gaspard reported that he was most unfavourably impressed with the way in which St. John's was being rebuilt. He criticized the revised version of the Act which now allowed wooden buildings to be erected on the north side of one of the principal streets. This amendment had been forced, he said, by popular pressure on members and by the commercial self-interest of some of the members. As a result, the fire insurance rates on all buildings had risen. There were already many deviations from a regular scheme of rebuilding, overcrowding of sites, and the erection of temporary wooden structures which he feared would not be replaced. He doubted if any other city in the Empire showed so complete a disregard for proper sanitation and water supply. The city seemed to him utterly squalid and the citizens to have learned no lesson from the fire.[89] Lord Grey suggested that there be local assessment for local objects, with wooden buildings subjected to double rates of taxation.[90] The Governor replied that the difficulty lay in the fact that the merchants had framed their leases so that any direct taxation levied by the Assembly or by a town corporation would fall upon their tenants. It was the rule rather than the exception, he said, for the actual owner of a mercantile establishment to be absent. Most tenants would, reportedly, be quite unable to meet rates. He had suggested to his Council that £5,000 might be raised by rates to build drains and sewers and had been told that it was impossible.[91]

By June 1847 the Governor believed that he had obtained a thorough knowledge of the "main springs of action" in the machinery of the island. He was convinced that the whole social and economic system must undergo a revolution and that it had never yet been adequately brought before the notice of the Home Government. The curse of Newfoundland was, he said, the fortune-hunting merchant who stayed only long enough to amass wealth and then departed, leaving a junior partner in his establishment. To avoid taxation was the interest of all, from the absentees who carried away some £35,000 a year and the wealthy landlords with their carefully drawn leases to the nine-tenths of the population who were supported by the other tenth as employers and suppliers. The whole situation had been crystallized for him by the fire which had crippled the resources of the merchants and by the potato failure which had brought the outports to the verge of pauperism. The merchants were now increasingly unwilling to advance winter supplies to the outports and were urging the Government to continue the paternalism shown after the fire, that is, to import and distribute provisions and to supply funds from the Treasury grant to enable the fishermen to buy. He believed that the Government should not take over the duties of the private trader or encourage the very evident readiness of the population to demand and expect support from the Government. There were, he said, about 80,000 people in the outports who were entirely dependent on the fisheries and on potato patches and were always, therefore, potential vagrants. There was no Poor Law and there were no hospitals. Instead there was a stream of paupers and petitions to the capital. It was evident to him that the "game" of the people and of the merchants was to declare their total inability to meet further taxation or to raise more supplies without the aid of the Government. He was being informed, in other words, that unless he drew upon the Home Government to alleviate the distress, his would be the responsibility for the starvation of thousands. As the potatoes had been planted in very short crop and provisions had doubled in price, he confessed himself very uneasy about the winter ahead.[92]

During 1847 and 1848 the Governor was concerned chiefly with alleviating the condition of the destitute poor and with providing incentives for increased cultivation of the soil. He used the relief funds for importing provisions, corn seed, and agricultural implements. The provisions he used in lieu of wages for the payment of paupers engaged in road construction, and the seed he distributed on condition that each recipient return an equal quantity after the harvest. Through the Agricultural Society he instituted prizes for corn-growing, cattle-raising, and cultivation of increased acreage. In August 1847 he made a cruise to the outports to see conditions for himself and to try to rouse the inhabitants to greater efforts and more self-reliance. In the autumn of 1847 the potato disease returned, and with it, renewed fears that starvation must ensue. He reported to the Colonial Office that there were increased efforts by the merchants to foist the dependent fishermen on the Government. Merchants were now, he said, almost invariably refusing to continue the winter supplies and in many cases were even lessening their imports in order to avoid having to dole out provisions should famine occur.[93]

At the end of 1847 the commercial depression in England and the extraordinary pressure on the money market had its effect on the transactions of the merchants in the Newfoundland trade in England and in the colony. In December one major firm in St. John's was obliged to suspend business, bringing down with it several smaller houses. The complex interconnections of all the establishments made further failures inevitable.[94] These increased the desire of the mercantile body to break away from the old system of maintaining the population and to throw the people upon their own resources. For a time in 1848 the Governor believed that he would have to use the authority granted him by Lord Grey to draw £20,000 for relief from the Treasury.[95] September, however, found the colony's fortunes improving. There had been a good seal fishery and an increased catch of cod, and there was the prospect of a satisfactory potato crop and a fair return from the experiments with grain. An election was to be held in November and the Assembly to be called in December. The Governor believed that he could persuade the Legislature to assume financial responsibility for the colony and to establish an effective system of poor relief.[96]

In June 1847 word had been received that a bill for reviving the former constitution was to be enacted that summer by Parliament. At that time LeMarchant had admitted that this would give the people satisfaction, but had confessed himself somewhat dismayed at the prospect of meeting the Legislature in 1848. This was a feeling shared, he said, by the "more sensible, wealthy, and intelligent part of the Community." He believed that the colony's interests would be advanced by an absence of all political excitement and that financial questions would be all too certain to give rise to warm, if not angry discussions in a body where, even in prosperous times, debate was often intemperate. He was not, in fact, ready to concede that a constitution was the "vehicle" required by the colony. Nor was he ready to concede that the Amalgamated Legislature, with its mutual bargains and profuse expenditure, had been beneficial. His predecessor's despatches seemed to him to have been written not from facts but from the "poetry of his imagination." LeMarchant reported that his own relations with the members of all parties were good, but that unless Grey had provided for the inclusion of official members in the Assembly, he feared that the Government would always be in a minority there.[97]

When the Act arrived in July 1847, it was found to provide only for a revival of the two bodies established by the Act of 1832, that is, for an assembly and for a single council with which the Governor was to consult and which should act as an upper house. It rendered permanent certain parts of the Act of 1842 which had been found useful, that is, the provisions for the qualifications for members and electors, for the Crown's initiative in money votes, and for simultaneous elections. It left untouched the question of increased representation and electoral divisions. It made no stipulation that there should be *ex officio* members representing the Government in the Assembly, or that certain members of the Assembly might have seats in the Executive Council, or that the Executive Council should be a distinct body.[98] Nor were these matters covered in the instruments giving effect to the Act.[99] These changes were presumably to be made as and if the Colonial Office felt they were warranted. The Instructions named nine councillors over whom the Governor had the power of suspension. These were the senior officer of the army, the Attorney-General, the Colonial Secretary, the Collector of Customs, William Thomas, Patrick Morris (Colonial Treasurer), W. B. Row, James Tobin, and Joseph Noad (Surveyor-General).

There were legal complexities in the virtual reversion to the constitution of 1832 and to the single Council which had been superseded in 1842, and more than a year elapsed before, on August 1, 1848, the instruments were dispatched in final form to Newfoundland.[100] The Governor had not pressed for speed since he was opposed to holding the election in June 1848, at the height of the fishing season, and in favour of postponing the session until the close of 1848, when commercial losses might be partly redeemed and the prospects of obtaining satisfactory Revenue and Loan Acts and a Poor Law much increased.[101] The year's delay was attributed by the *Patriot* on May 10 to a "base trick" on the part of the Governor and by the *Ledger* on April 11 to a prolonged consideration by the Home Government of the colony's former "transgressions."

Since 1832 representations had poured into the Colonial Office about defects in the constitution. There had been copious evidence of the incompatibility of the Assembly and the Council as legislative bodies, proposals for maintaining the Government's influence in the House, and intimations of the coming pressure for responsible government. There had been explanations of the need for more representatives, laborious schemes for procuring them, and insistence that alteration of the districts must, for political reasons, be made by Parliament. There had been advice about debarring the Colonial Secretary and the Collector of Customs from the Council. Events would seem to have demonstrated the need for a governor experienced in civil affairs and politically adroit. All these considerations had been put aside in favour of the reinstatement, with a few restraining provisos, of the constitution which Earl Grey, as Lord Howick, had originally helped to prepare, and the appointment of a distinguished soldier, untried in civil government. There was no attempt to provide a constitution which would be an alternative to responsible government, or to devise modifications which would be a preparation for that change. One concludes that, under the hypnosis of Canada and Nova Scotia, the Colonial Office was persuaded that the island's transition to self-government could be no more than briefly delayed.

The respite from party politics was over. Looking ahead with some apprehension to the general election of November 1848, the *Ledger* on September 5 wondered whether the electors and representatives had learned the essential lesson of moderation. Newfoundland, it said, "stood alone in the disreputable history of her self-government." The other view was that self-government had yet to be achieved.

PART III

RESPONSIBLE GOVERNMENT

CHAPTER EIGHT

THE REVIVAL OF POLITICS, 1848-1852

EVENTS of 1848—evolution in the colonies, revolution in Europe—had their echoes in St. John's. While the island awaited the restoration of its old constitution, responsible government was established in two of the mainland colonies of British North America. The principle had finally been conceded in Lord Grey's despatches of November 3, 1846, and March 31, 1847, to Sir John Harvey in Nova Scotia. Election victories in 1847 for the reformers in Nova Scotia and Canada had been followed by the establishment of the first responsible provincial cabinets early in 1848.[1] On May 24—the anniversary of the birth of the Queen—the advocates of responsible government for Newfoundland called a meeting in St. John's.

The purpose of this assembly was to pass a series of resolutions, to which considerable advance publicity had been given, and to endorse an address to the Queen asking that responsible government be extended to Newfoundland. The resolutions announced that the colony found itself "plunged into irretrievable debt," with expenditures increasing and revenue diminishing, with "educational institutions languishing and neglected" and with "widespread discontent pervading all classes of the community." It was asserted, however, that the colony's resources, if properly developed, could meet this emergency, provided only that a constitutional government like that of Nova Scotia were established.[2] The address attributed the colony's difficulties, not to the recent natural and commercial disasters, but to the Amalgamated Legislature. It declared:

That this unhappy and novel experiment . . . has shed a disastrous influence over our Fortunes. It has vitiated public opinion, emboldened executive usurpation, increased taxation, enlarged public expenditure, and has occasioned widespread discontent among all classes . . . .

That for the remedying of these evils and for the developing more fully the great resources of this colony . . . [we] . . . pray for a form of Government based upon enlarged and fairly divided Representation—with a departmental Government and Executive Responsibility similar in character to that form lately yielded to . . . Nova Scotia.[3]

John Kent, the Roman Catholic Liberal leader, who had joined forces with R. J. Parsons, editor of the *Patriot*, in the cause of responsible government, informed the meeting, in the words of Canning, that "inaction never yet begot repose, nor were the objects of human ambition ever yet attained but by human exertion." Although the address spoke of widespread discontent in the colony, Kent admitted and deplored the apathy of public opinion and called for agitation to concentrate and give a tone to the public mind. He admitted that agitation provoked intense bitterness in small communities, but he declared that Newfoundland would appear "sluggish" and "brutish" if it did not clamour for the progressive reforms of the other colonies. He could not endorse "slavish acquiescence" in things as they were. The merchants, he said, were indifferent to political progress, sulky about contested elections, and deprecating about the efforts of the reformers. Two legislative bodies were about to be re-established "without indentity, without sympathy, without cohesion." In their midst would be the executive, "supercilious, jealous, unyielding, conceding in fear, and grace-less in concession" and converted every four years into an electioneering machine in order to obtain a miserable minority in the Assembly. What he wanted was a cabinet of department heads, bearing an individual and general responsibility to the Assembly, and an end to the present system of elevation which silenced the colony's leaders and restricted its young men to the politics of place-hunting. He wanted the people, through their representatives, to have the means of restricting and revising public expenditure by removing old and useless burdens and replacing them with new and useful appropriations. It had been said that the colony was unfit for responsible government, but this seemed to him tanta-mount to charging unfitness for representative government altogether. He doubted the value of representative institutions which could not "in a moderate degree impose upon the Executive Government the force and direction of the public mind."[4]

The conservative mercantile press was flatly hostile to the proposed change. It disputed the assertions of the agitators, noted contradictions in their statements, and ridiculed their procedure.[5] The *Ledger* had made its position clear earlier in the year by describing the establishment of responsible government as a move towards republicanism, by declaring that the system could not work in Canada or Nova Scotia, and by denouncing it as totally inapplicable to New-foundland.[6] More temperate criticism came from the *Morning Courier*, a news-paper of moderate tone.[7] For this journal, Kent's sudden alliance with the ex-tremist Parsons, whom he had denounced as a mere obstructionist, was op-portunistic and discreditable. It suggested that there would be less apathy among the people if the Liberal leaders had not, in the Amalgamated Legislature, betrayed their own principles of economy and reform. It excepted Kent from its general charge of waste and self-aggrandizement, but suggested that Kent ought to prove himself a genuine reformer by reforming first his own party—that he should work for "the building of a solid structure of colonial government, not one which, resting on a rotten foundation and propped by needy partisans, who have not sufficient industry to earn their own substance, would crumble under its own weight in a few months." Kent was asking for "a ship of the build and rig of the Nova Scotia frigate," but without the ballast, that is, the forty-shilling freehold qualification. For the *Courier*, it would be time enough to ad-vocate responsible government when Newfoundland elected twenty-five mem-bers from twenty-five constituencies, when the mercantile clerks had been given the vote, when registration and election expenses had been transferred to the electors and candidates, when the pay of members had been halved, and when the educational level of the masses had been raised. It recommended, meantime, that the Government put down the agitation by taking the initiative in practical reforms.[8]

Believing that responsible government was totally inappropriate to the con-dition of Newfoundland, and subscribing to the view that the Roman Catholics acted from unscrupulous sectarian ambition, Governor LeMarchant informed Lord Grey that the whole of the "wealth and respectability" was entirely and unequivocally opposed to the change and that the mass of the population was apathetic. He charged that the agitators were trying, through the *Patriot*, to excite among the lower classes dissatisfaction and opposition to the existing order of government and that their aim was the establishment of Catholic power:

These parties under the cloke of inducing the people to attend public meetings for the purpose of petitioning ... for the introduction of the system of Responsible Government in this Colony (a state of things however desirable it may be elsewhere, totally incompatible to a small community like this, when its present advancement either in wealth or intelligence is taken into account) hope to withdraw all influence in the direction of the local affairs of the Colony from the hand of the Protestant portion of the Land and place themselves, the Roman Catholics, in full possession of every place of emolument throughout the entire of the Colony.

It seemed to him significant that, though Bishop Fleming disclaimed any part in the agitation, its promoter, Kent, was his nearest relative.[9] The Governor's relations with the Bishop had deteriorated with his successive refusals to meet the Bishop's request for a part of the Imperial grant to rebuild his convent and school. LeMarchant had indicated that depleted finances and general destitution were the grounds for his refusal, but he had not convinced Dr. Fleming, who was, he understood, both aggrieved and abusive.[10] On the basis of his experience with the Bishop, and on other information, the Governor asserted that the members of the Roman Catholic party ascribed every concession to their power of extortion and none to the good will and enlightenment of the Colonial Office. Forwarding the address for responsible government to Grey, he dismissed it as the emanation of a much-advertised meeting which had drawn its attendance only from the sponsors and some members of the lower orders. This statement was contradicted by one of his own newspaper enclosures, which described the crowd as dense and the meeting as one of the most interesting, respectable, and orderly ever held in the colony.[11]

The colony's first demand for responsible government was dismissed by the Colonial Office as premature. To Lord Grey, the institutions just granted to Newfoundland appeared "well calculated to meet the wants of the present state of society in that colony."[12] Nor did the reformers succeed in winning support from the House of Commons. Having lost, through death, their staunch ally, O'Connell, they had entrusted a copy of their address to the "young Irelander," T. F. Meagher, a spokesman for repeal of the Union. Meagher passed on the petition, but wrote that the case needed strengthening. He recommended that another address be prepared and forwarded for presentation by a member of high standing and long service in the Commons.[13] The task of overpowering opposition and apathy had only begun.

With no change in the electoral divisions, the Liberals again returned nine members to the House (Appendix B, Table V). The election contests were pacific, due, the *Ledger* suggested on November 17, to the experimental silence of the Roman Catholic clergy on this occasion and to the conviction of respectable persons that it was useless either to stand or to vote. No Conservative candidates came forward for St. John's and of the five Liberals who offered themselves there, two were defeated (J. V. Nugent, Inspector of Schools, and James

Douglas, Supervisor of Streets), apparently because they held appointments under the Government.[14] The *Times* had urged the merchants that there was more to be gained by a substantial representation in the Assembly than by membership in, or reliance on, the Council in its unceasing warfare with the House.[15] While it sympathized with the reluctance of respectable mercantile and professional men to associate themselves with such members as had sat in the past, there were very practical reasons why they should do so:

We are essentially a trading community; and measures bearing upon the business of the country, such as the removal of unnecessary restrictions on commerce, the repeal of any act under which partial or unjust taxation is enforced,—the protection of the fisheries by enactments that may be beneficially carried out,—and a due but not overstrained encouragement to the agriculturist, are much more necessary than ridiculous contentions about responsible government which nobody here understands.[16]

Nevertheless, the two principal merchants who had represented Conception Bay in the Amalgamated Legislature refused to offer themselves for election.[17] Protestant merchants and professional men would not expose themselves to defeat by Liberals in St. John's, but in Trinity Bay a contest occurred between two principal merchants and in Fortune Bay between two Protestant barristers.[18] The *Times* of December 2 deplored the apathy which had resulted in over 4,000 unpolled votes in St. John's and Conception Bay. Whether it could be ascribed to too much confidence in the Council, or to none in the Assembly, it had revealed, said this journal, an unhealthy political state and had allowed the return of a discreditable House. The *Times* had referred on November 25 to the hopes for abrogation of the constitution, but feared that the difficulty and delicacy of effecting this would mean that the island would continue for years to be burdened with the Assembly as a "wretched incubus" upon its resources and prosperity.

Although the Governor made no report to the Colonial Office about the election, he confessed, retrospectively, to considerable anxiety about the temper of the new House:

The disasters ... had fomented an excitement and an agitation of a very troublesome character among all classes for the amelioration of their condition; the absence also during this period of their usual channel of redress and relief, the Local Legislature, was artfully seized hold of by many of the leaders of the liberal party, and held up by them to the lower classes as a proof of the indifference of the Executive to the cries of a starving population; another topic, fruitful at all times of political commotion, the deprivation of their constitutional liberty and rights was made the subject of violent debate at the various public meetings.

The session, however, proved more amicable than the Governor had expected. He was gratified by the easy passage of the Appropriation, Contingency, and Indemnity Bills and by his success in maintaining the prerogative of executive administration of the funds voted in the Road Bill. Several of the candidates had pledged themselves to a systematic investigation of the distribution of the Imperial grant and the appropriation of part of the Letter Fund for the Church of England cathedral. Accordingly, with Parsons of the *Patriot* as principal instigator, the fire relief funds were the subject of prolonged debate and detailed returns were demanded and supplied. Eventually a majority of the Assembly declared themselves satisfied, and the matter was dropped without a vote impugning the Governor's conduct.[19] However, the Governor's hopes for a Poor Law were dashed when a measure brought in by the member for Fortune Bay, providing for local taxation, an asylum and workhouse for the permanent poor, and compulsory labour for the able-bodied, was rejected as inapplicable to the conditions of Newfoundland.[20] The members were more eager for retrenchment at the expense of the official class than of the poor. The question of the reduction of the reserved salaries had been revived by the receipt of the Imperial Act of 1846 extending to the colonies complete fiscal authority.[21] The Assembly altered and consolidated the tariff and provided for the collection of duties (12 Vict., c. 2, c. 3, and c. 4). However, opinion being divided as to whether the Civil List should be immediately or prospectively reduced, an application to the Home Government was postponed.[22]

Although the Governor did not credit the despatch of business to the presence of John Kent in the Speaker's chair, the *Times* on January 26 conceded freely that Kent made an able Speaker. Kent informed the House, however, that the session had provided several practical arguments for the establishment of responsible government. Whereas in the Amalgamated Legislature, members of the executive and representatives had been able to work closely together, proceedings were again being hampered, he said, by lack of harmony. On numerous occasions the House had had to move addresses for returns of information which could have readily been supplied had members of the Government been present in the House. He contended that for greater efficiency and despatch, legislative business should be conducted by departmental heads and that for the implementation of political theories, these should be members of a single party.[23]

In anticipation of the concession of responsible government, the Liberal majority passed an important resolution stipulating "that all persons who may be hereafter appointed to Offices within this Colony analogous to Offices held by a political tenure in those Colonies where Responsible Government prevails, should be notified by the Executive at the time of their appointment, that their Offices are to be held upon the like tenure in the event of Responsible Government being acceded to this Colony." An explanatory address to the Secretary of State pointed out that the intent was not to interfere with existing rights but to provide that persons thereafter appointed should be told that their tenure of office was contingent upon any change in the system of government. The members wished to ease the transition to responsible government and forestall the acrimonious dispute which had arisen in Nova Scotia, where the claims of vested rights were being urged by official incumbents as a reason for opposing the change.[24] The members did not, however, make any attempt to conciliate Protestant and mercantile opinion by advocating any of the changes which had been urged by the *Courier* as prerequisites of responsible government.

At the Colonial Office the Assembly's resolution was deemed to be a wise precaution against injustice to individuals and a shrewd attempt to force the pace towards responsible government.[25] Replying to the address, Grey commended the judgment and discretion of the Assembly and promised to issue the necessary instructions. But he wrote:

I am bound at the same time to express my conviction that until the wealth and population of the Colony shall have increased considerably beyond their present amount, the introduction of the system of what is termed "Responsible Government" will by no means prove to its advantage. From causes to which it is unnecessary for me to refer, the Institutions of Newfoundland have been, of late, in various ways modified and altered and some time must unavoidably elapse before they can acquire that amount of fixity and adaptation to the Political wants of

Society which seems an indispensable preliminary to the further extension of Popular Government.[26]

He refrained, tactfully, from any reference to the politico-religious difficulty cited by the Governor. In amplification of his sentiments upon responsible government, he sent Sir Gaspard a series of extracts from his despatches to Prince Edward Island, which was in the grip of a similar agitation. These set forth his belief that it was inadvisable that the salaried public officials of a small colony should sit in and be responsible to the Assembly. He had informed the Governor of Prince Edward Island that responsible government would be appropriate when the colony possessed a sufficient number of inhabitants qualified by property, intelligence, education, leisure, and public spirit to form two political parties, from either of which the Governor could form a competent administration, drawn not from a single town but from the several districts. These conditions, he had said, had been met by the continental colonies, but though Prince Edward Island was distinguished by a high degree of order and public spirit, it still lacked, he believed, the other prerequisites.[27] Similar arguments and the fact of Newfoundland's recent chequered constitutional history would, he hoped, fortify LeMarchant in discussions on responsible government in that colony.

In October 1849 the Governor made a private and complacent report on the political state of the island:

Politics are now a dead Letter, and the party which for years occasioned such serious embarrassment to the Government are broken—dispersed and annihilated. I have received the most cordial support from all parties, and I think on the closing of the next session I shall be able to say that the Government of Newfoundland is about the most orderly, quiet, and well-conducted Government in Her Majesty's Colonies.

There were several reasons for his optimism. The fisheries had been good, the potato crop had been abundant and free from blight, and his wheat had ripened well enough, he thought, to dispel prejudices against that crop. In an effort to instill habits of winter industry and self-sufficiency, he had established a factory for making homespun cloth, and in order to check the inroads on the colony's revenue and to decrease the winter influx of the outport poor into St. John's, he was administering and enforcing a Poor Law of his own, extracting compulsory labour from the able-bodied poor in exchange for outdoor relief.[28] He had made two appointments, neither of which had provoked party wrath. The Speaker, Kent, had accepted the office of Collector of Customs, which under the new fiscal arrangements, was no longer an Imperial one, and which, on the Governor's recommendation, did not carry with it the rank of Councillor.[29] Kent, who had supported the resolution of the Amalgamated Assembly declaring the offices of Speaker and Colonial Secretary to be incompatible, seems to have accepted the Collectorship on the understanding, and with the pledge, that he would be untrammelled in the advocacy of responsible government.[30] For the office of Colonial Treasurer, made vacant by the death of Patrick Morris,[31] the Governor chose Robert Carter, member for Bonavista and son of a former official, the Judge of the Vice-Admiralty Court.[32] Carter was considered a Conservative, but the fact that he was a native went far towards reconciling the *Patriot* to the choice.[33] As neither man was elevated to the Council, however, there were grounds for a controversy about inroads, through the gift of office, upon the independence of the Assembly.[34]

Ameliorated conditions and diversionary tactics brought a measure of tranquillity, but the proceedings of the Assembly in 1850 do not confirm the Governor's boast of the annihilation of the Liberal party. A select committee was appointed under Parsons to investigate further the vexed question of the fire relief funds.[35] This produced an address to the Queen complaining that some £14,000 of the Letter Fund had been diverted to the use of the Church of England and that some £15,000, or half the Imperial grant, had been misapplied to the construction of public works.[36] However, after rancorous discussion and personal vituperation, with some Liberals objecting to its phrases and imputations, the petition was voted down.[37] The members expressed their views about Crown appointments in the Assembly by passing a bill stipulating that in future any member appointed to office after election must vacate his seat and seek re-election. This, with its provision that the re-election must be at the member's expense, gained the assent of the Council.[38] Bills for the reduction of the reserved and other official salaries were introduced, debated at length, and postponed without being sent to the Council,[39] where, the *Times* on April 3 observed, they would certainly have been lost. In an effort to secure the prior consent of the Colonial Office to the Reserved Salaries Bill, which cut the reserved sum and the Governor's salary by one-tenth,[40] an address was despatched to Lord Grey. This was accompanied by the Governor's decided statement that the existing salaries were fair, except his own, which was too low.[41] The Colonial Secretary informed the House that it was a false economy to make official salaries, especially judicial ones, unattractive to able men, but that he would consider prospective reductions.[42]

Another step was attempted in the movement for responsible government by the introduction of a bill for increasing the representation. This would have doubled the number of members in the House by doubling the returns from the existing districts, but it was rejected by the Council as a device to double the majority party in the Assembly.[43] The allocation of public money to the "low class of persons" likely to be returned to an enlarged House seemed, to at least one observer in the Colonial Office, less likely to promote the welfare of the colony than a continuation of the salaries of what were deemed the "very effective" public servants.[44] Before prorogation Parsons gave notice that he would introduce in the next session a resolution for responsible government. On May 25, 1850, he began in the *Patriot* a series of twelve "Letters on Responsible Government" which appeared at regular intervals through the summer. The theme of these letters, as set forth on June 20, was twofold—the evil inflicted on the colony by an irresponsible, dual-purpose Council of seven members, none of whom now was a Liberal or a Catholic, and the need for intelligent agitation for responsible government. The editor suggested on July 6 that a petition to the Queen be forwarded immediately so that the reply would be received before the opening of the session. If this proved to be negative, he recommended that the Assembly follow the obstructive course lately adopted by Prince Edward Island and refuse to transact business or to vote supplies. A "disposition to parley", said his letter of July 13, would delay the change for a quarter of a century. He contended that no one in the colony was opposed to this change except the present office-holders and others who knew that they could not win the confidence of the people, and he declared that nothing but this concession could hold the colony to the British connection. He called on July 27 for scores of petitions as a demonstration to Lord Grey of the unanimity of public opinion, and, on August 17, suggested the formation of a Responsible Government Society to correspond with the Colonial Reform Society and with other reformers, to watch the turn of events in neighbouring colonies, and to draft petitions to the Assembly, to Parliament, and to the Queen. All that the Home Government required, he said, on August 31, was a "correct" representation of the situation in Newfoundland.

In what the *Patriot* greeted as a move to impair the concerted campaign for responsible government, the Governor called from the Assembly to the Council the Catholic merchant, O'Brien. This elevation made necessary a by-election in St. John's in the autumn of 1850. For the *Patriot* it was essential that the new member be for responsible government and that this principle should be the party distinction.[45] For the *Times* it was desirable that the member should be a merchant and above the paltry consideration of sessional pay.[46]

Two candidates appeared, both advocates of responsible government:[47] James Douglas, the Presbyterian merchant and liberal, and Philip F. Little, a Roman Catholic lawyer, a native of Prince Edward Island, and a resident of Newfoundland for only six years.[48] The *Ledger* noted that Little's support came from a newspaper under Kent's patronage (the *Morning Chronicle*) and from an "influence and interest" which the editor hoped had subsided. Having detected clerical support for Little, the *Ledger* was soon in full cry on the subject. It suggested that St. John's should be disfranchised for its "notorious submission to corrupt influences." It mocked the addresses to "free and independent" electors. It deplored Little's stress on his Irish Catholicism, on the wrongs of Ireland, and on corruption and Protestant ascendancy in the Government.[49] The *Times* was less certain that the election would expose the operation of secret influence, since Douglas, in receipt of a government salary, would be unlikely to draw votes. The truth about influence might be revealed, it said, if another merchant consented to run. But it noted that, as in 1848, the merchants were apathetic, abusing the Assembly, but refusing to enter it. With such indifference on the part of those who should be most interested, only a man possessed of a "higher order of principle, and of ability" than Sir Gaspard could resist the temptation of bringing members under his influence and of "purchasing peace to himself at the expense of the country."[50] Initially, the fact that Little was not a native seems to have troubled the *Patriot*. However, with the Protestant press raising the cry that "Papal Dominance" was curtailing British liberty, this newspaper on October 23 came out for Little as a responsible government man and against Douglas, as a government nominee. On nomination day, according to the *Times* of November 16, the Douglas supporters were refused a hearing by the crowd. When Little polled four hundred more votes than the Protestant liberal, the *Ledger* on November 20 declared that the result had proved its charges of influence. It suggested that the expense and farce of elections in St. John's could be avoided by waiting upon the new Roman Catholic Bishop, Dr. Mullock, and appointing his nominees.[51]

The return of Philip Little and the debates of the session of 1851 made mockery of the Governor's claim to have extinguished politics in Newfoundland. Lengthy and acrimonious discussions on almost every bill cut the volume of legislation to half what it had been in 1850, though it included important acts for the establishment of inland posts, an electric telegraph company, and a penitentiary, as well as other measures testifying to the island's advance as a colony.[52] Prolonged debates on the allocation of the grant for education split the House on sectarian lines. Several years of dissatisfaction about the absence of religious instruction had culminated in 1850 in the division of the St. John's Academy into three institutions, supervised respectively by a Roman Catholic, a Church of England, and a General Protestant board.[53] Pressure from the Puseyite party in the Church of England resulted in 1851 in an attempt to secure a proportional grant for separate Church of England elementary schools. However, since the Dissenters were, in general, opposed to a subdivision of the grant for Protestant education, the bill passed created two central boards, a Protestant and a Catholic.[54] The Conservative press agreed that the fruits of the four-month session were small. The *Times* on April 9 inveighed against the multiplication of offices, increased expenditure, and unprofitable discussions. The *Ledger* declared on May 20 that the Assembly was an "impossible" body and that the members for St. John's were the representatives of a savage mob. On June 6 it announced that the amount of useful legislation was too meagre to offset the "loathing ... engendered in the public mind against the accumulated details of individual political profligacy."

The Conservatives' indignation no doubt stemmed in part from Parsons' success in carrying an address to the Queen asking for the concession of responsible government. This was passed by a House reduced by the length of the session to eleven members, and it represented, according to the Governor, only the views of a small vexatious faction hostile to the executive.[55] In opening the session he had studiously avoided any mention of responsible government.[56] This omission was seized upon by Parsons who denounced the Speech from the Throne, the opponents of responsible government, the constitution, and the proposed Reply in a speech which lasted for five hours. His vehemence produced what the *Times* on January 29 called an "astounding uproar" in the gallery and drew from the Speaker a rebuke for bringing the constitutional cause into disrepute. Both parties agreed on the need for an increase in the number of members, but neither would yield on the method of achieving this. The Liberals insisted on the principle of doubling the representation and the Conservatives upon redivision of the districts and upon additional members for certain Protestant outports. The Liberals' bill, presented by Little, was lost when an independent Liberal, Prendergast, chose to vote against it. The Conservatives' bill, presented by H. W. Hoyles, was rejected when the majority decided that the proposed district of Bonne Bay on the south coast would be a closed Protestant borough.[57] The Governor advised Lord Grey to dismiss the petition for responsible government until the colony had declared itself at the general election of 1852 and until the Assembly and the Council had agreed on a measure for increasing the number of representatives.[58]

Sir Gaspard's request for delay evoked from the Minister a despatch setting forth multiple reasons for continuing to withold responsible government. Avoiding again any specific mention of the politico-religious division, he wrote that "even if there were less ground than actually exists for doubting the expediency of the measures proposed, I should consider it premature for the Queen to sanction changes of this magnitude ... without its having been ascertained in the first instance that their introduction would be in accordance with the deliberate wishes of its inhabitants." The address, he pointed out, had been passed in a thin House. He felt he must pay deference and attention to the opinion of the colonists them-selves—to "different orders of society" and to various public bodies. He was as yet unable to discern any general preponderance of opinion and he felt serious doubts about the applicability of responsible government to a community cir-cumstanced like Newfoundland. One practical obstacle was the limited number of members. What was wanted, he said, was not a mere increase, but an increase of members representing wealth, and these must be representative of the out-ports and not just of St. John's. He questioned whether the outports could yet produce a substantial leisured class from which candidates could be drawn. He pointed out that whereas representative institutions were some two centuries old in British North America, responsible government there had only a two-year history, and that in colonies with much greater population, wealth, and legislative experience than Newfoundland. The people of Newfoundland would have, he said, an opportunity of expressing themselves on the subject at the election of 1852. Finally, he cited what he considered two major financial deterrents. One was the necessity of providing for displaced public servants. Although the As-sembly had "very handsomely" intimated their readiness to meet any such claims, he believed the colony's finances unready for this burden. Further, if responsible government were conceded, it was only just that the colony assume the charges for maintaining the military force now paid for by the British Government. The purpose of this force was not defence against foreign attack but preservation of public order and this, under self-government, should be the colony's responsibil-ity.[59] In enumerating these difficulties, Grey's design was clearly to prolong deferment of the grant.[60]

When the session of 1852 began, the Governor promised, without intimating the contents, to lay the Colonial Secretary's reply before the House. There was much irritation among the Liberals because the Speech from the Throne had not an-nounced the immediate concession of responsible government, and the Reply incorporated an expression of regret at the omission.[61] But when Grey's despatch was sent down on February 4, preceded by a letter from the Governor saying that it would give satisfaction, irritation was replaced by fury. On February 6, Carter tried to postpone consideration of the despatch on the grounds that five members were absent. Little, however, alleged that their absences could be traced to the Governor's desire for delay, carried his motion for the debate, and introduced a series of resolutions as the basis for an address of protest. These announced that the House viewed the Minister's decision with "surprise and regret." They com-plained that Prince Edward Island, with a smaller population and a smaller annual revenue, had received the boon in 1851. They denied a lack of suitable candidates, declared that the colony could meet the necessary civil expenditure, and questioned the fairness of imposing upon Newfoundland defence charges not borne by the other colonies. Little charged that Grey's objections were the emanation of the local executive. His colleague, Ambrose Shea, defended the system of outport representation, pointing out that six of the twelve outport members were actual residents of their districts and that a seventh was a merchant with extensive connections in his. His opponent, Hoyles, found little but opportunism in the whole agitation. He questioned the existence of "surprise and regret." If there were regret, he thought it stemmed from the fact that the Liberal leaders had optimistically chosen their salaried offices. Despite the efforts of the Conservatives, the resolutions and the address were carried by six votes to four, the supporters being all Roman Catholics.[62]

On February 7, the day after the debate began, Bishop Mullock moved from the wings to the political stage for a dramatic denunciation of the Grey despatch. In a letter to his friend Little, which was given wide publicity in the press, he wrote:

I was never more pained in my life than when reading this evening the insulting document forwarded by the Colonial Secretary, in answer to the address for Responsible Government. Holding as I do an office of some consideration in Newfoundland, deeply anxious for the welfare of the country to which I am bound by so many ties, I feel the ill-judged and irritating Despatch an insult to myself and to my people.

Nothing since the days of the *Tea Tax* which raised the trampled provinces of the American colonies to the first rank among nations, as the Great Republic, has been perpetrated, so calculated to weaken the British connexion or cause the people of Newfoundland to look with longing eyes to the day when they can manage their own affairs, without the irresponsible control of some man in a back room in Downing Street, ignorant of the country and apparently only desirous of showing British colonists that they are but slaves to a petty, mercenary, intriguing clique.

Acquainted as I am with many forms of government, having lived and travelled in many lands, having paid some attention to the history of despotic and constitutional government, I solemnly declare that I never knew any settled government so bad, so weak, or so vile as that of our unfortunate country; irresponsible, drivelling despotism, wearing the mask of representative institutions and depending for support alone upon bigotry and bribery. I see the taxes, wrung from the sweat of the people, squandered in the payment of useless officials; the country, after three centuries of British possession, in a great part an impassable wilderness, its people depressed, its trade fettered, its mighty resources undeveloped, and all for what? To fatten up in idleness, by the creation of useless offices exorbitantly paid, the members of a clique. A tabular statement of the offices, the salaries, the families, and the religion of these state pensioners will show that I overstate nothing.

I was anxious, however, hoping for a reform, to give the present government, if it can be called one, a fair trial. As a matter of conscience, I can do so no longer. My silence would betray the cause of justice and the people. I hope that all honest men will unite in demanding justice, and by an appeal, not to the Colonial Office, but to the British Parliament.

Lord Grey's cautious retreat on the Treasury Note Bill [63] shows that justice must be done, if demanded by a united people. Should any petition for this object be forwarded before my return, I authorize you to put my name to it, and to state publicly to the people my sentiments. I do not aspire to the character of demagogue—every one in Newfoundland knows that in my position I need not do so. But it is the duty of a Bishop to aid and advise his people in all their struggles for justice, and I have no other desire than to see justice done in the country and equally administered to all classes of Her Majesty's subjects in this colony, irrespective of denominational distinctions, without seeking, or submitting to, the undue ascendancy of any class. And the people should know that government is made for them and not they for the government.

The puerile threat of withdrawing the Newfoundland Companies merits only supreme contempt. Gross as is the ignorance of the Colonial Office regarding the Colonies, no minister would dare advise such a suicidal act. Our present Governor, a brave and experienced soldier, knows full well that 500 Americans or French, occupying Signal Hill, one of the strongest maritime positions in the world, would jeopardize the Naval supremacy of Britain in these Northern seas. No, so long as Britain can spare a soldier, she will never give up Newfoundland. It is in all probability the last point of America where her flag will wave ....[64]

If the Bishop expected a favourable reaction from the Protestant community to this letter, he must have been gravely disappointed. For the *Ledger* of February 10 it served as proof that responsible government in Newfoundland would merely be government according to the "well understood wishes of the Romish Bishop." Comparing Dr. Mullock with his predecessor, the editor wrote on February 20: "Why, Dr. Fleming, in the worst of times, never committed himself half so egregiously; as objectionable upon public grounds as many of his proceedings unfortunately were, he never, as far as we remember, went the length of assigning the Government a probationary existence, nor attempted to constitute himself, even by the smallest fiction, *the* people and *the* Government of Newfoundland." The *Times* on February 14 believed that the Bishop's letter would be the "death thrust to the advocates of the obnoxious measure."

The Governor, describing to Grey the reaction to the refusal of responsible government, termed the Bishop's letter a "highly inflammatory" document. It was, he said, aimed at a public meeting convened by Roman Catholics for the purpose of petitioning Parliament. He predicted that a crisis was approaching and that the issue was whether the administration was to be removed from the Governor and placed in the hands of the Roman Catholic party under the direction of the Bishop. The councillors were opposed to responsible government, he reported, and were well satisfied with the Minister's reply. So too was the Protestant half of the community, including "all the higher grades of society among the merchants, the Legal and Professional Bodies, and the majority of ... the middle class of Tradesmen and Planters." He scouted the idea that there was sufficient administrative talent available for responsible government or that the outports would have a fair share in such an administration. Residents of St. John's hoped to "monopolize the whole power and patronage of the Colony." He recounted the abortive attempts to increase the representation and declared that the "war of creeds" was as bitter as in the time of Governor Prescott. Until the House was suitably augmented, the constitution would advance no interest connected with the general welfare, but would merely serve as a "vehicle always ready at the hands of the Roman Catholic Bishop and Priesthood to fan the flames of religious discord, and further excite those animosities which have on more than one occasion threatened to place the public peace ... in the greatest jeopardy."[65] Two weeks later he forwarded a petition from St. John's for responsible government, which he called a Roman Catholic production:

I may not inaptly term this address the personal application of the Roman Catholic Bishop, supported by the Representatives of his party in the ... Assembly, with a small fraction of the Bar, and a still smaller fraction of the minor Mercantile Interest, enlarged indeed by the signatures of several shopkeepers and finally augmented to its full size and bulk by the addition of a long array of fishermen, who as they approached their Cathedral on the Sabbath morning, were severally invited to subscribe the address, that they found spread out on tables placed in anticipation of the arrival of the congregation at the very entrance of the Building.[66]

The opponents of responsible government lost no time in expressing their views on the subject, as Lord Grey had suggested. The Commercial Society and the Law Society voted heavily against the grant.[67] They petitioned for its postponement, in the name of justice, until social conditions had changed and until a Representation Act had ensured that the Roman Catholic party would not secure preponderating power.[68]

For the Protestants, Little's Representation Bill of 1852 was further evidence that political power was the aim of the Roman Catholics. Once again the Liberals based their measure on the principle of doubling the return from the existing districts. This device, as the *Times* pointed out on April 3, would ensure that the Roman Catholic district of Placentia and St. Mary's would return four members and that the Protestant district of Trinity Bay, with a larger population and with much more capital invested in the trade, would return but two. The Council's amendments being rejected by the Assembly, the Bill was lost.[69]

While the controversy about the Representation Bill inflamed mutual suspicion in the colony, a third refusal of responsible government was being prepared in England. Since the Tories had come into office in February 1852, it had fallen to Sir John Pakington, the new Colonial Secretary, to reply to the Assembly's address. The Governor's dire predictions seem to have supplemented his own doubts about the wisdom of representative government for Newfoundland. He informed Sir Gaspard that events in the colony seemed to confirm the wisdom of Lord Grey's decision. The religious difficulty and the Bishop's disposition to be a party leader constituted, he thought, barriers to responsible government. He hoped that Dr. Mullock would realize the "impropriety and consequences" of such a course and he advised the Governor to stand firm should a collision occur. It might again prove necessary, he said, to ask Parliament to alter the constitution.[70]

Such a despatch was ill-calculated to restore harmony to the colony. It was greeted by the Conservatives with grateful satisfaction and by the Liberals with scathing denunciation. The *Ledger* described it on May 21 as a "total eclipse, an interminable extinguisher" of the hopes for responsible government, and suggested on May 25 that Sir John could be expected to withdraw or at least modify the constitution. He would do well, it said, to relieve the Roman Catholic electors from the burden of having to vote at all, since it seemed doubtful that they could ever vote freely. The *Times* of May 22 rejoiced at the rebuke to the Bishop and at the evidence that the Tories would refrain from "rash concessions to the discontented" and Whiggish "truckling" to radicalism. Little informed the Assembly that Pakington was a High Tory and that his reply was the stereotyped production of a Downing Street underling, occupied in misgoverning the colonies and driving their inhabitants to the United States. The Bishop, he said, would not be deterred from his duty by an "itinerant lecture," nor would the colony wait quietly for the boon. The Assembly must be cleansed of "trimmers" and the reformers must agitate so as to give the "vile" government no rest within or without the House. A colleague suggested that all responsible government candidates at the coming election pledge themselves to resist pressure to vote the supplies until responsible government had been granted.[71]

When the Governor went down to close the last session of the Assembly, he knew that he was to be transferred to another colony and that he might not be present for the election and the meeting of the new House.[72] Disdaining to offer the formal compliments usual on such an occasion, he administered instead a forthright rebuke:

I must express my deep regret that in place of the harmony and concord that marked the earlier part of your Legislative career, party contentions and acrimonious debates have occupied the time which might have been usefully devoted to the development of the resources of the Island and the promotion of the welfare of its inhabitants; and I must also add, that I feel disappointed that after four years' Legislation I have it not in my power to congratulate Newfoundland on the benefits derived from your labours being commensurate either with the length of time consumed in your deliberations, or with the necessary expense with which the same have been attended.[73]

For these frank sentiments Sir Gaspard was rewarded by the citizens of St. John's with a distinction not conferred on his predecessors, Cochrane and Prescott: he was blown up in effigy, in full regalia, clutching Pakington's despatch in one hand and his own speech in the other.[74] In June it was learned that the Governor was to go to Nova Scotia and his administration in Newfoundland closed amidst much vilification from the Liberals.[75]

Sir Gaspard had begun his administration with strong doubts about the wisdom of a representative constitution for Newfoundland. He closed it convinced that the time was fast approaching for a return to the system abandoned in 1832. He was certain that the election would produce a House overwhelmingly amenable to the Bishop and determined to achieve responsible government by the stoppage of supplies. Nothing had prevented the loss of the last Supply Bill, he said, but the Liberals' fear of losing their emoluments. The concession of responsible government, he declared, would involve the island in "irretrievable confusion and ruin," but he believed that the power of the Bishop and the Roman Catholic Church would finally be irresistible unless the Home Government consented to throw its weight into the scale. He asked that the local Government be supported in assisting the Protestant part of the population.[76]

To support his argument for the abolition of the Assembly, the Governor had called upon Attorney-General Archibald for an analysis of legislation and legislative costs. Archibald's report showed that there had been seventy-seven Acts in the last four sessions, of which about half were formal, continuing, or amending measures, and the remainder new, useful, or important. To secure these, over £18,000 had been required to meet election, registration, and contingent expenses. The legislative contingencies of the Fourth Assembly were almost four times greater than those of the first. The sum voted in the Appropriation Act of 1852 (excluding education and road grants, reserved salaries, and customs expenses) was £66,500, six times greater than that for 1834, which had included the road grant. Archibald did not deny that this sixfold increase had benefited the colony, but he maintained that the sums would have been more wisely spent under the executive's control. He described local and sectarian jealousies about the allocation of funds and the pressure on the Governor to initate money votes.[77] For the Governor, one of the most striking proofs of legislative inadequacy was that after twenty years the statute book showed "not one single enactment ... either for dividing the country into regular and convenient Districts, Counties, and Townships, or for raising local rates and assessments, or for defraying local charges and burthens, or for maintenance of the poor, or for the support of the police, or for the construction of courthouses and gaols." In the total absence of local rates not so much as a drain could be financed except from the public revenue, yet the Assembly could not be induced to legislate to remedy this situation.[78] The Governor informed Sir John Pakington, as he had informed the

House, that he did not think the amount or value of the legislation warranted the time and money it consumed.[79]

Despite these recommendations, the onus of solving its political difficulties was not removed from the colony in 1852 as it had been in 1841, when Governor Prescott had refused, in the absence of an electoral law, to take the responsibility for what might ensue at the election. The Colonial Office view was that the Protestant majority in Newfoundland must rouse itself to action. One member of the Office, noting the superiority of the Protestants in numbers and wealth and their conviction that they could not return a majority, traced the difficulty to the constitution itself. This, he pointed out, allowed them to lean on the Home Government and its official representation in the colony instead of encouraging them to take, openly, the unpopular side and to exert their energies in opposing democracy.[80] Another member wrote that it would be unjust to lend the Government's support to the Protestant party and difficult, if not impossible, to suspend the constitution. In his opinion, two decades of representative government, the talent and vigour displayed in the Assembly, the rapid diffusion of liberal ideas of government on the North American continent, and the operation of responsible government there, must make the Conservative Government at home hesitant about restricting the constitutional privileges of Newfoundland. What was needed, he thought, was not abolition of the Assembly but an enlargement of it which might improve the membership and allow the Protestant party to display such energies as they possessed.[81] As to how the Protestants might overcome the handicap of the electoral districts and the influence of the Catholic Bishop, the Colonial Office was silent.

CHAPTER NINE

THE WINNING OF RESPONSIBLE GOVERNMENT, 1852-1855

THE LIBERALS approached the election campaign of 1852 with a plan for concerted action, while the Conservatives were resigned to defeat. The Liberals' aim was to return their usual three-fifths of the Assembly as a solid bloc pledged to responsible government. Five months before the election the *Pilot*, a newspaper under the patronage of the Roman Catholic Bishop, warned the Liberals that the "enemy" was preparing to return executive hacks and called for a campaign organization. A central committee in St. John's, linked with committees in the districts, was to select and promote the return of Liberal candidates who would pledge themselves to do all in their power by constitutional means to force the concession. They were to stop the supplies until it had been attained and to refuse to accept office under the irresponsible system or to procure offices for others. They were also to lend full support to the cause of reciprocal free trade with the United States.[1] The opposing press did not advocate a counter-organization, but as the election drew nearer did issue warnings and exhort "respectable" men to stand.[2]

The Conservatives' tactics were essentially negative. The *Ledger* informed its readers on September 10 that there was no civil or religious liberty under the "Romish Church" and called their attention to the campaign of the Liberals:

There is an attempt by the Irish political Journalists in this town to revive and to invigorate the latent animosities which in Ireland were wont to be enkindled against everything that savours of British character, of British institutions, and generally of British Government. We have accordingly all sorts of rubbish gleaned from the Irish press in Ireland and the Irish press in America.... The electors ... are taught to believe that everything connected with the Government under which they live is hideous and oppressive, and that it is their first and paramount duty to obey the mandates of their clergy, in whom are concentrated the very venom of religious and political hostility to the powers that be ....

It now seemed to the *Ledger* (September 15) that there was warrant for the otherwise distasteful secret ballot. A fortnight later (October 1) it predicted that the general election would be another general "mockery," with few contests, truant voters subjected to the anathema of the Bishop, and St. John's once more a rotten borough whose leading interests would be unrepresented for another four years. A month later on November 5 it doubted that twenty Protestants would bother to vote in the capital, while the *Times* declared five days later that the sooner the "reign of oppression" were given full and undisturbed sway, the better it would be for the colony.

Once again the Liberals returned nine members (Appendix B, Table VI). In St. John's no Conservative candidates offered to oppose Kent, Little, and Parsons, so that city was once more, according to the November 10 *Times*, to be represented by "needy adventurers and hireling scribes." On Novembr 13 it did concede, however, that Kent had proved himself an able and consistent legislator whose political sentiments had matured and whose asperities had softened. At Conception Bay, Catholic and Protestant members were returned in equal numbers, but intimidation of voters was reported to have contributed to the defeat of Prendergast, the independent Roman Catholic favoured by the Protestants. Telegraph wires were cut between two polling places there and another poll in the district had to be closed early.[3] Coercion was reported also from Ferryland and Placentia, in both of which Roman Catholic candidates were returned. Conservative opinion was that the Protestant members were on the whole inferior in substance and ability to those in the fourth Assembly and the Catholic members more amenable to clerical direction.[4] The Governor deplored the loss of Robert Carter, the Colonial Treasurer and former member for Bonavista Bay, who was defeated at Ferryland, and T. B. Job who had represented Trinity, as well as the return of candidates more submissive to the Roman Catholic party. Liberal opinion was that the prospects of obtaining responsible government were good. The *Patriot* declared on January 22, 1853, that the election had shown what Lord Grey had asked—a clear desire for the responsible system—and that the recent supersession of the Derby by the Aberdeen Ministry, and of Sir John Pakington by the liberal Duke of Newcastle, augured well for the change.

Much would depend upon the disposition and recommendations of the new Governor, Ker Baillie Hamilton, appointed by Pakington. Little was known about Hamilton, save that after a military education and a military service in India he had held minor colonial posts in Mauritius and the Cape of Good Hope, and had risen to be Lieutenant-Governor of Grenada and later to be Administrator of the Barbados, neither colony having, as the *Patriot* had noted on August 30, 1852, responsible government (see Appendix A). The Conservatives apparently hoped, as was their habit, that the Governor's strength would supplement their weakness. The August 25 *Times* had written of the need for a "man of ability and experience—a man of firmness and cool determination—a man possessed of MIND . . . not to be played upon by artful demagogues."

The Speech from the Throne in January 1853, with its hopes for cordial cooperation and its reliance on divine mercy, made no mention of responsible government. Instead, the new Governor told the members that the true interests of the colony consisted "in the reasonable union and concurrence of the different branches of the Legislature in promoting the general welfare of the people, in the advancement of religion, the encouragement of education, the improvement of the administration of justice, obedience to the laws, and a steady perseverance in the healthy and remunerative occupations which are suitable to the climate and congenial to the inhabitants . . ."[5] Hamilton's failure to mention either responsible government or reciprocal free trade with the United States gave rise, like LeMarchant's parting rebuke, to much vehemence among the Liberals. Parsons proposed an amendment to the Reply declaring a want of confidence in the Council. When Kent declined to support this on the grounds that it would antagonize the Governor and give him a wrong impression of the members, Parsons turned upon him for his moderation.[6] The Reply, as passed, adverted to the necessity of conceding responsible government and to the desirability of securing reciprocity. Hamilton, commenting to Newcastle on the impropriety of introducing topics not touched upon in his Speech, interpreted the action as a censure of the Imperial Government.[7]

Reciprocal trade with the United States was not a straight party issue, although the Liberals by their endorsement made it a part of their programme. It had been first mooted in 1849 when Earl Grey had raised the question of whether the colony should be included in the reciprocal trade agreement between the British North American colonies and the United States, then in the early stages of negotiation.[8] LeMarchant's inquiries at that time had led him to believe that there would be great opposition to giving foreigners further rights of fishing off Newfoundland's coasts unless there were clear off-setting advantages to be gained from such a treaty. A free market in the United States for agricultural produce would obviously be of no use to Newfoundland, but he believed that access to the American market for fish might be a fair exchange for the cession of fishing rights to the Americans. Poor markets rather than poor catches were depressing the Newfoundland fisheries. Markets were poor in the United States because of the protective tariff and the bounty to American fishermen, and in Europe because of competition from the French. The demand in the British West Indies was insufficient to support the Newfoundland industry. He believed, however, that if the Americans were to be admitted to inshore fishing rights on the entire coast, the American bounty must be abolished and Newfoundland must, for her revenue, maintain a tariff on imports. It seemed to him that competition from the American fishermen would serve as a stimulus to the colony's fisheries and that the curing of American-caught fish in Newfoundland would set up a beneficial demand for land and labour. The merchants' opposition, he said, was based on the fear that the fishermen would grow increasingly independent.[9]

In April 1852, after a three-day debate in the Assembly, a large majority had passed a series of resolutions for "free trade." Americans were to be admitted to a participation in the fisheries "as an equivalent for the removal of their Bounties and prohibitory duties on Newfoundland produce; the produce of either country being admitted in the other, either free of duty, or at a rate not exceeding six per cent ad valorem." These resolutions were repassed unanimously in 1853, at which time Hamilton reported that a majority of the people seemed to favour the change because of the prospect of gaining remunerative markets and increased employment. Although the principal opponents were the merchants who feared that competition in trade and fisheries might follow a settlement of Americans in the outports, a minority of the merchants agreed with the resolutions of the Assembly. Hamilton's own opinion was that a reciprocal agreement should be reached.[10]

The Governor was entirely opposed to the other Liberal project—the establishment of responsible government. The allocation in the first ten days of the session of 1853, through appointments and patronage, of more than £1100 to Roman Catholic members and their relatives seemed to him, as he informed Newcastle, strong evidence of personal objects behind the agitation. His view was that of his predecessor and of the Protestants—that the concession would mean the establishment of a permanent oligarchy "totally destructive of that freedom which is the vaunted advantage of the desired change." Nor could he see any reason for the change:

There is no hindrance or obstruction whatever to the enactment by the Assembly of such useful measures as would promote the prosperity and well being of the Island: and the concession of Responsible Government would neither enlarge the capacity of the Members, nor add to the legislative powers of that Body, which are amply sufficient for all the powers of Legislation. Declamation, however, by the majority, on abstract theories of Government, and denunciation of all who dissent from them as hostile to what is termed "the cause of the people," occupy much valuable time to the exclusion of consideration of practical subjects for the good of the Country.[11]

Several considerations emerge from the Governor's assessment of the political situation. His administrative experience in the West Indies had clearly not prepared him to sympathize with or to appraise the strength of the democratic aspirations of these colonial reformers or to meet them in conciliatory fashion. A man of strong religious convictions, not averse to embroiling himself in the politics of his own Church,[12] he apparently shared the mid-century apprehension of the Church of Rome and of papal "aggression," which in England had produced the Ecclesiastical Titles Bill and which in Newfoundland was driving the Protestant press, especially the aging editor of the Ledger, to outbursts of despair.[13] Hamilton's very early strictures about men and motives in the colony suggest that his views owed much to the focus and interpretation supplied by his Protestant councillors and friends. With Hoyles, whom he made Solicitor-General,[14] and who was shortly to emerge as the spokesman and delegate of the Protestant community in the struggle against responsible government, he seems to have been particularly intimate.[15]

The advocates of responsible government, whether from a reluctance to lose their sessional pay or from a desire to impress the new Colonial Secretary with their moderation, did not in 1853 prevent the passage of the votes for supply. In the last month of the session they gave their attention to passing resolutions for responsible government and to incorporating these and their complaints against the composition and behaviour of the Council in addresses to the Queen and to both Houses of Parliament. One cause for complaint was the failure of the Representation Bill which had attempted to raise the membership to twenty-eight by doubling the representation of all districts except Placentia and St. Mary's and Conception Bay, which were to receive additions of one and three members respectively. The Bill was rejected by the Council because it seemed to ensure the return to the Assembly of sixteen Roman Catholics and twelve Protestants and so to give the minority in the population a large majority in the representation. Other measures rejected by the Council were those for poor relief and for the taking of a census, the former because the Council maintained that its provision to pay a group of officials in each outport would encourage pauperism, the latter because, a census having been taken in 1845, the Council deemed the expense unwarranted. The Assembly's charges about mutilated measures were reminiscent of the petitions despatched in the time of Governor Prescott. The principal arguments were that the elections had shown a clear desire for responsible government and that the session had demonstrated the need for the change.[16]

These contentions the Governor laboriously denied in his despatch to New-castle. He reiterated his fears of a permanent Catholic oligarchy and of a legis-lative council of the same complexion. He stressed the peculiar nature of the Newfoundland constituency, declaring it to consist almost entirely of fishermen of whom only a portion were literate, and that portion barely so. These, without the information necessary to enable them to judge rightly of their interests, were, he said, too easily led by those who, for their own purposes, flattered their feelings and exploited their prejudices.[17]

Realizing the disadvantage of having to submit their case through an un-sympathetic intermediary, the House appointed delegates to go to England. They asked the Governor to sanction expenses to the amount of £450, one-third for allocation to the Council. Instead of permitting this vote to be incorporated in the Supply Bill, the Governor, in the name of correctness, asked for a separate bill. This was rejected by the Council. The item was then "tacked" to the Supply Bill, from which it was, of course, struck by the Council. Little and Par-sons then agreed to proceed to England without the grant.[18]

The delegates, with Joseph Hume, had a sympathetic hearing from the Duke of Newcastle in July 1853.[19] Although Newcastle regretted the tone and manner in which many of the statements were made,[20] he does not seem to have dis-couraged the delegates from arguing their case further. He raised two objections to the concession of responsible government—"the difficulty of finding a sufficient number of persons in the Colony qualified to conduct that system and to justify an adequate increase of its representatives" and "the existence of such sectarian differences among the population as might interfere with its harmonious work-ing."[21] Both these problems the delegates alleged to be non-existent. They de-clared that contacts with neighbouring colonies had enlarged the inhabitants' knowledge and experience in trade and politics, that Newfoundland exceeded the other colonies in the "aggregate of intelligence," that the merchants, planters, and middle class had the capacity for legislation, and that the electors had "great morality, discretion, and peculiar genius and industry." As for the sectarian question, they produced figures indicating a proportional under-representation of Catholics and Dissenters in the Council and in public office. They denied that the reformers sought an "undue" sectarian ascendancy, contended that this would not be tolerated, if it were practicable, and pointed out that Catholic districts had sometimes returned non-Catholics. They claimed that there were six dis-tricts with Protestant majorities which could return nine Protestants, as compared with three districts able to return six Catholics.[22] After the interview Hume pre-sented the Assembly's petition to the House of Commons. He pressed Newcastle for a specific assurance which the delegates could report to the Assembly.[23] This assurance Newcastle was not prepared to give, on the grounds that his exhaustion after a laborious session left him unfit to give due consideration to the desired change.[24] He seems to have planned in August and in October to secure from the Governor privately, another report on the advisability of the concession and a statement on the truth or falsity of some of the charges made.[25] However, at the end of November the Governor was still in ignorance of his intentions.[26]

The delegates returned to Newfoundland confident that responsible govern-ment was about to be granted. In an open letter to the electors, Little wrote that judging from the assurances of the Colonial Secretary and from the tone of pubic opinion, particularly as expressed in Parliament, on questions of colonial government, it was unlikely that the members would be driven to follow the example of Jamaica in refusing to transact business in the Assembly.[27] The optimism of the Liberals was increased by a letter from Hume saying that Newcastle was giving the matter careful and favourable attention.[28] The Governor pressed the Colonial Office for a reply which he could communicate to the Assembly in January 1854. He urged that if Newcastle were actually contemplating the grant, the House should be required to make conditional provision for official pensions as stipulated by himself and that it then be dissolved so that the question of responsible government could be submitted to the electorate.[29] Since the Liberals had made this the issue in the election of 1852, the Governor was evidently asking for the Protestant party the chance to make a more forceful presentation of their case.

The requested despatch had not arrived from Newcastle when the session opened in 1854, and the Speech from the Throne again contained no reference to responsible government. This again provoked an impassioned discussion. Hoyles, for the Protestants, insisted that outside the Assembly people were not convinced that the time was ripe for the change. When Little had given the delegates' report, Hoyles presented the Protestant case. In other colonies, he said, responsible government was a political question, but in Newfoundland it was one of religion. It had been raised by a Church-directed party determined to take over the government. These remarks provoked much agitation among the members and an uproar from the packed gallery.[30] After a lengthy debate, the Assembly passed the Reply, which informed the Governor, in respectful terms, that the House intended to await the decision of the Imperial Government rather than to renew "fruitless attempts at legislation under the present constitution." The House was adjourned until February 20, the day on which the English mail packet was due. When the expected despatch did not arrive on that day, the Assembly passed an address explaining their course to the Duke and readjourned until a despatch had been received from him.[31]

In the month that elapsed before Newcastle's decision was learned, the Conservative press tried to arouse the opponents of responsible government into a display of energy and unity.[32] These exhortations to action were weakened, however, by reversions to the habit of reliance on the Home Government and to the spirit of defeatism. The *Times* of February 18 asked if the British Government was to be bullied by "some half dozen agitators," and on March 8 expressed the hope, as the *Ledger* had the previous day, that the Governor would dissolve the "cabal" and await instructions from England. When Little proposed a public meeting, promising that if four-fifths of the electors present were not in favour of the change, he would desist from the agitation, the *Times* on March 11 declared that he was perfectly safe in such a promise, since no respectable person would attend his meeting. One of its correspondents warned a week later that there would be a renewal of violence and outrage should Protestants attend the meeting and attempt to express their opinions. With Hoyles as the prime mover, 1,600 of the male adults of St. John's out of a total Protestant population of 6,210, joined in a petition against the unqualified grant of responsible government.[33]

Meantime, the Duke of Newcastle had been perusing two years' correspondence on the subject. By January 31 he had come, regretfully, to the conclusion that he could not maintain the adverse decisions of Lord Grey and Sir John Pakington. In a memorandum he wrote:

There are circumstances connected with the peculiar position of this Colony which render the proposed change unusually hazardous. It is perhaps about the severest test to which "responsible government" can be exposed. But the circumstances which militate against its adoption are not those which have hitherto been assigned by any Secretary of State or could with propriety be brought forward in a despatch—the unhappy antagonism and nearly equal power of two religious Creeds.

He had, nevertheless, been forced to the conclusion that the Government could not withhold from Newfoundland what had been conceded to the other colonies in British North America. He would, therefore, send instructions for the separation of the Executive and Legislative Councils when three indispensable conditions had been met. The first was the doubling of the representation by dividing large electoral districts as equally as geographical positions would permit. The second was the cessation of the practice of paying election expenses and sessional remuneration from the colony's Treasury. The third was the provision of perfectly guaranteed pensions for displaced officials.[34] The despatch setting out these prerequisites reached St. John's on March 22, 1854.[35]

To the Protestant portion of the community the principles laid down by Newcastle seemed eminently wise and just, being, in fact, the conditions asked for in a petition then on the way to London. The Liberals' view was quite other. The recalled House at once passed an address declaring that two of the conditions were unacceptable—the subdivision requirement being unjust because "it would create nomination boroughs for certain individuals notoriously opposed to free institutions," and the requirement that districts pay their own members and candidates their own expenses unfair, because it had not been imposed on the other colonies.[36] Hoyles brought in an amendment thanking the Home Government for a determination "not to permit injustice to be done to the Protestant people of this colony, nor to sacrifice its best interests to the aggrandizement of any class or order of the community." In view of the majority in the Assembly, this could be no more than an impotent and inflammatory gesture.[37] The address and the Governor's report were not answered by Newcastle, though they provoked comment in the Colonial Office. To the despatch with the Protestants' petition, which arrived at the same time as the Assembly's address, Newcastle appended the opinion that Hamilton's disposition to identify himself with the Protestant cause, as well as his alliance with one of the factions in his own Church, would do the colony a disservice. The Duke feared that the Roman Catholic party would read the Governor's bias and influence into the Colonial Office effort to secure a fair representation of all classes.[38]

In June 1854 the Governor refused to mediate between the Assembly and the Council to prevent the loss in the Council of yet another representation measure unsatisfactory to the Protestants. He maintained that mediation would be unconstitutional interference and that the Assembly had no warrant for assuming that he disagreed with the stand taken by the Council.[39] Although this reply earned him the gratitude of the Protestants,[40] it seems to have quickened doubts in the Colonial Office about his suitability for the colony. Peel, the Parliamentary Under-Secretary, was convinced that the politico-religious problem would never be solved under Hamilton:

> ... all this contention between the two Houses would have been avoided if there had been a moderate and sensible man acting as Governor. Governor Hamilton wants us to solve his difficulties by an Act of Parliament and instead of aiding the policy of Her Majesty's Government renews his old objections to the system of a responsible Executive. Imperial legislation seems to be out of the question, and if Governor Hamilton distrusts his ability to work the new system on its being introduced, he had much better come away ....
> ... it is really provoking to think that for want of tact on the part of the Governor an insignificant point ... has caused an indefinite postponement of the whole measure .... There would have been nothing "very absurd" in Governor Hamilton inducing the Council ... to abstain from pushing to extremities the little point on which they took their stand.[41]

The "little point" was, of course, the principle of a Protestant majority.

As devised by the Liberals in the Assembly, the Representation Bill provided, ostensibly, for the return of fifteen Protestants to fourteen Roman Catholics (see Appendix E, Tables III, IIIa). This seemed a fair reflection of the Protestant majority of 3,000 in the population. Hoyles and his associates contended, however, that the Bill was designed to permit the Protestants no more than fourteen representatives.[42] Newcastle's stipulation about geographical subdivision had not over-ruled the Roman Catholic fear of mercantile domination in small districts. The result had been that the principle of division had been applied only to St. John's and Conception Bay, the former being given six members who would, predictably, be Roman Catholic, the latter being given seven, of whom four would, presumably, be Protestant. Fortune Bay would certainly return a Protestant as would the new adjoining district, Burgeo and La Poile. Of the other Protestant districts, Trinity Bay had been given three members and Bonavista Bay and Twillingate and Fogo, two members each. Of the Catholic districts, Placentia and St. Mary's was given three members and Ferryland two. Burin, with a small Protestant majority, was given a second member.

The Protestants in the Assembly objected principally to the provision for Burin. While the Bill's proponents argued that Burin would automatically return two Protestant members, the Protestants felt that in the absence of church direction such as prevailed in Catholic districts, there was no certainty of such a return. Indeed they alleged that intimidation had resulted in the return of a Roman Catholic there and they pointed out that at Conception Bay, where there was also an over-all Protestant majority, that portion of the community had had in the past to settle with the Roman Catholics for the return of two members of each faith. Since it seemed useless to attempt amendments in the Assembly, the Protestant members spoke and voted against the Bill and left alterations to the Council.

The Council attempted to secure the return of fifteen Protestants. They provided that in Burin each elector should vote for only one candidate,. so that one of each faith should be returned, and that the Catholic district, Placentia and St. Mary's should have one less and the Protestant district, Bonavista one more member. The Assembly rejected the Burin amendment, saying that the principle of a divided vote was novel and a stigma to the colony. They agreed to a third member for the Protestant district, but not to a subtraction of one from the Catholic. The Council then gave way on Burin, trusting that the district would make a divided return, but they would not relinquish the principle of a Protestant majority. The Assembly remaining adamant and the Governor refusing to intervene, the Bill was lost. The Assembly resolved to transact no further business, and passed an address asking the Secretary of State for the immediate and unqualified concession of responsible government.

Both Houses decided upon delegations to England and the Legislature was prorogued on June 14. There had been no vote for supplies and the session had seen the completion of only five measures.[43] A week later the Central Protestant Committee authorized Hoyles to lay the Protestant case before the Home Government.[44]

When the delegations arrived in London, they found that Sir George Grey had become Colonial Secretary and Newcastle, Secretary of State for War. Although the delegates from the Assembly saw Grey and put their case into his hands, at Hume's suggestion they submitted it to Newcastle as well. They acknowledged the irregularity of this, but hoped that his friendly disposition and sense of fair play would lead him to interpose. What they asked was that responsible government be put into operation at once, upon the understanding that one of the new Government's first acts would be to pass the Representation Bill agreed upon by the Assembly. Their statement set forth their most recent complaints about the Council, especially on the representation question, and asserted that it was useless to ask the Assembly to renew the contest with that body. Newcastle's reply, friendly and reassuring, was that Grey had given him to understand that the contest would soon be brought to an end.[45] Hume declined to present the Assembly's petition to Parliament because he too was convinced that Grey was intent on the speedy establishment of responsible government.[46] With these replies the delegates had to be content, though they maintained that Grey should signify to the Governor his approval of the Representation Bill and his intention, if obstruction continued, to order the reconstruction of the Council on the responsible principle.[47]

The Council's defence was put by Attorney-General Archibald and W. B. Row and the specifically Protestant case by Hoyles.[48] The latter had prepared an able and comprehensive printed statement, detailing the history of the responsible government struggle and the reasons the Protestants feared its unconditional concession. They would have no objection to the system, he said, if steps were taken to prevent the establishment of a perpetual Catholic despotism. The Representation Bill was obnoxious to the Protestants because of its omissions. It did not provide for the subdivision of all the districts, or for the representation of the Protestant commercial community of St. John's, upon whom lay the responsibility of managing the island's trade and fishery, or for the clear definition of the property qualification for members, or for the payment of members by local assessment. He claimed that the controversy was a purely religious question, that officials in the Council were more than willing to retire on pension if they could do so without sacrifice of principle, and that the days of non-resident merchants, uninterested in the permanent prosperity of the colony, were over.[49]

The outcome of the various representations was a mediating despatch from

Sir George Grey. He thought that there was still a chance for a peaceful solution and he pointed out to the Governor his duty to act as an impartial arbitrator. He declined to aggravate the existing differences by asking Parliament to interfere, but he intimated that he was ready, as a last resort, to remodel the Council. On the Representation Bill he would only say that the application of a special principle to Burin seemed wrong. He was prepared to waive Newcastle's condition of local assessment to pay members, and advised that the Legislature be recalled at an early date to settle these questions.[50]

When the Legislature opened in October, the Assembly announced that they would bring forward the Bill that had failed, would make no further concessions to the Council, and would hold up the supplies until the Bill had passed.[51] The Council met this challenge by rejecting the Bill almost unanimously and by passing another which subtracted a member each from Bonavista and Placentia and St. Mary's, reducing the total to twenty-eight.[52] To this, the Assembly would not agree and the stalemate continued until November 9. Then, Colonial Secretary Crowdy succeeded in convincing a majority of the Council that unless they gave way there was a clear danger of suspension, new councillors, and a less satisfactory Act. This view was supported by the Attorney-General and opposed by three of the merchants.[53] It seems probable that satisfaction with the scale of the retiring allowances proposed by the Governor and sanctioned by Grey contributed to the decision of the officials to withdraw their opposition to the Bill.[54] The outcome was the passage of the Bill which the Council had refused in June. To this, the Governor gave his reluctant assent, reporting his own and the Protestants' dissatisfaction with its provisions and their anticipation of election violence.[55] The Council's refusal to sanction a census had put the Protestants at a disadvantage, for, as the census of 1857 was to confirm, their proportion of the population was out-distancing the Catholic (see Appendix E, Table IV).

For a few days it seemed that the grounds for controversy had been removed and the members of the Assembly applied themselves to the Pension and Supply Bills. Then the excitement was rekindled by Governor Hamilton's refusal to hold an immediate election. He reported to Grey that he intended to hold the general election in May 1855 in order to give time for the revision of the registration lists and the first registration in the new south coast district.[56] The majority of the Assembly was very anxious that the election be held immediately, but the minority was strongly opposed because the remote districts of the north and south, purely Protestant, would be unable, due to the lateness of the season, to send their elected representatives to the ensuing session.[57]

The news that there was to be a six-month delay before they could hope for office angered the Liberals. One member called the Governor a "villain" and there was talk of withholding the supplies and of despatching another delegation.[58] Little, armed with documents showing Hume's support, tried to force the Governor to reverse his decision, declaring, according to the Governor, that Hamilton would suffer "consequences injurious to himself personally" if he did not. The threat stiffened the Governor's determination not to yield. He wrote Grey:

The results of the improper and avowed attempts on the part of both Mr. Hume and Mr. Little to seek to control me in my official conduct by a fear of personal considerations, and of the endeavour, however absurd, to substitute Mr. Hume for the responsible adviser of the Crown, have unquestionably been to derogate from the true position of the Governor, and to foster that arrogancy which has just emboldened Mr. Little to threaten the Colony with another Crisis, and the withholding of Supplies.[59]

On November 21 Little gave notice of a resolution to address the Imperial Government for the removal of Governor Hamilton "for his mismanagement of this Colony, and his partizanship with his Council in their united opposition to the Assembly and the best interests of the Country." He referred to proofs discovered in London of the Governor's "collusion with the enemies of reform and progress" in the colony and alleged a new attempt to impede the establishment of responsible government. Hamilton was now, he said, protesting that he had not been advised by his Council that registration was necessary. Yet when the Assembly had tried to rectify this omission by providing in the supply vote for registration in the new district and for waiving revision in the other districts, these provisions had been expunged by the Council. A special bill then prepared for the same purpose had been tabled by the Council for six months.[60] Little's resolutions, as passed on November 25, formed a lengthy indictment of the Governor and the Council. They charged that there had been a wilful failure to arrange for registration and a deliberate delay of a month in passing the Representation Bill. They declared that May, when supplies were being advanced, was an unsuitable month for the election because the fishing population was then peculiarly subject to mercantile influence, and that an election held between March 1 and November 1 would disfranchise much of this population. They announced the rejection of the Supply Bill and the postponement of the Reciprocity Bill. As for the Governor, it was resolved that he must be removed because he had demonstrated that his sympathy with the "obstruction party" was paramount.[61]

It seems likely that neither the Liberals nor the Governor were free from sectarian motives in their respective insistence on haste and delay. However, Hamilton's lengthy explanation, accompanied by a protest against an immediate election from nine prospective Protestant candidates, seems to have convinced the Colonial Office that the Assembly, in this instance, were the unreasonable party.[62] While Grey found their disappointment understandable, he assured the Governor that his reasons seemed quite satisfactory.[63]

Before Grey's despatch arrived, the session had come to an end in an abrupt and unprecedented manner. The Assembly had passed an address informing him that Little was again proceeding to England as a delegate.[64] Then, when the Governor gave notice of his intention to prorogue the Legislature, the Assembly, in a demonstration of independence, adjourned until January 10. In obvious retaliation, the Governor signed the only four bills passed and dissolved the House. This dissolution, he pointed out to Grey, automatically deprived Little of his status as a member.[65] A few days later he wrote that Hoyles was leaving to place the Governor's case before the Colonial Office and that, in order to be in a strong position, that gentleman had temporarily resumed the position of Solicitor-General which he had relinquished during his fight against responsible government.[66] Neither of the delegates seems to have received a cordial reception from Grey, who deemed their missions unnecessary.[67] He refused, impartially, to hear oral statements from either and referred them and the Governor to the decision he had already made in the dispute.[68]

While the Colonial Secretary was prepared to exonerate Hamilton from the charge of partisanship in delaying the election, he considered it necessary to stay his hand in the selection of members for the Legislative Council. The Executive Council would, of course, be chosen after the election from the majority party in the Assembly and the new Legislative Council appointed by warrant. Since the councils in the other North American colonies had been separated when responsible government came into effect, they offered no precedent for the construction of an entire upper house with which to initiate the new system.[69] When the Governor submitted a slate of recommendations for the Legislative Council in December 1854, there was some conjecture as to his motive. Was he trying to forestall the advice of his ministers and to pack this Council with persons hostile to the party likely to dominate the Assembly? Sydney Herbert, very briefly Secretary of State during February 1855, suggested that this was the Governor's intention and that to accept his nominations would be to invite the failure of responsible government.[70] The Governor's selections were four merchants—of whom two were Roman Catholic, one Wesleyan, and the other Anglican—an Anglican barrister, and four merchants of the old Council.[71] It is unlikely that these gentlemen were in much sympathy with the Liberal party. One member of the Colonial Office, acquainted with Hamilton, believed that Herbert's suspicions were unwarranted and that most of the Governor's nominees held liberal views.[72] However, only one of Hamilton's selections was to figure in the Executive Council in the first eight years of responsible government. When Grey resumed the seals of office in March, he declined to give instructions for the separation of the councils until the political complexion of the Executive Council was known.[73]

It was by now apparent that if the experiment were to succeed it must not be conducted by Governor Hamilton. The Governor himself did not admit that his usefulness had been impaired. On the contrary, he wrote that whether the majority in the new House was Liberal or not, his record of firmness and determination would very probably procure respect for his office in the future.[74] In Herbert's opinion, however, it was scarcely just to the colony to entrust the experiment to these "prejudiced and adverse hands."[75] To remove the Governor might appear a concession to party feeling, but fortunately for the Colonial Office the Government of Antigua had fallen vacant. This had been offered to and accepted by Lieutenant-Governor Charles Darling of the Cape of Good Hope, but when it was suggested to Darling that he might take Newfoundland instead, he agreed. Accordingly, Grey informed Hamilton in March 1855 of his transfer to Antigua.[76] This decision anticipated by four days an adjournment debate in the House of Commons in which Radicals and Repealers, armed with material supplied by delegates and petitioners, accused the Palmerston Government of a want of good faith with Newfoundland and made out a strong case for the removal of Hamilton.[77] Grey's despatch, less blunt, and apparently designed to soothe the Governor's feelings, did not conceal the Minister's view that Hamilton had failed in his brief administration:

> ... I regret to find that serious differences still exist between the contending parties in which you have been unavoidably implicated and although I have considered myself fully authorized to uphold the course which you had pursued in adjourning the period of the Elections, it is impossible for me not to feel the difficulty of the position in which you would be placed if you had to meet the Assembly when thus reconstituted. The transition from the old form of Government to "responsible" Government can scarcely fail to be attended with much political as well as personal controversy, and in your case the ordinary difficulties would be aggravated by the hostile position in which you have been placed towards a large section if not the majority of the late Assembly, in opposing what you have considered their unreasonable demands. Whatever the precise results of the coming election may be, there can be unfortunately but little doubt that it will leave Newfoundland, as before, divided between two strong parties. Conciliation or compromise between these parties is the best object towards which a Governor can direct his efforts whatever the prospect may be of soon attaining it: and with the best intentions on your part (in which I am sure you would not fail) it would be extremely difficult for you now to succeed in such endeavours.
> ... Lieutenant-Governor Darling, on the other hand, will have the advantage of meeting the new Assembly, and commencing the responsible system without any former connexion with the Politics of the Island.[78]

For the fourth time since the establishment of representative government in the colony an inadequate governor had been caught and defeated by the political strife. It would be difficult to dispute the judgment of Prowse, for whom Hamilton—pious, shy, inarticulate, and unconciliatory—was "as unfit a man as the British Government could possibly have selected to fill a difficult position."[79] In the struggle of the Protestants to forestall government by the Catholics, Hamilton had played a role like that of Boulton in the battle of the merchants and officials to prevent the ascendancy of the House.

CHAPTER TEN

GOVERNMENT BY PARTY, 1855-1860

WHEN the Assembly met on May 22, 1855, following the general election of that month, the Liberals designated themselves the proper party to form the Administration. They were able to command for their resolution sixteen votes, exclusive of those of the Speaker and one absent adherent, demonstrating thus that they had doubled their membership in the House.[1] There had been few contests for the thirty seats, nomination being equivalent to election in most districts.[2] In St. John's a slate of six Liberals had been returned unopposed.[3] In the key district of Burin, Wesleyans had disappointed the expectations of the Protestant party by joining forces with the Roman Catholics to return two Catholic Liberals.[4] Elsewhere, the sectarian pattern of voting had persisted. (Appendix B, Table VII).

Although there could be no doubt that the Administration must be Liberal, there were two difficulties to be overcome. Fortunately for the colony, Governor Darling was not the man to allow these to generate a bitter and protracted dispute. When he arrived in Newfoundland on May 3 to establish responsible government, he had behind him the strength of twenty-eight years in colonial government (see Appendix A). E. M. Archibald, the retiring Attorney-General, was much impressed with Darling's suitability for his task, and described him as frank, manly, firm, tactful, and sensible—a man who would give the new Ministry all legitimate scope, but who would have a mind of his own. The Speech from the Throne, delivered, Archibald said, in stentorian voice and in the style of that arch-conciliator Sir John Harvey,[5] announced the inauguration of responsible government and congratulated the colony on its achievement. It announced, too, that the system would be established at once, despite the fact that the Instructions authorizing the two councils had not yet arrived from the Colonial Office.[6] Having learned before the House met that the Governor had not been provided with the requisite Instructions, the Liberals had been threatening obstruction and retaliation if he dared to meet the new House with the old Council. His predecessor, Hamilton, would undoubtedly have met this challenge with unconciliatory determination, but Darling, with the Crown officials, the latter now weary of warfare and waiting to leave the colony, devised instead a means of allowing the Liberals to take office. The Attorney-General, the Colonial Secretary, and the Surveyor-General tendered resignations which were to be accepted after a resolution had formally tested Liberal preponderance in the House. This resolution, however, posed for Darling another problem. In a direct encroachment on his prerogative, stemming from arrogance or ignorance, the Assembly informed him that Little was to lead and name the Administration. Darling, unwilling that the new system should begin with the establishment of such a precedent, was not at first prepared to overlook this breach of propriety or to seem to submit to unconstitutional dictation, but he was dissuaded by Kent from sending a message of reprimand.[7] However, in calling upon Little to form the Government Darling gave notice that he did so despite the irregularity committed. Provisional appointments were then made to both councils so that the Revenue Act, which the Liberals had threatened to refuse, might be renewed.[8] For his combination of firmness and flexibility in overcoming these initial difficulties, the Governor was commended by the Colonial Office.[9]

The first Liberal Cabinet contained six members, of whom four were Roman Catholic, while the Legislative Council was constructed on the principle that a working majority should be undoubted supporters of the Government.[10] The membership of, and the method of forming, the second chamber were sources of grievance to the Opposition. The *Times,* which had earlier (March 28) declared itself resigned to responsible government, now (June 16) deplored the blending of talent and mercantile experience with what it called "consummate ignorance." H. W. Hoyles contended in a series of unsuccessful resolutions that the Governor's course in choosing first the members of the Government and heeding, then, their advice in forming the Legislative Council was unconstitutional and contrary to his Instructions. He urged the Assembly to refuse to legislate with an illegally formed upper house. He was, of course, voted down by the Liberals.[11]

When the early irritations and obstructions had been overcome the Assembly embarked on an ambitious programme of legislation. During the first session under responsible government, with sympathy and guidance from the Governor and co-operation from the Legislative Council, the energy and talent of the Administration found expression in many useful and overdue measures of reform. In the session of 1855, which lasted just over two months, twenty-one significant bills were enacted, including measures for the consolidation of offices, for the establishment of boards of Revenue and Works, and for the immediate and prospective reduction of official and judicial salaries.[12] A bill (18 and 19 Vict., c. 9 (Nfld.)) was passed reducing the salary of future governors to £2,000, and, though he thought the sum scarcely adequate, Darling, to avoid a quarrel with his advisers, gave his assent.[13] Another bill (c. 2), delayed by the legislative stoppages of 1854, gave effect to the Reciprocity Treaty with the United States. Under this agreement, American fishermen, though still supported by bounties, were to be admitted to inshore fishing rights along the whole coast, while fish and fish products of all kinds, and a number of other items, were to be imported on a reciprocal duty-free basis.[14] To compensate for the deficiency of revenue which would arise from these exemptions, the Assembly passed a bill (c. 3) raising the *ad valorem* duties on a range of imported foodstuffs and manufactures. In following years, the Government, anxious for the maintenance of the revenue, resisted the appeals from the Home Government that Newfoundland should conform to free trade principles and abolish discriminatory duties on foreign imports, when similar goods were admitted duty-free from the United States and from British North America.[15] The year 1856 under the Reciprocity Treaty was one of rising prosperity, with exports and imports the highest in history and with the augmented tariff giving a high revenue.[16] Five good years were to follow (see Appendix F).[17] There were, from time to time, rumours that the beneficial effects of the reciprocal agreement, supplemented by the efforts of the American promoters of the cable connection with the United States, might induce the Liberals to complete the island's "liberation" from colonial status by attaching it to the United States.[18] In Darling's opinion, the loyalty of the general populace to Great Britain and mercantile reluctance to admit competition with their importing monopoly were sufficient to counteract the little annexationist sentiment he could detect.[19]

The harmony and productivity of the first session under the Liberal Government seems to have alarmed the unreconciled mercantile journal, the *Ledger*. The inclusion of several Protestant merchants in the Government did not prevent the editor from renewing his warnings about the establishment of a permanent Roman Catholic despotism. Commenting on the Government, the allocation of offices, and the events of the session, he suggested that Protestant support for the Catholic Liberals was a dangerous and dishonourable defection:

... the Roman Catholic clergy are upheld in their endeavours after the political ascendancy by a few nominal Protestants; but these are to be found among the needy, poverty-stricken "any-thingarians" who would support Atheism as soon as Romanism if thereby their purses felt the heavier. It is true, also, that there are a few unfortunate Wesleyans among their upholders, who have joined them for the sake of that paltry honour which is purchased with the sacrifice of an upright principle; or from ignorance of that bitter and insidious spirit which they maintain; or from that greed of gain, which is a far more culpable motive.[20]

Liberal satisfaction with the session and with the Governor was reflected in the August 6 *Newfoundlander's* unstinted praise for his closing speech, which it contrasted with the "miserable evasions" of the past.

The session of 1856 saw the passage of several laws which the Governor hoped would be beneficial to class and commercial relations in the island.[21] Two questions which had vexed the Assembly since the days of Chief Justice Boulton were set at rest. The Jury Act (19 Vict., c. 13) dispensed with the old qualification that grand jurors must be "gentlemen and principal merchants" and laid down property qualifications for grand and petty jurors. The Insolvency Act (c. 14) gave servants a prior claim to fish and oil for the recovery of their wages and provided that every creditor for fishery supplies was a privileged creditor. Other commercial Acts were those providing for limited partnerships (c. 15) and for the compromise or composition of joint debts (c. 16). On one point the Legislature remained adamant. Despite the Governor's advice, the majority would not accept the necessity for direct taxation. This refusal not only made local management of St. John's impossible, but closed off what seemed to the Governor an appropriate means of reducing the public debt which had climbed from £106,701 in 1850 to £167,257 in 1856.[22]

The unwonted political tranquillity in Newfoundland came to an end in 1857 with the receipt of the Fishery Convention signed by Britain and France.[23] Since 1844 negotiations, with intermissions, had been taking place between the two powers for the settlement of the French claim to exclusive, and the British claim to concurrent, fishing rights on the Treaty shore, as well as for the admission of the French to northern fishing grounds, and for the regulation of the traffic in bait on the southern coast. Although concessions had been offered by both sides, previous proposals had foundered on the French demand for extensive fishing privileges elsewhere to offset their admission of the British to concurrent rights on part of the disputed shore.[24] Stimulated by increased bounties, the French fishery had expanded after 1851 at a rate which alarmed the fishing interests of Newfoundland. In 1852 the colony had added another to the many protests on the fishery grievances despatched to the Imperial Government since 1832. It had complained of unfair French competition through bounties, invasion of traditional European markets, mass-hauling methods, and trespass on the fishing grounds of Labrador, Belle Isle, and elsewhere. It had also asked for increased naval protection to safeguard the colony's fishing rights and to prevent the illegal traffic in bait with its consequent losses to the colonial revenue. The Imperial Government had indicated unwillingness to bear any cost but that of the annual naval supervision. In 1856 the Assembly had reiterated these complaints.[25] In July of that year, with Anglo-French negotiations about to be renewed, Governor Darling, on the basis of a year's study of the question, had submitted his considered opinion on the nature of French rights. His view, in opposition to that held by the Commercial Society and enunciated by his predecessor,[26] was that concurrent rights could not and did not exist—that there was no room for the fishermen of both nations to fish and dry on the same shore without interfering with one another, and that the French had always had, therefore, in practice, an exclusive right as complete as if it had been confirmed to them in express terms. But Darling declared himself in very decided opposition to further concessions.[27] His report, after despatch to London, had been submitted to and unanimously approved by his Ministers.[28] Negotiations were begun in July 1856 and were terminated in London in January 1857 when the two powers signed the Convention.

The Convention stipulated an exclusive right for the French to fish in the season and to use the strand for fishery purposes from Cape St. John on the east to Cape Norman on the north, and in and upon five major harbours on the west coast. In exchange for this limitation in extent of the French exclusive rights, the British were to enjoy on the western shore an unquestioned right of concurrent fishery with the French, save that the French were now to have exclusive use of the strand for fishery purposes from Cape Norman south to a point in the Bay of Islands, as well as at the five points mentioned. The French were to enjoy what they had long sought, concurrent rights on the Labrador coast and North Belle Isle, with liberty to dry and cure on the unsettled coasts of the latter. No buildings were to be erected by British subjects on the French strand and those standing were to be removed through negotiation and compensation. The French were to be permitted to purchase bait on the south coast and, under certain circumstances, to catch it there.[29] Thus they were confirmed in their claim to exclusive rights on the northern and eastern Treaty shore, as well as on shrewdly selected fishing grounds on the western shore. They were also to be admitted to new grounds in the north and were to be assured a sufficient supply of bait.

In view of concessions so extensive in exchange for so little real equivalent, it is little wonder that opinion was unanimous in St. John's that the mother country proposed to victimize her colony in the interests of a settlement with her ally of the Crimean War. In the great surge of excitement which greeted the terms of the Convention, there was, reported the Governor, not one "dissentient voice." American flags were hoisted in St. John's and the British ensign was flown "Union down" over the Colonial Building and mercantile houses in St. John's.[30] The Convention had been submitted to Newfoundland with a despatch in which the Colonial Secretary, Henry Labouchere, stressed the Imperial Government's very strong desire to effect the settlement. He pointed out that should the lengthy negotiations prove fruitless, the compromising spirit shown by France might be replaced by a more strenuous and inconvenient insistence on exclusive rights on the Treaty shore. The despatch suggests strong apprehension about the course the Legislature might pursue and a paragraph deleted from the final draft contained a thinly veiled threat of over-riding Imperial action.[31] On February 6 the Governor sent the Convention for ratification to the waiting Council and Assembly where it had a stormy reception. The Assembly immediately passed a resolution and address to the Governor expressing their "extreme" regret and surprise at the concessions made and their "unanimous and unalterable determination never to give their assent to a measure so unjust."[32] Adopting the report of a select committee, they resolved unanimously to condemn the Convention, to ask for the support of the other North American colonies, to despatch addresses to the Colonial Secretary and to both Houses of Parliament, and to appoint delegates to London. A similar course was followed by the Legislative Council.[33] The latter adopted a report denouncing the Convention in its entirety and declaring: "We should be either more or less than men if bitterness were not added to our disappointment, when we find that the Parent which would not stretch out her hand to help will do so to despoil her own household; and would fain take her children's bread to give it unto strangers."[34] The Assembly in former days might have expressed their displeasure by the stoppage of supplies for the public service, but under responsible government this form of obstruction did not, of course, suggest itself. After passing the money bills and several others, the Legislature asked for prorogation on March 17 so that delegates of both parties might proceed to England.[35] The delegates were P. F. Little and H. W. Hoyles from the Assembly and Lawrence O'Brien and James Tobin from the Legislative Council, As no member of either party concurred with his views, the Governor was, under responsible government, absolutely helpless.[36] Such was the unanimity of opinion, however, that no form of representative government, he reported, could have secured the requested enactment. In reporting to the Colonial Office the rejection of the Convention, he gave full weight to the unanimity of opinion and to the right of the colony to resist any alienation of its maritime and territorial privileges. His purpose was to forestall the effort to raise a sympathetic agitation in the other colonies and to strengthen the Imperial Government's position in announcing to France the failure of ratification.[37]

The Legislature's veto not only quashed the Fishery Convention, but drew from the Colonial Secretary a despatch of recession which was long to be celebrated in Newfoundland as a sort of colonial Magna Carta. Labouchere's despatch, circulated also to the other North American colonies, said:

When Her Majesty's Government entered into the Convention with that of France, ... they did so in the hope of bringing to a satisfactory arrangement the many complicated and difficult questions which have arisen between the two countries on the ... Newfoundland Fisheries. But they did so with the full intention of adhering to two principles which have guided them; namely that the rights at present enjoyed by the community of Newfoundland are not to be ceded or exchanged without their assent and that the constitutional mode of submitting measures for that assent is by laying them before the Colonial legislature. For this reason, they pursued the same form of proceeding which had been before pursued in the case of the Reciprocity Convention with the United States and which was in that case adopted and acted upon by the Newfoundland Legislature. It was in perfect uniformity with the same precedent that it appeared necessary in the present instance to add a condition respecting Parliamentary Enactment, in order that, if necessary, any existing obstacles to the arrangement in the series of Imperial Statutes might be subsequently removed.

The proposals contained in the Convention having been unequivocally refused by the Colony, they will of course fall to the ground. And you are authorized to give such assurance as you may think proper that the consent of the community of Newfoundland is regarded by Her Majesty's Government as the essential preliminary to any modification of their territorial or maritime rights.[38]

This despatch, when published in St. John's, was greeted, according to Governor Darling, with "perfect satisfaction."[39] The Assembly's address of thanks construed the Labouchere despatch as a guarantee forced from the Imperial Government that, in the fishery question, the colony would be completely independent of Crown and Parliament, irrespective of Great Britain's treaty obligations with other powers.[40] It should be noted, however, that the despatch, though hailed and afterwards adverted to as a great triumph over the mother country, did not say that the Imperial Government was bound to share the colony's view of what constituted its "territorial or maritime rights" or a modification of these, or guarantee to lay interpretations of the treaties before its Legislature.

Shortly after receipt of the despatch Governor Darling left the colony for Jamaica, to which Government he had been appointed in February 1857. His early popularity had been much dispelled by his alleged betrayal of Newfoundland's fishing rights. One rumour had it that he had been bribed by the French while on a visit to St. Pierre and another that he had been appointed to supersede Hamilton because the latter's views on the fishery question were inconvenient to the Home Government. One member of the Assembly described Darling as a "mere agent of the Imperial Government, bound to conceal any designs that Government had in view, however injurious to the Colony," while another called him a traitor.[41]

The unanimity with which the colony faced Great Britain and France was not duplicated in the political arena where the Opposition seized the opportunity of branding the ministers with charges of treachery and betrayal.[42] When it was known early in the session of 1857, before the Convention arrived, that additional fishing privileges were to be granted, the Opposition denounced the Ministry on the grounds that they had not acted with sufficient vigour in respect to an address originated in 1856 by the former and that in concealing what must be known to them, the nature of the Anglo-French negotiations, they were failing in their duty to the inhabitants. While the Opposition seemed to grant that the Governor might have the right to be silent until the moment for formal disclosure, they contended that the Ministry had not. The Ministry found themselves threatened with a defection of their own supporters which would have placed them in a minority had there been a motion of want of confidence on the question. When the Convention and the relevant correspondence were tabled, party tactics changed. The Ministry pointed in self-defence to Darling's despatch opposing further concessions and the Opposition took up the long-established mercantile position that concurrent rights did exist, which position they declared Darling had abandoned with ministerial advice or sanction. Party division was reflected in the selection of the delegates for London. Although all were chosen to urge that the Convention be set aside, they represented, according to the Governor, two distinct points of view, Tobin of the Legislative Council, Hoyles of the Assembly, and Bryan Robinson of the Commercial Society standing for the mercantile, extreme "Newfoundland rights" group, and Little and O'Brien of the Government for the less adamant elements.[43]

With the Opposition disposed to make capital out of the alleged ministerial betrayal, two avenues were open to the Liberal party: either they could justify their stand to the colony and to their dissatisfied members and adherents and seek another Convention more favourable to the island, or they could allow themselves to be driven, in self-defence and love of office, to the unconciliatory stand of their opponents. Anxious not to leave the fishery question in its vexatious unsettled state, the French Government pressed the British Foreign Office to ascertain to what terms the colony would agree. In December 1857 Labouchere asked the new Governor, Sir Alexander Bannerman, to suggest any terms which he and his advisers thought might form the basis of a satisfactory agreement.[44] Sir Alexander, a substantial shipowner and merchant of Aberdeen with interests in seal and whale fisheries,[45] had had some acquaintance with Newfoundland and came to the colony with the idea that he might be able to find a solution to the fishery question.[46] Apart from his interest in the trade and his experience in governing Prince Edward Island, Sir Alexander had a further qualification for his duties in Newfoundland which might offset some of his seventy-four years. He was a veteran politician who had represented Aberdeen for sixteen years in the Liberal interest (see Appendix A). He found his Liberal Ministry in the colony mute with caution on the fishery question and unwilling to offer any proposition whatever for the reopening of negotiations.[47] Upon the attitude taken by these colonial politicians, the new Governor made this scathing comment:

... the Governors [*sic*] *Constitutional Advisers* have refused to offer any suggestions .... The truth is, they are frightened out of their wits, that they might lose their places by their opponents pouncing on their proceedings of last year and their *daring* the British Government to interfere in their local affairs at any future time. They carry this doctrine to a great extent to serve party purposes, as they well know the paramount powers of the Imperial Parliament. All former Governors have been asked for their opinions on the fishery question, and the best way in my opinion to deal with *my advisers* is to ask me, now that I have obtained all the information I can acquire, whether I can offer any suggestions to form the basis of a new Convention with France, as the question cannot be allowed to remain unsettled. I should be *desired* to submit such suggestions to the Council for any remarks or *suggestions of theirs* for the consideration of Her Majesty's Government and perhaps that of Parliament.[48]

In April 1858 he offered to express his views to the Colonial Office, provided he received an official instruction which could be shown to his Council.[49] He was asked instead to make a confidential statement.[50] This course Bannerman repeatedly refused to adopt, on the grounds that excitement would be aroused if, as was probable, he were forced to disclose that he was engaged in private correspondence on the fishery question.[51]

Exasperated with what he considered the Governor's evasion of his "imperative duty" and the "improper exercise of his discretion," E. B. Lytton, Colonial Secretary of State in the Derby Ministry, believed that it might be necessary to order his recall.[52] The Governor was unquestionably in an awkward situation, with his superiors at home pressing him for confidential opinions which he felt it injudicious to give, his ministers too fearful for their popularity to give advice about terms, and the inhabitants elated by success and apparently not averse to a quarrel with France. In this impasse, Sir Alexander did not conceal his belief that both the Palmerston and Derby governments were at fault, the one in giving and the other in maintaining the impression that the colony having spoken, the question of the treaties had ceased to be one which the Imperial Parliament might settle.[53] Lytton had felt it sufficient to say that the new Government concurred in the "language" of the Labouchere despatch.[54]

What Labouchere had forecast, a more stringent attitude on the part of the French about the concurrent fishery claim and the presence of British settlers on the Treaty shore, was confirmed by evidence which arrived in St. John's in the summer of 1858. The Commander-in-Chief of the French naval force informed the Governor that the forbearance of France had come to an end and that he would enforce the French interpretation of the treaties. French naval officers were reported to be ordering residents and fishermen to leave. These events led Bannerman to propose, in September, a mixed commission of enquiry to investigate rival claims and to formulate regulations for the control of the fishery. Faced with these reports of encroachment and with those presented by Bishop Mullock about privation and the need for winter relief at St. George's Bay, the Council now resolved that the colonists ought to have the opportunity to show what their rights were and to insist that these be respected.[55] British discussions with the French Government showed them willing to resume negotiations, if they could be assured that the conclusions reached would not again be frustrated by the action of the colony. The British Government felt unable to give such an assurance or to promise coercion, but, encouraged by evident alarm in the colony about the notices served, undertook to persuade the French that the prospects for conclusive negotiations were favourable.[56]

In January 1859 Governor Bannerman was informed that a joint Anglo-French commission would go to Newfoundland to investigate the operation of the treaties and to suggest, if possible, a permanent settlement. The Governor was asked to appoint one of the two British delegates by selecting, with the advice of his Executive Council, a competent and conciliatory person who should be paid expenses and who should proceed to England at once for instructions. If the Council refused to co-operate, the Governor was himself to make the selection. The Council agreed that it was expedient to make the appointment, but insisted upon consulting first both branches of the Legislature. After considering the proposal, the Assembly adopted a series of resolutions setting out the conditions of participation in the Commission and the colony's interpretation of the treaties: the Commission should be limited strictly to an enquiry into the facts of infringement and the colony was to retain intact its right to deal independently with any proposal contemplating a change in maritime or territorial rights. When, after these proceedings, the Council appointed as commissioner, Kent, now leader of the Government, with instructions based on the Assembly's resolutions, the Governor entered a protest about sending the commissioner fettered to the enquiry. The Assembly adopted a further resolution saying

That the British Coastal Fisheries within the jurisdiction of the Colonial Government, although common and free to all British subjects, are yet, in a peculiar manner, the undoubted property of the people of Newfoundland; and while they are subject to the Sovereignty of Her Gracious Majety and Her legal prerogatives, they cannot be alienated or shared with any Foreign Power without the consent of the Local Legislature.[57]

Believing that Kent's usefulness as Commissioner had been impaired, Bannerman furnished him with an open letter to the Secretary of State expressing the Governor's confidence that should Kent find that the instructions given him in London compromised his character as a colonist and a member of the Government, he would resign an appointment he could not conscientiously fulfil.[58] The Governor apparently believed that if Kent chose to remain on the Commission and to sign the Report, this letter in the hands of the Colonial Secretary would be evidence of Kent's tacit consent to the instructions of the Imperial Government. Political and financial considerations seem to have induced Kent not to surrender this document, for when the Governor enquired, the Colonial Office could find no record of its receipt.[59]

Kent was officially dropped from the Commission in the spring of 1860 after serving from March to September 1859 without making, according to his naval colleague, any contribution whatever, apart from signing the Report.[60] The Governor informed the Assembly bluntly that the colony had treated the Commission as a "mere political juggle."[61] Rumour that the Convention had been completed in June 1860 was followed by pressure on the Governor to disclose its terms and reiterated emphasis on the right of veto from the press, the Executive Council, and the Assembly.[62] The terms of the Convention gave rise to considerable anxiety in the Colonial Office. These provided for a mixed commission for the settlement of fishery disputes, the punishment of offenders, and the removal of obstructing buildings on the French shore. They sanctioned certain existing usages of French fishermen and conceded their right to buy bait.[63] The question raised was whether the colony would accept the provisions as machinery designed to secure the rights of both parties to the treaties or condemn them as infringements of maritime and territorial rights.[64] In the end, however, the Convention was not submitted to the test, being nullified by the Anglo-French failure to reach agreement on the instructions to the permanent joint commissioners.[65] Had it been completed, one may suspect that, however it had been submitted, it would have produced popular and political excitement, if not a crisis for the Liberal Government.

The halcyon period of the Liberal Government was brief. The first clouds appeared in 1858 when the census of 1857 revealed that since 1845 the Protestants had increased in numerical strength by 29 per cent, compared with a 17 per cent increase by the Catholics. Roman Catholics were now 45.9 per cent of the total population, compared with 48.6 per cent in 1845. Wesleyan strength had also increased significantly, Dissenters, of whom Wesleyans formed the bulk, now comprising 17 per cent of the total population and one-third of the Protestant community (Appendix E, Tables II-IV). The Wesleyan increase was reflected in an increasing solidarity in this group, which became in 1855 part of the Methodist Conference of Eastern British America,[66] and which secured in 1858 an Act of Incorporation and an allocation for the maintenance of a Wesleyan Academy in St. John's.[67] These changes in the religious balance of the population, together with the increase of the middle class and the growth of the proportion of the native-born, were outmoding the old political dichotomy of semi-resident Protestant merchants and liberal-led immigrant Irish. Consciousness and statistical evidence of growing strength could scarcely fail to make the Protestant community in general restive under a Catholic-directed regime and to stimulate the political ambitions of Wesleyans and of independent natives, Catholic and Protestant. Conversely, the decline in Catholic strength and the danger of new affiliations increased the desire of that party to consolidate their position by holding their Protestant supporters and by discouraging the breaking away of independent Catholic candidates and voters. This involved, on the one hand, the denial of Church influence, and, on the other, its use, and the branding of all opposing elements as non-liberal by identifying them with the political ogres of the past. During the fishery controversy the quest for invulnerability had bred a caution which exasperated Bannerman, but it does not seem to have impelled the Liberals to a corresponding caution in reaping and bestowing the fruits of office. When Bannerman arrived in St. John's, he found, he was later to report, that he was surrounded by councillors as arrogant as they appeared to be ignorant about responsible government. Construing it as a "system of Government which would enable them, once in power, to aggrandize themselves," they must eventually, he said, make it a "curse instead of a blessing to the people."[68]

With the retirement of Little to the Bench of the Supreme Court after the session of 1858 and his replacement by Kent as leader of the Government and by G. J. Hogsett as Attorney-General, the Liberals entered upon a period of unease and conflict with the Governor, in which anxiety was coupled with arrogance, and corrupt practice with constitutional dogma. The storm over the Fishery Convention was followed in 1858 by the defection of the Catholic merchant and legislative councillor, James Tobin, who held the political appointment of Financial Secretary. Tobin, after private advice to the opposite effect to successive governors, had propounded in the Legislative Council the doctrine of concurrent fishing rights in its most extreme form, allying himself thereby with the Opposition.[69] His motives seem to have been, at least in part, opportunistic. Having served for five years as stipendiary magistrate at St. George's Bay, he could claim an exceptional familiarity with conditions on the west coast, and his office having been, to his discomfiture, cancelled by the Legislature in 1855, he was understood to be anxious to be appointed Permanent Fishery Commissioner, should the British Government create such a post.[70] The Liberal press in St. John's charged that Tobin was the source of certain offensive paragraphs supplied from Paris to the London *Globe*. These announced that the Liberal party and Bishop Mullock had fallen foul of the inhabitants through their false interpretation of the treaties and that a collision "between the bark Peter and the cod smacks" was impending.[71] Tobin, after vain efforts to obtain editorial retraction and apology, protested to the Bishop that he was denied legal redress. He implied that Dr. Mullock's authority protected the editor of the *Newfoundlander* (E. D. Shea, brother of the Speaker, Ambrose Shea), and that it was useless to expect justice from the Supreme Court when two members of the Bench and the jury would be Roman Catholic. This allegation, and Tobin's remarks about the power wielded by the Bishop through his influence over five of the seven executive councillors, evoked much indignation in the Liberal party. A public meeting was convened and attended by Catholic leaders and inhabitants, and resolutions were passed condemning Tobin's conduct.[72] Tobin's charges and his effort to discredit the Government suggest Protestant encouragement. However, the *Ledger* declared on December 4, 1858, that the Liberals, by giving much publicity to the quarrel, were seeking to convert embarrassment into advantage by involving Tobin with his Bishop and coupling political with religious loyalty.

The ministers requisitioned the Governor unanimously for Tobin's suspension from the office of Financial Secretary and from the Legislative Council. This demand, and Kent's "dictatorial tone," the Governor resisted on the grounds that the question was a constitutional one affecting the relative position in which the Governor was placed with his advisers and that he would not be induced to comply by considerations of political expediency. Kent thereupon tendered his resignation. This the Governor did not accept, having decided to suspend Tobin in repudiation of his doctrine that the Bishop's authority could and did influence the Supreme Court. While he had no doubt that the man would attribute the suspension to the pressure of the councillors, Bannerman informed Lytton emphatically that he had not attended to their advice and that he never did so when he considered it erroneous. Members of the Colonial Office were in some doubt about the constitutional correctness of the Governor's action and the sufficiency of the grounds given for Tobin's suspension. It was recognized, however, that if the Governor were not supported by the Secretary of State he might be faced with the resignation of his Council and the problem of finding successors able to command the confidence of the House. It was also felt that it would be inconsistent as well as impolitic to interfere with such removals in responsibly governed colonies. Further, in view of the fishery dispute, it was desirable that the Colonial Office be popular with the Legislature and the people of Newfoundland.[73] Since Tobin's political office was not a Crown creation or appointment, the Governor was left to confirm that suspension, but he was advised that Tobin's offence did not warrant his removal by the Queen from the Legislative Council.[74]

The obdurate attitude of the Government in 1859 may be seen in an attempt to secure assent to an act for direct taxation whose principle the Colonial Office had condemned earlier in the year. An act of 1858 providing for a property assessment in St. John's for the liquidation of the public debt and for other purposes had been disallowed on the grounds that it was "oppressive class legislation against unrepresented persons" who required the Queen's protection.[75] A similar act was passed in 1859 providing for a tax upon owners for the construction of water works. This was also disallowed, since it too was clearly framed to thrust the burden of direct taxation upon absentee landlords and to exempt specifically the consumers of dutiable goods, that is, the residents who were to benefit from the tax.[76]

The legal term of the sixth Assembly came to an end in 1859 and a general election was set for November. In announcing this, the Governor gave tacit recognition of and encouragement to changing sentiments in the electorate by expressing his confidence that the election would be conducted "in that quiet and constitutional manner which should always prevail where the blessings of Civil and Religious liberty exist."[77] Unsuccessful efforts to throw off the Government yoke were made in Harbour Grace and Burin. In the former, since 1856 a separate Catholic diocese, violence and intimidation led to the retirement of the independent Catholic candidate, who had been repudiated from the altar, and to the return of his opponent, Prendergast, who had been backed by Bishop Dalton and his clergy.[78] In the latter, the Liberals, with one Roman Catholic and one Wesleyan candidate, defeated two Protestants, one of them Hoyles, leader of the Opposition, through intimidation and the expenditure of some £2,000 raised by levy in the party.[79] The party standings in the House remained unchanged (see Appendix B, Table VIII).

There were repercussions from the election struggle at Harbour Grace. For reasons of their own, the ministers chose to withhold from the Governor for ten days the information they had about the cause and extent of the disorders. This failure of duty, deliberate in the Governor's opinion, seemed to him ample justification for their dismissal, but since the Liberal party had just achieved a majority, that course seemed neither prudent nor safe. However, the attitude of his Council spurred him to vigorous action. He appointed three investigators —T. Bennett, a magistrate, and C. Simms, a barrister, who were not members of the Government, and G. J. Hogsett, the Attorney-General. These examined forty witnesses and submitted reports, the Attorney-General's being at complete variance with the other two. The latter cited numerous acts of intimidation and injury to the persons and property of the electors, the defeated candidate, and his friends. They reported the forcible entry of four polling booths, the seizure of poll books and registers, the routing of the police, and, finally, the dispersal of the mob through the efforts of the Roman Catholic clergy. According to these reports, several of the witnesses failed to appear because of intimidation and one of the injured dared not come to Harbour Grace to give his evidence. In no case had there been legal proceedings because there was insufficient guarantee of protection to property. There appeared to be widespread fear of continuing intimidation and disorder and the investigators advised the despatch of a small permanent military force. The Attorney-General, on the contrary, declared that the disorders, though regrettable, occurred in most countries and ceased with the occasion, that life and property were otherwise secure in Harbour Grace, and that complaints to the contrary were the "groundless fears of a few timid individuals." He contended that the fault lay with the magistrates and that the trouble had stemmed from their failure to swear in temporary constables. He said that in a district in which the people were "proverbially peaceable, industrious, and loyal" what was needed was an enlarged constabulary rather than a detachment of troops. The three local magistrates, two of them leading Protestant merchants and legislative councillors, asked for troops, reporting that the district was, and had been for some years, insecure, that there were frequent outbreaks prejudicial to trade, and that the disorders were "fearfully" aggravated at election times. The councillors, like the Attorney-General, were disposed to minimize the disturbances and to dismiss contrary evidence as partisan. The Governor took the opposite view. After studying the reports, he declared that the outbreak had been very bad and "similar to what took place in the disturbed districts in Ireland in the worst times."[80]

There were repercussions, too, from the Liberal victory at Burin. On the recommendation of the Council after the election, the Governor appointed as stipendiary magistrate at Trinity Bay the man who had served as Returning Officer at Burin. This appointment drew protests from residents at Trinity Bay on the grounds that impartial justice could not be expected from a man who had shown violent political partisanship after taking the election oath at Burin and who had boasted of his bias from the Bench. After investigation the Governor declared himself bound to suspend the man, dismissing as "mere subterfuge" the Council's threat of resignation if the man were not given a chance to reply.[81] In adopting this course Sir Alexander was, in fact, ignoring one of his Instructions.[82] However, as events were to show, strict adherence to the letter of these was not one of the aging Governor's characteristics and, in the absence of an impartial legal adviser, he chose to act in such crises with the determination of good sense.

In the Colonial Office, despite the conviction that constitutional correctness must always be a paramount consideration, there was appreciation of the Governor's honesty, vigour, and single-mindedness in acting against the pressure of advisers whom he felt to be unscrupulous partisans.[83] After mature consideration with the Duke of Newcastle during the visit of the Prince of Wales to Newfoundland in 1860, the Governor decided to take upon himself the responsibility for the supersession of the magistrate.[84] Upon his return to the Colonial Office, Newcastle set down his conviction that the extremely low moral tone of the colony made it necessary to support the Governor in this matter. But he stressed that it must be understood that in future the Instructions were to be strictly observed.[85] Thus the Governor, as in the Tobin case, won his point and the Council chose not to resign.

In the light of subsequent events, Sir Alexander's comment on the elections of 1859 and on the attitude of his ministers is significant:

Great responsibility may attach to me situated as I am, with feeble, or rather, no support from where I ought to get it; but if I am obliged to resort to extreme measures I have no fear of results. The Elections have brought out feelings which were slumbering, of a fixed determination that a certain party should carry everything before them; I am not sorry for this, as I shall know on whom I can depend.[86]

Despite the Attorney-General's strictures about the need for an increased constabulary, neither he nor any member of the Council responded in 1860 to the Governor's pressure for such an increase. However, anticipating that the election of Prendergast must be declared null and void, Sir Alexander secured the reluctant consent of Newcastle for the stationing of a small body of troops near Harbour Grace. These were to aid the civil power at a second election if this were absolutely necessary to prevent the recurrence of rioting.[87] When the facts of intimidation were considered by the election committees of the Assembly, it was decided that the return of 1859 was invalid. Another election was set for November 1860. This time Prendergast and a Protestant opponent came forward. On the advice of the magistrates, Sir Alexander arranged to send a detachment of troops after nomination day and four days before the polls were to open. But his determination to prevent the exertion of mob influence at this election was well-known. Prendergast's friends set themselves on nomination day to force the withdrawal of the other candidate, succeeding in their intimidation, the Governor believed, through the "vacillating and pusillanimous" conduct of the magistrates.[88]

The Liberals' victory and a weakening in the revenue position in 1859 (see Appendix F) were reflected in their attitude towards expenditure in the session of 1860. Opposed to measures for maintaining civil peace and good order—a Police Act or an increased allocation for constables—the councillors were equally resistant to making any provision for the military defence of the colony. In response to requests from the Home Government that Newfoundland should establish a militia and contribute to the maintenance of the Imperial forces in the Island, the Governor, over the objections of his ministers, called these matters to the attention of the Legislature in 1860.[89] Despite his recommendation that some action be taken, the Council refused to express an opinion. A repetition of his views to the Legislature produced from both branches the meagre response that a militia was not practicable, but that they would consider anything consistent with the state of the revenue and the "imperative" claims for public improvement. Even this equivocal reply was opposed by the Ministers in the Assembly, the Attorney-General moving an amendment, narrowly defeated, that no portion of the revenue could be contributed to an Imperial force in the colony. This amendment he supported with a series of observations about Britain's resources and responsibilities and the advantage the mother country enjoyed in being able to keep part of her standing army in Newfoundland's invigorating climate.[90] The Governor, thwarted, established instead several companies of a Volunteer Rifle Corps, but he considered it useless to ask for legislation on this or any defence measure until he could counter a refusal by dissolving the Assembly.[91] The Assembly refused to meet another charge which the Home Government believed should justly be borne by a self-governing colony—the expense of the fog gun at the entrance to the Harbour of St. John's. This attitude in a colony notorious for its fogs and dependent upon sea-trade was viewed by the Colonial Office as irresponsible, disgraceful, and contemptible. Great Britain necessarily assumed the expense for the year but Newfoundland was warned that the charge must be met thereafter from the colony's revenue.[92]

The Liberals might flout the wishes of the Home Government and the Governor without losing electoral support, but they found at the close of the session that they could not administer a direct rebuff to Dr. Mullock without forfeiting the support and influence of that prelate. An act (23 Vict., c. 9) had been passed providing a grant for the establishment of steam communication with the outports. Unauthorized by the Government, the Bishop and Judge Little had in New York entered into a virtual contract for a vessel, which contract the Government refused to honour. This refusal, coupled with the rewards to political minions and the failure to curtail relief to the able-bodied poor (see Appendix F), gave the Bishop material for a denunciation of the Kent Administration which was as scathing as his famous manifesto on Grey's refusal of responsible government. In June 1860, as political mentor to the Roman Catholics of St. John's, he published his repudiation of the party in power:

I address you this letter on a matter of vital importance to your interests, and I consider that my advocacy of everything connected with the improvement of the country gives me a right to offer you a few words of advice. The great and paramount want of Newfoundland is a facility of communication between the capital and the outports; as long as the outports are left isolated, so long will education, religion, and civilization be left in the background. Newfoundland must remain in that state of darkness to which ages of bad government have reduced it. I solemnly declare that without steam communication the people must remain poor, degraded, and ignorant. Forced by the indignant voice of the people, those whom you call your representatives passed a Bill granting £3,000 a year for five years for outport steam. It appears that by a dishonest quibble, intended to defeat the project, two steamers were smuggled into the Bill so as to render the offer illusory, in plain English, a humbug.

A beautiful steamer, in every way adapted for the purpose, engaged to do the service north and south twice a month, was offered in New York; I visited the ship myself, and if she was not all that was specified the contract could be terminated at three months' notice. She had every accommodation for passengers, and would have done more to develop the interests of the out-harbours than all the Houses of Assembly that ever met on the Island.

The Government, when they saw the matter brought to a point, refused to engage her. What was intended only to delude the people was about to become a reality, and the contract was repudiated. How does it happen that an enormous revenue, wasted in providing useless places for State paupers, cannot afford the sum of £3,000 a year for outport accommodation? Year by year every improvement is put off for want of means, though every infant in Newfoundland pays in taxes £1 a head. Will strangers believe that in a British Colony the shire town of Fortune Bay is in reality further from us than Constantinople? But then we have the satisfaction of seeing thousands upon thousands of pounds distributed among our *locust-like officials*. We pay heavy taxes, but get comparatively no return; almost all goes in salaries and pretended compensations, and I have no hesitation in saying that the collection of a revenue under the present system is nothing but *legalized robbery*. I am aware that my name has been made use of to prop up the supporters of this system, but I consider it due to myself, and to those whose interests I advocate, to repudiate any connexion with a party who take care of themselves, but do nothing for the people. This is not a political or religious question, it is one of civilization, in which Catholics and Protestants, priests and ministers, are equally interested.[93]

In the early phase of representative government, Kent had enjoyed the support of his relative, Bishop Fleming, but unlike Little, had apparently never won the whole-hearted confidence of Dr. Mullock. Though a veteran Liberal politician and office-holder, Kent seems to have been the victim of past compromises, parasitic supporters, and an uncertain temper. His efforts to command the loyalty and maintain the coherence of the Liberal party were impaired, too, by his rivalry for the leadership with the Speaker of the House, Ambrose Shea.[94] The Bishop's manifesto on the corruption of the Administration was, therefore, a signal to the Governor that the day was approaching when he might safely dismiss his ministers and hope for their replacement by worthier men. When Dr. Mullock called at Government House, Sir Alexander informed him that the men to whom he had lent his support for five years were indeed "legalized robbers," but that the Governor must await his constitutional time.[95] His conviction that this time was approaching is apparent in his despatches after Dr. Mullock's manifesto. He informed Newcastle that he was certain he could carry abrogation of certain duties in opposition to the Government or any which might be formed should such an event take place before the next meeting of the

Legislature. He closed the session without introducing a Volunteers Bill because he was not yet in a "condition to consider it advisable to adopt such a course as would have been a proper answer to . . . a refusal."[96]

CHAPTER ELEVEN

THE OUSTING OF THE LIBERALS, 1860-1861

STRENGTHENED by Bishop Mullock's denunciation of the Liberal Government, the Governor opened a special session in December 1860 with a series of blunt criticisms and proposals. He condemned as extravagant and demoralizing the system of poor relief which, without due investigation, dispensed aid to the able-bodied and recognized applicants as paupers without debarring them as electors. He commented sternly on the public debt, saying: "That system must be a wrong one which increases the permanent debt of a Colony by appropriating from its ordinary revenue, raised by indirect taxation, large sums for purposes which benefit the few at the expense of the many, and which are, therefore, legitimate objects for direct taxation . . . ." He pointed once more to the need for an increased constabulary.[1] With the Opposition gleefully applying Dr. Mullock's labels of derogation to the members of the Government, uneasiness and disunity were evident in the leaders and ranks of the Liberal party.[2] Through a resignation of singular convenience, the leader of the Opposition, Hoyles, who had failed to gain a seat in 1859, was able to resume his place in the Assembly.[3]

The session had been called early to consider means of meeting the heavy demand for poor relief. Despite recent years of prosperity, pauperism had become an entrenched social evil, the allocation for relief averaging one-third of the annual supply vote and amounting in 1860 to almost £15,000 (Appendix F). In that year, seal and cod fisheries less productive than expected had been followed in many districts by failure of the potato crop and for 1861 the Government proposed a relief vote of £20,000.

No decision had been reached on retrenchment or reform in the system of poor relief by the time the Legislature adjourned for the Christmas recess, but on January 22, the day after the session was resumed, an advertisement was published in the *Royal Gazette* in the name of the Relief Commissioners setting out more stringent regulations for the distribution of relief:

The Commissioners for the Relief of the Poor hereby give notice that henceforth all persons applying to the Stipendiary Commissioner for relief shall, when possible, produce a Certificate signed by a Magistrate or Clergyman of the locality or district to which the applicant belongs, setting forth the cause of distress, the number of family, and place of residence, and other particulars; and that a printed List of the names of all persons receiving relief, whether in St. John's or in Outports, including those persons in the Sheds or Poor House, with the number of their families and place of residence, together with the names of the parties by whom recommended, shall be deposited by the Stipendiary Commissioner at the Colonial Secretary's Office, for the use of the Commissioners.

Dissident elements in the Liberal party at once showed signs of a desire to promote and capitalize on popular resentment of this action by the

Government. Nowlan, a Roman Catholic member for Harbour Main, announced two anti-Government resolutions condemning the regulations as unjust and inapplicable to the circumstances of the colony, advocating road employment in all practicable cases for the able-bodied poor, and declaring that "any regulations made on the subject of Poor Relief should not ignore the just influence of the Representatives of the people." Next day Kent gave notice of three counter-resolutions which defended the revised regulations and the right of the Government to make them. They condemned indiscriminate relief for the able-bodied poor as demoralizing and a vicious principle which the Legislature should not acknowledge, but declared that in exceptional cases, where distress arose from the failure of the fishery or the crops, the Legislature had a duty to provide relief through employment.[4] He defended himself and his resolutions in an impassioned speech to the House and the crowded, hostile gallery. He was being attacked, he said, by a "miserable faction who sought his political destruction; a set of frozen serpents which having been warmed into life had stung the breast which gave it vitality." He saw behind the scenes "same designing, cozening, cunning rogue" who for ambition or vindictive purposes had devised this treason against the Government.[5] He enlarged upon the theme of his long personal service to the party and the country and the financial straits in which he would be placed if now removed from office. His eloquence and his resolutions rallied sufficient support and the business of the session continued.[6] In a private letter of March 8, 1861 Newcastle remarked to the Governor: "Your Ministers and Parliament seem resolved to prove to the world their unfitness for their position. Some of the recent scenes would be highly amusing, if they were not so disgraceful. Mr. Secretary Kent is a grand specimen. I can picture him as the indignant Senator, having seen him as the dancing Courtier."[7] The Bishop's comment to the Governor on the proceedings seemed unequivocal:

... the members in a great measure were chosen only as the representative-beggars of a set of paupers, and he who could get most flour was the best member. The whole system was one of robbery and demoralization on all sides, for the distribution of Poor Relief among the idle and the improvident and for political purposes is the worst species of political robbery, for it not only debases the distributors (if anything could do that) but debases and demoralizes the recipients nearly to the level of their corruptors.[8]

Mutual desire for the ousting of the Kent Administration strongly suggests, though it does not prove, collusion between the Governor and the Opposition for this end. During February 1861 members of the Opposition followed up the controversy about poor relief with efforts to expose mal-distribution.[9] On February 27 the Governor wrote a long confidential despatch to Newcastle which seemed to hint at his intention to dismiss his ministers as soon as the ground had been prepared by disclosures about public expenditure. It was clear, he said, that

nothing but a change of men was likely to bring about a change of measures. An appeal to the people, in any other Colony, might have effected the object; but in Newfoundland, the ignorance of the people and the powerful influences which prevail over them have induced me to act with caution, and to wait for a time (I hope not far distant) when even ignorant people will find out what profligate expenditure and corruption mean,—and when the respectable population shall find out that it will be their interest to bestir themselves, and be less apathetic than they hitherto have been in supporting a system of Government long sought for, and which, if fairly and honestly administered, and understood by the people,—is one which I think is well adapted for these Provinces.[10]

He was later to declare that in February 1861 he had been certain that disrepute would bring down the Ministry within six months.[11]

If the Governor had charted for himself a cautious course, he would seem to have been provoked from it by the sudden, open defiance of Kent. In the poor relief crisis of January, Kent had managed to prevent the splintering of the Liberal party, but in February he betrayed himself into the hands of the Governor and the Opposition. A bill had been introduced by the Receiver-General on February 6 which provided for the payment of the public accounts, including official salaries, in colonial currency at a reduced rate—4s. 4d. to the dollar instead of the sterling rate of 4s. 2d. This provision ran counter to the long-standing claim of the judges and the Governor who were not willing to accept the financial loss involved without testing the legality of the change in a court of law. The test case which Judge Robinson proposed to bring had been deferred until the competence of the Supreme Court to decide the matter had been ascertained.[12] This being the position, the introduction of the Currency Bill evoked a protest from the judges and arrayed the Opposition against it.[13] The vocal rage with which Kent greeted this obstruction may have been spontaneously indiscreet, or its purpose may have been to reinstate himself after the poor relief controversy and to heal the schism in his party by producing a cause for unity. He announced to the Assembly that the Governor had entered into a conspiracy with the judges, the lawyers, and the minority in the House to defeat a useful bill. When this speech was reported in the press, the Governor wrote to Kent asking for his explanation as Premier and Colonial Secretary. Kent replied that as an independent member of the Legislature he did not consider himself called upon to account for his utterances there to the Governor.[14] The Governor's reaction was swift. After consulting with Hugh Hoyles and Frederick Carter, Queen's Counsellors and members of the Opposition, on the sufficiency of the grounds, and with the former on his willingness to form the Government, he dismissed his Liberal ministers and called upon Hoyles.[15] He drew Hoyles's attention, he said, to his own support for civil and religious liberty and toleration.[16]

Setting on one side for a moment the questions of constitutional correctness, legal right, and political prudence raised by the dismissal, the chronology of events which led swiftly to the dissolution of the Assembly may be briefly stated. In the construction of the new Ministry, Hoyles attempted to obtain four Protestants, of whom two should be Anglican and two Wesleyan, and three Roman Catholics. He approached two Catholics, Lawrence O'Brien, President of the Legislative Council, and Ambrose Shea, Speaker of the Assembly, to whom he offered any departmental position he chose to name. O'Brien accepted, but Shea, who had presumably hoped to head a new Liberal Ministry, refused. Hoyles was then apparently unable to find Roman Catholics willing to take the two remaining seats in his attempted coalition.[17] On March, as Attorney-General, he met the Assembly with only three other ministers. These were Captain Robert Carter, also of the Church of England, Nicholas Stabb and John Bemister, Wesleyans, and Lawrence O'Brien, Roman Catholic. He suggested that the business of the session should be completed, but this the displaced ministers, the Liberal majority, and the tumultuous crowd filling the gallery and most of the body of the House, would not permit. The scenes in the Assembly, wrote Chichester Fortescue, Parliamentary Under-Secretary for Colonies and member for County Louth, Ireland (1847-1874), were like those at a contested election. Henry Winton, in St. John's, compared them to those enacted in the early stages of the French Revolution.[18] Resolutions were moved by Kent that his outgoing Ministry had the confidence of the House; that the new Ministry wanted to satisfy a craving for power; that an election would be unfair at that season; and that, with a fishery convention impending, any measure which would weaken and disunite the people of the colony must be concocted as a "gross act of treachery" towards the people of Newfoundland. Next day these resolutions were carried on division by sixteen votes to twelve.[19] Two days later the Governor dissolved the House, leaving the Liberal party to face the unwelcome prospect of fighting a general election in the approaching supplying season and the Liberal press to indulge in furious denunciations of conspirators at Government House.[20]

Had the Governor constitutional justification and had he legal power for this summary removal of a whole Government possessing the confidence of the Assembly? These were questions which troubled the Colonial Office. One view was that the Governor had allowed himself to be distracted by annoyance and dislike of his ministers from the constitutional avenues open to him and that he should have attempted instead to induce Kent or his whole Ministry to resign, failing which he should have resorted to suspension of the Council or dissolution of the Assembly. A trial of strength in the newly elected House might then have necessitated the resignation of Kent and his colleagues. Another view was that in extreme cases political intervention by the Governor was desirable, but that considering colonial habits of speech, Kent's conduct did not seem to warrant what amounted to an extra-constitutional *coup d'état* by the Governor. As far as legal right was concerned, it was believed that the Governor had ignored or misinterpreted his Instructions. He had been given the power to suspend executive councillors but, unlike the other governors of British North America, not the power to remove them, and though he could suspend the holders of political office who were appointed by royal warrant, he had not the power of direct removal.[21] The attention of the Colonial Office having been focused on the defects in the power of the Governor, it was decided that Sir Alexander should be empowered by a new Instruction to dismiss his executive councillors. His successor was to be granted, under his Commission, the right to remove all officers appointed by or under the authority of the Crown and the "unnecessary and misleading formality" of issuing warrants in responsibly governed colonies was to cease. That the Governor lacked legal authority for his action does not appear to have been suspected by the ministers he dismissed.[22] These urged rather that his course had been unconstitutional and conspiratorial.[23]

Of greatest concern to the Colonial Office was the political prudence of the Governor's step and the realization that the return of the Liberals to power might make it impossible to retain him in office. The principal minute on this subject, that of Elliot of April 19, pointed out two dangerous possibilities: Kent and his colleagues, if reinstated, might choose to flout Sir Alexander at will, he having exhausted his only remedy; or the Liberals as a party might decide to refuse office and to create a deadlock by denying support to any government that might be formed. In either case, the recall of the Governor might be imperative, but such a recall, forced by collision and deadlock, could establish an inconvenient precedent and destroy the little independent authority still retained by governors of "responsible" colonies. In a candid and realistic note to his colleagues, Newcastle remarked that nothing could justify the Governor's extreme step except what was generally held to justify strong measures—success. While he hoped that Hoyles and his party would be returned, leaving Kent to "spit fire and fury" as much as he liked, he was convinced that all would depend upon the course taken in the elections by the Roman Catholic Bishop. To Sir Alexander he expressed no opinion about the constitutionality of his course, but referred to the serious embarrassments in which he might shortly be involved.[24]

The sudden dismissal of the Ministry he had himself repudiated, and the establishment of a Protestant-led rather than another Catholic-led Government, forced Dr. Mullock into the tortuous paths of retraction. In June 1860, he had accused the Liberal party of using their power for self-aggrandizement rather than for the progress of the colony and had declared, in effect, that the claims of civilization must be put before those of political and religious party. In March 1861, faced with the danger that a division of the Catholic vote would bring in a Government less amenable to his influence, he made it clear that, though the Liberals had lately incurred his displeasure, episcopal sanction had not been given for a change in political allegiance. In a letter to the editor of the *Record*, designed to be read by the Catholic electors of St. John's, he denounced the election as a reckless experiment which would give rise to years of evil and disruption. He endorsed the Liberals as the party of civilization and as the vehicle through which the Catholic clergy, and they alone, had effected every improvement thus far made in Newfoundland. The policy of their opponents was that of the enemies of Catholicism everywhere—to divide, conquer, and enslave. If progress was to continue and if subjugation was to be avoided, Catholics must support the candidates chosen by their priests; independent Catholic candidates would be merely hungry expectants of place. Mullock suggested that mercantile influence in the election—an "Irish landlord trick"—could be nullified by a specific financial threat:

The interest of the planters and merchants is identical; the merchants trade in great measure on the planters' money; an attempt then to coerce the people might induce the independent Catholic planter to call for his money (and the planters have been so often scalded that very little would induce them to do so); one call of the kind would immediately produce others; and we know what embarrassments, of not ruin, a run of this kind would cause.

It would therefore be impolitic, he said, for the merchants to arouse the religious feelings of Roman Catholics. His letter ended with the peroration: "If you reject this advice you will deservedly be the tools of unprincipled schemers, and the slaves of a ruthless faction who have always, when they could crushed you, and hope by dividing you to do so again."[25]

Whatever his motives, the language and theme of the Bishop's letter were not likely to quell sectarian alarm and jealousy or promote a peaceful election. His effort to equate Catholic power in Newfoundland with the cause of civil and religious liberty and material progress, his references to old fears and prejudices, and his implication that a Protestant-led Government would be an anti-Catholic conspiracy, stemmed no doubt from benevolent concern, but they suggest, too, personal ambition—a desire to hold the political reins and a reluctance to yield them to others. One political journalist, contrasting the Bishop's letters, declared that Dr. Mullock, staggered by the catastrophe he had helped to bring about, could not afford to be very nice.[26]

A general election in which the Bishop and the Governor were political rivals and which would sustain the influence of the one or vindicate the stand of the other could hardly be other than disruptive. The Bishop's concern was apparently the return of a Liberal majority deferential to himself, the Governor's the election of an Assembly which would support the Government he had installed. Both men agreed that the electors were highly susceptible to influence, but their inferences were different. The Governor informed the Bishop that great responsibility would attach to those who attempted to deter the electors from freely exercising the privilege which was their undoubted right—"to choose and vote for the object or objects of their preference." The Bishop replied that irresponsible bribers would buy their return from an unguided electorate of paupers.[27] For the Bishop it seemed essential to discourage what the Governor believed would ultimately benefit the colony—the spread of an independent spirit in the Catholic laity.[28] The Governor was concerned to prevent the intimidation which had repeatedly led to the withdrawal of candidates and electors. For him, as for the Hoyles party, the immediate issue was the return of four additional members so as to give that party sixteen seats in the Assembly and allow them to form a Government.

The most significant events in the election struggle occurred in five districts— Burin, St. John's, Carbonear, Harbour Grace, and Harbour Main.[29] In Burin, Hoyles and a Protestant colleague were nominated and returned without contest, a change in the district's adherence which seemed to ensure that the Conservatives would have a minimum of fourteen seats. Presumably the Liberals were unwilling or unable to repeat their financial battle for this district. In St. John's, where there were two rival Catholic Liberal factions, designated respectively the "priests' party" and the "natives' party," the Bishop found it discreet to withdraw one of his nominees and to substitute a native. A contest appeared likely in the western division of the district when five candidates, one of them a Protestant merchant, were nominated for the three seats, but the tactics which had so often proved successful forced the withdrawal of the Protestant and one of the Catholics. A priest addressed the crowd from the hustings and they dispersed in what became a window-breaking procession through the streets of the city. There was an attack on the premises of the mercantile candidate which was repelled by gun-fire from the occupants, who had armed themselves in anticipation of such an event, and who succeeded in wounding several of the assailants. As a result of this nomination day violence and the threat of more, the Protestant and the independent Catholic declined to expose themselves and their supporters to the perils of polling day. Similar tactics ensured the withdrawal of the protestant candidate for Carbonear.

Harbour Grace had lately been represented by one Protestant and one Catholic, but in view of the district's Protestant majority there seemed a good chance, if disorders could be prevented, that two Protestants, one of them a mercantile candidate, might be returned. The problem, according to the Governor, was that the Protestant population was scattered through the district, whereas the Catholics were concentrated in the town itself and could call for support from Catholic allies in nearby Carbonear.[30] The Catholic candidate was Prendergast who had been returned by mob tactics in 1859 and 1860, and, anticipating trouble on nomination day, the magistrates induced the Governor to send a detachment of a hundred soldiers. It is significant that the Governor, notifying the Colonial Office of this step, invited the Secretary of State to make a statement of intention to disfranchise the district for disturbances which demanded the presence of troops at every election. The power of disfranchising the district rested with the Newfoundland Legislature, so that the Governor appears to have been seeking Colonial Office approval in anticipation of an emergency course he might adopt. He had earlier sought advice from Newcastle about the possibility of declaring martial law in Harbour Grace, but had been warned that the Assembly would be unlikely to pass for him a subsequent Act of Indemnity and that if lives were lost under martial law, he would probably be tried as an accessory to murder. The Legislature might be induced to grant him a temporary increase in powers. However, Newcastle had added, "in an *extreme case* ... a Man in Authority must dare anything that his sense of duty dictates rather than risk the safety of the Country."[31] On April 29 a Roman Catholic inhabitant of Spaniard's Bay near Harbour Grace was sent by Bishop Mullock to the Governor to report that anti-Catholic violence had obliged him to flee the place and to ask that military protection be provided for his house and for the Roman Catholic church. The Governor's enquiries satisfied him that the man's tale was fabricated and that the alleged crowd of Protestant besiegers had been a mixed group assembled to repel an anticipated attack from Harbour Grace. The request for a military detachment the Governor dismissed as a crude feint—a ruse into which he presumed the Bishop had unwittingly been drawn—to draw from Harbour Grace the troops sent to ensure a peaceful election.[32] In the event, however, despite the presence of troops, the magistrates deemed it unwise to open the polls on May 2 and the district made no return. Since there is evidence that the mercantile candidate had already resigned,[33] the district would appear to have been disfranchised to avoid the uncontested return of the Catholic candidate.

At Harbour Main there were four Roman Catholic candidates for the two seats. Hogsett, the former Attorney-General, and Furey were backed by Bishop Dalton and accompanied by Father Walsh of that place, while Nowlan and Byrne were reportedly supported by a priest of a neighbouring parish. In these circumstances, polling day produced brawling, threats, and intimidation. When Father Walsh and a contingent of three hundred men from Harbour Main descended upon Cat's Cove, a polling place where there was strong support for Nowlan and Byrne, the people of the Cove assumed, or affected to assume, that it was an attack rather than an attempt to cast three dozen votes. Anticipating the arrival of the invaders, they had secured firearms; before the visitors had withdrawn one had been killed and others wounded, some severely. The Roman Catholic Returning Officer at Harbour Main, under duress, furnished candidates Hogsett and Furey with a certificate of return, but also endorsed the writ which said that the other candidates had a majority of the votes.[34]

The general election ended with Harbour Grace virtually disfranchised, with a double and therefore invalid return from Harbour Main, and with the Hoyles party, because of the Burin return, numbering fourteen in a House of twenty-six. (Appendix B, Table II). This was a situation which could hardly fail to suggest to the Liberals that there had been a conspiracy to rob them of a majority by contriving imperfect returns from districts where their victory was assured.[35] The ability of Hoyles and his colleagues to carry on the Government would hinge upon the subsequent returns from Harbour Main and Harbour Grace, the former to be decided by an electoral committee of the House, the latter by the electorate when a re-election was called. It would not have been rash, therefore, to predict, in the first fortnight of May 1861, that the convening of the new Assembly would be followed by scenes like those which had preceded the dissolution of the old, and that the Liberals, wrathful and suspicious, would bend every effort to force the resignation of the Government.

The attempt to wrest from Hoyles his precarious victory began on May 13, the opening day of the first session of the eighth Assembly.[36] Armed with the Returning Officer's certificate, former Attorney-General Hogsett and his colleague, Furey, took the two seats for Harbour Main for which there had been the invalid double return. Since they refused all orders to withdraw, proceedings could not begin until Hogsett had been forcibly removed by the police and Furey had had the prudence to retire. When the Governor arrived with his military guard to deliver the Speech from the Throne, he found some 2,000 persons milling about the Colonial Building. News that Hogsett had been ejected was soon circulated through the crowd. Its immediate effect was an attempt by an excited rabble to break into the House. The violence was such that the commander of the guard, Colonel Grant, felt obliged to order his men to prepare to use their weapons, and for a time the crowd was awed. When the Governor emerged he was hooted and his carriage was stoned, but his departure was followed by a period of relative quiet, the troops being withdrawn and many of the citizens dispersing. The exodus of the members, however, was a signal for the renewal of disorder. As members of the Government appeared, there were cries of "run them," and some of these members and some of the legislative councillors were unable to gain their homes until a military escort had been provided.

The violence of the mob was then turned upon the premises of relatives and friends of the other pair of "returned" candidates from Harbour Main. Two establishments were attacked, damaged, and looted. For an hour and a half outbreaks of destruction continued, with the mob swelling in size. Then, on requisition of the magistrates, ninety soldiers under Colonel Grant arrived to quell the disorders and to clear the streets. For another hour and a half this small body of troops was hemmed in by a turbulent crowd of thousands, upon whom the reading of the Riot Act and the persuasion of Colonel Grant, the magistrates, Judge Little, and several priests had no effect. Those who dispersed up one street rejoined the throng down another. An attempt was made to drag the Colonel from his horse and he and his soldiers were repeatedly stoned. But, according to the testimony at the inquest, the troops were not given the order to fire until finally, at about eight in the evening, a shot was fired at them. The military order once given, shooting lasted only a few minutes, but in that time three people were killed and twenty wounded, including one of the priests who had been most earnestly entreating the crowd to desist. Then—but not till then— the bells of the Roman Catholic cathedral rang out to summon the rioters away.

Bishop Mullock could scarcely have been unaware that disorders had been raging for four hours, but whether from an access of spiritual detachment or from motives of political strategy, he had chosen to delay intervention until the troops had been forced into decisive action and until his people were falling in the streets. At that moment, before general panic could be replaced by concerted vengeance, he emerged from his seclusion to restore the peace. In a dramatic demonstration of obedience, the Roman Catholic citizens of St. John's surged up to the cathedral to hear the Bishop, in pontificals, exhort them from the altar to eschew revenge and to murmur a pledge of peace as he raised the Host.

The Bishop's course on the night of May 15 was a striking illustration of a propensity for delay upon which the Governor had commented. A fortnight earlier, in an exchange of views with Dr. Mullock about the pacifying influence which the Catholic clergy could wield, Sir Alexander had remarked: "From my experience here, I have invariably seen the influence to which you allude predominant at the *height* of a storm, when men's passions were strongly excited,— but I have never seen the influence used at the *beginning* of that storm, when it might prove so very beneficial to society."[37] The Bishop's belated use of his pastoral power on the night of the riot did not escape the Duke of Newcastle, to whom Dr. Mullock lost no time in forwarding a long version of the affair, its cause, and its suppression. The Duke replied, carefully, that the Bishop's letter had been forwarded in natural excitement, so that it seemed very probable that many of his statements were based on imperfect information and therefore much exaggerated. He was, he said, much impressed with the way in which the Bishop had been able to summon his thousands to the cathedral and deeply grateful for his action, but he expressed his concern that "an influence of so paramount a character was not exercised sooner." "I imagine," he wrote, "that a word from you before the storm began might have saved the sad scenes which it required the whole force of your sacred office to stay when it had reached its height." He said also: "More than once in your letter you complain that the Police were not employed. Surely it is notorious that those whose duty it has been to organize a Police have hitherto refused to do so, and that the force, which as you rightly say, ought to have stopped those riots *in limine*, does not exist."[38]

The *Ledger,* disposed always to put the least favourable construction on the motives and actions of political priests, thought it very probable that the letter which the Bishop had chosen to publish two days before the opening of the Legislature had been an instigating factor in the riot. In this Dr. Mullock had written that "a war of extermination" had apparently been commenced against the Catholics of Newfoundland and had suggested that the power of the priests would soon be unable to "restrain the feelings of their people, whose lives are threatened and their blood spilt by ruffians, as it appears, with impunity."[39]

The Governor was convinced that the violence of May 13 and subsequent representations of terror to come were part of a concerted effort to intimidate the Hoyles Ministry into resigning. On May 14 Bishop Mullock called upon Bannerman to remonstrate about the shooting of the priest and the use of the troops. If the soldiers were not used again, the Bishop said that he and his clergy would do all in their power to keep the people quiet. He informed the Governor that riots were intended for that night and that 10,000 men armed with sealing guns were ready to wreak vengeance by plundering and destroying the town. On the same day he wrote to advise Sir Alexander that a deputation had besought him "on their knees" to permit them to call out such a force.[40] The Governor assured him that the troops would not be used unless there were a repetition of violence and that he deeply regretted the wounding of an estimable priest. The threat of terrorism was not implemented and, save for sporadic fires of suspicious origin, one of which destroyed the country home of Premier Hoyles, the town was quiet, though some of the merchants maintained armed guards on their premises for several weeks. The acquiescence of St. John's was no doubt due in part to the influence of Dr. Mullock, though the Governor believed it could be ascribed to the fact that for the first time in Newfoundland a mob had been opposed with fairness and determination.

During May there were reports of sporadic disorder and gun-fire from Harbour Grace and Carbonear, but with the fisheries about to draw away a large part of the male population, the Governor did not again despatch troops. The uneasy situation in these districts was produced by post-election bitterness. Two of the leading merchants refused to hire, or advance supplies to, those who had played a notorious part in the violence. There were threats of recrimination from those who were denied credit, a descent on the jail to rescue a prisoner, and a severing of telegraphic communication with the capital. The Executive Council urged the need for a larger military force, part of which should be permanently stationed at Conception Bay. The Colonial Office, however, reiterated the view that the maintenance of civil order was the colony's responsibility and that any supplement to the strength of the garrison must be paid for from the local Treasury. At the same time it was recognized that persons who saw their opinions promoted by violence were unlikely to vote funds for its suppression. The Governor was not disposed to attempt the formation of a force of Sea Fencibles or a militia, believing that the influence of the "predominant" power made it inadvisable to arm and drill the fishermen for naval and military service.[41]

If the city were subdued after the riot, the press was not. There were columns of attack in the Liberal newspapers on the Governor and his new ministers, stories about conspiracies at Government House, and allegations that Sir Alexander and the Duke of Newcastle had schemed for the ousting of the Liberals during the royal visit of 1860. The favourite theme, the Governor reported to the Duke, was to add ten years to his age and to suggest that in his judgment and actions he must be a prey to influences. The Governor remarked that he cared little for such attacks; he would greet a parliamentary investigation with satisfaction, and he was certain that those who accused him of senility would find him quite young enough to disappoint their expectations.[42]

Acting as transmitter of the grievances of the defeated party, Dr. Mullock turned his attention to the double return from Harbour Main from which the violence at St. John's had stemmed. He alleged that Attorney-General Hoyles had caused the trouble by establishing a poll at Cat's Cove. The Governor promptly notified him that Hoyles had agreed to establish the Harbour Main polls at places agreed on by both sets of candidates, but that since these could not agree on the sites, he had retained the polls used in the past.[43] The Bishop then informed the Governor that the Returning Officer at Harbour Main was fit neither for that office nor for that of magistrate. The Governor replied with some satisfaction that the man had been selected for both posts by the Government supported by Dr. Mullock—for one post by Attorney-General Hogsett and for the other by Attorney-General Little.[44]

On May 18, five days after the St. John's riot, the Returning Officer's house at Harbour Main was pulled to the ground and his cattle killed—an act of vengeance at which Father Walsh, so the Governor was told, was an unprotesting spectator. The telegraph poles and wires having been destroyed, news of this attack did not reach St. John's until next day, when the Governor promptly despatched troops by steamer. The homes of the culprits were surrounded, several arrests were made, and the prisoners were conveyed to the jail in St. John's. However, when they came up for trial they were acquitted by the jury in the face of what the Governor termed "clearest evidence." For this acquittal, the Returning Officer himself seems to have been partly responsible, since he and his family could not be persuaded to supply the evidence which would have made the case. Fear of retaliation may have inspired this silence: to some Protestants it apparently suggested that the family was in spiritual fear of the local priest.[45]

The outcome of the disputed return from Harbour Main caused violent chagrin among the Liberals. Petitions having been presented to the House by the four claimants, an election committee of seven was selected by ballot. On June 25 this committee returned a majority and two dissenting reports. Five members declared that having examined all the evidence available, and having allotted to each candidate the votes indisputably lost through intimidation, they must recommend that Nowlan and Byrne be pronounced duly elected. Of the two dissenting members, both Liberals, one found that Hogsett and Furey should be returned, or that, alternatively, the election should be declared null and void. The other, contending that to admit these uncast votes was to condone the principle of intimidation, called for another election. There were vehement Liberal attacks on the integrity and proceedings of the committee, but even the authors of the dissenting reports maintained stoutly that the committee had made an objective examination of evidence unavailable to the denigrators.[46]

The session of the Legislature was short. Steps had been taken to ensure that the proceedings of the Assembly would not be obstructed as in the past by an invasion of spectators. Each member was allotted nine tickets for visitors and a rule was made for the summary ejection of the disorderly. Obstruction came, however, from members of the Opposition and with the close standing of the parties and the uncertain affiliation of the two members for Harbour Main, exposed as they were to the hostility of the other Liberals, only five bills were passed and the Legislature was prorogued on June 27.[47] The House would not assemble again until an election had brought in two members for Harbour Grace and had defined the majority party.

The inquests into the deaths of May 13 provided the Liberals with further complaints for relay by Dr. Mullock. He presented charges that the inquests had been conducted in secrecy, that the jury had been improperly constituted, and that its foreman had been the chairman of the committee of the House which had declared for Nowlan and Byrne. The charges of a partial jury, far from novel in the island, astonished the Governor. The circumstantial statement on the inquests supplied by Attorney-General Hoyles suggests that in this instance a temporary inadvertence had been magnified, for party purposes, into a deliberate impropriety. The Attorney-General disposed of the charge of secrecy and exclusion by informing the Governor that the hearings had been open in the usual way to orderly members of the public, as space became available, that several of Dr. Mullock's clergy had been present throughout, and that the Bishop himself had been invited to occupy a reserved seat, but had refused to appear.

The jury found that one of the victims of May 13 had been killed by a soldier and another by persons unknown; the family of the third refused to allow an inquest. Much evidence was brought forward on the provocation to which the troops had been subjected, and indeed the evidence was so copious that both Newcastle and his Under-Secretary, Fortescue, quailed before the task of reading it, Fortescue departing for the August recess and Newcastle perusing only as much of it as the state of his eyes would permit. A résumé was prepared by the Permanent Under-Secretary, Sir Frederic Rogers, who advised that the Governor's position be strengthened by words of commendation for the behaviour of the troops.[48] Accordingly, Newcastle wrote praising their exemplary forbearance and stating his belief that the inquests had been conducted with perfect fairness. Any complaint on the latter score could, he said, be brought before the Assembly.[49]

After the inquests and the prorogation of the House, Hogsett and his colleagues began work on a petition to the Queen for the removal of the Governor and for the dissolution of the Assembly. The meetings called to pass the resolutions were, according to the Governor, ill attended, and the petition was therefore brought on successive Sundays to the cathedral for signatures.[50] Some 8,000 of these were obtained, including those of ten priests, two members of the Assembly, and some members of the late Government. The petition announced that the Governor had decided in November 1859 to throw his influence into the scales of the opponents of his sworn advisers, that he had countenanced the most sectarian and inflammatory attacks on the latter in the newspapers in the pay of the minority, that he had made no secret of his antipathy to the Liberal party, and that their opponents in the Assembly were fully advised of his designs on all occasions. It then reviewed subsequent events in relation to this premise and declared that the Governor and Hoyles had set up a "Reign of Terror, Tyranny, and Fraud" unexampled in the history of any British Colony. The petition was not entrusted to Sir Alexander for transmission, but he sent a printed copy to Newcastle, expressing his surprise that it did not call for a public investigation or for a parliamentary enquiry. In his opinion, the Bishop, knowing that Parliament would be prorogued, had drawn up the document for its publicity value.[51] It was not, in fact, laid before Parliament. When the original of the petition reached Newcastle through the member for Limerick, he laid it before the Queen, but did not deem it his duty to advise her to take any steps on the contents.[52]

The Governor believed that the petition was meant to be shown in Ireland as proof that "Orangeism" was rampant in Newfoundland. To the best of his knowledge, he said, there was not an Orange Society in the island. From the *Record*, which had been established with Dr. Mullock's endorsement in October 1860, he extracted for Newcastle a typical statement, intended, he thought, for the Galway *Vindicator*. This announced that there was a "most virulent Orange faction" in Newfoundland which owed its vital existence and its practical evils to the "driviling [*sic*] bigotry and inherent depravity of Sir Alexander Bannerman." The Governor interpreted the language of this newspaper as an attempt to convince the Roman Catholics that they were justified in their late actions and to ensure the same proceedings at the autumn election at Harbour Grace. The Bishop, he said, spoke openly of long dark nights and the return of the fishermen from Labrador.[53] In August, he submitted to the Colonial Office a further sample of the inflammatory matter "read in pot-houses to ignorant people." This declared that unless an enquiry were soon made into the "Orange tyranny," Her Majesty would find that she had lost the "key to the St. Lawrence." Dr. Mullock, he said, had frequently expressed a wish that Great Britain should become a third-rate power and an earnest hope that she would soon be involved in a war with France and America.[54] Of the Bishop's behaviour, Sir Alexander wrote: "The sudden impulses which come over him, the violent and outrageous language which appears in the press under his control, sometimes impress me with the idea that he was labouring under temporary insanity."[55]

A sample of the "violent and outrageous" matter being distributed in the island is quoted by the chronicler of the year 1861. This was an appeal for the "Commemoration of the Bloody Thirteenth of May" and was headed "Attention! Make Ready!! Prime and Load!!! It read:

The 13th of August next will be the first quarter of the year since the butchery and slaughter of the people of St. John's were committed by the Orange Party. It is intended to celebrate the day by a Public Meeting; and we beg to apprize our friends of the Outports all around, that it is expected every man will come into the city on that day to take part in the proceedings.

This celebration is to be the first of a series which the Liberal Party intend to celebrate every quarter while the present Governor remains in office. We expect it to be a *great* gathering even at this time of the year for no Liberal will absent himself unless absolute illness prevent him. At this meeting you will hear truth told which will startle the dirty birds from their Orange nests.

A subsequent notice, postponing the meeting until November to permit the participation of the fishermen, termed May 13 a day of "legalized murder and premeditated bloodshed."[56] The same chronicler summarized the course adopted by the *Record* after March 1861. As the organ of Dr. Mullock's views, it had been attacking the Liberal Government; from this, it turned to attack the "common foe." It stimulated the passions of the lower orders by hints that sealing guns should in future be used against the troops. It described the military intervention both as a wanton action and as a premeditated martial tyranny. It reduced the disorders to the pranks of a "few harmless boys amusing themselves in the public thoroughfare." It called the Governor an Orangeman and an arch-Tory—and this despite his known liberal antecedents, his friendship with O'Connell, and his association in Parliament with O'Connell's adherents. It stigmatized all supporters of the new Government as members of a Federal Orange

Organization.[57] The prospects of the Government, the *Record* announced in September, were a public resistance, "fierce and unmitigable."[58]

By September the *Record* was able to report that journals in several countries were agreed that the Governor of Newfoundland was both illiberal and anti-Catholic.[59] In Ireland and England organs of Irish nationalism and of Catholic freedom, like the Galway *Vindicator,* had seized upon the material supplied by the *Record* as the basis for inflammatory articles on the outcropping in Newfoundland of a vast and sinister Orange conspiracy. These articles the *Record* did not fail to reproduce as proof to the populace of Sir Alexander's Orange plot.[60] Translations from the *Record* found their way into Italian journals which were critical of Britain's role in the struggle against Austrian and papal power in Italy. These, the Governor understood, were supplied by the "Italian priest" in St. John's,[61] Father Henry Carfagnini of the Franciscan Order, who was President of St. Bonaventure's College and later (1869) Bishop of Harbour Grace.[62] One of the Italian newspapers, a Tuscan journal (*Arraldo Cattolica* of Lucca), presumably disillusioned by British support for the anti-clerical Garibaldi, found in events in the colony an illustration of the perfidy of Great Britain. That power pretended, it said, to sympathize with the cause of liberty in the Italian peninsula, but sought "by sword and bayonet ... to extirpate the smallest growth of freedom among her own subjects, when that freedom was in alliance with a devoted attachment to the Catholic faith."[63] The *Record* was able to quote and cite this and other Italian journals, horrified, it said, by the persecutions they had discerned in Newfoundland. Foreign observers regarded the "unconstitutional eccentricities" of Sir Alexander and his faction, not as aberrations from the law confined to themselves, but as "part and parcel of British policy and practice," invariably resorted to where there was any hope of impunity. These observers, looked upon the British constitution, in its theory, as a blind behind which the grossest outrages upon public liberty and private conscience were perpetrated. The evidence, it said, went far to support what it believed to be the universal opinion among enlightened foreigners.[64]

In view of the blatant incitements to violence, the Governor and the Attorney-General were understandably anxious about the autumn election at Harbour Grace. In August, Hoyles wrote to the Governor to express his conviction that unless the electors were afforded protection the occasion would be marked by unprecedented outrages and intimidation. Tactics of violence, he predicted, would ensure the return of one Roman Catholic candidate, equalize the party standings in the House, and prevent him from carrying on the Government. Even a majority of one in the Assembly would be sufficient, he thought, to win him the support of those Roman Catholics who would not otherwise be bold enough to transfer their allegiance. But he assured the Governor that party strength was only part of the issue and that what he hoped to avert from Newfoundland was government by a "purely Romish despotism, masked by *nominally* free institutions." Forwarding this letter to Newcastle, the Governor wrote that he was persuaded that if the law were upheld in Harbour Grace, the Bishop's agitation would fail and Catholics in the Assembly would no longer hesitate to vote for and enter a non-sectarian Administration. He proposed to send a military detachment to the district and to have a naval vessel in Conception Bay.[65]

The disorders of May and the threats of terrorism had led him in that month to requisition several companies of troops from Halifax with which to augment the garrison.[66] Although the question of their payment awaited the decision of the Assembly, he had retained part of this force on the grounds that it would be folly to reduce his strength.[67]

The protection the Governor was determined to afford at Harbour Grace, the *Record* sought to prevent. In the past, troops had been passive observers of election violence in this town, but now a precedent for active intervention had been set in St. John's. Anticipating the despatch of troops, the *Record* set itself to stay the Governor's hand. In October it published the following challenge:

Will the Catholics and protestants [*sic*] of that district, those who have hitherto united their exertions for their mutual benefit, their mutual prosperity, commence the work which Sir Alexander has assigned them, namely to cut each other's throats for the special gratification and profit of his Excellence and his Excellency's little contemptible Orange faction of St. John's? Will they do this, we ask? Never: be assured, never. But, says somebody, Sir Alexander will repeat his former experiment, and send Queen's troops to force compliance with his wishes. We challenge him to do it. His Excellency cannot, dare not do it. The first moment he moved a body of troops against the constitutional independence of the people—that moment a civil war was proclaimed, his allegiance to the Crown became forfeited, he stood before the country a traitor to his Sovereign; and as a traitor should have to be dealt with by the people. Repeat this experiment! Ah, such an experiment cannot afford a repetition. Try it, Sir Alexander,—*if you dare*.[68]

A month later, in a letter published in the *Royal Gazette*, the Governor gave notice of his intention to defy this "treasonable threat." His letter was a reply to an application for a protective force from the stipendiary magistrate at Harbour Grace, who had informed him that there were indications of trouble to come. The Governor wrote that in the light of the published threat and of certain verbal communications, the magistrate's apprehensions seemed well-founded. He referred, too, to daily reports about disorders in the district and to the slaying of a policeman on duty in Harbour Grace. He assured the magistrate that troops would be sent.[69]

Four days after this assurance, Bishop Mullock wrote to Sir Alexander to deny that he had any connection with the *Record*, or with the "treasonable threat," and to declare that he had never written or spoken a word to incite his flock to violence. His relationship with the *Record*, he said, was simply that of a subscriber. The Governor, replying, pointed out that there was a general belief in St. John's that the Bishop was the patron of this journal and had selected its editor. He alluded to the notorious fashion in which it had deviated from the prospectus of October 1860, in which it had been defined as a politically independent Roman Catholic journal whose precept was the golden rule. He did not ask why Bishop Mullock had failed until the eve of the election to disavow the opinions expressed in its columns and to dissociate himself from its policy.

The Bishop sent for the Governor's perusal a pastoral letter which he proposed to publish and read before the election. In this, he coupled a strong and eloquent plea for peace with an assurance that the sympathy of the clergy was with the people in their "wrongs and misfortunes." Upon the Governor's questioning the use of the word "wrongs" in a letter of pacific intent, the Bishop agreed, with some demur, to its deletion. Dr. Mullock's prescriptions for the ills of the colony were the establishment of a strong police force and the elimination of indiscriminate poor relief. He promised his co-operation to further these ends. He declared also that he would use his influence to prevent a repetition of the sad scenes of the past year. He proposed to make it known that the penalty of excommunication would apply to persons who carried deadly weapons with unlawful intent or who engaged in the malicious destruction of property.

These intimations that the Bishop intended to put civil peace and religious harmony before sectarian party, vindicating, as they seemed to do, the vigour of Sir Alexander's course, could not but be satisfactory to the Governor. Transmitting the Bishop's letters to Newcastle, he called his attention to the "pacific and Christian tone" in which they were written. The Duke expressed his pleasure with their tenor and their promises. He wrote to the Governor privately to say that he only awaited word of a quiet election at Harbour Grace to be convinced that Sir Alexander had "broken the neck of the disorders."[70]

The Governor's absolute refusal to be deterred by threats or promises from affording protection at Harbour Grace ensured a peaceful election, the return of the two Protestant candidates, and an accession of strength sufficient to allow the Hoyles party to carry on the Government. With a military detachment in the town and two naval vessels in the Bay, nomination and polling proceeded with none of the violence and intimidation of the past. More than 1300 of the 1400 registered electors were able to cast their votes in safety and to return the Protestant candidates by double the vote of their single Catholic opponent.[71] Sir Alexander's success in achieving an undisturbed election at Harbour Grace evoked from Newcastle an expression of official gratification.[72] At the opening of the Legislature the Governor, too, spoke of his gratification, pointing out that for the first time in four years an election in that town had not been marred by violence, and voicing the hope that naval and military protection would never again prove necessary for the free and independent exercise of the franchise in Newfoundland.[73]

The elation of one party and the chagrin of the other was such that it proved impossible to free the post-election trials in the Supreme Court from the intrusion of politics and the suspicion of bias. Chief Justice Brady, a Roman Catholic, informed the jurors that to carry sectarian and party spirit into the jury box would make the name of Newfoundland a "lasting by-word and a shame."[74] Yet, in the face of strong evidence, several of the leading spirits in the riot at St. John's secured acquittal, as did those charged with malicious destruction at Harbour Main. The eleven men charged with manslaughter in repelling the descent on Cat's Cove challenged the Roman Catholic jury on the grounds that justice could not be expected from members of the Bishop's party; though Catholics, they elected to leave their fate in Protestant hands. The Protestant jury brought in a verdict of guilty and left it to the Chief Justice to weigh the factors of mitigation. He condemned as "far worse than silly and foolish" those who had organized and had taken part in the march on the Cove. Since the fact of provocation had been established and the identity of the culprit had not, and since the men had been confined for some months, he pronounced sentences of less than two years. Four of the men were sentenced to twelve months' imprisonment from May, and five of them to nine months' from December 1861.

This judgment, with its light sentences and its thinly veiled censure of the Roman Catholic priest, stung Dr. Mullock as pastor and, one may suspect, as politician. He had awaited the outcome of the trials to issue his promised directive for the excommunication of all those who used firearms, stones, or other deadly weapons with intent to wound or kill. The letter he now circulated privately to his clergy was scarcely devised to promote confidence in the civil power in Newfoundland or to induce his priests to allay the fear and prejudice of their flocks. Instead of underlining Chief Justice Brady's condemnation of those who had organized the march, Dr. Mullock informed his clergy, in effect, that the Bench of the Supreme Court could not be relied upon for an impartial administration of justice and that they must therefore exhort their people to commit no offence against the law—"not only for wrath, (and that in this country should be a sufficient motive), but also for conscience' sake." To this end, he empowered them to announce that the sentence of excommunication would be passed on any person "using firearms with the unlawful intention of killing or wounding." From this sentence, persons who used pickets and stones—weapons notorious in Newfoundland—would seem to have been excluded.

The language of this confidential directive, not intended for the eye of the Governor, was very different from that which the Bishop had so recently employed. He told his clergy that life had been sacred in Newfoundland until assassination had been preached by a vile press, until murder had been made familiar to the people, and until doctrines subversive of all law had been "authoritatively" promulgated. The events of May 1861 had been commented on by every civilized people in Europe and America and the shooting of the priest had received the judgment of the world. These things could be borne, but the doctrine which had just been published suggested an end to the security of human life: that, if not lawful, it was "in great measure excusable to fire on unarmed people lawfully engaged, lest perhaps they might do some harm, though none was threatened." It was, he said, awful to contemplate the fact that an ignorant and isolated people had been led to kill, but worse to realize that persons with "some pretence to knowledge and refinement" should try to excuse them. For him, it showed a state of society in which "the whole head is sick and the whole heart is sad." Thousands of people now believed that crime might be committed with impunity if they belonged to a certain party. He would not say that this opinion had a "just foundation," but he held that

as long as the most awful crime that man can commit is punished in the same Court with a less penalty than petty larceny; as [long as] deliberate manslaughter, to call it by the mildest name, is a bailable offence, and minor ones are punished by 7 or 8 months previous imprisonment through the delay of justice, and those legally innocent and acquitted are obliged to suffer an incarceration which would be a great penalty for their crime if convicted; as long as warrants are allowed to become waste paper, and as long as the public have no confidence in the selection of jurors, and religion is supposed to be the test of qualification, so long will the people have no confidence in the administration of law.

He reminded his clergy that the highest tribunal was the Holy Catholic Church which knew no party, whose law was eternal justice, and by whom judges were condemned when the guilty were pardoned.

Before the prelate's condemnation of the Supreme Court reached the Governor,

Sir Alexander had decided to exercise his prerogative and to liberate the men from Cat's Cove. He announced that the extenuating circumstances cited by the Chief Justice had induced him to reply thus to the petition for release. As soon as his decision was known, the *Record* following the line of Dr. Mullock, published a vehement attack. It called the crime "murder," questioned the Governor's right of release, condemned the Catholics who had signed the petition, and pronounced all the signatories guilty of the crime at Cat's Cove.

A more decisive denunciation was to come. When the liberated men returned to their tiny village, a celebration was held, like that for the acquitted of Harbour Main. The latter had apparently been ignored by Dr. Mullock, but the demonstration at Cat's Cove drew from him the following decree:

> Having made the necessary enquiries we have been convinced of the truth of an outrage on Religion and humanity, perpetrated in Cat's Cove, by public rejoicing and hoisting Flags, not only in the Harbour, but at the place where George Furey was murdered, on the return of the "Convicts from St. John's Jail." Brutal and savage as that act itself was, this last outrage shows that the perpetrators are a disgrace to human nature and that the place they inhabit is branded with the curse of Cain. Therefore invoking the Holy Name of God, etc., we ordain that no Mass be said, no Station held, and no Sacrament, unless to the dying (and Baptism in the case of extreme necessity) be administered in Cat's Cove, for the next twelve months, from this date. The Church will remain closed for the same time.
>
> We pray that God may enlighten the darkened understanding, and soften the stony hearts of these people, that by sincere repentance they may escape the awful judgment which His judgment holds over them.

This document the Governor regarded as worthy of the "Dark Ages of the Church." It seemed wrong to him that the Bishop could denounce with impunity the Governor, the Supreme Court, and the laws of the colony, as well as the troops of the Queen, and could accuse persons of murder who had never been tried for such a crime. Although he took no official notice of the charges, he arranged for the publication of the two letters in the press. He intended thus, he said, to forestall their appearance in the colony in newspapers from Ireland which argued that he was following a policy marked out by the British Government for the extermination of Roman Catholics.

For Sir Alexander, the Bishop was as much the aggrieved politician as the grieved man of God. In the despatch of February 28 he told Newcastle that loss of influence prompted Dr. Mullock's outbursts and that the Bishop had failed to secure the return of Hogsett over a rival Catholic in a by-election in St. John's. He thought that the absence that summer of both bishops at a convention in Rome would be conducive to the peace of the island. In an aside which was rather unusual in an official despatch, the Governor hoped the bishops might "fall in with Garibaldi."[75] When the prelates sailed for Europe in May, they were "crestfallen," he said, at the reply to the petition for his recall.[76] During the summer Newcastle had a conversation with the Roman Catholic Archbishop of Halifax, Dr. Connolly, who, according to the Duke, condemned Dr. Mullock's conduct as that of a "firebrand and disturber of the peace" and regretted that his own jurisdiction did not extend to Newfoundland.[77]

The elections of 1861 had annihilated the hopes of the great political-ecclesiastical confederacy which for three decades had dominated representative government in Newfoundland. Since 1859 the Liberal party, weakened by the corruptions and jealousies of office and threatened by the pressure of their rivals, had trembled on the verge of disunity. Dr. Mullock had sought to promote this division, to re-form the party under episcopal patronage, and to secure their election. His thesis was that none but a Liberal-Catholic Administration would protect the rights of Catholics and foster civilization in the colony. Sir Alexander had sought to promote conditions which would give the lie to this sectarian argument. He had adopted a boldly political and dubiously constitutional course in dismissing his ministers and had afforded the security which would allow the electors to return a new set of men. He had set himself to counteract the circumstances and influences which had for so long excluded one party from power. He had given this party the opportunity to emerge from their inertia and pessimism, to exhibit their energies in the cause of Newfoundland, to win new adherents, and to break the sectarian pattern in the formation of ministries and the distribution of office. His intervention had fanned religious jealousy to white heat; his vindication must come from an abatement of this feeling and from a decrease in the sectarian ingredient in party politics.

CHAPTER TWELVE

AFTERMATH

THE EVENTS of 1861 had blasted the politics of class, sect, and "race", but shock and suspicion were such that a new structure could not immediately be raised. Nor were its architects those who had cleared the way, for H. W. Hoyles retired from politics and Governor Bannerman from the colony in 1864.

Although proceedings in the Assembly in 1862 were, inevitably, marked by party acrimony, Hoyles was able to command a steady majority and some Catholic support and by firm direction to cut the session to half the usual length.[1] Most of the members seemed to recognize that for the safety and reputation of Newfoundland, disorders must be suppressed.[2] Hoyles piloted through the House a series of measures designed to remove some of the sources of the recent excitement and to prevent its repetition. The police establishment at Harbour Grace and Carbonear was almost doubled. The Appropriation Act (26 Vict., c. 13) provided for 99 constables in Newfoundland, 13 of them at Harbour Grace, and 8 at Carbonear. The figures in 1859 (22 Vict., c. 20) had been, respectively 84, 7, and 4. The districts in which destruction had occurred were penalized by making payment of damages a first charge on their grant for roads.[3] A custom of the Christmas festive season, which had become the cloak for vandalism and assault, was made illegal (c. 4) by providing for the summary arrest and sentencing of all persons masked and disguised as "mummers." Several alterations were made in the jury regulations (c. 6) to decrease the role of petty jurors and the chances of a partisan panel.[4] Two questions which had for some time vexed the House were settled. A measure (c. 9) modelled on those of the other colonies for securing the independence of the Assembly disabled from membership, with named exceptions, the holders of government office. Those not debarred from membership were the Attorney-General, Colonial Secretary, Receiver-General, Solicitor-General, Surveyor-General, Financial Secretary, the chairmen of committees, and the directors of the Savings Bank. Contractors with the Government were to be ineligible but not members of corporations contracting with the government or holders of debentures for the public debt. The controversy about the meaning of "sterling" in previous legislation was brought to an end, it being enacted (c. 10) that all salaries, with four exceptions, were to be paid at the Newfoundland currency rate. The exceptions were the salaries of the Governor and the Chief Justice and the pensions of two retired judges which were to be paid at the sterling rate. The Governor's report on the session seemed to the Colonial Office to justify his *coup d'etat* of 1861 and to inspire the hope that he had opened a new and happier chapter in the history of the colony.[5]

Again in 1863 the Governor derived much satisfaction from proceedings in the Assembly and from the passage of twenty useful bills in a session less than two months in length. He attributed this productivity to the "perseverance and business habits" of Attorney-General Hoyles who gave "ample scope to Mr. Kent and his friends to state their objections at length to every measure brought forward, but took care that the business was finished before prorogation at night."[6] Among the displaced Liberals there seems to have been some nostalgia for the bear-garden scenes of the past. The editor of the Liberal *Newfoundlander* wrote that nothing could be expected from the session of 1864 but the "dull" despatch of business.[7]

The new Government was handicapped by a depleted treasury, by heavy demands, and by successive poor fisheries from 1861 to 1864. The *Record*, blending piety with politics, announced that failing fisheries and pauperism were the just chastisement of Newfoundland.[8] Retrenchment in the expenditure for poor relief proved easier to preach than to effect. The successive failures in the fisheries and growing indebtedness led to a decreased consumption of dutiable goods and so to a fall in imports, but upon the reduced revenue there was increasing pressure for relief.[9] In the period of high revenue the Liberals had voted one-tenth of the annual income for relief; in the recession which followed the vote rose to one-fifth (see Appendix F). The enormous drain was not stopped until 1868 when the Administration announced the suppression of relief to the able-bodied poor, a decision which the excellent fishery of 1869 made it possible to sustain.[10] The need for revenue led the Hoyles Government to add to the import duties on rum and spirits (27 Vict., c. 1). They also provided (c. 1, c. 2) for the appointment of customs officers and the collection of duties on the Labrador coast, and for the establishment of a Court of Record for summary proceedings in Labrador with the right of appeal to the Supreme Court (c. 2, c. 3), measures unsuccessfully opposed by certain West Coast merchants who had long resorted to the Labrador coast.[11] The wedge of direct taxation was entered in 1863 with provisions for assessment for water rates in St. John's and Harbour Grace (c. 4, c. 5), as well as for sewerage and a fire brigade in the capital (c. 6, c. 9). Other financial measures of the Hoyles Administration were an Act (c. 17) consolidating and reducing the interest on the public debt, the debt amounting in 1864 to £177,000; and an Act (c. 18) by which the dollar replaced the pound as the medium of exchange, the public accounts being converted to the decimal system in 1865. There were a number of material advances during the eighteen-sixties: the use of steam in the seal fishery (1862); the opening of a copper mine at Tilt Cove (1864); the beginning of a geological survey (1865); the landing of the Atlantic cable (1866); and the establishment of a permanent direct steam service with England. Prosperity returned in 1868.[12]

In September 1864 Sir Alexander Bannerman, who had reached the age of eighty-one, completed his term of office in Newfoundland. His farewell message to his ministers made explicit reference to the unresolved sectarian controversy. He hoped that the ministers would be able to surmount their great financial problems until the general election of 1865 and that the electors would then decide that, under representative government, representatives of no one particular sect should be allowed to claim an "hereditary title" to rule over the colony.[13] His active intervention in the island's political struggle made it inevitable that one party should applaud and the other regret his departure. Kent, who had been succeeded by Ambrose Shea as leader of the Opposition, used· the occasion to publish a denunciation of the Governor's whole course from arrival to departure, with special attention to his own dismissal from office in 1861.[14] For the Liberal press, the many farewell testimonials to the Governor were merely the "thanks of faction for services to faction."[15] The *Ledger* filled its columns with these addresses of tribute and regret, and deplored the loss of a gentleman of "deep penetration, sound judgment, and a firm hand."[16] Three decades after Sir Alexander's departure this opinion was echoed in the pages of Prowse, who as a young man had known the aged Governor, and who declared that he was honoured, and long would be, as an honest, straightforward administrator and as a genial, kindly, and liberal old Scot.[17] Sir Alexander died almost immediately after his return to Scotland.

The retirement of Hoyles in 1864 and his appointment to be Chief Justice in 1865 removed from the political scene the other protagonist in what Catholic Liberals believed to be a plot for a Protestant ascendancy, and prepared the stage for new political affiliations. His tasks as leader of his very small Government had been arduous and had apparently made inroads upon his health. Whatever the degree of truth in the charges of a Protestant bias in politics, his industry and impartiality on the Bench seem to have gone far to dispel animosity against him and to win him the esteem of all classes in the colony. As the century drew to a close Prowse wrote of Hoyles that "he made a model judge, the most painstaking, able and impartial administrator that ever graced the Bench of any British colony—an indefatigable worker, he gave no complaint for the law's delays. His decision of character, his amiable manners, and his extreme courtesy endeared him to all. We are all proud of Sir Hugh as the most distinguished Newfoundlander of our day."[18] Hoyles was succeeded as leader of the Government by F. B. T. Carter, Q.C., Speaker of the House, a Protestant and a native.

The general election of 1865 brought Carter increased support and, with the mitigation of the rancour of 1861, it proved possible as well as expedient to put into effect the principle of a fair representation of all religious parties in the formation of the Administration.[19] The Government formed by Carter in 1866 after the election was an "amalgamated" one containing representatives of the three major religious groups, among them members of the old Liberal party, including John Kent, Lawrence O'Brien, and Ambrose Shea (see Appendix C). The amalgamation principle had long been indicated by the religious proportions in the population, by the stormy record of sectarian politics, and by the need for administrative talent. It was virtually dictated during the eighteen-sixties by the weakening of exclusive sectarian attitudes and the growth in "native" sentiment,[20] and by the willingness of a significant number of Catholic politicians and electors to break away from the party patronized by the Church. Although the sectarian ingredient did not disappear from politics, the violence of 1861 seems to have demonstrated the folly of a struggle for religious ascendancy in government.[21] There was a brief reversion to the old exclusive sectarian principle in the Thorburn "Protestant" Government of 1885, but by 1887 it was found expedient to bring in some Catholics. In 1896 Prowse could declare that as a direct result of the disorders of 1861, "sectarianism in politics, bigotry, and intolerance" had year by year diminished, and that from the advent of the Carter Government denominational amalgamation had become the "settled rule" in the formation of ministeries and in the distribution of offices.[22]

"Out of evil sometimes comes good," wrote Prowse in 1896, but thirty-seven years later a Royal Commission, investigating at Newfoundland's request the collapse of public finance and credit, was to report that the "settled rule" had become a settled evil. Discussing the careful distribution of departmental offices and government posts among members of the three principal denominations, Church of England, United Church, and Roman Catholic, the commissioners recorded that this practice was a major factor in the several decades of misgovernment which had contributed to the economic chaos they found. Of the "settled rule," they said:

. . . while doubtless achieving the salutary object of avoiding overt rivalry between the Churches, it must necessarily be a handicap to good administration. Moreover, the underlying principle of equality between the Churches has been extended and amplified in some directions and modified in others, to the detriment, it must be said, of the best interests of the country. Thus, if a member of one denomination obtains a contract from the Government, then members of the other main denominations must be selected for some compensating favour. All appointments, not merely to the Civil Service, but to Boards and Committees, must be equally allotted. On the other hand, the Minister in charge of a Department is commonly expected to show special consideration to the members of his own denomination, and here the principle of equality takes a different form.

It might have been expected that the influence of the Churches, so strong in Newfoundland, would have acted as a check to political malpractices. It is clear from our investigations that this is not the case, and we have reluctantly come to the conclusion that the denominational divisions, of which the people are daily reminded, so far from exercising a beneficent influence in the direction of cleaner politics, have failed to check, if indeed they have not contributed to the general demoralisation. For members of successive Administrations have been led, consciously or sub-consciously, to place the interests of particular sections of the Church before the good of the country as a whole; and the desire to serve those interests, and to promote the welfare of individual members of the same denomination, has conduced to a disregard of the proprieties which would never have reached such proportions had Newfoundland been united in one religious community, or if sectarianism had not assumed such political influence.

Public life in Newfoundland, the commissioners said, was "confused by many obligations, political, denominational, and domestic; in gratification of these the obligations of good government were apt to be ignored."[23] Among the political factors contributing to misgovernment, they cited: the operation of a brazen "spoils system"; the reluctance of the very small educated class to enter the arena of corruption and personal abuse; the disposition of the electorate, conditioned to the demoralizing credit system, to regard the merchants as exploiters rather than as friends and co-operators; the election of candidates whose records or promises indicated a willingness to put the interests of their districts and their constituents before the general welfare of the island; and an ingrained tendency to look to the Government as a paternal provider and to the members of the Assembly as the channels of Government funds. They reported that the whole tone of public life was unhealthy, the party awaiting power generally condoning the greed, graft, and corruption of the other, politicians seeking and gaining personal enrichment, and successive governments, in the name of modernization and progress, putting the demands of outside investing interests and "concession hunters" before the requirements of sound and economical government. The rule of amassing benefits during a party's tenure of office had contributed, they said, to twelve successive unbalanced budgets, to misgovernment, to *ad hoc* increases in the tariff, and to exorbitant prices for imported goods.

The commissioners reported adversely, too, on the political maturity of the electors and upon the political integrity of the candidates. They found no real distinction of principle between the parties, despite the use of the labels "Liberal," "Conservative," and "Labour," and they found that candidates tended to secure election by exploiting the naivety of the outport voters. These they characterized as easy-going, law-abiding individualists, marked by a sense of patriotism, but by an absence of community spirit.[24] In 1933 there was not a municipal government in the island except that established in St. John's by the Act of 1888. By 1945 nine other municipalities had been incorporated. Municipal government was resisted and delayed for a number of reasons: the original settlers of the outports, unlike those of other areas of North America, had had no experience with municipal institutions; the littoral settlements were sparsely populated and widely separated; the fishing industry drew the male population away from their homes; and dread of direct taxation was reinforced by the chronic scarcity of currency in the outports. The Commissioners reported that the credit system had had a deleterious psychological effect in that it bred distrust and suspicion rather than a spirit of co-operation between supplier and supplied. They quoted with approval an earlier finding which had blamed the credit system for "dishonesty, extravagance, luxury, carelessness, recklessness, want of energy, laziness, and dependence" amongst the fishing population. They found that, in general, the people tended to be shrewd and suspicious in their business dealings, but in other matters, as simple as children. In this they echoed the opinion of Sir Thomas Cochrane who a century earlier had written that the people of the outports were "merely children of a larger growth" in need of guardianship rather than representative government.[25]

The economic depression of the nineteen-thirties, with its disastrous effect on the market for the island's staples, reduced the ill-governed country to a desperate position. With enormous annual deficits, with a huge public debt at high interest rates, and with credit almost impossible to obtain, Newfoundland had ceased by 1933 to be an economically viable entity. After an investigation into the causes of the collapse, the Royal Commission recommended a temporary cessation of party politics, the suspension of responsible government, and its replacement by a Commission of Government—in effect, the reversion of Newfoundland to the status of a Crown colony. This arrangement went into effect in February 1934.[26] Then, with the United Kingdom shouldering the budgetary deficits, the Commission devoted itself to the task of increasing the national income and of improving public administration and welfare. Its economic policies, which did not differ radically from those of previous governments, and which had only limited success, were designed to increase the productivity of old industries and to encourage the establishment of new. The establishment of advanced scientific and technical services, through which Newfoundland might improve its competitive position in world markets, proved beyond the means of the small community. But significant improvements were made in the administrative organization and in the civil service. The maintenance of highways was removed from the sphere of political patronage. Partisan interference in appointments to office and in administrative practice were eliminated under the Commission. Some experienced persons from Britain were brought into the civil service and a beginning was made in the recruitment of able young Newfound-landers.[27] The Commission continued to govern through the years of depression and war until, after a popular referendum, which showed much anti-Confederation sentiment, the island joined the Dominion of Canada in April 1949.

CHAPTER THIRTEEN

RETROSPECT

IN RETROSPECT, one sees Newfoundland in the first three decades of representative government as an embittered little Ireland and as a rudimentary North
American colony; it had the grievances and prejudices of the one and the ambitions and frustrations of the other. "Racial" and religious animosities against
the English smouldered in half the population of 1832, for conditions in the new
land fostered memories of wrongs in the old. In Ireland the Irish had known
defeat and coercion, plantation and union, eviction and famine; they had suffered
the absence of landlords and the presence of agents; they had resented the
privileges of an alien church and the restrictions on national industry. In Newfoundland they found the English still their masters in industry and government,
still their betters in wealth and status; they faced monopolistic suppliers and
ruthless agents, high prices and perpetuating debts, curtailed credit and recurrent
famine; they saw the English church established in effect, if not in fact, and their
livelihood limited by English concessions to the French. In Ireland they had
met arrogance with defiance and had looked to their demagogues as spokesmen
and to their clergy as guides; in Newfoundland, too, they resorted to the intimidation of Protestants and relied upon the leadership of democrats and priests.
A handful of Irish and Scottish liberals was ready, like the French in Lower
Canada, to struggle with the English at home and in the colony for the rights
won by Englishmen in the seventeenth century. These frontier democrats, imi-
tating prematurely their counterparts in the neighbouring colonies and their
predecessors in England, were not content that the representative body should
have the mere shadow of power. They sought to control the purse, to curtail the
power of the executive and the judiciary, to extend the area of colonial autonomy,
and to win appointments to office. They had to contend, like their colonial
contemporaries, with the irritations of government from a distance—with delays
and refusals, with referred complaints and deferred replies, with galling appointments and antipathetic governors, with the slow evolution of colonial policy and
the rapid succession of colonial secretaries.

Their complaints were in the colonial pattern that followed the concession of
representative government, but in the concession itself there seems, in retrospect,
more to complain of from haste than from delay. The resentment sown in the
years of prohibited settlement and slow recognition might never have sprung
to such height and vigour had the Whig ministers chosen to withhold the sudden
change and to devote a few years to fostering harmony and co-operation. In
recognizing the need for change and in rejecting the need for experience, in
yielding to the pressure of the colonists and in dismissing the advice of the

Governor, in equating the island with British North America and in missing the analogy with Ireland, in embracing the panacea of a wide franchise and in ignoring the danger of a poor electorate, in condemning legislative councils for the colonies and in establishing one in Newfoundland, the Colonial Office ensured for that island three decades of political disorder.

The initial folly having been committed, ten years elapsed before the constitution was suspended, the electoral qualifications raised, and the quarrelling chambers replaced by the amalgamated body so ineffectually broached in 1832. These were the years in which clerical direction and coercion, and mob violence and intimidation, ensured a united Catholic vote and a Catholic-dominated House—the years in which the tactics of the Catholics consolidated the Protestants in defeat and opposition and goaded them from conservative principles to obstruction to the representative principle itself. These were the years in which sectarian parties, Catholic and Protestant, established themselves in the districts and entrenched themselves, respectively, in the Assembly and the Council. This was the decade in which the Catholic party in the Assembly sought to expand colonial rights and to diminish Imperial control, in which the Protestant party in the Council fought to curb the assumptions of the Assembly and to support the prerogatives of the Crown, and in which the Governor tried to obey his Instructions and to devise remedies which his superiors would accept. This was the decade in which the Colonial Office, beset with problems from all the North American colonies and loth to expose them to Parliament, aware that the constitution had brought evils to the island and convinced that its abridgement would mean embarrassment for the Government, urged Governor Prescott to seek legislative amendments from the very body most unlikely to accede.

In this period, the unhappy Colonial Secretary, Glenelg, vulnerable to criticism and anxious to placate, veered, in a slow retreat before the pressure of the Assembly, between irresolution, decision, and delay, irritating alike the Governor and the contending parties in the island. His decision to invalidate the election of 1836 on a minor legal point brought the return of a more hostile Liberal majority, while the subsequent reversal of this decision by the Law Officers of the Crown gave the victorious party further grounds for accusation and complaint. The removal of Chief Justice Boulton from the Council and the Bench gratified the Liberals, who had seen him as an enemy, but it mortified their rivals, who had used him as a prop. The support afforded the Council in the struggle over the voting of supply strengthened their will to oppose, but it hardened the Assembly's determination to deny them the right to amend. The representations to the Papal Court and the enquiry into the activities of Bishop Fleming induced the Bishop to end his political career, but they estranged this leader from the Governor, enlarged the Catholics' sense of grievance, and embittered those who had hoped the prelate would be removed.

This period of inept intervention saw the establishment of the politics of class, sect, and "race." It saw, too, the inflammation of jealously and suspicion by a scurrilous political press. In these years, Roman Catholics defined the Protestants as the party of mercantile privilege and religious bigotry, of executive obstruction and economic stagnation, while they designated themselves the party of popular freedom and religious liberty, of democratic progress and material advance. In these year, the Protestants conjured up the spectre of Catholic ascendancy and sought Imperial protection as a shelter from political defeat. While these prejudices were deepening their roots, the Whigs continued to hope that they would be eradicated by time. Only the violence of 1841, the despair of the Governor, and the questions of the Opposition convinced them that action was required.

It fell to the Tories to provide a representative constitution for New South Wales and a new constitution for Newfoundland in 1842; on both colonies an amalgamated legislature was bestowed. For one it was a reward for patience and for the other a penalty for haste. The Australian colony had had separated councils since 1825 and a bare majority of officials in the Legislative Council since 1828, because of the cleavage in the population—half convict-settlers and half free. The cleavage in opinion and population had been cited as grounds for deferring representative institutions, while the unity of opinion and interest in Newfoundland had been given as reasons for establishing such bodies. This unity had soon proved more apparent than real and the religious factor as significant in that colony as the factor of transportation in New South Wales. It is tempting to surmise that had Newfoundland been set twenty years earlier on a parallel course with New South Wales, sectarian politics might have been avoided. Had the novel constitution been given in 1832, it would have been greeted as an advance in status rather than as a punitive change.

Religious parties having been established, the apprenticeship of amalgamation came late, nor could its term be extended long enough for attitudes in the colony to change. Initially, the chastening effect of the suspension, the novelty of the arrangements, and the adroitness of Sir John Harvey resulted in sessions which, if not free from carping and abuse, produced the basic legislation. But the influence of the island's past and the impact of the Canadian example proved too strong. Mutual suspicions were not removed, but overlaid by mutual bargaining; with a political press to reproach and remind, neither side could forget that they had laid aside principles for peace. As the experiment continued, the Assembly fell into increasing disrepute and the constitution seemed more of a stigma. The constitutionalists, looking to the past, pressed for a return to the old system, with modifications to increase and improve the House; Catholic suspicions revived. The Liberals, looking to the future, pressed for the concession of responsible government, which Canada was about to extract; Protestant anxiety returned. The Conservatives, deploring the lack of an upper chamber, felt their interests were endangered; the constitutionalists, denouncing the anomalies of the system, said the colony was degraded; and the Liberals, discerning the future in Canada, claimed that justice was withheld.

When the Whigs restored their provocative constitution in 1848, sectarian efforts to win and to resist responsible government had already begun. For six years the Protestants urged that the colony was unready for the concession and that the Catholics would win perpetual and unwarranted power. With this view the governors concurred. The Catholics urged that it was invidious to refuse what had been conceded elsewhere. To this pressure the Colonial Office succumbed. Having come to the decision reluctantly, the Office then over-ruled colonial dissent. A bitter party struggle was provoked by the condition that there must first be a fair bill for increasing the membership of the House. Under the threat of suspension, the Council gave assent to a bill; under the terms of the measure, the Catholics came easily to power.

Thus Newfoundland began self-government with rival sectarian parties and with sectarian ascendancy an aim. But native, as opposed to Catholic, liberalism was awaiting the chance to emerge. Before the Catholics began their second term of office, factionalism in the party suggested that the old pattern must presently break. Governor Bannerman, advised by the Opposition, precipitated the change by abruptly dismissing his ministers and by contributing to their narrow defeat in the sudden election of 1861. A brief period of chagrin and suspicion followed in which it seemed that permanent damage had been done and that non-sectarian governments might never be installed. But the growth of native sentiment had prepared the ground for the change. Four years later, with a new leader and a new governor, there was a more decisive victory at the polls and a non-sectarian government could be formed. Expediency then dictated to both parties the principle of religious representation in government. This principle, with results both good and evil, became the permanent rule of political life.

The adoption of this rule meant the end of sectarian parties, as such, and the pervasion of sectarian politics through the whole of public life. Overt rivalry between the churches was replaced by a rigid equality of denominational representation which, as the Royal Commission of 1933 found, was as detrimental to good government as the former system had been disruptive to public peace. Summoned in 1933 to investigate the factors which had led to the expansion of the island's debt and to exhaustion of the public credit, the Commission found a history of maladministration and mismanagement of the revenue to which denominational rule and denominational zeal had contributed much. It called for a cessation of party politics and representative government until solvency was restored. A century after the granting of an Assembly, the island reverted to a colonial status which was essentially that of 1832.

Surveying the chequered career of representative government in Newfoundland—the constitution suspended after a decade, revoked again when it was a century old, responsible government opposed for six years by the Protestants, the Catholics ousted under protest when they had been for six years in power—one is forced to conclude that the island's institutions, when given, were not suited to the population's needs. A system demanding population, experience, and a revenue was applied to a community where no middle class had emerged, where no municipal institutions had been established, and where no direct tax could be imposed. Institutions suitable to a population with an acquired homogeneity were given to a colony in which peace had been preserved by the infrequency of occasions for clash. Responsibilities borne by the classically educated of England, schooled in the civilities of political strife, were transferred to colonial democrats whose formal schooling was narrow, but whose political ambitions were high. The wide franchise, suggested by the sparsity of the population and by the temper of the times, fostered rivalry between the two small segments of the community which had joined in seeking the change—between the intellectual liberals and radicals, patently in advance of the unlettered mass, and the supplying merchants, to whom the majority of the populace was in the bondage of debt. Electoral districts, suggested by the confines of geography and by the claims of equality, promoted, rather than prevented, the division of the population into the political halves suggested by the bisecting line of pre- judice, tradition, religion, and "race." Open voting, suggested by custom in Eng- land and by distrust of the ballot, raised the fear of economic coercion by Protestant merchants and permitted the use of spiritual coercion by Irish priests; it allowed that physical intimidation by the Catholics which united the Protes- tants in defeat; and it inhibited that potential liberalism among the Protestants whose absence sustained the Catholic claim to a monopoly of that political creed. The dual chamber system, suggested by the models in England and by their transfer to British settlements abroad, encouraged the Catholic party to seek domination of the Assembly and prompted the Catholic Bishop to take an active political role; it tempted the Protestants to abandon the fight for election and to entrench themselves in the Council; and it invited them to lean on the Governor and to look to the Home Government for support. Governors who were re- sponsible, whatever their politics, to those who directed from London, were forced into conflict with reformers who were responsive, whatever their motives, to changes in the colonies nearby. A system which was essentially evolutionary was bestowed on a colony unready to evolve.

The alternative had lain in the hands of the Whigs; they had admired it and had laid it timidly aside. They had seen the merits of a united legislature, but they had declined to innovate. Ten years which might have been devoted to founding mutual trust, to establishing political civility, and to advancing the good of the colony, were spent in cultivating the seeds of suspicion, in creating a tradition of violence, and in obstructing the designs of the House. When legislative union was imposed, the former rivals felt their demotion in status; when constitutional checks were removed, the political veterans found the means to corrupt. But the early harmony of the joint House and the enlightened legis- lation which was passed suggest that the political pattern in Newfoundland could have been other than it was.

Had the colony graduated from the tutelage of legislative co-operation directly or indirectly into the era of responsible government, it might have had the personnel for alternative party administrations which were distinguished by political principles not parallel with distinctions of religion and "race." Had there been, at the beginning of party government, a choice of administrations which were "representative" and "responsible" alike, less disruptive political develop- ments would surely have ensued. The concession of 1855 might not have been divisive; the dismissal of 1861 might not have been evoked; the "rule" of 1865 might not have been established; the suspension of 1933 might not have been required.

Two failures of perception at the Colonial Office seem to have brought New- foundland the constitution of 1832 which provoked its latent dissensions and which overlooked its special needs. One was the failure to realize that a colony which had long felt retarded and deprived was less likely to relinquish parlia- mentary models, once they had been secured, then was Parliament to modify them, once the need had been explained. The other was the failure to see that the analogy was not with Upper Canada, Nova Scotia, and New Brunswick, but with the old French colony, Quebec.

In his constitutional memorandum of 1832, Stephen had pronounced the assembly a boon to all colonies not divided into different "castes," as in the West Indies, or composed of different "nations," as in Lower Canada and the Cape of Good Hope. He had declared that the assemblies of Upper Canada, Nova Scotia, and New Brunswick, in meeting the ends for which they had been devised, were unmatched by any other legislature which, to his knowledge, had appeared. But, though he had termed the legislative council uncongenial and unnecessary to these colonies, he had not gone on to delineate the factors which might make it even less suited to the situation in Newfoundland. Yet these factors were there to be discerned. The mainland colonies had received a great infusion of Loyalists in 1783. Their education, their experience in public offices, colonial legislatures, and the professions, and their familiarity with popularly elected local government had had a significant effect. The newcomers had assumed prominent places in the councils and the assemblies; parties had been formed on the basis of privilege and conservatism to oppose parties of democratic aspiration and reform; these rivalries had proved vexatious but not disruptive to societies where pressures towards homogeneity were at work.

The situation was different in Newfoundland. Since the opening of the nineteenth century there had been an influx of population comparable to the Loyalist migration in numbers, but not in civilizing weight. The mass of Irish emigrants had brought not education, or executive ability, or means, but, rather, a low standard of life; they knew nothing of elective local government, but they had seen violence at the hustings and the polls; they were predisposed by past experience to dislike the English and to distrust the Protestants they found. Thus Newfoundland in 1832 was less a colonial version of England than a colonial Ireland with the Irish potential for strife.

There were parallels with Lower Canada, too. Stephen observed the divisive tendency of the representative institutions in that colony, where the French majority was divided from the minority by language, religion, tradition, and culture. He clearly did not regard as a "nation" the Irish community in Newfoundland. But the elements of nationalism were unmistakably there, and for both French and Irish the old enemy was the same. In Lower Canada, where England had gone some way towards establishing harmony by recognizing the Roman Catholic Church and the French language and civil law in 1774, the Church had proved a conservative force. In Ireland, where old grievances still festered, despite the Acts of Union and Emancipation, the Church was ranged on the side of the aggrieved. In Newfoundland, where Catholics had been emancipated on paper but where discrimination had not been erased, the identification of emigrant clergy and people had always been significantly close. But no time was spent in rectifying the past; the transition from neglect and bias was abrupt. One concludes that it was not a dearth of information but an absence of vision that produced the constitution of 1832—that fancied analogies obscured valid parallels and that the claims of theory outweighed those of fact.

In the longer view, of course, the disorders of the nineteenth century stemmed from older decisions devised to meet situations in centuries past. Policies for the domination of Ireland had made the Irish hostile at home; subsequent emigration made the Irish problem a truly Imperial one. Mercantilist legislation and navigation laws had made settlement illicit in Newfoundland; slow abandonment of the policy allowed a little Ireland to establish its roots and to grow despite neglect. Efforts to appease the French had planted a thorn in the island's side; belated efforts to ease the irritation provoked the self-governing colony's rage. Since these policies and decisions were adopted to meet the needs of England, and not to prepare the ground for representative government in a colony which did not legitimately exist, it is absurd to condemn them as short-sighted and ill-advised. It is the failure to give due weight to the situation they had created that may properly be deplored.

Policies, geography, and economy have kept Newfoundland eccentric and peripheral in the British North American scene. The island never really belonged to the old colonial system, in that it was not a colony until 1824. It did not really resemble the colonies of the Second Empire, with their American components, in that its roots were in the Old World, though its aspirations were in the New. It was not ready to federate with its neighbours in 1867, for it was held back by the bonds of its own origin, history, and way of life—by insular patriotism and pride, prejudice, and fear. It could not retain its Dominion status, for it had lost its viability by 1933. When Confederation was finally accepted, almost half the population was still against the change.

It has been contended here that political strife and constitutional change in Newfoundland stemmed from consecutive colonial policies inappropriate in their timing to the place. The first was the imposition of the post-Revolution formula for the maintenance of colonial peace. The second was the adherence to the Canadian example in establishing responsible government. If there is a lesson to be derived for an evolving colony in the political history of Newfoundland, it would seem to be the somewhat unpalatable one that there is folly in slavish emulation of one colony by another and wisdom in refraining from premature efforts to leave colonial status behind. Through the chequered pattern of Newfoundland's history since 1832 light falls upon the need in each colony for close investigation on the spot; for a constitution relevant to the state of the colony and not to the status of another; for a governor who is sympathetic and capable and for government tutelage that is wise; for evidence that leaders are responsible and that the colony is stable and sound; and, finally, for gradualism, firmness, and patience when the transition to self-government is coming to a close.

APPENDIXES

BIOGRAPHICAL NOTES ON GOVERNORS
OF NEWFOUNDLAND

Sir Thomas Cochrane	1825-34
Captain Henry Prescott	1834-41
Sir John Harvey	1841-47
Sir John Gaspard LeMarchant	1847-52
Mr. Ker Baillie Hamilton	1852-55
Sir Charles Darling	1855-57
Sir Alexander Bannerman	1857-64

BANNERMAN, Sir Alexander, Knight. 1783-1864. Cousin of baronet of same name; extensive shipowner, merchant, and banker at Aberdeen. 1832-47, Liberal M.P. for Aberdeen. 1837, Dean of the Faculty of Marischal College, Aberdeen. 1841, Commissioner of Greenwich Hospital. 1851, Lieutenant-Governor of Prince Edward Island. 1854, Governor of Bahamas. 1857-64, Governor of Newfoundland. (*Men of the Reign*, 1885.)

COCHRANE, Sir Thomas, C.B., K.C.B., G.C.B. 1789-1872. Eldest son of Admiral Sir Alexander Forrest Inglis Cochrane. 1796, entered as volunteer on "Thetis." 1805, Lieutenant on "Jason." 1806, Captain of "Jason" — rapid promotions through father's influence. 1806-9, service in West Indies. 1809-11, naval half-pay. 1811-15, Commander of frigate "Surprise" on North Atlantic Station. 1820-24, Commander of "Forte" on North Atlantic Station. 1825-34, Governor of Newfoundland. 1841, Rear-Admiral. 1839-41, Conservative M.P. for Ipswich. 1842-45, Second-in-Command on China Station. 1845-47, Commander-in-Chief on China Station. 1852-55, Commander-in-Chief, Portsmouth. 1850, Vice-Admiral. 1856, Admiral. 1856, Admiral of the Fleet. (*Dictionary of National Biography*; O'Byrne's *Naval Biography*; Marshall's *Naval Biography*.)

DARLING, Sir Charles, K.C.B. 1809-70. Born Annapolis Royal, Nova Scotia, son of a former Lieutenant-Governor of Tobago and grandson of a former Governor of Bahamas; educated at Royal Military College, Sandhurst. 1827-47, colonial service—various posts in New South Wales, Barbados and Windward Islands, and Jamaica. 1847, Lieutenant-Governor of St. Lucia. 1851-54, Lieutenant-Governor (civil) of Cape of Good Hope. 1855-57, Governor of Newfoundland. 1857, Governor of Jamaica. 1862-66, Governor of Victoria. (*DNB*.)

HAMILTON, Ker Baillie, C.B. 1804(?)-(?). Educated at Royal Military Academy, Woolwich. 1822, entered Indian military service. 1826, writer in civil service, Mauritius, and assistant private secretary to Governor. 1829, Clerk of Council, later Colonial Secretary, at Cape of Good Hope. 1846, Lieutenant-Governor of Granada. 1851, Administrator of Barbados and Windward Islands. 1852-55, Governor of Newfoundland. 1855-63, Governor of Antigua and Leeward Islands. (Prowse, *History*, p. 465, n. 2.)

HARVEY, Sir John, K.C.H., K.C.B. 1778-1852. 1794, entered 80th Regiment as Ensign. 1794-95, military service in Holland under Duke of York. 1796, Lieutenant. Served at Cape of Good Hope and was present at surrender of Dutch Fleet. 1797-98, Ceylon. 1801, Egyptian campaign. 1812, Deputy Adjutant-General, Upper Canada. 1813-14, campaign in North America. Subsequently Inspector of Police in Ireland. 1835-37, Lieutenant-Governor of Prince Edward Island. 1837-41, Lieutenant-Governor of New Brunswick. 1841-46, Governor of Newfoundland. 1846-52, Lieutenant-Governor of Nova Scotia. (*Men of the Reign*.)

LeMARCHANT, Sir John Gaspard, G.C.M.G., K.C.B. 1803-74. 1820, entered army. 1851, Colonel. 1858, Major-General. For services in Spain, made a Knight of the First Class and a Knight Commander of the Orders of San Fernando and Charles III of Spain. 1847-52, Governor of Newfoundland. 1852-57, Lieutenant-Governor of Nova Scotia. 1859-64, Governor of Malta. 1865-68, Commander-in-Chief at Madras. (*DNB*.)

PRESCOTT, Sir Henry, G.C.B. 1783-1874. Son of Admiral Sir Isaac Prescott who was on Newfoundland Station, 1781. Entered Navy. Action in Mediterranean during Napoleonic Wars. 1834-41, Governor of Newfoundland. 1847-52, Admiral Superintendent, Portsmouth Dockyard. 1862, Admiral of the Blue and J.P. for Surrey. (*DNB*.; O'Byrne; Marshall.)

MEMBERS OF HOUSE OF ASSEMBLY

TABLE I
1832

District	Member	°Religion	°Denomination	°Occupation
St. John's	Patrick Kough	R.C.	–	carpenter
	John Kent (L)°°	R.C.	–	auctioneer, commission agent
	William Thomas	Prot.	C.E.	merchant
	replaced 1833 by			
	William Carson (L)	Prot.	Unitarian	physician
Conception Bay	Peter Brown (L)	R.C.	–	dealer, small shopkeeper
	James Power (L)	R.C.	–	dealer
	Charles Cozens	Prot.	–	merchant
	Robert Pack	Prot.	–	merchant, farmer
Twillingate and Fogo	T. R. Bennett	Prot.	C.E.	merchant
Bonavista Bay	William Brown	Prot.	–	–
Trinity Bay	J. B. Garland	Prot.	C.E.	merchant
	replaced 1833 by			
	W. B. Row	Prot.	C.E.	barrister
Ferryland	Robert Carter	Prot.	C.E.	ex-naval officer
Burin	William Hooper	Prot.	–	–
Fortune Bay	Newman Hoyles	Prot.	C.E.	Colonial Treasurer
Placentia-St. Mary's	Roger Sweetman	R.C.	–	merchant
	John Martin	Prot.	C.E.	merchant's agent

* Religious affiliation and occupation for this and the tables following have been derived from miscellaneous sources, principally newspapers, Governor's despatches, and petitions. Some inaccuracies are inevitable.
°° Liberal party.

TABLE II
1836: Invalidated Election

District	Member	Religion	Denomination	Occupation
St. John's	William Carson (L)	Prot.	Unitarian	physician
	John Kent (L)	R.C.	–	commission agent
	Patrick Morris (L)	R.C.	–	merchant
Conception Bay	Robert Pack	Prot.	–	merchant
	John McCarthy (L)	R.C.	–	planter
	Anthony Godfrey (L)	R.C.	–	dealer
	James Power (L)	R.C.	–	dealer
Twillingate and Fogo	T. R. Bennett	Prot.	C.E.	merchant
Bonavista Bay	Robert Job	Prot.	Congreg.	merchant
Trinity Bay	T. F. Moore (L)	Prot.(?)	–	fisherman, constable
Ferryland	Patrick Morris (L)	R.C.	–	merchant
Burin	J. Shea (L)	R.C.	–	–
Fortune Bay	W. B. Row	Prot.	C.E.	barrister
Placentia-St. Mary's	Patrick Doyle (L)	R.C.	–	master of vessel
	J. V. Nugent (L)	R.C.	–	retailer, schoolmaster

[194]

TABLE III

1837

District	Member	Religion	Denomination	Occupation
St. John's	William Carson (L)	Prot.	Unitarian	physician
	John Kent (L)	R.C.	—	commission agent
	Patrick Morris (L)	R.C.	—	merchant
	replaced 1840 by			
	Lawrence O'Brien (L)	R.C.	—	merchant
Conception Bay	Peter Brown (L)	R.C.	—	dealer, small shopkeeper
	John McCarthy (L)	R.C.	—	planter
	Anthony Godfrey (L) d. 1840	R.C.	—	dealer
	James Power (L)	R.C.	—	dealer
Twillingate and Fogo	E. J. Dwyer (L)	—	—	fisherman
Bonavista Bay	H. A. Emerson	Prot.	—	lawyer, Solicitor-General
Trinity Bay	T. F. Moore (L)	Prot.(?)	—	fisherman, constable
Ferryland	Peter Winser (L)	R.C.	—	planter
Burin	H. G. Butler (L)	—	—	small business man
Fortune Bay	W. B. Row	Prot.	C.E.	barrister
Placentia-St. Mary's	Patrick Doyle (L)	R.C.	—	master of vessel
	J. V. Nugent (L)	R.C.	—	retailer, schoolmaster

TABLE IV

1842: AMALGAMATED LEGISLATURE

A. *Elected Members*

District	Member	Religion	Denomination	Occupation
St. John's	William Carson (L) *replaced 1843 by*	Prot.	Unitarian	physician
	R. J. Parsons (L)	Prot.	Presbyt.	proprietor of *Patriot*
	Lawrence O'Brien (L)	R.C.	–	merchant
	J. V. Nugent (L)	R.C.	–	merchant
Conception Bay	Thomas Ridley	Prot.	C.E.	merchant
	John Munn	Prot.	Wesleyan	merchant
	J. L. Prendergast (L)	R.C.	–	–
	E. Hanrahan (L)	R.C.	–	–
Twillingate and Fogo	J. Slade	Prot.	–	merchant
Bonavista Bay	Robert Carter	Prot.	C.E.	ex-naval officer
Trinity Bay	Richard Barnes *replaced 1846 by* T. B. Job	Prot.	Wesleyan	–
		Prot.	Congreg.	merchant
Ferryland	Thomas Glen (L)	Prot.	Wesleyan(?)	–
Burin	C. Benning (L)	R.C.	–	–
Fortune Bay	Bryan Robinson	Prot.	C.E.	barrister
Placentia-St. Mary's	J. Dillon (L)	R.C.	–	–
	Simon Morris (L)	R.C.	–	–

[196]

TABLE IV (cont'd)

1842: AMALGAMATED LEGISLATURE

Member	Religion	Denomination	Occupation
B. Nominated Members			
J. A. Simms	Prot.	C.E.	Attorney-General
J. A. Crowdy	Prot.	C.E.	Colonial Secretary and Speaker of the House
Patrick Morris	R.C.	–	Colonial Treasurer
J. Noad *replaced 1845 by* H. A. Emerson	Prot.	Congreg.	Surveyor-General
William Thomas	Prot.	–	Solicitor-General
	Prot.	C.E.	merchant
W. B. Row	Prot.	C.E.	barrister
J. Dunscombe *replaced 1845 by* J. Stuart	Prot.	Presbyt.	merchant
	Prot.	Presbyt.	merchant
James Tobin	R.C.	–	merchant
C. F. Bennett	Prot.	C.E.	merchant
John Kent	R.C.	–	commission agent

TABLE V

1848

District	Member	Religion	Denomination	Occupation
St. John's	John Kent (L)	R.C.	—	commission agent
	Lawrence O'Brien (L) *replaced 1850 by*	R.C.	—	merchant
	P. F. Little (L)	R.C.	—	barrister
	R. J. Parsons (L)	Prot.	Presbyt.	proprietor of *Patriot*
Conception Bay	J. L. Prendergast (L)	R.C.	—	—
	E. Hanrahan (L)	R.C.	—	—
	N. Molloy (L)	R.C.	—	physician
	R. Rankin	Prot.	—	merchant
Twillingate and Fogo	G. H. Emerson	Prot.	—	lawyer
Bonavista Bay	R. Carter	Prot.	C.E.	ex-naval officer
Trinity Bay	T. B. Job	Prot.	Congreg.	merchant
Ferryland	Peter Winser (L)	R.C.	—	planter
Burin	J. G. Falle	Prot.	—	—
Fortune Bay	H. W. Hoyles	Prot.	C.E.	barrister
Placentia-St. Mary's	J. Delany (L)	R.C.	—	—
	Ambrose Shea (L)	R.C.	—	merchant

[198]

TABLE VI

1852

District	Member	Religion	Denomination	Occupation
St. John's	John Kent (L)	R.C.	–	commission agent
	P. F. Little (L)	R.C.	–	barrister
	R. J. Parsons	Prot.	Presbyt.	proprietor of *Patriot*
Conception Bay	J. Bemister	Prot.	Wesleyan	–
	E. Hanrahan (L)	R.C.	–	–
	J. Hayward	Prot.	–	–
	T. Talbot (L)	R.C.	–	teacher
Twillingate and Fogo	G. H. Emerson	Prot.	–	lawyer
Bonavista Bay	J. H. Warren	Prot.	–	merchant
Trinity Bay	S. March	Prot.	Wesleyan	planter
Ferryland	Peter Winser (L)	R.C.	–	planter
Burin	C. Benning (L)	R.C.	–	–
Fortune Bay	H. W. Hoyles	Prot.	C.E.	barrister
Placentia-St. Mary's	G. H. Hogsett (L)	R.C.	–	barrister
	Ambrose Shea (L)	R.C.	–	merchant

TABLE VII

1855

District	Member	Religion	Denomination	Occupation
St. John's East	John Kent (L)	R.C.	–	commission agent
	R. J. Parsons (L)	Prot.	Presbyt.	proprietor of *Patriot*
	Peter Winser (L)	R.C.	–	planter
St. John's West	P. F. Little (L)	R.C.	–	barrister
	Ambrose Shea	R.C.	–	merchant
	John Fox (L)	R.C.	–	–
Conception Bay:				
Harbour Grace	J. L. Prendergast (L)	R.C.	–	–
	J. Hayward (L)	Prot.	–	–
Carbonear	E. Hanrahan (L)	R.C.	–	–
Bay de Verde	J. Bemister	Prot.	Wesleyan	–
Harbour Main	T. Talbot (L)	R.C.	–	teacher
	T. Byrne (L)	R.C.	–	–
Port de Grave	Robert Brown	Prot.	–	–
Twillingate and Fogo	W. H. Ellis	Prot.	–	–
	T. Knight	Prot.	–	–
Bonavista Bay	Robert Carter	Prot.	C.E.	ex-naval officer
	J. H. Warren	Prot.	–	merchant
	M. Walbank	Prot.	–	planter
Trinity Bay	S. March	Prot.	Wesleyan	planter
	J. Winter	Prot.	–	–
	F. B. T. Carter	Prot.	C.E.	barrister
Ferryland	Thomas Glen (L)	Prot.	Congreg.	editor, *Newfoundlander*
	E. Shea (L)	R.C.	–	–
Burin	C. Benning (L)	R.C.	–	–
	S. Morris (L)	R.C.	–	–
Fortune Bay	H. W. Hoyles	Prot.	C.E.	barrister
Placentia-St. Mary's	G. J. Hogsett (L)	R.C.	–	barrister
	J. Delany (L)	R.C.	–	–
	M. Kelley	R.C.	–	–
Burgeo and La Poile	Robert Prowse	Prot.	–	–

[200]

TABLE VIII
1859

District	Member	Religion	Denomination	Occupation
St. John's East	John Kent (L)	R.C.	—	commission agent
	J. Kavanagh (L)	R.C.	—	—
	R. J. Parsons (L)	Prot.	Presbyt.	proprietor of *Patriot*
St. John's West	J. Casey (L)	R.C.	—	—
	T. S. Dwyer (L)	R.C.	—	—
	P. M. Barron (L)	R.C.	—	—
Conception Bay:				
Harbour Grace	J. Hayward (L)	Prot.	—	—
	J. L. Prendergast (L)	R.C.	—	—
Carbonear	E. Hanrahan (L)	R.C.	—	—
Bay de Verde	J. Bemister	Prot.	—	—
Harbour Main	P. Nowlan (L)	R.C.	—	—
	C. Furey (L)	R.C.	—	—
Port de Grave	J. Leamon	Prot.	—	—
Twillingate and Fogo	W. V. Whiteway	Prot.	—	—
	T. Knight	Prot.	—	—
Bonavista Bay	S. March	Prot.	Wesleyan	planter
	J. H. Warren	Prot.	—	merchant
	M. Walbank	Prot.	—	planter
Trinity Bay	F. B. T. Carter	Prot.	C.E.	barrister
	S. Rendell	Prot.	—	merchant
	J. Winter	Prot.	—	—
Ferryland	Thomas Glen (L)	Prot.	Congreg.	—
	E. Shea (L)	R.C.	—	editor, *Newfoundlander*
Burin	Ambrose Shea (L)	R.C.	—	merchant
	J. J. Rogerson (L)	Prot.	Wesleyan	—
Fortune Bay	Robert Carter	Prot.	C.E.	ex-naval officer
Placentia-St. Mary's	G. J. Hogsett (L)	R.C.	—	barrister
	J. Delany (L)	R.C.	—	—
	J. English (L)	R.C.	—	—
Burgeo and La Poile	J. Seaton *replaced 1860 by*	Prot.	—	editor, *Express*
	H. W. Hoyles	Prot.	C.E.	barrister

TABLE IX

1881

District	Member	Religion	Denomination	Occupation
St. John's East	John Kent (L)	R.C.	—	commission agent
	J. Kavanagh (L)	R.C.	—	—
	R. J. Parsons (L)	Prot.	Presbyt.	proprietor of *Patriot*
St. John's West	J. Casey (L)	R.C.	—	teacher; editor, *Record*
	T. Talbot (L)	R.C.	—	—
	H. Renouf (L)	R.C.	—	—
Conception Bay:				
Harbour Grace	J. Hayward	Prot.	—	—
	H. Moore	Prot.	—	—
Carbonear	E. Hanrahan (L) *replaced 1863 by* J. Rorke	R.C.	—	—
Bay de Verde	J. Bemister	Prot.	Wesleyan	—
Harbour Main	P. Nowlan (L)	R.C.	—	—
	T. Byrne (L)	R.C.	—	—
Port de Grave	J. Leamon	Prot.	—	—
Twillingate and Fogo	W. V. Whiteway	Prot.	—	—
	T. Knight	Prot.	—	—
Bonavista Bay	S. March	Prot.	Wesleyan	planter
	J. H. Warren	Prot.	—	merchant
	M. Walbank	Prot.	—	planter
Trinity Bay	F. B. T. Carter	Prot.	C.E.	barrister
	S. Rendell	Prot.	—	merchant
	J. Winter	Prot.	—	—
Ferryland	Thomas Glen (L)	Prot.	Congreg.	editor, *Newfoundlander*
	E. Shea (L)	R.C.	—	barrister
Burin	H. W. Hoyles	Prot.	C.E.	—
	E. Evans	Prot.	—	ex-naval officer
Fortune Bay	R. Carter	Prot.	C.E.	merchant
Placentia-St. Mary's	Ambrose Shea (L)	R.C.	—	—
	R. McGrath (L)	R.C.	—	—
	W. G. Flood (L)	R.C.	—	—
Burgeo and La Poile	D. W. Prowse	Prot.	—	barrister

APPENDIX C

MEMBERS OF EXECUTIVE COUNCIL

1832:	R. A. Tucker, President and Chief Justice *replaced 1833 by* H. J. Boulton, President and Chief Justice Commander Sall J. A. Simms, Attorney-General J. Crowdy, Colonial Secretary J. M. Spearman, Collector of Customs Colonel Haly
added 1833:	W. Thomas J. B. Garland *replaced 1836 by* J. Sinclair J. Dunscombe
added 1834:	J. B. Bland
1838:	Commander Sall, President J. A. Simms, Attorney-General J. Crowdy, Colonial Secretary J. M. Spearman, Collector of Customs W. Thomas J. Dunscombe J. B. Bland *replaced 1840 by* J. Tobin J. Sinclair *replaced 1840 by* W. B. Row
added 1840:	P. Morris, Colonial Treasurer
1842:	J. A. Simms, President J. Crowdy, Colonial Secretary and Speaker of Assembly P. Morris, Colonial Treasurer W. B. Row J. Noad, Surveyor-General *replaced 1845 by* Walter Grieve W. Carson (d. 1843) *replaced 1843 by* L. O'Brien W. Thomas
added 1843:	B. Robinson T. Bennett R. Job T. Ridley
1848:	Lieutenant-Colonel Law E. M. Archibald, Attorney-General J. Crowdy, Colonial Secretary J. M. Spearman, Collector of Customs (dropped 1849) W. Thomas

P. Morris, Colonial Treasurer (d. 1849)
W. B. Row
J. Tobin
J. Noad, Surveyor-General

added 1850:   C. F. Bennett
L. O'Brien

added 1852:   J. J. Grieve
T. B. Job

June 1855:   P. F. Little, Premier and Attorney-General until 1858
J. Kent, Colonial Secretary; Premier in 1858
T. Glen, Treasurer and Collector of Customs
E. Hanrahan, Surveyor-General
G. H. Emerson, Solicitor-General
replaced 1857 by
J. J. Rogerson
L. O'Brien, President of Legislative Council

added 1858:   G. J. Hogsett, Attorney-General
E. D. Shea

March 1860:   J. Kent, Premier and Colonial Secretary
G. J. Hogsett, Attorney-General
T. Glen, Receiver General
E. Hanrahan, Surveyor-General
J. J. Rogerson
L. O'Brien, President of Legislative Council
E. D. Shea

May 1861:   H. W. Hoyles, Premier and Attorney-General
R. Carter, Colonial Secretary
J. Bemister, Receiver-General
J. Warren, Surveyor-General
L. O'Brien, President of Legislative Council
N. Stabb

1866:   F. B. T. Carter, Premier and Attorney-General
J. Bemister, Colonial Secretary
J. Kent, Receiver-General
J. Hayward, Solicitor-General
L. O'Brien, President of Legislative Council
N. Stabb
A. Shea

POPULATION*

District	1827	1836	1845	1857
St. John's:	15,165	18,926	25,196	—
East	—	—	—	17,352
West	—	—	—	13,124
Conception Bay:	17,859	23,215	28,026	—
Harbour Grace	—	—	—	10,067
Carbonear	—	—	—	5,233
Bay de Verde	—	—	—	6,221
Harbour Main	—	—	—	5,386
Port de Grave	—	—	—	6,489
Twillingate and Fogo	3,547	3,497	6,744	9,717
Bonavista Bay	4,154	5,183	7,227	8,850
Trinity Bay	5,153	6,803	8,801	10,736
Ferryland	3,116	5,111	4,581	5,228
Burin	2,120	3,140	4,358	5,529
Fortune Bay	2,808	3,129	5,100	3,493
Placentia and St. Mary's	3,649	4,701	6,473	8,334
Burgeo and La Poile	—	—	—	2,545
Scattered	2,000	—	—	—
French Shore	—	—	—	3,334
TOTALS	59,571	73,705	96,506	122,638

* Census figures from Blue Books of 1827, 1836, 1845, and 1857.

DISTRIBUTION OF POPULATION BY CONSTITUENCY
AND RELIGION

TABLE I*
1827

District	R.C.	C.E.	Diss.	Prot.	Members of Assembly
St. John's	10,214	—	—	4,951	3
Conception Bay	7,230	—	—	10,629	4
Twillingate-Fogo	669	—	—	2,878	1
Bonavista Bay	950	—	—	3,721	1
Trinity Bay	903	—	—	4,250	1
Ferryland	2,902	—	—	214	1
Burin	1,152	—	—	968	1
Fortune Bay	207	—	—	2,601	1
Placentia - St. Mary's	3,985	—	—	716	2
TOTALS	30,928	—	—	28,212	15

* Figures from *JHA*, 1833, Appendix, p. 64.

TABLE II*
1836

District	R.C.	C.E.	Diss.	Prot.	Members of Assembly
St. John's	14,056	3,813	1,057	4,870	3
Conception Bay	10,063	6,819	6,333	13,152	4
Twillingate-Fogo	669	2,878	—	2,878	1 (1827)
Bonavista Bay	1,249	3,473	461	3,934	1
Trinity Bay	1,066	4,098	1,639	5,737	1
Ferryland	4,798	213	—	213	1
Burin	1,374	671	1,095	1,766	1
Fortune Bay	308	2,823	—	2,823	1
Placentia-St. Mary's	3,985	710	6	716	2
TOTALS	37,568	25,498	10,591	36,089	15

* Figures from *JHA*, 1837, Appendix, p. 417.

TABLE III*

1845

District	R.C.	C.E.	Diss.	Prot.	Members of Assembly
St. John's	18,986	—	—	6,210	3
Conception Bay	11,580	—	—	16,446	4
Twillingate-Fogo	1,128	—	—	5,616	1
Bonavista Bay	1,809	—	—	5,418	1
Trinity Bay	1,283	—	—	7,518	1
Ferryland	4,399	—	—	182	1
Burin	1,951	—	—	2,407	1
Fortune Bay	392	—	—	4,708	1
Placentia-St. Mary's	5,455	—	—	1,018	2
TOTALS	46,983	—	—	49,523	15

* Figures from Hoyles, *Case of Protestant Inhabitants*, Table A.

TABLE IIIa*

REPRESENTATION BILLS AND REPRESENTATION ACT OF 1854

District	Members				Probable Religions	
	Bill A	Bill A(1)	Bill A(2) Enacted	Bill B	R.C.	Prot.
St. John's	6	6	6	6	6	—
Conception Bay	7	7	7	7	3	4
Twillingate-Fogo	2	2	2	2	—	2
Bonavista Bay	2	3	3	2	—	3
Trinity Bay	3	3	3	3	—	3
Ferryland	2	2	2	2	2	—
Burin	2	1-Prot. 1-R.C.	2	2	1	1
Fortune Bay	1	1	1	1	—	1
Placentia-St. Mary's	3	2	3	2	3	—
Burgeo and La Poile	1	1	1	1	—	1
TOTALS	29	29	30	28	15	15

A: Passed by Assembly.
A(1): Amended by Council.
A(2): Amended by Assembly; finally accepted by Council, Nov., 1854.
B: Passed by Council.

* Figures from Hoyles, *Case of Protestant Inhabitants*; *Times*, Oct. 25, 1854, Proceedings of Council, Oct. 24; and CO 194/142, Hamilton to Grey, Nov. 14, 1854.

APPENDIX E

TABLE IV*

1857

District	R.C.	C.E.	Diss.	Prot.	Members of Assembly
St. John's East	11,867	3,493	1,992	5,485	3
St. John's West	10,033	2,162	929	3,091	3
Conception Bay:					
Harbour Grace	3,390	5,490	1,187	6,677	2
Carbonear	2,582	791	1,860	2,651	1
Bay de Verde	1,583	446	4,192	4,638	1
Harbour Main	4,153	1,160	73	1,233	2
Port de Grave	1,637	2,726	2,126	4,852	1
Twillingate-Fogo	1,442	6,232	2,043	8,275	2
Bonavista Bay	2,030	5,714	1,106	6,820	3
Trinity Bay	1,253	6,016	3,467	9,483	3
Ferryland	5,093	127	8	135	2
Burin	2,354	1,356	1,819	3,175	2
Fortune Bay	647	2,787	59	2,846	1
Placentia-St. Mary's	7,156	966	212	1,178	3
Burgeo-La Poile	89	3,172	284	3,456	1
TOTALS	55,309	42,638	21,357**	63,995	30

* Figures from *JHA*, 1858, Appendix, p. 125.

** Breakdown of total of dissenters:

Wesleyans	20,144
Kirk of Scotland	302
Free Kirk	520
Congregationalists	347
Baptists	44
	21,357

COMPARATIVE FINANCIAL TABLE, 1855-1865*

	Trade		Revenue	Supply Act **	Poor Relief	
Year	Exports	Imports	Total	Total	Permanent and Casual	Total
1855	£1,142,212	£1,152,804	£126,448	£49,447	£ 400	£17,100
1856	1,338,797	1,271,604	118,831	32,215	7,500	11,000
1857	1,651,171	1,414,432	149,324	40,753	7,250	13,493
1858	1,318,836	1,172,862	141,128	54,258	7,250	11,086
1859	1,357,113	1,323,288	124,799	50,265	7,250	11,976
1860	1,271,712	1,254,128	133,608	37,012	7,250	14,901
1861	1,092,551	1,152,857	90,043	52,732	18,000	23,280
1862	1,171,723	1,007,082	116,929	46,950	15,000	21,934
1863	1,233,353	1,077,272	102,174	53,673	20,000	27,234
1864	1,111,330	1,067,062	116,770	48,048	10,000	16,534
1865	1,373,251	1,324,900	142,040	56,765	10,000	16,534
			AVERAGES			
1855-1860	1,346,640	1,264,686	132,356	43,991	6,150	13,259
1861-1865	1,194,441	1,125,834	113,591	51,633	14,600	21,103

* Data compiled from Blue Books and Supply Acts.
** Including Poor Relief.

BIBLIOGRAPHY

THE CHIEF SOURCES have been the Colonial Office volumes in the Public Record Office, London, which comprise: (1) despatches from the secretaries of state for the colonies; (2) letters from the governors, with copious enclosures, minutes by the Colonial Office staff, and draft versions of replies; (3) Colonial Office correspondence with offices of the Home Government; (4) letters and memorials from Newfoundland; (5) the files of Newfoundland newspapers; (6) bound volumes of the Newfoundland Sessional Papers; and (7) acts of the legislature.

Other sources have been *Parliamentary Debates* and *Parliamentary Papers* on Newfoundland, in particular, the papers of the Select Committee of 1841 and the Newfoundland Royal Commission *Report* of 1933. The latter is useful for its historical review as well as for its analysis of the island's economy, government, and politics. Material was found in the private papers of Sir Robert Peel, Lord John Russell, and the fifth Duke of Newcastle and in a number of pamphlets and monographs of the nineteenth century. The holdings of the Provincial Archives in St. John's are described in the *American Archivist*, vol. XXI, Jan. 1958, pp. 43-53. Useful bibliographies are found in the *Cambridge History of the British Empire*, vol. VI, and in Evans Lewin's *Subject Catalogue of the Royal Empire Society*, vol. III. Little has been published in books and periodicals on the political history of the period, but secondary sources have been valuable for the diplomacy of the cod fisheries, and for background material generally.

I. MANUSCRIPT SOURCES AND OFFICIAL PAPERS AND PUBLICATIONS

A. PUBLIC RECORD OFFICE

1. *Colonial Office Documents*

Correspondence

CO 194. Newfoundland. Original Correspondence, Secretary of State: Despatches from Governors, Offices and Individuals; Minutes and Draft Replies. Vols. 83-173.

CO 195. Newfoundland. Entry Book of Outgoing Despatches from Secretary of State to Governor. Vols. 18-23.

CO 43. North America General. Entry Book of Letters from Secretary of State (Domestic). Vols. 75-87.

CO 323. Colonies General. Original Correspondence. (i) Law Officers' Reports: on Colonial Acts, vols. 48-61; on Newfoundland Acts, vols. 63, 69, 71, 73, 75, 77, 78, 83, 84, 87. (ii) Private Letters to R. W. Hay. Vols. 168-75.

CO 324. North America. Entry Book of Private Letters from R. W. Hay. Vols. 89 and 90.

CO 325. Colonies General. Vol. 40: "State of the Roman Catholic Church in the Colonies, 1833-1851."

CO 199. Miscellaneous. Vol. 19: "Appeal to the Privy Council, 1838, Kielly v. Carson and Others."

Commissions, Instructions, etc.

CO 380. Drafts. Vols. 13-15.
CO 381. Entry Book. Vols. 53-54.

Acts of Newfoundland Legislature

CO 196. Acts. Vols. 1-5.
CO 383. Register of Acts. Vol. 59.

Newfoundland Sessional Papers

CO 197. *Journals of House of Assembly. Journals of Legislative Council.* Minutes of Executive Council. Vols. 1-71.

Newfoundland Blue Books

CO 199. Vols. 29-60.

Newfoundland Newspapers

CO 199. Vols. 1-15 (*see* Part II. NEWSPAPERS).

2. *Other*

Russell Papers. PRO/30/22. Boxes 3-5.

B. BRITISH MUSEUM

Peel Papers. Add. MSS 40467, vol. CCLXXXVII; 40468, vol. CCLXXXVIII; 40470, vol. CCXC.

C. UNIVERSITY OF NOTTINGHAM

Newcastle Papers (5th Duke). Original Correspondence and Entry Books, Colonial.

D. SELECT LIST OF PARLIAMENTARY PAPERS

Instructions to the Governor of Nfld. and Despatches to him transmitting the Commission. 1831-32 (704) XXII, 261.
Addresses Received at the Colonial Office from the Legislative Council or Assembly of Nfld. 1839 (525) XXXIV, 565.
So much of a despatch from . . . Sir John Harvey . . . Secretary of State . . . June 24, 1842 as relates to the Bill for the Government of Newfoundland. 1842 (478) XXVIII, 159.
Correspondence between . . . Secretary of State . . . and Governor of Nfld. upon . . . assumption of the title of Bishop of Nfld. by the Roman Catholic Bishop. 1851 (169) XXXVI, 619.
Correspondence between Secretary of State and Governor of Nfld. on the recent changes in the constitution. 1854-55 (273) XXXVI, 583.
Correspondence re-appropriation of subscriptions raised for the relief of sufferers at St. John's by the fire in 1846. 1851 (679) XXXVI, 621.
Select Committee on Newfoundland, 1841, House of Commons: Minutes and Papers printed for Committee. Unnumbered. No Report presented. (Colonial Office Library.)
Newfoundland Royal Commission, 1933. *Report.* Cmd. 4480.

E. PARLIAMENTARY DEBATES

Motion for a Select Committee, 1830. 2nd series. Vol. 24, cc. 580-93. George Robinson.

3rd series

Introduction of Nfld. Constitution Bill, 1832. Vol. 12, cc. 506-7. Howick.
Plea for a Legislature, 1831. Vol. 55, cc. 283-91. Robinson, Howick and Joseph Hume.
Possible Motion for a Legislature, 1831. Vol. 66, cc. 1377-88. Hume, Lord Althorp, H. Labouchere, D. O'Connell, et al.
Introduction of Nfld. Constitution Bill, 1832. Vol. 112, cc. 506-7. Howick.
Petition on Administration of Justice and Chief Justice Boulton, 1835. Vol. 30, cc. 672-75. O'Connell.
Petition from Roman Catholics, 1837. Vol. 39, cc. 978-79. Hume and O'Connell.

Petition for Repeal of Constitution, 1839. Vol. 47, ll. 552-63. Lords Aberdeen, Durham, Normanby, Ripon and Brougham.
Petition for Constitutional Change, 1841. Vol. 57, ll. 391-94. Lords Aberdeen and Normanby.
Possible Motion for a Select Committee, 1841. Vol. 57, cc. 611-12. Sir John Pakington and Lord John Russell. Cc. 657-59. Pakington, Russell, Lord Stanley, and Sir R. Peel.
Motion for a Select Committee, 1841. Vol. 57, cc. 705-20. Pakington and others.
Introduction of Nfld. Constitution Bill, 1842. Vol. 63, cc. 875-80.
Second Reading Debate on Constitution Bill, 1842. Vol. 65, cc. 871-88. O'Connell, Stanley, Hume, et al. Cc. 979-1006. Pakington, Buller, Sir Howard Douglas, R. V. Smith, et al.
Committee on Bill, 1842. Vol. 65, cc. 1064-69.
Second Reading Debate on Bill, Lords, 1842. Vol. 65, ll. 1178-79. Lords Campbell, Ripon, and Clanricarde.
Disposal of Queen's Letter Fund for Fire Relief, 1847. Vol. 92, ll. 1241-45. Lords Portman and Grey and the Bishop of London.
Delay in establishing responsible government, 1855. Vol. 137, cc. 883-92. J. Roebuck, Lord Palmerston, J. Bright, et al.

F. ACTS OF IMPERIAL PARLIAMENT

Fisheries, 4 and 5 Geo. IV, c. 51.
Judicature, 4 and 5 Geo. IV, c. 67.
Marriage, 4 and 5 Geo. IV, c. 68.
Representative Government, 2 and 3 Wm. IV, c. 78.
Amending Constitution, 5 and 6 Vict., c. 120.
Continuing Amended Constitution, 9 and 10 Vict., c. 45.
Restoring Legislative Council, 10 and 11 Vict., c. 44.

II. NEWSPAPERS

1. Newfoundland newspapers

A. PUBLIC RECORD OFFICE

CO 199. Vols. 1-15. Royal Gazette, 1844-53; Patriot, 1838-53; Public Ledger, 1838-55; Times, 1842-55.
CO 194. Vols. 83-173. Governor's Despatches, 1832-64. Many single copies of newspapers and newspaper extracts.

B. GOSLING MEMORIAL LIBRARY, ST. JOHN'S

Conception Bay Man, 1857; Courier, 1856-64; Daily News, 1860-64; Day Book, 1862-64; Express, 1855-64; Weekly Express, 1858, 1859; Public Ledger, 1855-60, 1862-64; Morning Courier, 1855; Royal Gazette, 1855-64; Newfoundlander, 1855-59, 1861-64; Patriot, 1855-61; Post, 1855-56, 1859-62; Record, 1862, 1863; Reporter, 1856; Harbour Grace Standard, 1860, 1863-64; Telegraph, 1857-64; Times, 1855-64.

C. BRITISH MUSEUM NEWSPAPER LIBRARY, COLINDALE

Royal Gazette, Courier, Newfoundlander, Patriot, Public Ledger, Times—each for the year 1864.

D. BRITISH MUSEUM

Add. MSS 8155. ee. 6. Newspaper cuttings from Newfoundland newspapers, chiefly 1824 and 1833.

2. Other

The Times (London), 1832-64.

Apart from Newfoundland news reports, there are the following leading articles on politics and government in Newfoundland: "Newfoundland," July 21, 1835, p. 5; "Newfoundland," Sept. 25, 1838, p. 4; "Popish Priests in Ireland and Newfoundland," Jan. 11, 1841, p. 4; "Newfoundland Bill," Aug. 4. 1841, p. 4; "Newfoundland Bill," Aug. 6, 1842, p. 4; "Newfoundland Bill," Aug. 8, 1842, p. 4; "Assembly of Newfoundland and its Power to Commit for Contempt," Jan. 13, 1843, p. 4.

III. BOOKS, PAMPHLETS AND THESES

ANSPACH, LEWIS. *A History of Newfoundland.* London, 1827.
ARCHIBALD, EDITH J. *Life and Letters of Sir Edward Mortimer Archibald.* Toronto, 1924.
BLACHFORD, LORD (previously Sir Frederic Rogers). *Letters.* Ed. G. MARINDIN. London, 1896.
BONNYCASTLE, R. H. *Newfoundland in 1842.* 2 vols. London, 1842.
BROWNE, C. A. *Letters and Extracts from the Addresses and Occasional Writings of J. B. Jukes.* London, 1871.
Cambridge History of the British Empire. Ed. J. HOLLAND ROSE, A. P. NEWTON, and E. A. BENIANS. Vol. II: *The Growth of the New Empire, 1783-1870.* Cambridge, 1940. Vol. VI: *Canada and Newfoundland* (chap. 5, "Newfoundland to 1783," by A. P. NEWTON; chap. 17, "Newfoundland, 1783-1867," by SIR C. A. HARRIS.) Cambridge, 1930.
CARSON, W. *Letter to Members of Parliament,* 1812. *Reasons for Colonizing the Island of Newfoundland.* 1813. (Pamphlets in CO 194/52 and 194/54.)
CLARKE, DOROTHY. "The Attitude of the Colonial Office towards the Working of Responsible Government, 1854-1868." Unpublished Ph.D. thesis at the University of London, 1953.
CORMACK, W. E. *Narrative of a Journey across the Island of Newfoundland.* St. John's, 1822.
Creevey Papers. Ed. SIR HERBERT MAXWELL. Vol. II, London, 1904.
DECELLES, A. D. *Papineau.* (Makers of Canada.) Oxford, 1926.
—— *The Patriotes of '37.* (Chronicles of Canada.) Toronto, 1916.
DENT, J. C. *The Story of the Upper Canadian Rebellion.* 2 vols. Toronto, 1855.
DUNHAM, AILEEN, *Political Unrest in Upper Canada, 1815-1836.* London, 1927.
EGERTON, H. E. *A Short History of British Colonial Policy.* Ninth ed., rev. A. P. NEWTON. London, 1932.
FAY, C. R. *Life and Labour in Newfoundland.* Cambridge, 1956.
GOSSE, EDMUND. *The Life of Philip Henry Gosse.* London, 1890.
GREVILLE, C. C. F. *The Greville Memoirs.* London, 1880.
GREY, HENRY, 3rd Earl. *The Colonial Policy of Lord John Russell's Administration.* 2 vols. London, 1853.
HARVEY, M. *A Short History of Newfoundland.* Second ed., rev. London, 1890.
HARVEY, M., and HATTON, J. *Newfoundland.* London, 1883.
HOYLES, H. W. *The Case of the Protestant Inhabitants ... against ... the Unconditional Concession of Responsible Government.* 1854. (Pamphlet in Colonial Office Library.)
INNIS, HAROLD A. *The Cod Fisheries: The History of an International Economy.* New Haven, 1940; second ed., rev., Toronto, 1954.
JOB, R. B. *John Job's Family, Devon–Newfoundland–Liverpool, 1730-1953.* St. John's, 1953.
JUKES, J. B. *Excursions in and about Newfoundland during the years 1839 and 1840.* 2 vols. London, 1842.
KENNEDY, W. P. M., ed. *Statutes, Treaties, and Documents of the Canadian Constitution, 1713-1926.* New and rev. ed. Oxford, 1929.
LEWIN, EVANS, comp. *Subject Catalogue of the Royal Empire Society.* Vol. III: *The Dominion of Canada and Its Provinces: The Dominion of Newfoundland, the West Indies and Colonial America.* London, 1932.
LITTLE, J. *Constitution of the Government in its Executive and Legislative Departments.* St. John's, 1855.
LUCAS, Sir C. P., ed. *Lord Durham's Report on the Affairs of British North America.* 3 vols. Oxford, 1912.
McCREA, R. B. *Lost Amid the Fogs: Sketches of Life in Newfoundland.* London, 1869.
MACKAY, R. A., ed. *Newfoundland: Economic, Diplomatic and Strategic Studies.* (Contributors: S. A. SAUNDERS, A. M. FRASER, G. S. GRAHAM, A. R. M. LOWER, G. W. WATTS.) Toronto, 1946.
McLINTOCK, A. H. *The Establishment of Constitutional Government in Newfoundland, 1783-1832.* London, 1941.
MORRIS, PATRICK. *Observations on the Present State of Newfoundland.* 1823.
—— *Remarks on the State of Society, Religion, Morality, and Education at Newfoundland.* 1827.
—— *Arguments to prove the Policy and Necessity of granting to Newfoundland a Constitutional Government: A Letter to Hon. William Huskisson, M.P.* 1828.
—— *Legislative Councils proved to be the Root of all the Evils of the Colonies: A Short Address to the Earl of Durham.* 1838.
—— *A Short Reply to the Speech of Earl Aberdeen on the State of Newfoundland.* 1839.
—— *A Letter to the ... Marquis of Normanby in Reply to the Statements of a Member of the House of Assembly of Newfoundland.* 1839.

——— *Memorial to Lord Glenelg.* 1839.
(The Morris pamphlets are in the Colonial Office Library.)
O'Byrne's Naval Biography. London, 1849.
PAGE, F. R. *History and Description of Newfoundland.* London, 1860.
PEDLEY, C. *The History of Newfoundland from the Earliest Times to 1860.* London, 1863.
PRESCOTT, H. *A Sketch of the State of Affairs in Newfoundland.* 1841. (Pamphlet in Colonial Office Library.)
PROWSE, D. W. *History of Newfoundland from English, Colonial, and Foreign Records.* London, 1896.
REEVES, J. *History of the Government of Newfoundland.* London, 1793.
ROGERS, J. D. *Newfoundland.* (Vol. V, part 4, of SIR C. P. LUCAS, ed., *Historical Geography of the British Colonies.*) Oxford, 1911.
SMALLWOOD, J. R., ed. *The Book of Newfoundland.* 2 vols. St. John's, 1937. (Vol. I contains "Newfoundland Statesmen of the Past" by E. B. FORAN.)
THOMPSON, FREDERIC F. "The Background to the Newfoundland Clauses of the Anglo-French Agreement of 1904." Ph.D. thesis at the University of Oxford, 1953.
——— *The French Shore Problem in Newfoundland.* Canadian Studies in History and Government, no. 2. Toronto, 1961.
TOCQUE, P. *Newfoundland: As it was and as it is in 1877.* Toronto, 1878.
WALLACE, W. S., ed. *Encyclopedia of Canada: Newfoundland Supplement.* Ed. R. BLACKBURN. Toronto, 1949.
WARDLE, A. C. *Benjamin Bowring and His Descendants.* London, 1940.
WILLSON, H. B. *The Tenth Island: Being some Account of Newfoundland, its People, its Prolixities, its Problems, and its Peculiarities.* London, 1897.
WINTON, H. *A Chapter in the History of Newfoundland for the year 1861.* 1861. (Pamphlet in British Museum and in Commonwealth Relations Office Library.)
WOODWARD, E. L. *The Age of Reform, 1815-1870.* Oxford, 1938.
WRONG, E. M. *Charles Buller and Responsible Government.* Oxford, 1926.

IV. ARTICLES

Canadian Historical Association Reports

INNIS, H. A. "An Introduction to the Economic History of the Maritimes (including Newfoundland and New England)," 1931, pp. 85-96.
MACDONELL, MALCOLM. "The Conflict between Sir John Harvey and Chief Justice John Gervase Hutchinson Bourne," 1956, pp. 45-54.
NEW, CHESTER. "The Rebellion of 1837 in its Larger Setting," 1947, pp. 5-17.

Canadian Historical Review

MACNUTT W. S. "New Brunswick's Age of Harmony — The Administration of Sir John Harvey," XXXII, no. 2 (June 1951), pp. 105-25.
MANNING, HELEN TAFT. "The Colonial Policy of Whig Ministers, 1830-1837," XXXIII, no. 3 (Sept. 1952), pp. 203-36.
MAYO, H. B. "Newfoundland and Confederation in the Eighteen Sixties," XXIX, no. 2 (June 1948), pp. 125-42.
STANLEY, G. F. G. "Sir Stephen Hill's Observations on the 1869 Election," XXIX, no. 3 (Sept. 1948), pp. 278-85.

Newfoundland Quarterly

PROWSE, D. W. "The History of Responsible Government," III, no. 1.
——— "Progress in Newfoundland," VIII, no. 2.

Royal Colonial Institute Proceedings

PINSENT, SIR R. "Our Oldest Colony," XVI (1884-85).

Simmond's Colonial Magazine and Foreign Miscellany

MORRIS, PATRICK. "A Short Review of the History, Government and Constitutions of Newfoundland in a series of Letters to Earl Grey," Letters I and II, XIII (1848), pp. 362-64; Letter III, XIV (1848), pp. 269-94; Letter III cont'd, XV (1848), pp. 181-96.

University of Toronto Studies, History and Economics

PROWSE, D. W. "Local Government in Newfoundland," II (1907), pp. 269-77.

NOTES

ABBREVIATIONS used in these notes are as follows: *CHBE — Cambridge History of the British Empire*; CO — Colonial Office Documents; *DNB — Dictionary of National Biography*; *JHA — Journals of the House of Assembly*, Newfoundland; MHA — Members of the House of Assembly, Newfoundland; *NRCR* — Newfoundland Royal Commission, 1933, *Report*; *PD — Parliamentary Debates*, 3rd series, unless specified.

CHAPTER ONE

1. See A. H. McLintock, *The Establishment of Constitutional Government in Newfoundland, 1783-1832* (London, 1941), pp. 177-84.
2. *Ibid.*, pp. 162-77.
3. W. Carson, 1770-1843, began practice in St. John's in 1808. P. Morris, 1789-1849, arrived in St. John's in 1800 and became Colonial Treasurer in 1840.
4. W. Carson, *Letter to Members of Parliament* (1812); *Reasons for Colonising the Island of Newfoundland* (1813).
5. Patrick Morris, *Remarks on the State of Society, Religion, Morality, and Education at Newfoundland* (1827); *Arguments to prove the Policy and Necessity of granting to Newfoundland a Constitutional Government: A Letter to Hon. William Huskisson, M.P.* (1828).
6. McLintock, p. 176.
7. Select Committee, House of Commons, 1841 (unnumbered), I, p. 1, memorial, Sept. 15, 1830.
8. CO 194/80, Goderich to Cochrane, Jan. 1, 1831.
9. McLintock, pp. 164-72.
10. CO 324/89, R. W. Hay to Cochrane, Priv. and Conf., Dec. 28, 1830.
11. CO 194/81, Cochrane to Goderich, Secret and Conf., April 14, 1831.
12. *Ibid.*, May 4, 1831.
13. C. R. Fay, *Life and Labour in Newfoundland* (Cambridge, 1956), pp. 48-49.
14. CO 194/81, Cochrane to Goderich, Secret and Conf., May 31, 1831, encl., J. Simms, "Observations on the propriety of initiating a Local Legislative Assembly for Newfoundland," May 4, 1831.
15. *NRCR*, pp. 79-80.
16. J. D. Rogers, *Newfoundland*, p. 204.
17. Edmund Gosse, *The Life of Philip Henry Gosse* (London, 1890), pp. 48-51.
18. *Ibid.*, p. 47.
19. *NRCR*, pp. 78-79.
20. McLintock, p. 173.
21. Gosse, p. 51.
22. McLintock, p. 123.
23. CO 197/1, minute of Council, Feb. 21, 1832.
24. Harold A. Innis, *The Cod Fisheries: The History of an International Economy* (New Haven, 1940), p. 386.
25. P. Tocque, *Newfoundland as it was and as it is in 1877* (Toronto, 1878), p. 86.
26. McLintock, p. 169.
27. CO 194/81, Cochrane to Goderich, Secret and Conf., April 14, May 14, 1831.
28. Blue Book of 1832 shows a school attendance of about 1,800 in a population of 60,000.
29. Gosse, pp. 51, 43.
30. *CHBE*, VI, p. 422.
31. C. Pedley, *The History of Newfoundland from the Earliest Times to 1860* (London,

1863), p. 205; Rogers, p. 121; McLintock, p. 9; D. W. Prowse, *History of Newfoundland from English, Colonial, and Foreign Records* (London, 1896), p. 343, n. 1, and pp. 355-58. On the courts, see McLintock, pp. 53-71, *et passim*.

32. *CHBE*,VI, pp. 424, 426.
33. Prowse, p. 364.
34. McLintock, p. 127.
35. Innis, p. 306, n. 64.
36. McLintock, p. 127.
37. *Ibid.*, p. 166.
38. P. Morris, *Remarks on the State of Society . . . at Newfoundland.*
39. P. Morris, *Arguments to prove the Policy and Necessity of granting . . . a Constitutional Government.*
40. Select Committee, 1841, I, p. 1, memorial, Sept. 15, 1830.
41. CO 194/81, Cochrane to Goderich, Secret and Conf., April 14, 1831.
42. W. E. Cormack, *Narrative of a Journey across the Island of Newfoundland* (St. John's, 1822). Cormack traversed the country from Trinity Bay to St. George's Bay in the first reported overland trip.
43. *NRCR*, p. 5. The soil was said to be generally light and shallow, over large areas being of vegetable and peaty composition, deficient in lime and drainage, and unsuited to crop production. Sand and sandy loam is found in the west and excellent soil for agriculture in the chief river valleys and in parts of certain bays. However, in 1933, 90 per cent of the population still lived on the littoral (p. 3).
44. Area 42,000 square miles, coastline 6,000 miles, tenth largest island in the world.
45. CO 194/81, Cochrane to Goderich, Secret and Conf., April 14, 1831.
46. *Ibid.*, May 4, 1831.
47. *Ibid.*, May 31, 1831, encl., J. Simms, "Observations," May 4, 1831.
48. *PD*, vol. 4, 1831, June 27, p. 360, Howick; CO 324/19, Hay to Cochrane, Priv., July 6, 1831.
49. *PD*, vol. 5, 1831, July 25, pp. 283-84; vol. 6, 1831, Sept. 13, pp. 1377-81; pp. 1383-84, J. Hume; p. 1388, Lord Althorp.
50. Select Committee, 1841, I, Evidence, p. 5, Cochrane; p. 25, Brooking.
51. CO 194/82, #21, memorandum, Dec. 19, 1831.
52. CO 43/75, Howick to G. Robinson, Jan. 25, 1832.
53. CO 194/83, Cochrane to Goderich, Jan.23, 1832.
54. 2 and 3 Wm. IV, c. 78; Royal Commission, March 2; Instructions, July 26; Proclamation, July 26, 1832.
55. CO 194/82, #21, memorandum, Dec. 19, 1831.
56. CO 195/18, Goderich to Cochrane, July 27; Howick to Cochrane, July 27, 1832.
57. CO 194/82, #21, memorandum, Dec. 19, 1831.
58. CO 195/18, Goderich to Cochrane, July 27, 1832.
59. *Ibid.*, Howick to Cochrane, July 27, 1832.
60. *PD*, vol. 4, 1831, June 27, p. 260; vol. 5, 1831, July 25, p. 285.
61. CO 43/75, Howick to R. Slade, Feb. 4, 1832.
62. CO 195/18, Stanley to Cochrane, March 1, 1834; CO 324/90, Hay to Cochrane, March 8, April 5, 1834.
63. H. E. Egerton, *British Colonial Policy* (London, 1932), p. 218.
64. C. C. F. Greville, *The Greville Memoirs*, part 2, vol. 3 (London, 1890), p. 303.
65. CO 323/172, Cochrane to Hay, Feb. 18, 1832.
66. *Ibid.*; CO 323/170, Cochrane to Hay, Dec. 18, 1833.

CHAPTER TWO

1. *Public Ledger*, Nov. 6, 1832.
2. Prowse, pp. 430, 432.
3. *Ibid.*, pp. 427, 429.
4. CO 194/99, Prescott to Glenelg, Oct. 14, 1837, encl. 2, P. Kough to J. Crowdy, Sept. 12.
5. Prowse, pp. 432-33.
6. McLintock, pp. 145-48; R. B. Job, *John Job's Family, Devon–Newfoundland–Liverpool, 1750-1953* (St. John's, 1953), pp. 65-83.
7. Quoted by Prowse, p. 430.
8. CO 323/168, Cochrane to Hay, Oct. 20, 1832.

9. W. D. Wallace, ed., *Encyclopedia of Canada: Newfoundland Supplement* (Toronto, 1949), p. 21.

10. *Public Ledger*, Nov. 13, 1832.

11. *Newfoundlander*, Sept. 13, 1832, Kent to Editor, Sept. 12.

12. *Ibid.*, Sept. 20, 1832, Bishop Fleming to Editor, Sept. 19.

13. *Newfoundlander*, Oct. 4, 1832, report of meeting, Sept. 27.

14. Select Committee, 1841, I, Evidence, p. 5, Cochrane.

15. CO 194/85, Cochrane to Stanley, Dec. 26, 1833.

16. CO 195/19, Glenelg to Prescott, Jan. 1, 1837, requests regular transmission of representative newspapers. The CO files begin in 1838.

17. CO 194/88, Cochrane to Stanley, July 28, 1834, is such a despatch.

18. CO 195/18, Goderich to Cochrane, July 27, 1832.

19. CO 194/85, Cochrane to Goderich, Jan. 3, 1833, encl., Speech from Throne, Jan. 1; Prowse, p. 431.

20. *JHA*, 1833, Jan. 1, p. 9.

21. *Ibid.*, July 8, p. 57, July 12, p. 68.

22. *Ibid.*, Jan. 5, p. 14; April 16, p. 51.

23. CO 194/105, Prescott to Normanby, June 12, 1839, encl. 4, MHA to Prescott, June 3.

24. *JHA*, 1833, Jan. 15, p. 18; Cochrane to MHA, March 16, p. 41.

25. *Ibid.*, Jan. 9, p. 15.

26. CO 194/85, Cochrane to Goderich, Feb. 13, 1833.

27. *Ibid.*

28. CO 194/85, Cochrane to Goderich, March 12, 1833.

29. Public Ledger, March 15, 1833, Speech of R. A. Tucker in Council, Feb. 26.

30. CO 194/85, Cochrane to Goderich, March 12, 1833.

31. *Public Ledger*, March 15, 1833, MHA to His Majesty, March 11.

32. CO 194/85, Cochrane to Goderich, March 12, 1833.

33. CO 195/18, Stanley to Cochrane, May 4, 1833; CO 43/77, Howick to Tucker, May 3, 1833.

34. CO 195/18, Stanley to Cochrane, May 3, 1833.

35. *Ibid.*, May 4, 1833.

36. *Ibid.*

37. CO 195/18, Goderich to Cochrane, July 27, 1832, had stressed the inconvenience of having the leading inhabitants in the Council rather than in the Assembly.

38. CO 194/85, Cochrane to Stanley, Dec. 26, 1833; CO 194/87, Cochrane to Stanley, May 1, April 6, 1834.

39. Until 1855 only four Roman Catholic residents of St. John's had been chosen as councillors—Patrick Morris, James Tobin, John Kent, and Lawrence O'Brien. In the same period there were six councillors who were Protestant Dissenters.

40. *DNB*, XVIII, pp. 942-43, Stanley.

41. CO 194/103, Privy Council, Case of Henry John Boulton, 1838.

42. *Ibid.*; CO 43/77, Hay to Boulton, June 17, 1833.

43. CO 324/90, Hay to Cochrane, May 4, 1833.

44. CO 194/85, Cochrane to Goderich, Jan. 3, 1833, encl., memorandum.

45. CO 324/90, Hay to Cochrane, July 4, 1833.

46. *Ibid.*, Hay to Cochrane, Priv., Jan. 3, 1834.

47. W. P. Morrell, *British Colonial Policy in the Age of Peel and Russell* (Oxford, 1930), p. 35.

48. CO. 194/85, Cochrane to Goderich, Oct. 22, 1833, and encls., Acts and comments.

49. CO 383/59, Acts, 1833.

50. CO 194/85, Cochrane to Goderich, Jan. 3, 1833, encl., memorandum; *JHA*, 1834, Jan. 29, p. 9, Cochrane to MHA.

51. W. B. Row, barrister, replaced J. B. Garland, apparently without contest, for Protestant Trinity Bay (*JHA*, 1834, Jan. 29, p. 5).

52. CO 194/85, Cochrane to Stanley, Dec. 26, 1833.

53. *Ibid.*

54. CO 194/99, Prescott to Glenelg, Oct. 14, 1837, encl. 1, Fleming to Glenelg, Jan. 10, 1837; encl. 4, A. Shea (editor, *Newfoundlander*) to J. Crowdy, Sept. 9, 1837.

55. CO 194/85, Cochrane to Stanley, Dec. 26, 1833; CO 194/99, Prescott to Glenelg, Oct. 14, 1837, encls. 1-10, newspaper extracts, 6-17.

56. CO 195/18, Stanley to Cochrane, March 1, 1834.

57. CO 324/90, Hay to Cochrane, March 8, April 5, 1834.

58. CO 194/87, Cochrane to Stanley, May 1, 1834.

59. *Ibid.*, April 6, 1834, and encl., resolutions, Dec. 26, 1833; July 28, 1834, and encls., Bishop Fleming to Roman Catholics of St. John's, Dec. 27, 1833, Crowdy to Fleming, Dec. 28, 1833.

60. *Ibid.*, April 6, 1834.

61. CO 194/88, Cochrane to Spring Rice, Oct. 22, 1834.

62. *Ibid.*, encl., memorial, W. Carson.

63. *JHA*, 1834, Jan. 29, p. 6.

64. CO. 194/87, Cochrane to Stanley, April 6, 1834, and encl., address, March.

65. *Ibid.*, encl., Att.-Gen. Simms to Cochrane.

66. CO 194/89, Stephen to Hay, May 8, 1834.

67. CO 194/87, Cochrane to Stanley, May 23, 1834, encl., Rules of Supreme Court; *JHA*, 1837, Oct. 10, p. 246, Report of Committee on Administration of Justice; CO 194/102, Morris to Glenelg, April 26, 1838.

68. CO 325/172, Boulton to Hay, Jan. 31, 1834.

69. Pedley, p. 400; *JHA*, 1837, Oct. 10, p. 247, Report ... Justice.

70. CO 323/172, Boulton to Hay, Jan. 31, 1834.

71. CO 43/78, Hay to D. O'Connell, March 13, 1834, acknowledging documents.

72. CO 194/93, Fleming to O'Connell, June 5, 1835, and encl., address to His Majesty.

73. CO 194/102, Morris to Glenelg, April 26, 1838.

74. CO 323/51, Stephen to Aberdeen, March 10, 1835.

75. CO 194/102, Morris to Glenelg, April 26, 1838; CO 194/97, Prescott to Glenelg, July 31, 1837, encls. 1-4, petitions, St. John's, Carbonear, Brigus, Harbour Grace, June 1837.

76. *JHA*, 1834, Feb. 6, p. 14.

77. Prowse, pp. 431-32. See Edith J. Archibald, *Life and Letters of Sir Edward Mortimer Archibald* (Toronto, 1924).

78. CO 383/59, Acts, 1834.

79. CO 323/172, Cochrane to Hay, Feb. 18, 1834.

80. CO 194/88, Cochrane to Spring Rice, Oct. 22, 1834.

81. CO 194/95, Prescott to Glenelg, Dec. 10, 1836.

82. CO 324/90, Hay to Cochrane, May 9, 1834. Prowse, p. 427, asserts inaccurately that he was superseded without notice.

83. CO 194/87, Cochrane to Stanley, Priv., June 12, 1834; CO 195/18, Spring Rice to Cochrane, Priv., Aug. 14, 1834; Co 324/90, Hay to Cochrane, Aug. 4, 1834.

84. CO 194/87, Cochrane to Stanley, Priv., June 12, 1834; CO 194/88, Cochrane to Spring Rice, Oct. 22, 1834.

85. CO 195/18, Spring Rice to Cochrane, Aug. 3, 1834.

86. CO 323/173, J. V. G. Martin to Hay, Sept. 24, 1834.

87. CO 194/106, Prescott to Normanby, Conf., July 4, 1839, a detailed report on the state of the colony, is an example.

88. *Ibid.*, minute, Stephen to Labouchere, Aug. 6, 1839.

89. CO 194/88, Cochrane to Spring Rice, Nov. 3, 1834.

90. Prowse, p. 436.

91. CO 194/88, Cochrane to Spring Rice, Nov. 7, 1834, encl., J. Shea to Cochrane, Nov. 3.

92. CO 194/90, Prescott to Aberdeen, May 14, 1835.

93. CO 194/88, Prescott to Spring Rice, Nov. 11, 1834.

94. CO 194/90, Prescott to Aberdeen, May 14, 1835.

95. CO 194/93, Boulton to Hay, Jan. 7, 1835, and encl., Cochrane to Boulton, Nov. 10, 1834.

96. *Ibid.*, Boulton to George Grey, Aug. 20; Boulton to Stephen, Aug. 26, 1835.

97. CO 194/102, Morris to Glenelg, April 26, 1838.

98. *JHA*, 1837, Oct. 10, pp. 248-49, Report ... Justice.

99. CO 194/90, Prescott to Glenelg, Priv., May 29, 1836.

100. *Ibid.*, May 29, May 30, 1835.

101. *Ibid.*, June 22, 1835, encl., R. J. Parsons to Prescott; CO 194/91, Prescott to Glenelg, July 1, 1835, encl., petition.

102. CO 195/18, Glenelg to Prescott, Aug. 13, 1835.

103. CO 194/93, Boulton to Grey, Aug. 20, 1835.

104. *Ibid.*, Boulton to Stephen, Aug. 26, 1835.

105. CO 194/90, Prescott to Aberdeen, May 21, 1835, and encls. 1-4.

106. *Ibid.*, May 14, 1835, and encl., McLean Little to Prescott, March 21.

107. Select Committee, 1841, I, Evidence, pp. 82-87, Dr. Joseph Shea.

108. CO 194/90, Prescott to Aberdeen, May 21, 1835.

109. *Ibid.*, Prescott to Glenelg, May 29, 1835.

110. Prowse, p. 439, n. 4; Gosse, pp. 60-63.

111. CO 194/94, Prescott to Glenelg, Jan. 4, 1836, and encl., report, J. Martin, Dec. 22, 1835.

112. *Ibid.*, Jan. 11, Jan. 17, 1836, and encls. 1-7; *JHA*, 1837, Oct. 10, p. 251, Report . . . Justice.

113. CO 194/94, Prescott to Glenelg, Feb. 15, 1836, encl., address, Feb. 8.

114. CO 194/95, Prescott to Glenelg, July 20, 1836, encl., address.

115. CO 195/18, Glenelg to Prescott, Aug. 21, 1836.

116. CO 194/94, Prescott to Glenelg, Jan. 4, 1836; CO 195/18, Glenelg to Prescott, Feb. 5, 1836.

117. CO 194/94, Prescott to Glenelg, May 21, 1836, and encl., *Patriot*, pastoral letter.

118. *Patriot*, Oct. 22, 1836, Fleming to Dr. Sprott, Aug. 24.

119. CO 194/101, Prescott to Glenelg, Oct. 2, 1838.

120. CO 43/79, Spring Rice to Palmerston, July 11, 1834.

121. CO 194/89, Palmerston to Spring Rice, Conf., Sept. 12, 1834, and encl., G. H. Seymour to Palmerston, Conf., Aug. 22, and encls. (a) Seymour to T. Aubin, Conf., Aug. 13, and (b) Aubin to Seymour, Conf., Aug. 19.

122. *Ibid.*, J. Bidwell to Hay, Dec. 3, 1834, and encls., Aubin to Seymour, Nov. 12 (extract), and F. Capaccini to Fleming, Nov. 9.

123. CO 194/92, W. F. Strangways to Hay, Oct. 25, 1835, encl., Fleming to Capaccini, June 13.

124. CO 194/90, Prescott to Aberdeen, May 1835, and encl., McLean Little to Prescott, March 21.

125. Select Committee, 1841, I, pp. 66-67, Ewen Stabb, merchant, on cases of Lawrence Barron, Patrick Stafford, and McLean Little; pp. 82-87, Dr. Joseph Shea, physician, on his own and other cases; CO 194/99, Prescott to Glenelg, Oct. 14, 1837, encl., Kough to Crowdy, Sept. 12, on his own case; CO 194/102 H. Simms to Glenelg, Jan. 3, 1838, asking for passage to New South Wales, his school and shop having failed through proscription by the clergy; CO 194/102, Strangways to Stephen, March 18, 1838, and encls., conf. statement and annex, T. Aubin, Dec. 28, 1837.

126. CO 195/19, Glenelg to Prescott, Dec. 1835.

127. CO 194/96, J. Y. Bramston to Fleming, July 27, 1835.

128. CO 194/90, Prescott to Glenelg, Nov. 30, 1835, encl., Fleming to Prescott, Nov. 20.

129. CO 194/96, Fleming to Bramston, Jan. 25, 1836.

130. *Ibid.*, Glenelg to Palmerston, Feb. 4, 1836.

131. *Ibid.*, Stephen to Strangways, Feb. 18, 1836.

132. CO 195/18, Glenelg to Prescott, May 20, 1836.

133. CO 194/95, Prescott to Glenelg, July 2, 1836.

134. CO 195/19, Glenelg to Prescott, Feb. 9, 1837.

135. CO 194/109, Prescott to Russell, June 10, 1841, minute, Stephen to R. V. Smith, July 16.

136. CO 194/90, Prescott to Aberdeen, Feb. 16, 1835.

137. CO 194/95, Prescott to Glenelg, Conf., July 16, 1836.

138. CO 195/18, Glenelg to Prescott, Aug. 20, 1836.

139. CO 194/95, Prescott to Glenelg, Conf., July 16, 1836.

140. CO 194/108, Prescott to Russell, March 7, 1840.

141. CO 194/91, Prescott to Glenelg, Nov. 28, 1835.

142. CO 194/94, Prescott to Glenelg, April 11, 1836.

143. CO 194/90, Prescott to Aberdeen, Feb. 16, 1835.

144. CO 195/18, Aberdeen to Prescott, April 15, 1835.

145. *Ibid.*, Glenelg to Prescott, July 24, 1835.

146. CO 194/94, Prescott to Glenelg, April 11, 1836, 6 Wm. IV, c. 7 (Nfld.).

147. CO 194/90, Prescott to Glenelg, Feb. 16, 1835.

148. CO 195/19, Aberdeen to Prescott. April 15, 1835.

149. CO 194/90, Prescott to Aberdeen, Feb. 16, 1835.

150. CO 195/18, Glenelg to Prescott, Sept. 27, 1835.

151. CO 194/94, Prescott to Glenelg, April 11, 1836, and encl., address, MHA to Prescott, April 8.

CHAPTER THREE

1. CO 194/103, Privy Council, Case of Henry John Boulton, Appendix 27, p. 34; CO 194/106, Prescott to Normanby, Conf., July 4, 1839.

2. CO 194/95, Prescott to Glenelg, Dec. 9, 1836; Select Committee, 1841, I, Evidence, p. 55, Robert Job; p. 65, Ewen Stabb.
3. CO 194/95, Prescott to Glenelg, Dec. 9, 1836.
4. *Ibid.*, Nov. 11, 1836; CO 194/101, Prescott to Glenelg, Oct. 2, 1838.
5. CO 194/95, Prescott to Glenelg, Nov. 11, 1836, and draft reply, J. Stephen. The paragraph of criticism was omitted in the amended despatch of Dec. 15.
6. CO 195/19, Glenelg to Prescott, Dec. 15, 1836.
7. CO 194/97, Prescott to Glenelg, Jan. 23, 1836, and encls., memorial, Jan. 16, and J. V. Nugent to Glenelg, Jan. 16.
8. CO 195/19, Glenelg to Prescott, Feb. 20, 1837.
9. CO 194/95, Prescott to Glenelg, Dec. 10, 1836.
10. *Ibid.*
11. CO 195/19, Glenelg to Prescott, Jan. 12, 1837.
12. CO 194/95, Prescott to Glenelg, Dec. 12, Dec. 13, 1836.
13. CO 195/19, Glenelg to Prescott, Jan. 12, Jan. 26, 1837.
14. CO 194/97, Prescott to Glenelg, March 2, 1837, and encl., report of Attorney-General, Feb.; *ibid.*, April 11, 1837, encls. 1-12, petitions; *JHA*, 1837, Oct. 10, pp. 249-53, Report ... Justice; CO 194/102, Morris to Glenelg, April 26, 1838.
15. CO 195/19, Glenelg to Prescott, May 31; Conf., May 31, 1837.
16. CO 194/106, Prescott to Normanby, Conf., July 4, 1839.
17. *PD*, vol. 65, 1842, July 30, pp. 878-79; Select Committee, 1841, I, Evidence, p. 35; T. H. Brooking.
18. H. of C., Parl. Papers (525) XXXIV, 565, addresses #5, #12, #13.
19. CO 194/97, Prescott to Glenelg, July 10, 1837.
20. CO 194/106, Prescott to Glenelg, Conf., July 4, 1839.
21. *Ibid.*
22. *JHA*, 1837, July 3, pp. 12-18.
23. CO 195/18, Glenelg to Prescott, Aug. 18, 1836.
24. *JHA*, 1837, July 4, pp. 19-20.
25. *Ibid.*, July 6, pp. 29-32.
26. CO 194/97, Prescott to Glenelg, July 10, 1837, and encls. 1-14, correspondence with the Assembly.
27. CO 195/19, Glenelg to Prescott, Aug. 12; Conf., Aug. 12; 1837.
28. *JHA*, 1837, July 6, p. 23, Nugent; pp. 24-25, Brown; July 10, p. 39, Nugent.
29. CO 194/101, Prescott to Glenelg, Oct. 2, 1838.
30. CO 194/97, Prescott to Glenelg, July 14, 1837.
31. CO 195/19, Glenelg to Prescott, Feb. 20, 1837.
32. *JHA*, 1837, July 14, p. 45.
33. *Ibid.*, July 6, p. 26, Address in Reply to Speech from Throne.
34. *JHA*, 1837, July 12, p. 52; July 18, p. 59; July 21, p. 63, Crowdy to Prescott, July 21; Aug. 2, p. 83; Aug. 9, pp. 97-98.
35. CO 194/103, Nugent to Glenelg, July 9, 1838.
36. CO 194/98, Prescott to Glenelg, Sept. 9, 1837.
37. CO 195/19, Glenelg to Prescott, Nov. 10, 1837.
38. CO 194/106, Prescott to Normanby, Conf., July 4, 1839.
39. *JHA*, 1837, Aug. 25, p. 25, Resolutions ... Justice; Appendix, pp. 459-540, Enquiry and Papers; Oct. 10, pp. 244-52, Report ... Justice.
40. *JHA*, 1837, Sept. 1, p. 135, Nugent; Sept. 5, p. 145; Sept. 8, p. 155 (see *Royal Gazette*, Nov. 26, 1833); Oct. 12, pp. 271-72; CO 194/98, Prescott to Glenelg, Dec. 9, 1837, encl., address, Oct. 18.
41. CO 194/98, Prescott to Glenelg, Nov. 21, 1837.
42. *JHA*, 1837, Nov. 18, pp. 361-65, address; also p. 71 *et passim* to p. 361.
43. *Ibid.*, Sept. 19, p. 185; Sept. 28, p. 215; Sept. 29, pp. 219, 222.
44. *Ibid.*, July 3, p. 15, Speech from Throne.
45. CO 194/113, delegates to Lord John Russell, Sept. 4, 1841.
46. *JHA*, 1837, Oct. 4, p. 230.
47. On road controversy see: *JHA*, 1837, Oct. 6, p. 239; Oct. 11, p. 261; Oct. 16, p. 275, Oct. 18, pp. 286-87; Oct. 21, p. 296; Oct. 23, p. 313.
48. *JHA*, Nov. 18, pp. 361-65, address.
49. Innis, p. 387, n. 38, quotes Thomas Talbot, *Newfoundland* (London, 1882), p. 43, to this effect.
50. CO 194/88, Prescott to Glenelg, Nov. 21, 1837.
51. *JHA*, Oct. 26, pp. 318-19.

52. Select Committee, 1841, I, Evidence, p. 74, Ewen Stabb.
53. *JHA*, Oct. 26, pp. 318-19.
54. CO 194/97, Prescott to Glenelg, March 2, 1837, encl., report, Chief Justice Boulton.
55. CO 194/98, Prescott to Glenelg, Nov. 22, 1837, encl., address of Council, Nov. 18.
56. *JHA*, 1837, Oct. 27, pp. 321-24; Nov. 1, p. 331; Nov. 3, p. 333; Nov. 15, pp. 347-50;
Nov. 17, p. 354.
57. CO 195/19, Glenelg to Prescott, Feb. 1, 1838.
58. *JHA*, 1837, Oct. 10, pp. 244-52, Report . . . Justice.
59. CO 194/98, Prescott to Glenelg, Nov. 24, 1837, encl., address from Assembly, Nov. 6;
CO 194/102, Morris to Glenelg, April 2, 1838.
60. CO 194/103, Privy Council, Case of Henry John Boulton, 1838, Assembly's Case, p. 11.

CHAPTER FOUR

1. For events in the Canadian provinces, see Aileen Dunham, *Political Unrest in Upper
Canada, 1815-1836* (London, 1927); A. D. Decelles, *Papineau* (Oxford, 1926), and *The Patriotes of 1837* (Toronto, 1916). For a more general treatment, see *CHBE*, VI, pp. 235-50.
Lower Canada; pp. 251-70, Upper Canada; see also pp. 856-57, Bibliography.
2. *CHBE*, VI, pp. 237, 246.
3. CO 194/107, Morris to Normanby, March 20, 1839.
4. CO 194/103, delegates to Glenelg, Feb. 12, 1838; *Patriot*, May 5, 1838.
5. Feb. 9, 1838, quoted by *Patriot*, April 7, 1838.
6. CO 194/103, delegates to Glenelg, Jan. 31, 1838.
7. CO 195/19, Glenelg to Prescott, Jan. 2, 1838.
8. CO 194/102, Morris to Glenelg, April 26, 1838.
9. CO 194/100, Prescott to Glenelg, Conf., Jan. 5, 1838, minute, Stephen, Jan. 30.
10. CO 195/19, Glenelg to Prescott, March 6, 1838.
11. CO 194/103, Privy Council, Case of Henry John Boulton, 1838, Case of Chief Justice,
pp. 1-22; Appendix 6, p. 3.
12. *Patriot*, June 23, 1838, Morris to Kent, May 7.
13. CO 194/103, Order-in-Council, July 5, 1838, embodying and confirming Report of
Privy Council committee, July 5.
14. CO 194/103, Boulton to Glenelg, July 12; Grey to Boulton, July 23, 1838.
15. *Patriot*, Oct. 26, 1839.
16. CO 195/19, Glenelg to Prescott, July 28, 1838; Prowse, p. 457.
17. CO 194/98, Prescott to Glenelg, Jan. 3, 1838, encl., address, Oct. 3, 1837.
18. CO 194/103, delegates to Glenelg, Jan. 31, March 26, 1838.
19. CO 195/19, Glenelg to Prescott, Jan. 3, 1838; CO 194/103, Glenelg to delegates, March
2, May 25, 1838.
20. 5 and 6 Vict., c. 1 (Nfld.).
21. CO 194/103, Glenelg to delegates, March 2, 1838.
22. *Ibid.*, delegates to Glenelg, Jan. 31, 1838.
23. *Ibid.*, Glenelg to delegates, March 2, May 25, 1838.
24. *Ibid.*, delegates to Glenelg, Jan. 31, 1838.
25. CO 194/102, Stanley to Stephen, June 23, 1838.
26. CO 194/103, delegates to Glenelg, Jan. 31, 1838.
27. *Ibid.*, Glenelg to delegates, March 2, 1838.
28. *Ibid.*, Nugent to Glenelg, March 26, 1838.
29. CO 194/101, Prescott to Glenelg, Aug. 29, 1838; CO 195/19, Glenelg to Prescott, Sept.
29, 1838.
30. CO 194/103, address, Oct. 25, 1838, based on Report of Fishery Committee in *JHA*,
1837, Oct. 3, pp. 225-26.
31. CO 195/19, Glenelg to Prescott, Feb. 14, 1838; CO 194/103, Nugent to Glenelg,
March 26, 1838.
32. CO 194/100, Prescott to Glenelg, Jan. 3, 1838, encl., address; Conf., Jan. 5, and
minute, Stephen, Jan. 30.
33. CO 195/19, Glenelg to Prescott, May 18, 1838.
34. CO 194/98, address, Nov. 18, 1837.
35. *CHBE*, II, p. 285; VI, pp. 279, 283.
36. CO 194/98, address, Nov. 18, 1837.
37. Patrick Morris, *Legislative Councils proved to be the Root of all the Evils of the
Colonies: A Short Address to the Earl of Durham* (1839), pp. 27-45.

38. CO 194/103, Prescott to Glenelg, Oct. 3, 1838.
39. *Ibid.*, minute, J. W. C. Murdoch to G. Grey, Nov. 9, 1838.
40. CO 195/19, Glenelg to Prescott, Nov. 25, 1838.
41. CO 194/105, Prescott to Glenelg, Jan. 15, 1839.
42. CO 194/99, Prescott to Glenelg, Oct. 14, 1837, and encls.; CO 195/19, Glenelg to Prescott, Feb. 9, 1837.
43. CO 194/102, Fleming to Glenelg, Feb. 1, 1838.
44. CO 194/97, Prescott to Glenelg, Aug. 10, 1837.
45. CO 43/87, Stephen to J. Backhouse, Nov. 29, 1837; CO 194/102, Strangways to Stephen, Feb. 1, 1838, and encls.
46. CO 195/19, Glenelg to Prescott, Conf., Nov. 23, 1837.
47. Jan. 30, 1838, on CO 194/100, Prescott to Glenelg, Jan. 4, 1838.
48. CO 194/102, Strangways to Stephen, March 18, 1838, and encls., Aubin to R. Abercrombie, Feb. 17, and encls. (*a*) conf. statement and (*b*) annex, Dec. 28, 1837; Aubin to Abercrombie, Priv. and Conf., Feb. 19, 1838.
49. *Ibid.*, Fleming to Glenelg, Feb. 25, 1838, minutes, Murdoch to Stephen, March 1, and Stephen, March 2.
50. *PD*, vol. 39, 1837, Dec. 12, pp. 978-79, Hume and O'Connell; vol. 41, 1838, March 6, pp. 476-512, Molesworth.
51. CO 194/102, Grey to Fleming, March 3; Fleming to Glenelg, March 21, 1838, and minute, Stephen to Murdoch, March 31; Grey to Fleming, Aug. 2; CO 195/19, Glenelg to Prescott, Aug. 12, 1838.
52. CO 195/19, Glenelg to Prescott, Conf., May 18, 1838.
53. *Patriot*, Oct. 27, 1838, letter of Bishop Fleming.
54. CO 194/106, Prescott to Normanby, Conf., July 4, 1839.
55. *Patriot*, May 23, 1838, quoting *Public Ledger*.

CHAPTER FIVE

1. *Patriot*, July 7, 1838.
2. *Public Ledger*, July 10, 1838, protest of Councillors Dunscombe, Bland, and Sinclair.
3. CO 194/100 Prescott to Glenelg, Aug. 14, 1838.
4. CO 194/102, address of Assembly to Her Majesty, Oct. 25, 1838.
5. *JHA*, 1838, Oct. 24, p. 138, resolutions and protest of Legislative Council.
6. *Ibid.*, Oct. 25, pp. 139-47, address of Assembly to Her Majesty.
7. CO 194/101, Prescott to Glenelg, Nov. 2, 1838.
8. *JHA*, 1838, Oct. 25, pp. 139-47, address of Assembly to Her Majesty.
9. CO 194/102, address of Assembly to Her Majesty, Oct. 25, 1838.
10. CO 195/19, Glenelg to Prescott, Jan. 12, 1839.
11. CO 194/100, Prescott to Glenelg, Aug. 16, 1838, and encls. 1-9.
12. *Ibid.*, Aug. 16, Aug. 30, 1838; Prowse, pp. 446-47.
13. *Public Ledger*, May 28, 1839, "Case of Kielly v. Assembly in Supreme Court," reprinted from *Monthly Law Magazine*, March 1839.
14. *Public Ledger*, Jan. 9, 1839, Judge Lilly's judgment; CO 195/19, Glenelg to Prescott, Secret and Conf., Feb. 2, 1839; CO 194/105, Prescott to Glenelg, Conf., April 30, 1839.
15. CO 194/105, Prescott to Glenelg, Conf., Jan. 10, 1839.
16. *Ibid.*, Feb. 21, 1839, and encl., petition, E. Kielly to Lords of Privy Council.
17. Quoted in Pedley, p. 408.
18. CO 194/106, Prescott to Normanby, Conf., July 4, 1839.
19. CO 195/19, Glenelg to Prescott, Jan. 8, 1839, and encl., Law Officers' report, Dec. 3, 1838. The despatch seems to have been delayed in transit.
20. CO 194/106, Prescott to Normanby, Conf., July 4, 1839; Prescott to Russell, Dec. 9, 1839, encl., address of Assembly to Her Majesty, Oct. 10.
21. CO 194/105, Prescott to Glenelg, Conf., Jan. 10, 1839.
22. CO 195/19, Glenelg to Prescott, March 1, 1839.
23. CO 194/101, Prescott to Glenelg, Dec. 24, 1838, encl., address, Dec. 1838.
24. CO 195/19, Glenelg to Prescott, Jan. 21, 1839.
25. CO 194/102, address, Feb. 20, 1839.
26. *Ibid.*, addresses to Secretary of State from Liverpool, Sept. 25, Oct. 12; from Poole, Oct. 5; from Bristol, Oct. 24, 1838.
27. *Public Ledger*, Nov. 20, 1838, extracts from the *Constitutional* (Glasgow), the *Gazette* (Exeter), the *Courier* (Liverpool), and the *Conservative Journal* (London).

28. CO 194/102, addresses to Secretary of State from Liverpool, March 7; from Torquay, Feb. 28; from Dartmouth, March 8; from Teignmouth, March 12, 1839.
29. *Ibid.*, address, Carson, Kent, Nugent, and Doyle to Her Majesty, Jan. 7, 1839.
30. *Ibid.*, address, Dec. 11, 1838.
31. *Ibid.*, address, Dec. 1838.
32. CO 194/107, Morris to Normanby, March 20, 1839.
33. *PD*, vol. 47, 1839, April 26, pp. 551-56.
34. CO 195/19, Normanby to Prescott, Conf., April 25, 1839.
35. *PD*, vol. 47, 1839, April 26, pp. 556-57.
36. *Ibid.*, 1838, pp. 557-58.
37. *JHA*, 1838, Sept. 17, p. 43.
38. Sir C. P. Lucas, ed., *Lord Durham's Report on the Affairs of British North America*, II (Oxford, 1912), p. 202.
39. On the matter of a parliamentary inquiry see *PD*, vol. 47, 1839, April 26, pp. 558-63.
40. Patrick Morris, *A Short Reply to the Speech of Earl Aberdeen on the State of Newfoundland* (1839).
41. *Patriot*, April 13, 1839.
42. *DNB*, XV, pp. 1116-17 (Normanby).
43. *Patriot*, April 13, 1839, quoting *Public Ledger*.
44. CO 194/106, Prescott to Normanby, Conf., July 4, 1839.
45. *Ibid.*, minute, Stephen to H. Labouchere, Aug. 6.
46. *Ibid.*, July 5, 1839.
47. CO 195/19, Russell to Prescott, Oct. 6, 1839.
48. CO 194/108, Prescott to Russell, Conf., Jan. 6, 1840.
49. CO 195/19, Russell to Prescott, Conf., March 9, 1840.
50. H. Prescott, *A Sketch of the State of Affairs in Newfoundland*. This consists of two letters, dated 1839 and 1842, the first of which was printed in the *Metropolitan Magazine*, Aug. 1839, and reprinted in the *Patriot*, Nov. 23, 1839. CO 194/115, Prescott to A. Blackwood, June 27, 1842, enclosing the pamphlet, apparently acknowledges authorship.
51. CO 194/105, Prescott to Normanby, May 25, 1839, and encls. 1-7.
52. CO 195/19, Normanby to Prescott, June 23, 1839.
53. CO 194/105, Prescott to Normanby, June 3, Aug. 13, 1839.
54. CO 195/19, Normanby to Prescott, Aug. 31, 1839.
55. CO 194/105, Prescott to Normanby, June 12, 1839, and encls. 3 and 4.
56. CO 194/107, Law Officers' report, July 20, 1839.
57. CO 194/106, Prescott to Russell, Oct. 17, 1839.
58. CO 195/19, Glenelg to Prescott, Dec. 10, 1838; CO 194/108, Prescott to Russell, Jan. 3, 1840, encl., Assembly's minute of conference.
59. CO 195/19, Normanby to Prescott, June 4, 1839.
60. CO 194/108, Prescott to Russell, Jan. 3, 1840, encls., Council's minute of conference, and Assembly's minute of conference.
61. CO 195/19, Russell to Prescott, May 4, 1840.
62. *JHA*, 1840, Feb. 20, p. 75; Feb. 24, p. 76.
63. *Patriot*, Nov. 9, 1839; Jan. 11, Feb. 1, 1840.
64. CO 194/106, Prescott to Normanby, Oct. 17, 1839.
65. *Ibid.*, Prescott to Russell, Dec. 9, 1839, encl., address of Assembly to Her Majesty, Oct. 10; CO 194/108, Prescott to Russell, Jan. 18, 1840; encl., Address in Reply to Speech from Throne.
66. *Patriot*, Jan. 11, 1840, Proceedings of Assembly, Jan. 3.
67. *JHA*, 1840, April 27, pp. 193-96.
68. CO 194/108, Prescott to Russell, May 18, 1840.
69. CO 194/106, Prescott to Normanby, Oct. 17, 1839.
70. *Patriot*, Jan. 11, 1840, Proceedings of Assembly, Jan. 2; *JHA*, 1840, Feb. 3, p. 57; Feb. 10, p. 65.
71. *Public Ledger*, July 26, 1839.
72. *JHA*, 1840, p. 22 *et passim* to p. 196. Compare CO 383/59, Acts, 1840.
73. *JHA*, 1840, April 29, p. 212, Speech of Prorogation.
74. CO 194/106, Prescott to Russell, Dec. 9, 1839, and encl., address of Assembly to Her Majesty, Oct. 10; CO 194/108, Prescott to Russell, Jan. 30, 1840, encl., address; CO 195/19, Russell to Prescott, Feb. 19, March 9, 1840.
75. CO 194/106, Prescott to Russell, Dec. 9, 1839, encl., address, Oct. 10.
76. W. P. M. Kennedy, ed., *Statutes, Treaties, and Documents of the Canadian Constitution, 1713-1926* (Oxford, 1929), pp. 480 *seqq.*

77. *CHBE*, VI, pp. 285-86.
78. *Patriot*, Jan. 4; Jan. 11, 1840, Proceedings of Assembly, Jan. 3.
79. *Ibid.*, Jan. 11, 1840, Proceedings of Assembly, Jan. 8.
80. CO 194/108, Prescott to Russell, March 7, 1840.
81. *JHA*, 1840, March 24, p. 114.
82. *Patriot*, May 9, 1840.
83. CO 194/109, Prescott to Russell, June 10, 1840.
84. *Ibid.*
85. *Patriot*, May 16, May 20, May 27, 1840; CO 194/109, Prescott to Russell, June 10, 1840.
86. CO 194/109, Prescott to Russell, June 12, 1840, encl., petition, *Patriot*, June 6.
87. *Ibid.*, June 9, 1840.
88. *Ibid.*, minutes, Stephen to R. V. Smith, Stephen to J. Backhouse, July 16.
89. CO 325/40, State of the Roman Catholic Church in the Colonies, 1833-1851, Precis #14, Sept. 1843, "Ionian Islands and Conduct of Dr. Fleming."
90. CO 194/113, Fleming to Russell, Nov. 16, 1840; March 24, 1841; CO 195/19, Russell to Prescott, Feb. 21, 1841.
91. Prowse, p. 608.
92. *Public Ledger*, June 9, 1840.
93. *Patriot*, July 11, 1840.
94. *Ibid.*, June 12, May 27, June 6, Aug. 25, 1840.
95. *Ibid.*, Sept. 15, 1840, report of meeting; Aug. 25, Oct. 1, 1840.
96. Reference to the election and pre-election atmosphere: CO 194/109, Prescott to Russell, June 12; Nov. 7, encl. 1, and minute, Stephen to Smith; Dec. 10, #70, encls. 1-18; Dec. 10, #71; Dec. 11, #72; Dec. 19, 1840.
97. CO 195/19, Russell to Prescott, Jan. 14, 1841, #80.
98. CO 194/111, Prescott to Russell, March 3, 1841.
99. CO 194/109, Prescott to Russell, Dec. 10, 1840, #70, minute, Stephen to Smith.
100. CO 195/19, Russell to Prescott, Jan. 14, 1841, #80.
101. CO 195/111, Prescott to Russell, March 3, 1841.
102. CO 195/19, Russell to Prescott, Jan. 14, #81; Feb. 2, 1841.
103. CO 194/111 Prescott to Russell, March 3, 1841.
104. *Patriot*, Jan. 2, 1841.
105. *JHA*, 1841, Jan. 2, p. 7, Speech from Throne; Jan. 8, p. 12, Address in Reply.
106. CO 194/111, Prescott to Russell, Jan. 12, 1841.
107. *JHA*, 1841, Feb. 9, p. 60; Feb. 12, p. 71.
108. CO 194/111, Prescott to Russell, Feb. 16, 1841.
109. *JHA*, 1841, April 23, pp. 209-16, address of Assembly to Her Majesty.
110. *Ibid.*, Feb. 5, p. 55, address.
111. CO 194/111, Prescott to Russell, Feb. 11, 1841.
112. CO 195/19, Russell to Prescott, March 30, 1841.
113. *PD*, vol. 57, 1841, March 27, pp. 611-12.

CHAPTER SIX

1. CO 194/111, Prescott to Russell, Feb. 16, 1841, minute, Stephen to Smith.
2. Peel Papers, BM Add. MSS 40467, vol. cclxxxvii, f. 21, Stanley to Peel, March 18, 1841.
3. *PD*, vol. 57, 1841, March 19, pp. 391-94.
4. Peel Papers, *loc. cit.*, f. 162, Stanley to Peel (dated from internal evidence between March 19 and March 26, 1841).
5. *PD*, vol. 57, 1841, March 19, p. 711; March 26, pp. 611-12; March 29, pp. 657-59, 705-20.
6. *Ibid.*, vol. 65, 1842, July 30, p. 881, Stanley.
7. CO 194/111, Prescott to Russell, April 27, 1841; CO 194/112, Commander Sall to Russell, May 25, 1841.
8. Members: Lord Ashley, Mr. Colquhoun, Mr. Gladstone, Sir James Graham, Sir George Grey, Lord Howick, Mr. Lascelles, Mr. Langdale, Mr. O'Connell, Sir John Pakington (chair), Lord John Russell, Lord Sandon, and Lord Stanley.
9. Select Committee, 1841, I, Evidence.
10. CO 194/113, delegates to Russell, Aug. 20, Aug. 24, and n.d., received Sept. 20, 1841.
11. Select Committee, 1841, II, Papers, Section 6, pp. 1-23, R. Bonnycastle, "Considerations upon the Political Position and Natural Advantages of Newfoundland," 1841. (Submitted

in CO 194/113, Bonnycastle to Russell, Jan. 14, 1841.)
  12.   CO 194/113, Archibald to Stanley, Sept. 16, 1841.
  13.   W. S. MacNutt, "New Brunswick's Age of Harmony—The Administration of Sir John Harvey," *CHR*, XXXII, no. 2 (June 1951), p. 106.
  14.   *CHBE*, VI, p. 280.
  15.   Russell Papers, Anglesey to Russell, April 5, 1841, and encl., Harvey to Anglesey, Feb. 25; Anglesey to Russell, April 18, 1841.
  16.   *Ibid.*, Russell to Queen Victoria, April 26, 1841.
  17.   CO 194/112, Harvey to Russell, Sept. 17, 1841.
  18.   CO 194/114, Harvey to Stanley, Conf., March 17, 1842.
  19.   MacNutt, pp. 105-25. See also *CHBE*, VI, pp. 279-80, 285.
  20.   CO 194/112, Harvey to Russell, Sept. 24, 1841, and encls., addresses, various.
  21.   CO 323/55, Stephen to Russell, Feb. 11, 1840; CO 323/56, Stephen to Russell, Aug. 24, 1841.
  22.   CO 194/112, Harvey to Russell, Oct. 25, 1841.
  23.   *Ibid.*, Harvey to Stanley, Sep. and Conf., Dec. 21, 1841, and minute, Stephen to G. W. Hope, Jan. 18, 1842.
  24.   CO 194/112, Harvey to Russell, Conf., Oct. 6, 1841.
  25.   *Ibid.*, minutes, Stephen to Hope, Nov. 19, and Stanley.
  26.   CO 195/19, Stanley to Harvey, Conf., Nov. 19, 1841.
  27.   *Ibid.*
  28.   CO 194/112, Harvey to Stanley, Sep. and Conf., Dec. 21, 1841.
  29.   *Ibid.*, minute, Stephen to Hope, Jan. 18, 1842.
  30.   Morrell, *British Colonial Policy*, pp. 83, 96; 5 and 6 Vict., c. 76.
  31.   CO 194/114, Harvey to Stanley, Conf., Jan. 10, 1842, minutes, Stanley to Hope, March 19; Stephen to Hope, March 23; Stanley to Hope, March 25; Stanley, March 31.
  32.   *PD*, vol. 63, 1842, May 26, pp. 875-79.
  33.   *PD*, vol. 65, 1842, July 30, pp. 873-87.
  34.   Morrell, p. 83.
  35.   *PD*, vol. 65, 1842, Aug. 3, pp. 983-89, 990-1007; Aug. 5, p. 1070.
  36.   *PD*, vol. 64, June 24, p. 538.
  37.   *PD*, vol. 65, 1842, Aug. 9, pp. 1178-79; Aug. 10, p. 1214; Aug. 12, p. 1300.
  38.   *Ibid.*, July 30, pp. 873-80, O'Connell quoting from Fleming to O'Connell, June 25.
  39.   CO 194/115, Prescott to A. J. Blackwood, June 27, 1842.
  40.   CO 194/111, Prescott to Stanley, Sept. 16, 1841.
  41.   CO 194/115, Prescott to Hope, July 1, 1842.

CHAPTER SEVEN

  1.   CO 195/20, Stanley to Harvey, Conf., Sept. 3, 1842.
  2.   CO 194/115, Harvey to Stanley, Sept., Dec. 21, 1842.
  3.   CO 194/114, Harvey to Stanley, Conf., April 6, 1842.
  4.   CO 194/115, Harvey to Stanley, Priv. and Conf., Oct. 5, 1842.
  5.   CO 194/116, Harvey to Stanley, Sep. and Conf., Jan. 16, 1843.
  6.   CO 194/116, Harvey to Stanley, Sep. and Conf., Jan. 16, 1843, and encls., circular memorandum, Dec. 21, 1842, and address, Jan. 11, 1843; minutes, Stephen and Stanley.
  7.   CO 194/115, Harvey to Stanley, Priv. and Conf., Oct. 5, Oct. 18, 1842.
  8.   CO 195/20, Stanley to Harvey, Conf., Sept. 3, 1842.
  9.   CO 194/116, Harvey to Stanley, Sep. and Conf., Jan. 19, 1843.
  10.   CO 195/20, Stanley to Harvey, March 19, 1843.
  11.   *Ibid.*, Dec. 27, 1842.
  12.   CO 194/116, Harvey to Stanley, Jan. 18, 1843, encl., Speech from Throne, Jan 14; Sep., Jan. 25, 1843, encl., Address in Reply.
  13.   CO 194/116, Harvey to Stanley, Sep., March 15, 1843, encl., message.
  14.   *Ibid.*, May 11, 1843.
  15.   *Public Ledger*, May 22, 1843, Speech of Prorogation.
  16.   CO 194/116, Harvey to Stanley, Sep., May 22; Conf., May 30, 1843.
  17.   *Ibid.*, Conf., May 30, 1843.
  18.   *Public Ledger*, June 19, 1843.
  19.   CO 194/116, Harvey to Stanley, Sep. and Conf., March 2, 1843.
  20.   *Ibid.*, Aug. 22, 1843.
  21.   *Ibid.*, June 30, 1843.

22. CO 194/115, Harvey to Stanley, Priv. and Conf., Oct. 5, 1842.
23. CO 194/119, Robinson to Stanley, Feb. 21, 1843; Robinson to Harvey, July 3; Harvey to Stanley, Dec. 18, encl., Bourne to Stanley, Dec. 9; Harvey to Stanley, Dec. 28; Crowdy to Harvey, Dec. 22; Robinson to Harvey, Dec. 23; Harvey to Stanley, Feb. 21, 1844.
24. For a treatment of the intricacies of this controversy, see Rev. Malcolm MacDonell, "The Conflict between Sir. John Harvey and Chief Justice ... Bourne," *Canadian Historical Association Report*, 1956, pp. 45-54.
25. CO 195/20, Stanley to Harvey, May 5, 1844.
26. *Ibid.*, Aug. 1, 1844.
27. CO 194/116, Harvey to Stanley, Sep., May 22, 1843.
28. MacNutt, p. 115.
29. *Public Ledger*, March 4, 1842; July 6, 1844; March 11, Dec. 2, 1845. *Patriot*, Feb. 16, 1842; Aug. 7, 1844.
30. CO 194/117, Harvey to Stanley, July 4, 1843, and minute, Stephen.
31. CO 195/20, Stanley to Harvey, Sept. 13; Priv., Sept. 13, 1843.
32. CO 194/120, Harvey to Stanley, Conf., March 30, 1844.
33. *Ibid.*, April 20, 1844.
34. *Ibid.*, May 21, 1844.
35. CO 195/20, Stanley to Harvey, July 4, 1844.
36. CO 194/120, Harvey to Stanley, May 1, 1844.
37. *Ibid.*, Conf., April 20, 1844.
38. *Ibid.*
39. *Ibid.*, July 9, 1844, encl., *Newfoundlander*, Feb. 8, Proceedings of Assembly.
40. *Ibid.*
41. *Patriot*, Feb. 28, 1843, report of meeting.
42. *Newfoundlander*, Feb. 8, 1844, Proceedings of Assembly.
43. *Patriot*, Feb. 28, 1843, report of meeting.
44. CO 194/120, Harvey to Stanley, July 9, 1844, encl., *Newfoundlander*, April 18, Proceedings of Assembly, April 1.
45. *Ibid.*
46. CO 194/120, Harvey to Stanley, Conf., April 20, 1844.
47. CO 195/20, Stanley to Harvey, Sept. 3, 1844.
48. CO 194/121, Harvey to Stanley, Oct. 18, 1844.
49. CO 196/2, Acts, 1845.
50. CO 194/122, Harvey to Stanley, Sep. and Conf., April 23, 1845, and minute, Stephen to Hope, May 15.
51. *Ibid.*, Harvey to Stanley, Priv., April 23; Priv., May 29, 1845.
52. CO 195/20, Stanley to Harvey, July 3, 1845.
53. CO 194/122, Harvey to Stanley, Oct. 12, 1845.
54. CO 195/20, Stanley to Harvey, Nov. 22, 1845.
55. *Public Ledger*, Jan. 16, 1846, Speech from Throne and Proceedings of Assembly, Jan. 15.
56. *Times*, Feb. 18, 1846, Proceedings of Assembly, Feb. 10.
57. *CHBE*, VI, p. 314.
58. *Public Ledger*, Jan. 23, 1846, resolutions.
59. *Patriot*, March 11, March 18, 1846, Proceedings of Assembly, Feb. 10.
60. *Times*, Feb. 28, 1846, Proceedings of Assembly, Feb. 16.
61. *Ibid.*, Feb. 21, 1846, Proceedings of Assembly, Feb. 12.
62. CO 194/125, Harvey to Gladstone, Conf., Feb. 16, 1846, and encl. "A," Dec. 1839.
63. CO 195/20, Gladstone to Harvey, May 18, 1846.
64. *Patriot*, March 25, 1846.
65. CO 194/125, Harvey to Stanley, March 17, 1846.
66. *Public Ledger*, March 24, 1846.
67. *Ibid.*, March 26, 1846, Proceedings of Assembly, March 23.
68. CO 194/125, Harvey to Gladstone, March 25, 1846.
69. *Times*, April 1, 1846.
70. *Public Ledger*, April 7, 1846, Proceedings of Assembly, March 30; April 17, Proceedings, March 30; April 28; May 15, Proceedings, April 7 and April 15.
71. CO 194/125, Harvey to Gladstone, Conf., April 22; Sep. and Conf., April 22; Priv. and Conf., June 24, 1846.
72. CO 194/125, Harvey to Gladstone, April 22, 1846, and encl., draft bill.
73. *Ibid.*, minute, Stephen to Lord Lyttelton, May 20, 1846, Queries, Gladstone, and answers, Blackwood and Stephen; minute, Gladstone to Stephen, June 8.

74. CO 194/125, Harvey to Gladstone, May 15, 1846, and minutes, Stephen, June 15, and Lyttelton to Gladstone, June 18.
75. *PD*, vol. 87, 1846, June 25, p. 964.
76. E. L. Woodward, *The Age of Reform, 1815-1870* (Oxford, 1938), p. 118.
77. 9 and 10 Vict., c. 45.
78. Prowse, pp. 457-61.
79. *Ibid.*; CO 194/125, Harvey to Gladstone, June 10, 1846.
80. 9 and 10 Vict., c. 3 (Nfld.)
81. Prowse, pp. 460-61.
82. CO 194/125, Harvey to Gladstone, Personal, March 3, 1846; CO 195/20, Gladstone to Harvey, June 18, 1846.
83. CO 194/126, Law to Grey, Sept. 25, Nov. 26, 1846.
84. *PD*, vol. 92, 1847, May 28, pp. 1241-45; Earl Grey, *The Colonial Policy of Lord John Russell's Administration*, I (London, 1853), pp. 295-96.
85. *Royal Gazette*, Dec. 8, 1846.
86. CO 194/127, LeMarchant to Grey, May 10, 1847, #7 and #8.
87. CO 195/21, Grey to LeMarchant, June 3, 1847.
88. CO 194/127, LeMarchant to Grey, June 24, 1847; CO 195/21, Grey to LeMarchant, July 19, 1847.
89. CO 194/127, LeMarchant to Grey, May 10, 1847, #6.
90. CO 195/21, Grey to LeMarchant, June 24, 1847.
91. CO 194/127, LeMarchant to Grey, Aug. 24, 1847.
92. *Ibid.*, LeMarchant to Blackwood, Priv., June 10, 1847.
93. *Ibid.*, LeMarchant to Grey, Aug, 9, Aug. 24, Oct. 14, Oct. 18, Dec. 13, 1847.
94. *Ibid.*, Priv. and Conf., Dec. 13, 1847.
95. CO 194/129, LeMarchant to Grey, May 1, 1848.
96. *Ibid.*, Sept. 27, 1848; *Public Ledger*, Aug. 1, 1848.
97. CO 194/127, LeMarchant to Blackwood, Priv., June 10, June 17, 1847.
98. CO 195/21, Grey to LeMarchant, July 3, 1847, and encl., 10 and 11 Vict., c. 44.
99. CO 381/54, Commission, July 5; Instructions, July 19, 1848.
100. CO 194/127, LeMarchant to Grey, July 24, 1847, encl., Archibald to LeMarchant, July 23; CO 194/129, LeMarchant to Grey, Feb. 4, 1848, and encls., minutes and drafts; CO 195/21, Grey to LeMarchant, Aug. 1, 1848.
101. CO 194/129, LeMarchant to Grey, May 1, 1848.

CHAPTER EIGHT

1. *CHBE*, VI, 357 (Nova Scotia); pp. 324-26 (Canada).
2. *Public Ledger*, May 26, 1848, resolutions 1-3.
3. *Ibid.*, address, May 24.
4. CO 194/129, LeMarchant to Grey, June 8, 1848, encl., *Terra Nova Herald*, May 31, Kent's speech.
5. *Times*, May 27; *Public Ledger*, May 26, 1848.
6. *Public Ledger*, Feb. 18, Feb. 25, April 21, April 25, 1848.
7. The editor, James Seaton, was to serve for six months in 1849 as editor of the *Times*, during which time its policy was "Moderation and Independence of Party Bias" and its motto, "Political Freedom is a Plant of Slow Growth." (*Times*, Jan. 3, 1849.) Seaton was displaced because his opinions were not those of the proprietor. (*Times*, July 4, 1849.)
8. CO 194/129, LeMarchant to Grey, June 8, 1848, encl., *Morning Courier*, May 30.
9. *Ibid.*, Priv. and Conf., May 22, 1848.
10. *Ibid.*, Jan. 24, 1848.
11. *Ibid.*, Priv. and Conf., May 22, 1848; June 8, and encl., *Terra Nova Herald*, May 31.
12. CO 195/21, Grey to LeMarchant, July 6, 1848.
13. *Times*, Aug. 12, 1848, T. P. Meagher to S. Morris, July 13.
14. *Times*, Nov. 18, 1848.
15. *Ibid.*, Sept. 4, 1847; Sept. 20, 1848.
16. *Ibid.*, Oct. 7, 1848.
17. *Ibid.*, Nov. 11, 1848.
18. *Patriot*, Dec. 6, 1848.
19. CO 194/131, LeMarchant to Grey, April 30, 1849.
20. *Ibid.*, April 28, 1849; *Patriot*, Feb. 3, 1849, Proceedings of Assembly, Jan. 27.
21. CO 194/29, LeMarchant to Grey, Dec. 21, 1848, encl., Speech from Throne, Dec. 14.

22. *Times,* Feb. 28, 1849.
23. *Ibid.,* April 18, 1849, Proceedings of Assembly, March 29.
24. CO 194/131, LeMarchant to Grey, April 10, 1849, encl., address, March 29.
25. *Ibid.,* minutes, Blackwood to H. Merivale, May 2; Merivale to B. Hawes, May 3.
26. CO 195/21, Grey to LeMarchant, May 10, 1849.
27. *Ibid.,* Conf., May 10, 1849, encls., Grey to Campbell, Conf., Nov. 12, 1847; March 27, 1848; Conf., Sept. 22, 1848; Jan. 1, 1849. (See CO 227/9 for the Grey-Campbell despatches.)
28. CO 194/132, LeMarchant to Blackwood, Oct. 18, 1849, extract.
29. *Ibid.,* LeMarchant to Grey, Sept. 4, 1849, #1.
30. *Times,* Feb. 2, 1853, Proceedings of Assembly, Jan. 31.
31. CO 194/132, LeMarchant to Grey, Sept. 4, Oct. 7, 1849; LeMarchant to Blackwood, Oct. 18, 1849. After Morris' death, defalcations to the amount of £6,000 were discovered. These seem to have been facilitated by the fact that the Assembly did not conduct simultaneous audits of the accounts and funds of the Treasury and the Savings Bank. The offices of Treasurer and Cashier were subsequently separated. (It may be significant that a few months after the appointment of Morris, Bishop Fleming had asked to be released as one of his sureties. *Patriot,* Nov. 28, 1840.)
32. CO 194/132, LeMarchant to Grey, Oct. 17, 1849.
33. *Patriot,* Sept. 1, 1849.
34. *Ibid.; Ledger,* Jan. 18, 1850.
35. *Patriot,* Feb. 2, 1850, Proceedings of Assembly, Jan. 29.
36. *JHA,* 1850, pp. 141-43.
37. *Ibid.,* April 25, p. 199.
38. 13 Vict., c. 13 (Nfld.).
39. *JHA,* 1850, pp. 94, 98.
40. *Patriot,* March 16, 1850, draft bill.
41. CO 194/133, LeMarchant to Grey, May 4, 1850, and encl., address, April 20.
42. CO 195/21, Grey to LeMarchant, June 10, 1850.
43. *Public Ledger,* April 30, 1850.
44. CO 194/133, LeMarchant to Grey, May 4, 1850, minute, Blackwood to Merivale, June 29.
45. *Patriot,* July 27, 1850.
46. *Times,* Sept. 4, 1850.
47. *Ibid.,* Oct. 2, 1850.
48. *Public Ledger,* Sept. 17, Sept. 27, 1850.
49. *Ibid.,* Sept. 27, Oct. 4, Oct. 15, Nov. 19, 1850.
50. *Times,* Oct. 19, Oct. 12, 1850.
51. Dr. Fleming had died on July 14. His successor, Dr. John Thomas Mullock, also of the Franciscan Order, had arrived as coadjutor on May 6, 1848. One of his successors, Dr. M. F. Howley, described him as a "man of rare ability, vast erudition, and great strength of character." See Prowse, pp. 607-8.
52. CO 196/2, Acts, 1851.
53. *JHA,* 1850, Appendix, pp. 133-42, reports on Academy; 13 Vict., c. 5 (Nfld.).
54. *Public Ledger,* Feb. 18, 1851; 14 Vict., c. 2 (Nfld.).
55. CO 194/134, LeMarchant to Grey, June 4, 1851, and encl., address.
56. *Times,* Jan. 25, 1851, Speech from Throne, Jan. 23.
57. *Times,* Feb. 26, 1851. Population was spreading along the south coast, drawn by the opportunities of selling bait to the Americans and French.
58. CO 194/134, LeMarchant to Grey, June 4, 1851.
59. CO 195/21, Grey to LeMarchant, Dec. 13, 1851.
60. Grey, *Colonial Policy,* I, pp. 33-35, 294.
61. *Public Ledger,* Jan. 30, 1852, Speech from Throne, Jan. 29; Feb. 3, 1853, Proceedings of Assembly, Jan. 30.
62. CO 194/136, LeMarchant to Grey, Feb. 13, 1852, encl., *Newfoundland Express:* Feb. 7, Proceedings of Assembly, Feb. 6; Feb. 10, Proceedings, Feb. 9; Feb. 13, Proceedings, Feb. 12.
63. A bill for the issue of Treasury notes and for the reduction of the public debt was disallowed in 1850, but repassed and allowed in 1851; 14 Vict., c. 5 (Nfld.). CO 323/71, C. A. Wood to Merivale, Aug. 11, 1851.
64. CO 194/136, LeMarchant to Grey, Feb. 13, 1852, encl., Dr. J. T. Mullock to P. F. Little, Feb. 7.
65. CO 194/136, LeMarchant to Grey, Feb. 13, 1852.
66. *Ibid.,* Feb. 27, 1852.

67. *Ibid.*, Feb. 26, 1852, encls., addresses of Chamber of Commerce and Law Society.
68. *Times*, Feb. 21, 1852.
69. CO 195/21, Pakington to LeMarchant, April 6, 1852.
70. *Ibid.*
71. CO 194/136, LeMarchant to Pakington, June 28, 1852, encl., Proceedings of Assembly, May 2.
72. *Ibid.*, April 20, 1852.
73. *Royal Gazette*, June 15, 1852, Speech of Prorogation.
74. *Times*, June 19; *Patriot*, June 21, 1852.
75. *Patriot*, June 21, Aug. 2; *Public Ledger*, July 16; *Times*, July 7, 1852.
76. CO 194/136, LeMarchant to Pakington, June 15, 1852.
77. *Ibid.*, June 28, 1852, encl., report of Attorney-General.
78. CO 194/136, LeMarchant to Pakington, June 28, 1852.
79. *Ibid.*, June 15, 1852.
80. *Ibid.*, Feb. 13, 1852, minute, Merivale to Earl Desart, March 18.
81. *Ibid.*, June 15, 1852, minute, Blackwood to Merivale, July 21.

CHAPTER NINE

1. CO 194/136, LeMarchant to Pakington, June 28, 1852, encl., extract from the *Pilot*. For reciprocal trade, see pp. 130.
2. *Public Ledger*, Sept. 10; *Times*, Sept. 15, 1852.
3. *Public Ledger*, Nov. 19, 1852.
4. CO 194/139, Hamilton to Newcastle, Conf., Feb. 21, 1853.
5. *Ibid.*, encl., Speech from Throne, Jan. 31.
6. *Times*, Feb. 5, 1853, Proceedings of Assembly, Feb. 4.
7. CO 194/139, Hamilton to Newcastle, Conf., Feb. 21, 1853.
8. CO 195/21, Grey to LeMarchant, Priv., Nov. 10, 1849.
9. CO 194/132, LeMarchant to Grey, Conf., Dec. 31, 1849.
10. CO 194/139, Hamilton to Newcastle, June 28, 1853.
11. *Ibid.*, Conf., Feb. 21, 1853.
12. CO 194/140, Hamilton to Newcastle, Nov. 19, 1853, and encls. These relate Hamilton's controversy with the Newfoundland Church Society (Church of England) over alleged coercive methods of collection.
13. In the *Public Ledger*, May 21, 1852, is a typical pronouncement: "... we have the Church of Rome among us, which is thoroughly anti-British, and concedes no abatement of its politico-religious pretensions unless wrung from it by a Government which ... it has not the power successfully to resist." The colony's newspapers at this period contained long doctrinal discussions and reports of conversions to Rome.
14. CO 194/139, Hamilton to Newcastle, Feb. 22, 1853.
15. *Ibid.*, May 4, 1853, encloses a commentary on charges levelled by the Assembly which indicates close collaboration between Hoyles and Hamilton.
16. *Ibid.*, encls., address to Her Majesty; commentary, K. B. Hamilton and H. W. Hoyles.
17. *Ibid.*
18. *Ibid.*, June 28, 1853, encl., address of Assembly to Her Majesty.
19. CO 194/140, Hume to Newcastle, July 25, 1853; delegates to Newcastle, July 25, July 28, 1853.
20. Newcastle Papers, Newcastle to Hamilton, Aug. 5, 1853, draft letter, not sent.
21. CO 194/140, delegates to Newcastle, July 28, 1853.
22. *Ibid.* Compare Tables III and IV, Appendix E. Such a return was theoretically possible, but in practice it had not been occurring.
23. CO 194/140, Hume to Newcastle, Aug. 4, 1853.
24. *Ibid.*, Newcastle to Hume, Aug. 5, 1853.
25. Newcastle Papers, Newcastle to Hamilton, Aug. 5, Oct. 7, 1853—drafts of letters apparently not sent.
26. CO 194/140, Hamilton to Blackwood, Priv., Nov. 30, 1853.
27. *Patriot*, Oct. 15, 1853, Little to electors, Sept. 30.
28. *Public Ledger*, Dec. 20; *Times*, Dec. 28, 1853.
29. CO 194/140, Hamilton to Blackwood, Priv., Nov. 3, Nov. 30, 1853.
30. *Times*, Feb. 1, 1854, Speech from Throne and Proceedings of Assembly, Jan. 31; Feb. 4, Proceedings, Feb. 1.
31. CO 194/141, Hamilton to Newcastle, Feb. 26. 1854, and encls., Address in Reply, Feb. 13; address to Newcastle, Feb. 22.

32. *Times*, Feb. 18, Feb. 22, Feb. 25, March 8; *Public Ledger*, Feb. 21, March 7, 1854.
33. *Times*, March 25, 1854; CO 194/141, Hamilton to Newcastle, March 23, 1854, encl., address.
34. CO 194/139, Hamilton to Newcastle, June 28, 1853, minute, Newcastle, Jan. 31, 1854.
35. CO 195/21, Newcastle to Hamilton, Feb. 21, 1854.
36. CO 194/141, Hamilton to Newcastle, March 24, 1854, encl., address to Newcastle.
37. *Times*, March 29, 1854.
38. CO 194/141, Hamilton to Newcastle, March 23, 1854, minute, Newcastle, April 14.
39. *Times*, June 3, 1854, Governor's message, June 2.
40. *Times*, June 3, 1854.
41. CO 194/141, Hamilton to Newcastle, June 15, 1854, marginal note and minute, F. Peel.
42. For the representation struggle of 1854 see H. W. Hoyles, *The Case of the Protestant Inhabitants ... against the Unconditional Concession of Responsible Government* (1854), pp. 5-9, and Table A.
43. CO 194/141, Hamilton to Newcastle, June 15, 1854.
44. Hoyles, *op. cit.*, resolutions, June 20, 1854.
45. Newcastle Papers, P. F. Little and G. H. Emerson to Newcastle, Aug. 1, 1854, and encl., delegates' statement to Sir George Grey, July 28; Newcastle to Little and Emerson, July 28, 1854.
46. CO 194/143, Hume to Little and Emerson, Aug. 11, 1854.
47. *Ibid.*, Little and Emerson to Hume, Aug. 12, 1854.
48. Both sets of correspondence are in CO 194/143.
49. Hoyles, pp. 6-10.
50. CO 195/22, Grey to Hamilton, Aug. 14, 1854.
51. *Times*, Oct. 14, 1854, Address in Reply, Oct. 12.
52. *Ibid.*, Oct. 25, 1854, Proceedings of Council, Oct. 24.
53. CO 194/143, Hamilton to Grey, Dec. 9, 1854, encl., *Newfoundland Express*, Nov. 21.
54. CO 194/141, Hamilton to Newcastle, June 26, 1854; CO 195/22, Grey to Hamilton, Aug. 14, 1854. The Colonial Secretary was to receive £400, the Attorney-General, £350.
55. CO 194/142, Hamilton to Grey, Nov. 14, 1854.
56. *Ibid.*
57. *Ibid.*, Nov. 23, 1854.
58. *Times*, Nov. 25, 1854, Proceedings of Assembly, Nov. 24.
59. CO 194/142, Hamilton to Grey, Nov. 23, 1854.
60. *Ibid.*, encl., *Newfoundland Express*, Nov. 28, Proceedings of Assembly, Nov. 21.
61. *Times*, Nov. 29, 1854, resolutions, Nov. 25.
62. CO 194/142, Hamilton to Grey, Nov. 29, 1854, and encl., petition. Also, minutes, Merivale to Peel, Dec. 18; Peel, Dec. 21, 1854.
63. CO 195/22, Grey to Hamilton, Jan. 18, 1855.
64. CO 194/142, Hamilton to Grey, Nov. 20, 1854, encl., address, Nov. 27.
65. *Ibid.*, Dec. 9, 1854.
66. *Ibid.*, Dec. 14, 1854.
67. *Ibid.*, Dec. 26, 1854; minute, Grey, Jan. 20, 1855.
68. CO 195/22, Grey to Hamilton, Jan. 24, 1855.
69. CO 325/41, memorandum, Blackwood to Merivale, Feb. 20, 1855.
70. CO 325/41, memorandum, Herbert to Merivale, Feb. 17, 1855.
71. CO 194/142, Hamilton to Grey, Dec. 29, 1854, named R. F. Sweetman, William Donnelly, Nicholas Stabb, Eugenius Harvey, Bryan Robinson, C. F. Bennett, L. O'Brien, T. B. Job, and J. J. Grieve.
72. CO 325/41, memorandum, Blackwood to Merivale, Feb. 20, 1855.
73. CO 195/22, Grey to Hamilton, Conf., March 3, 1855.
74. CO 194/142, Hamilton to Grey, Dec. 9, 1854.
75. CO 325/41, memorandum, Herbert to Merivale, Feb. 17, 1855.
76. CO 195/22, Grey to Hamilton, Priv., March 16, 1855.
77. *PD*, vol. 137, 1855, March 20, pp. 883-92.
78. CO 195/22, Grey to Hamilton, Priv., March 16, 1855.
79. Prowse, pp. 465-66.

CHAPTER TEN

1. CO 194/144, Darling to Russell, May 29, 1855.
2. CO 194/148, Darling to Labouchere, Aug. 31, 1856.

3. *Times*, May 9, 1855.
4. *Public Ledger*, May 22, 1855.
5. Archibald, *Life and Letters*, pp. 73-74.
6. CO 194/144, Darling to Russell, May 29, 1855, encl., Speech from Throne, May 22.
7. Archibald, pp. 71-72, 74.
8. CO 194/144, Darling to Russell, May 29, 1855.
9. CO 195/22, Russell to Darling, July 6, 1855.
10. CO 194/144, Darling to Russell, June 25, 1855. The Cabinet: P. F. Little, Attorney-General; John Kent, Colonial Secretary; E. Hanrahan, Surveyor-General; L. O'Brien, President of Legislative Council; Thomas Glen, Receiver-General; G. H. Emerson, Solicitor-General. The Legislative Council: L. O'Brien, President; J. Tobin, John Rochford, M.D., G. H. Emerson, John Munn, T. H. Ridley, J. J. Rogerson, James Furlong, Phillip Duggan, James Cormack, S. Carson, M.D., T. Row.
11. *Times*, June 20, 1855, Proceedings of Assembly, June 18.
12. CO 196/2, Acts, 1855.
13. CO 194/145, Darling to Molesworth, Sept. 4, 1855.
14. MacKay, *Newfoundland*, pp. 338-41.
15. CO 195/22, Labouchere to Darling, July 29, 1856, July 16, 1857; CO 194/148, Darling to Labouchere, Oct. 27, 1856; CO 194/150, Bannerman to Labouchere, Sept. 1, 1857.
16. CO 194/150, Darling to Labouchere, Feb. 4, 1857, encl., Speech from Throne, Jan. 29.
17. Prowse, p. 573.
18. *Times*, Sept. 15, 1855; CO 195/22, Labouchere to Darling, Conf., Oct. 15, Dec. 10, 1856.
19. CO 194/150, Darling to Labouchere, March 3, 1857.
20. *Public Ledger*, Oct. 2, 1855. Among the Protestants who supported Little were: Assembly—R. J. Parsons, J. Hayward (Board of Revenue), T. Glen (Colonial Treasurer); Council —J. Munn, T. H. Ridley, J. J. Rogerson, G. H. Emerson (Solicitor-General); Board of Revenue —Walter Grieve. (Prowse p. 468; CO 194/145, Darling to Molesworth, Sept. 3, 1855.)
21. CO194/147, Darling to Labouchere, May 12, 1856; CO 194/148, Darling to Labouchere, July 7, 1856, #56, encl., report on legislation.
22. CO 194/147, Darling to Labouchere, May 12, 1856; Prowse, p. 573.
23. No attempt is made here to treat the subject of the French fishery in Newfoundland except in so far as it has a direct bearing upon political developments. For a general treatment see the chapter "The French Shore" by A. M. Fraser in MacKay, *Newfoundland*, pp. 275-332, and Prowse. For an exhaustive treatment see Frederic F. Thompson, *The French Shore Problem in Newfoundland* (Toronto, 1961).
24. MacKay, pp. 278-81; Prowse, pp. 471-72.
25. Thompson, pp. 32-34.
26. CO 194/138, Hamilton to Newcastle, Sept. 28, 1853.
27. CO 194/148, Darling to Labouchere, July 23, 1856.
28. CO 194/150, Darling to Labouchere, Priv. and Conf., March 30, 1857, and encl., minute of Executive Council, July 25, 1856.
29. Thompson, pp. 35-36.
30. CO 194/150, Darling to Labouchere, March 3, 1857.
31. CO 195/22, Labouchere to Darling, Jan. 16, 1857. Draft is in CO 194/151.
32. CO 194/150, Darling to Labouchere, Feb. 7, 1857, encl., resolution, Feb. 6.
33. CO 194/151, statement for Foreign Office, April 10, 1857, summarizing legislative proceedings in Newfoundland after receipt of the Convention.
34. CO 195/22, Darling to Labouchere, March 5, 1857, encl., report, March 2.
35. *Ibid.*, Priv. and Conf., March 30, 1857.
36. *Ibid.*, March 3, 1857.
37. *Ibid.*, Priv. and Conf., March 30, 1857.
38. CO 195/22, Labouchere to Darling, March 26, 1857.
39. CO 194/150, Darling to Labouchere, April 15, 1857.
40. CO 194/152, Bannerman to Stanley, Priv. and Conf., May 12, 1858, and encl., address to Secretary of State, May 8.
41. CO 194/150, Darling to Labouchere, Priv. and Conf., March 30, 1857.
42. *Ibid.*, March 3, 1857.
43. *Ibid.*, Priv. and Conf., March 30, 1857.
44. CO 195/22, Labouchere to Bannerman, Conf., Dec. 6, 1857.
45. R. B. McCrea, *Lost Amid the Fogs: Sketches of Life in Newfoundland* (London, 1869), p. 120.
46. CO 194/153, Bannerman to Lytton, Conf., Aug. 30, 1858, minute, Merivale to Carnarvon, Sept. 18.

47. CO 194/153, Bannerman to Labouchere, Jan. 21, 1858, encl., minute of Executive Council, Jan. 15.

48. CO 194/152, Bannerman to Merivale, Priv., Jan. 22, 1858.

49. *Ibid.*, Bannerman to Stanley, Priv., April 13, 1858.

50. CO 195/22, Lytton to Bannerman, Priv. and Conf., June 17, 1858.

51. CO 194/153, Bannerman to Lytton, July 5, Aug. 19, Conf., Aug. 30, 1858.

52. *Ibid.*, Aug. 19, 1858, minute, Lytton, Sept. 16.

53. CO 194/152, Bannerman to Stanley, Priv. and Conf., May 13, 1858; CO 194/153, Bannerman to Lytton, July 6, Aug. 19, 1858.

54. CO 195/22, Lytton to Bannerman, June 14, 1858.

55. CO 194/153, Bannerman to Lytton, Sep., Sept. 27, 1858, and encl., LeNowry to Bannerman, Sept. 11; Aug. 3, encl., Captain Paisley's report, Aug. 2; Sept. 13, encls., various; Nov. 11, encl., reports of Bishop Mullock (2), and minute of Executive Council, Nov. 10.

56. CO 194/154, Hammond to Merivale, Dec. 15, 1858, and Foreign Office encls., Colonial Office minutes and drafts, and minute, Carnarvon to Lytton, Dec. 15.

57. CO 195/22, Lytton to Bannerman, Conf., Jan. 14, 1859; CO 194/155, Bannerman to Lytton, Priv. and Conf., Feb. 4, 1859, encl., minute of Executive Council, Feb. 3; Sep., Feb. 4; March 4, encl., resolutions, Feb. 16; March 5, and encls., minute of Executive Council, Feb. 25, and Bannerman to Council, Feb. 26. In a minute of April 6 Lord Carnarvon, Parliamentary Under-Secretary, consistently unsympathetic to the colony's view of its rights, termed the Assembly's resolutions "violent" and "very indefensible" at this stage in the negotiations.

58. CO 194/165, Bannerman to Newcastle, Sep., March 5, 1861, quoting from Bannerman to Lytton, March 19, 1859.

59. CO 195/23, Newcastle to Bannerman, Sep., Aug. 26, 1861.

60. CO 194/165, Bannerman to Newcastle, Priv., Feb. 21, 1861, minute, T. F. Elliot, March 9.

61. CO 194/161, Bannerman to Newcastle, May 28, 1860, encl., Speech of Prorogation, May 14.

62. *Ibid.*, Bannerman to C. Fortescue, Priv., Aug. 17; Priv., Dec. 19, 1860; CO 194/165, Bannerman to Newcastle, Jan. 1; Jan. 30, #11; Jan. 30, #12, 1861, and encls., various.

63. CO 194/165, Bannerman to Newcastle, Jan. 30, 1861, #11, minute, F. Rogers, Feb. 24, summary of terms.

64. CO 195/23, Newcastle to Bannerman, March 4, 1861.

65. Thompson, pp. 37-38.

66. Prowse, p. 619.

67. 22 Vict., c. 9 and c. 19 (Nfld.).

68. CO 194/165, Bannerman to Newcastle, Conf., Feb. 27, 1861.

69. CO 194/150, Darling to Lytton, Priv. and Conf., March 20, 1857, quoting Tobin in the Legislative Council, Feb. 20; CO 194/154, Bannerman to Lytton, Priv. and Conf., Jan. 6, 1859.

70. CO 194/154, Bannerman to Lytton, Priv. and Conf., Jan. 6, 1859.

71. CO 194/155, Bannerman to Lytton, Dec. 10, 1858, encl., extract reprinted from the *Globe* (London).

72. *Ibid.*, Dec. 31, 1858, #100, and encls., newspaper extracts, correspondence with J. Tobin, minutes of Executive Council, December 1858. Tobin's correspondence with the Colonial Office is in CO 194/167.

73. *Ibid.*, Dec. 31, 1858, #100; Sep., Dec. 31, and encl., Bannerman to Kent, Dec. 20, and minutes, Blackwood to Merivale, Jan 27, Merivale to Carnarvon, Jan. 29, Lytton, Feb. 9, 1859.

74. CO 195/22, Lytton to Bannerman, Feb. 17, 1859.

75. *Ibid.*, Nov. 17, 1858, re 21 Vict., c. 15 (Nfld.).

76. CO 195/23, Newcastle to Bannerman, Oct. 29, 1859; March 19, 1860, re 21 Vict., c. 9 (Nfld.).

77. CO 194/155, Bannerman to Lytton, April 21, 1859, encl., Speech of Prorogation.

78. CO 194/161, Bannerman to Newcastle, Conf., Jan. 16, 1860; Prowse, p. 607.

79. *Ibid.*, March 5, 1860, and encl., petitions and correspondence. See also Prowse, p. 485.

80. CO 194/161, Bannerman to Newcastle, Conf., Jan. 16, 1860, and encl., petition of T. Ridley, J. Munn, and J. Stack, J.P.'s; Conf., Jan. 17, encls., reports of T. Bennett, C. Simms, and G. J. Hogsett, Dec. 29, 1859; Conf., Feb. 8, 1860, encls., minute of Executive Council, Jan. 16, and Governor's comments.

81. CO 194/161, Bannerman to Newcastle, March 5, 1860, and encls., petitions, correspondence, and minute of Executive Council, Feb. 24.

82. CO 381/54, Instructions, Feb. 14, 1857, article 36.

83. CO 194/161, Bannerman to Newcastle, March 5, 1860, minutes, Merivale to Fortescue, March 17; Carnarvon, March 19.
84. *Ibid.*, Bannerman to Under-Secretary of State, Aug. 29, 1860.
85. *Ibid.*, minute, Newcastle, Dec. 12, 1860. In his letter of June 24, 1860 to the Queen on the visit to Newfoundland, Newcastle reported that the levee at St. John's was attended by 250 persons, "the greater part of them not very favourable specimens of the English Colonial Gentleman, but all anxious to show respect and loyalty." (Newcastle Papers, Entry Book of Letters written to Her Majesty during the Visit of the Prince of Wales to the British North American Provinces.)
86. CO 194/161, Bannerman to Newcastle, Conf., Feb. 8, 1860, Governor's comments on minute of Executive Council, Jan. 16.
87. *Ibid.*, Conf., Jan. 16, 1860; CO 195/23, Newcastle to Bannerman, Feb. 23, 1860.
88. CO 194/161, Bannerman to Newcastle, May 29, 1860; CO 194/165, Bannerman to Newcastle, Conf., Feb. 27, 1861.
89. CO 194/161, Bannerman to Newcastle, Feb. 8, 1860, and encl., Speech from Throne.
90. *Ibid.*, April 2, 1860, and encls., address of Legislative Council, March 16; Report of Select Committee of Assembly, March 7; extract from Proceedings of Assembly.
91. *Ibid.*, April 3, Aug. 9, 1860.
92. *Ibid.*, May 9, 1860, and minutes, H. Irving, C. Fortescue, May 31; CO 195/23, Newcastle to Bannerman, June 26, 1860; Feb. 16, 1861.
93. Dr. Mullock's letter to the Catholic people of the Diocese of St. John's, quoted in Prowse, p. 486, n. 1.
94. See Prowse, pp. 485-86.
95. CO 194/165, Bannerman to Newcastle, May 16, 1861.
96. CO 194/161, Bannerman to Newcastle, June 21, Aug. 9, 1860.

CHAPTER ELEVEN

1. CO 194/161, Bannerman to Newcastle, Dec. 5, 1860, encl., Speech from Throne, Dec. 3.
2. Prowse, p. 486; H. Winton, *A Chapter in the History of Newfoundland for the year 1861* (1861), p. 4.
3. *JHA*, 1860. Dec. 2, p. 1. Hoyles was sworn in to replace J. Seaton, resigned member for Burgeo and LaPoile.
4. *JHA*, 1861, Jan. 22, pp. 32-33; Jan. 23, p. 33.
5. Quoted in Prowse, p. 488, n. 1. Kent was apparently referring to the Speaker, Shea.
6. Winton, p. 4.
7. Newcastle papers, Letter Book of 1861.
8. CO 194/165, Bannerman to Newcastle, May 20, 1861, quoting extract from Mullock to Bannerman, Feb. 10.
9. *JHA*, 1861, Feb. 5, pp. 40, 45; Feb. 6, p. 49; Feb. 18, p. 62.
10. CO 194/165, Bannerman to Newcastle, Conf., Feb. 27, 1861.
11. *Ibid.*, May 20, 1861.
12. *JHA*, 1861, Feb. 18, p. 61, Message from the Governor; Appendix, pp. 491-98, Documents and Despatches on the Currency Question.
13. Winton, p. 4.
14. CO 194/165, Bannerman to Newcastle, March 14, 1861; Winton, p. 5; Prowse, p. 488.
15. CO 194/165, Bannerman to Newcastle, May 20, 1861.
16. *Ibid.*, March 14, 1861.
17. Winton, p. 5; Note B, pp. i-ii, extract from Hoyle's speech to Assembly.
18. CO 194/165, Bannerman to Newcastle, March 14, 1861, and minute, C. Fortescue to Newcastle, April 22; Winton, p. 6.
19. *JHA*, 1861, March 4, p. 70; March 5, p. 72.
20. CO 194/165, Bannerman to Newcastle March 14, 1861.
21. *Ibid.*, minutes, Blackwood, April 6; T. F. Elliot to Fortescue, April 19.
22. CO 195/23, Newcastle to Bannerman, June 15; Conf., Aug. 26, 1861; Sep., Jan. 18, 1862.
23. CO 194/165, Bannerman to Newcastle, March 13, 1861, encl., Hogsett to Bannerman; CO 194/167, Kent to Newcastle, June 15, 1861.
24. CO 194/165, Bannerman to Newcastle, March 14, 1861, minutes, Blackwood, April 6; Elliot to F. Rogers, April 9; Elliot to Fortescue, April 19; Newcastle, April 25; CO 195/23, Newcastle to Bannerman, May 3, 1861.

25. CO 194/165, Bannerman to Newcastle, May 16, 1861, encl., Bishop Mullock to editor of *Record*, March 21.

26. Winton, p. 6.

27. CO 194/165, Spaniard's Bay correspondence from the *Record* (no covering despatch): Bannerman to Mullock, April 29; Mullock to Bannerman, April 30, 1861.

28. CO 194/161, Bannerman to Newcastle, Conf., Jan. 16, 1860.

29. The ensuing account of the election, except where other references are indicated, is based on CO 194/165, Bannerman to Newcastle, May 8, 1861, and Winton, pp. 7-11, which corroborate and supplement each other. These sources have been checked against the copious documentary material on the election—newspapers, magistrates' statements, affidavits, etc.— enclosed with despatches in CO 194/165 and CO 194/166, the Harbour Grace affair being massively documented in the enclosures with CO 194/165, Bannerman to Newcastle, July 3, 1861.

30. CO 194/166, Bannerman to Newcastle, July 18, 1861.

31. CO 194/165, Bannerman to Newcastle, Priv., April 23, 1861, and minute, Blackwood to Elliot, May 16; Newcastle Papers, Letter Book of 1861, Newcastle to Bannerman, Priv., March 8.

32. CO 194/165, Spaniard's Bay correspondence: Mullock to Bannerman, April 29; Bannerman to Mullock, April 29; Gosse and Shepherd to Bannerman, May 13; memorandum, Bannerman, May 20, 1861.

33. CO 194/166, Bannerman to Newcastle, July 13, 1861, encl., J. Munn to Speaker, May 21; JHA, 1861, May 16, p. 13, petition; June 4, p. 74, counter-petition.

34. CO 194/165, Bannerman to Newcastle, Sep., May 17, 1861; JHA, 1861, May 16, p. 13, petition of Nowlan and Byrne.

35. CO 194/166, Bannerman to Newcastle, Conf., Aug. 12, 1861, encl., petition (8,000 signatures) for removal of the Governor.

36. The ensuing account of the events is based on CO 194/165, Bannerman to Newcastle, Sep., May 17, 1861; CO 194/166, Bannerman to Newcastle, July 2, 1861, encls., evidence at inquest; Prowse, pp. 489-490; *Newfoundlander*, May 14, 1861, as quoted in Prowse, pp. 490-91; Winton, pp. 12-16.

37. CO 194/165, Spaniard's Bay correspondence: Bannerman to Mullock, April 29, 1861.

38. Newcastle Papers, Letter Book of 1861, Newcastle to Mullock, Priv., June 15, 1861.

39. CO 194/165, Spaniard's Bay correspondence: Mullock to Bannerman, April 29, 1861. The Bishop's covering letter to the editor of the *Record* is dated May 7, and the *Public Ledger*, May 17, notes that the correspondence appeared in the *Record* of May 11.

40. CO 194/165, Bannerman to Newcastle, Priv. and Conf., May 17, 1861, encl., Mullock to Bannerman, May 14.

41. *Ibid.*, June 4, 1861; CO 194/166, Bannerman to Newcastle, July 2, 1861, and encls., correspondence and petitions from Harbour Grace and statements from Carbonear, May 1861; minute of Executive Council, June 14; minute, Elliot to Fortescue, July 30; CO 195/23, Newcastle to Bannerman, May 31, Aug. 12.

42. CO 194/165, Bannerman to Newcastle, Priv. and Conf., May 17, 1861.

43. *Ibid.*, May 16, 1861, #30, and encl., Bannerman to Mullock, May 16.

44. *Ibid.*, June 4, 1861.

45. *Ibid.*; Winton, pp. 17, 25; CO 194/166, Bannerman to Newcastle, July 2, 1861.

46. CO 194/165, Bannerman to Newcastle, June 4, 1861, encl., *Daily News*, June 26, Proceedings of Assembly, June 25. The evidence taken by the committee appears in JHA, 1861, Appendix, pp. 41-124.

47. Winton, p. 18.

48. CO 194/166, Bannerman to Newcastle, July 2, 1861, and encls., Mullock to Bannerman; J. Little to Mullock, June 28; declaration, P. Brazil; statement by Attorney-General Hoyles; minutes, Newcastle; Rogers to Fortescue, Aug. 13.

49. CO 195/23, Newcastle to Bannerman, Sept. 3, 1861.

50. CO 194/166, Bannerman to Newcastle, Conf., July 31, 1861.

51. *Ibid.*, Conf., Aug. 13, 1861, and encl., petition.

52. CO 195/23, Newcastle to Bannerman, April 5, 1862.

53. CO 194/166, Bannerman to Newcastle, Conf., July 31, 1861, and encl., extract from the *Record*.

54. *Ibid.*, Priv. and Conf., Aug. 14, 1861, and encl., newspaper extract.

55. *Ibid.*, Conf., July 31, 1861.

56. Winton, note F, p. iv.

57. *Ibid.*, pp. 20-21.

58. CO 194/166, Bannerman to Blackwood, Priv., Sept. 25, 1861, encl., *Record*, Sept. 14.

59. *Ibid.*, encl., *Record*, Sept. 21.
60. Winton, p. 21.
61. CO 194/166, Bannerman to Blackwood, Conf., Sept. 25, 1861.
62. Prowse, p. 612.
63. Quoted in Winton, p. 21.
64. CO 194/166, Bannerman to Blackwood, Priv., Sept. 25, 1861, encl., *Record*, Sept. 21.
65. *Ibid.*, Bannerman to Newcastle, Priv. and Conf., Aug. 28, 1861, and encl., Hoyles to Bannerman, Aug. 26.
66. CO 194/165, Bannerman to Newcastle, Sep., May 16, 1861.
67. CO 194/166, Bannerman to Newcastle, July 2, Sept. 10, 1861.
68. *Ibid.*, Bannerman to Blackwood, Oct. 23, 1861, encl., *Record*, Oct. 12.
69. *Ibid.*, Nov. 8, 1861, encls., J. Peters to Bannerman; *Royal Gazette*, Nov. 5, Bannerman to Peters.
70. *Ibid.*, Nov. 19, 1861, and encls., Mullock to Bannerman, Nov. 9 (encl., pastoral letter); Bannerman to Mullock, Nov. 11; Mullock to Bannerman, Nov. 13; CO 195/23, Newcastle to Bannerman, Dec. 17, 1861; Newcastle Papers, Letter Book of 1861, Newcastle to Bannerman, Dec 14.
71. CO 194/166, Bannerman to Newcastle, Dec. 3, 1861.
72. CO 195/23, Newcastle to Bannerman, Jan. 1, 1862.
73. CO 194/168, Bannerman to Newcastle, Jan. 21, 1862, encl., Speech from Throne, Jan. 30.
74. CO 194/166, Bannerman to Blackwood, Oct. 23, 1861, encl., *Daily News*, Oct. 23, charge to jury, Oct. 20.
75. Winton, pp. 25-26. For the trials and their aftermath see CO 194/168, Bannerman to Newcastle, Conf., Feb. 28, 1862, and encls., Bannerman to F. B. T. Carter, quoting the judgment of Chief Justice Brady; Bishop Mullock to Roman Catholic clergy, Jan. 7; Bannerman to Carter, Jan. 11; *Public Ledger*, n.d. (letter quoting *Record*), and March 4; directive, Bishop Mullock, Feb. 6.
76. CO 194/168, Bannerman to Newcastle, Priv., May 8, 1862.
77. Newcastle Papers, Letter Book of 1862, Newcastle to Bannerman, Aug. 9.

CHAPTER TWELVE

1. CO 194/168, Bannerman to Newcastle, April 10, 1862, and encl., Speech of Prorogation, March 27.
2. *Ibid.*, Priv., May 8, 1862, and minute, Blackwood to Elliot, May 29.
3. *Ibid.*, Sept. 25, 1862, schedule of claims and damages:

District	Claim for Damages £	Award £	Road Grant (26 Vict., c.3) £
St. John's	4,599	1,132	1,277
Harbour Main	1,711	588	228
Harbour Grace	1,353	962	427
Carbonear	331	52	291

4. Compare 18 Vict., c. 13.
5. CO 194/168, Bannerman to Newcastle, Priv., May 8, 1862, minutes, Blackwood to Elliot, May 29; Fortescue, June 2; Newcastle, June 2.
6. CO 194/170, Bannerman to Newcastle, March 27, 1863.
7. Quoted in *Public Ledger*, Jan. 26, 1864.
8. CO 194/168, Bannerman to Newcastle, Conf., Oct. 20, 1862, encl., *Record*, Oct. 4.
9. CO 194/170, Bannerman to Newcastle, May 18, 1863.
10. Prowse, p. 496.
11. CO 194/170-73.
12. See Prowse, p. 574.
13. *Public Ledger*, Sept. 9, 1864, Governor's reply to Executive Council.
14. *Newfoundlander*, Sept. 8, 1864, Kent to editor.
15. *Ibid.*, and *Patriot*, Sept. 13.
16. *Public Ledger*, Sept. 6, Sept. 9, Sept. 13, 1864.
17. Prowse, p. 492.
18. *Ibid.*, p. 494.
19. CO 194/174, Musgrave to Cardwell, April 19, 1865.

20. The census of 1857 showed: total population of electoral districts, 119,304; native-born, 107,299; Irish-born, 7,383; English-born, 3,516; Scottish-born, 390; colonial-born, 475; and foreign-born, 136. (Figures from *JHA*, 1858, Appendix, p. 125.)

21. Prowse, pp. 513-14; Sir P. T. McGrath, "Some Recent Premiers of Newfoundland," *Canadian Magazine*, XI (1898), pp. 475-79.

22. Prowse, p. 491.

23. NRCR, pp. 88-89. For the commissioners' report on the political system, see pp. 77 *et seq.*

24. MacKay, *Newfoundland*, pp. 150-51.

25. CO 194/81, Cochrane to Goderich, Secret and Conf., April 14, 1831.

26. MacKay, pp. 71-74.

27. *Ibid.*, pp. 212-18.

INDEX

elected: 1842, 196; 1852, 199; 1855, 141,
143, 200; 1859, 159, 201; 1861, 202
West Country (England): and Newfoundland,
5, 8, 26
West Country merchants: and supply monopoly, 3, 40, 53–4, 70, 177, 182; as non-
residents, 5, 106, 136; urge abrogation
of representative government, 56, 86; and
direct taxation, 106, 151
West Indies, 131
Wexford (Ireland): settlers from, 14
Whig ministries (Great Britain): in 1830, 3,
18; and granting of representative government, 3, 11, 13, 182–3; in 1835, 31;
in 1838, 44, 50, 57, 59; in 1839, 59; and
Newfoundland question, 1839–41, 57–8,

60–1, 70, 73, 77, 86, 184; and New
foundland Act, 1842, 85–7; in 1846, 103,
105; and Newfoundland Act, 1846, 103,
184
Whig party (Great Britain), 19, 103; and
Newfoundland question, 11, 13, 31, 86–7
Whiteway, William Vallance Whiteway:
elected, 201, 202
Winser, Peter: elected, 37, 195, 198–200 passim
Winter, J.: elected 200–2 passim
Winton, Henry, 15, 66, 69, 159; and Kent, 15,
16; and Roman Catholicism in Newfoundland, 15, 16, 20, 26, 28, 69, 131,
143. See also Public Ledger

CANADIAN UNIVERSITY PAPERBOOKS
Of related interest

Also related

By Great Waters: A Newfoundland and Labrador Anthology
from 1000 to the Present
Edited and introduced by PETER NEARY and
PATRICK O'FLAHERTY

9 780802 063236